GLOBAL RALPH ELLISON

RACE AND RESISTANCE ACROSS BORDERS IN THE LONG TWENTIETH CENTURY

Volume 6

PETER LANG
Oxford • Bern • Berlin • Bruxelles • New York • Wien

GLOBAL RALPH ELLISON

Aesthetics and Politics Beyond US Borders

Edited by Tessa Roynon and Marc C. Conner

PETER LANG
Oxford • Bern • Berlin • Bruxelles • New York • Wien

Bibliographic information published by Die Deutsche Nationalbibliothek.
Die Deutsche Nationalbibliothek lists this publication in the Deutsche Nationalbibliografie; detailed bibliographic data is available on the Internet at http://dnb.d-nb.de.

A catalogue record for this book is available from the British Library.

Library of Congress Cataloging-in-Publication Data

Names: Roynon, Tessa, editor. | Conner, Marc C., 1965- editor.
Title: Global Ralph Ellison : aesthetics and politics beyond US borders / [edited by] Tessa Roynon, Marc C. Conner.
Description: Oxford ; New York : Peter Lang, [2021] | Series: Race and resistance across borders in the long twentieth century, 2297-2552 ; vol 6 | Includes bibliographical references and index.
Identifiers: LCCN 2020035077 (print) | LCCN 2020035078 (ebook) | ISBN 9781789974942 (hardback) | ISBN 9781789974959 (ebook) | ISBN 9781789974966 (epub)
Subjects: LCSH: Ellison, Ralph--Criticism and interpretation. | Ellison, Ralph--Appreciation. | Aesthetics in literature. | Politics in literature.
Classification: LCC PS3555.L625 Z69 2021 (print) | LCC PS3555.L625 (ebook) | DDC 813/.54--dc23
LC record available at https://lccn.loc.gov/2020035077
LC ebook record available at https://lccn.loc.gov/2020035078

Cover design by Brian Melville for Peter Lang, incorporating photographs taken by Tessa Roynon, of materials in the 'Foreign Rights and Translations' folder of the Ralph Ellison Papers, Manuscripts Division, Library of Congress, Washington DC.

ISSN 2297-2552
ISBN 978-1-78997-494-2 (print)
ISBN 978-1-78997-495-9 (ePDF)
ISBN 978-1-78997-496-6 (ePub)

Published by Peter Lang Ltd, International Academic Publishers,
52 St Giles, Oxford, OX1 3LU, United Kingdom
oxford@peterlang.com, www.peterlang.com

This publication has been peer reviewed.

Contents

Acknowledgements

The editors wish to thank the contributors to this volume for their painstaking research and dedicated commitment to this project over the last four years. They are also grateful to the following institutions, organizations and individuals for numerous different kinds of support, both for the International Ralph Ellison Symposium (Oxford, September 2017) and for this volume: the Library of Congress, Washington DC; The Ralph Ellison Trust; The Ralph Ellison Society; the Race and Resistance Programme at TORCH (The Oxford Research Centre in the Humanities); the Rothermere American Institute at the University of Oxford; the Vere Harmsworth Library at the University of Oxford; Merton College, Oxford; the anonymous reviewers and series editors for Peter Lang; Professor Elleke Boehmer; Dr Alexey Kostyanovsky; Dr Laurel Plapp and her colleagues at Peter Lang; and Professor Stephen Tuck.

TESSA ROYNON

Introduction

'Thinking about Ralph Ellison as an internationalist requires tinkering with some of our most closely guarded assumptions about his work', states Brent Hayes Edwards in his contribution to the 2010 essay collection, *Globalizing American Studies*. To do so 'might seem something close to perverse', he continues.[1] Edwards, like Jonathan Arac before him, persuasively attends to the often hidden and always complex elements of resistant black diasporic thinking in Ellison's work, locating in this most self-avowedly 'American' of writers what he terms a problematic 'grain' of 'radical internationalism'.[2] Taking a different but related tack, Sara Marzioli and Daniel Williams separately demonstrate that a comparativist engagement with Europe – whether with classical and renaissance Rome (Marzioli), with Cold War politics (Marzioli again) or with Wales and Welsh nationalism during World War II (Daniels) – is fundamental to Ellison's explorations of African American identity and American history.[3] The eight original chapters collected here, as *Global Ralph Ellison*, both build on and diverge from these prior scholarly insights in important ways.

1 Brent Hayes Edwards, 'Ralph Ellison and the Grain of Internationalism', in Brian T. Edwards and Dilip Parameshwar Gaonkar, eds, *Globalizing American Studies* (Chicago, IL: Chicago University Press, 2010), 115–16.

2 Ibid., 129. See also Jonathan Arac, 'Toward a Critical Genealogy of the U.S. Discourse of Identity: *Invisible Man* after Fifty Years', *boundary 2* 30/2 (2003), 195–216; and Jonathan Arac, 'Global and Babel: Language and Planet in American Literature', in Wai Chee Dimock and Lawrence Buell, eds, *Shades of the Planet: American Literature as World Literature* (Princeton, NJ: Princeton University Press, 2007), 19–38.

3 See Sara Marzioli, 'Ralph Ellison's Exceptional Diaspora: The View from Rome', *Atlantic Studies* 9/4 (2012), 447–66; Daniel Williams, '"If We Only Had Some of What They Have": Ralph Ellison in Wales', *Comparative American Studies: An International Journal* 4/1 (2006), 25–48.

As the first full-length work to consider the transnational dimensions of Ellison's life, intellect, literary works and reception, this volume challenges a truism that – despite the ground-breaking work of Edwards, Marzioli et al. – has continued to dominate Ellisonian scholarship. This truism is that Ellison, in his commitment to democratic ideals of the country of his birth, is 'exceptionally American' to the extent that both culture and politics outside of the USA are of only secondary importance in his writing. At the same time, Anglophone scholarship has until now paid regrettably scant attention to the infinitely varied and often counter-intuitive ways in which Ellison's work, in particular *Invisible Man* (1952), of course, has been translated and read, reformulated and even at times appropriated, in numerous different countries, continents and transnational constituencies. *Global Ralph Ellison* takes two specific approaches in its analyses of the Ellisonian oeuvre. First, in its focus on what the Library of Congress archives reveal about this writer's extensive reading in and responses to the work of four profoundly influential prior authors, it significantly advances our understanding of the truly international nature of Ellison's intellectual formation and of his cultural allusiveness. And second, in examining the reception histories of *Invisible Man* in four distinct non-American locales, it demonstrates this novel's apparently infinite adaptability and relevance to a range of contrasting intra- as well as international political struggles, right across the second half of the twentieth century and well into the twenty-first. In so doing, this volume as a whole contributes new complexity and nuance to abiding questions about both the nature of Ellison's aesthetics and their political implications.

The intellectual context and projects which have given rise to *Global Ralph Ellison* are various. One foundation, of course, is the transnational approach to American literature as a whole that primarily characterized the post-millennium wave of 'new' American studies: as theorized by Wai Chee Dimock and Lawrence Buell in *Shades of the Planet: American Literature as World Literature* (2007), for example, by Brian T. Edwards and Dilip Parameshwar Gaonkar in *Globalizing American Studies* (2010); and by Paul Giles in *The Global Remapping of American Literature* (2011).[4] As Gayle Rogers has argued in her useful discussion of 'American Modernisms in

4 Wai Chee Dimock and Lawrence Buell, eds, *Shades of the Planet: American Literature as World Literature* (Princeton, NJ: Princeton University Press, 2007); Brian T. Edwards and Dilip Parameshwar Gaonkar, eds, *Globalizing American Studies*

the World',[5] these recalibrations are by definition inseparable from the diasporic and black internationalist approaches to black culture and history exemplified by Paul Gilroy, Robin D. G. Kelley, Brent Hayes Edwards, Minkah Makalani and Imaobong Umoren, among others.[6] A specific formative influence on both this book and on the International Ralph Ellison Symposium that preceded it (held at the University of Oxford in 2017)[7] was a prior Oxford project: a workshop entitled 'The Global History of the Book (1780–the Present)'. This event, together with the publication that inspired it and those to which it gave rise, all explore the rich, chiasmic concept of 'the world in the book; the book in the world'. This concept has defined our own approach to Ralph Ellison, which we have conceptualized as both 'the world in Ellison' and 'Ellison in the world'.

While the concept of the 'global' is of course imperfect and contested,[8] in this volume we follow the way the term is used in Boehmer et al.'s invaluable publication deriving from the Oxford workshop: *The Global Histories of Books* (2017).[9] Drawing directly on this work's introduction, we argue

(Chicago, IL: Chicago University Press, 2010); Paul Giles, *The Global Remapping of American Literature* (Princeton, NJ: Princeton University Press, 2011).

5 Gayle Rogers, 'American Modernisms in the World', in Joshua Miller, ed., *The Cambridge Companion to the American Modernist Novel* (Cambridge, UK: Cambridge University Press, 2015), 227–44.

6 See Paul Gilroy, *The Black Atlantic: Modernity and Double Consciousness* (London: Verso, 1993); Robin D. G. Kelley, *Freedom Dreams: The Black Radical Imagination* (Boston, MA: Beacon Press, 2002); Brent Hayes Edwards, *The Practice of Diaspora: Literature, Translation and the Rise of Black Internationalism* (Cambridge, MA: Harvard University Press, 2003); Minkah Makalani, *In the Cause of Freedom: Radical Black Internationalism from Harlem to London, 1917–39* (Chapel Hill: University of North Carolina Press, 2011); Imaobong Umoren, *Race Women Internationalists: Activist-Intellectuals and Global Freedom Struggles* (Oakland: University of California Press, 2018).

7 The International Ralph Ellison Symposium, directed by Marc Conner and Tessa Roynon, was held at the Rothermere American Institute and St Anne's College, University of Oxford, 28–30 September 2017.

8 For one useful discussion of the benefits and limitations of the concepts of 'transnationalism' and the 'global' see Ian Tyrrell, 'Reflections on the Transnational Turn in United States History: Theory and Practice', *Journal of Global History* 4/3 (2009), 453–74.

9 The workshop, 'The Global History of the Book (1780–the Present)', directed by Elleke Boehmer et al., took place at the University of Oxford in December 2014.

that both Ellison's own works and the cultural forms that shape them are 'errant texts', texts that wander from their originating locale.[10] Ellison's writing and the literatures that inform it both clearly exemplify the 'capacity for mobility, migration and mutability' that define the 'global lives of books'.[11] Our implicit critique of the exclusively Americanist lens through which Ellison is too often viewed, and of his Americanist self-fashioning, is indubitably part of what Boehmer et al. (building on Martin Lyons) describe as 'the transnational or global challenge to the national histories of the book emerging with particular vigour since the 1990s'.[12]

In suggesting that Ellison's oeuvre be viewed as a collection of 'global books', and in positing that a 'global' approach to his reception is instructive, we do not of course make any claims for geographical or linguistic comprehensiveness in terms of the reach of his work, its reception, or our coverage.[13] Nor does our volume engage in any detail with the capitalist-oriented implications of the recent and current usage of the term 'globalization'. As Boehmer et al. discuss, books and their circulation can never be distinct from capitalist structures, from the market forces that drive circulation and consumption and that they in turn influence.[14] Indeed, there exist numerous important questions surrounding the status of *Invisible Man* as a 'monumental book' and Ellison's particular negotiations of individualism, the cultural and socio-economic privileges he enjoyed following the success of this publication, and neo-liberalism. Yet while two of the chapters in this volume touch briefly on these issues, these concerns are

This event was in part inspired by Antoinette Burton and Isabel Hofmeyr, eds, *Ten Books that Shaped the British Empire: Creating an Imperial Commons* (Durham, NC: Duke University Press, 2014), and it gave rise to Elleke Boehmer, Rouven Kunstmann, Priyasha Mukhopadhyay and Asha Rogers, eds, *The Global Histories of Books: Methods and Practices* (London: Palgrave Macmillan, 2017), and Dominic Davies, Erica Lombard and Benjamin Mountford, eds, *Fighting Words: Fifteen Books that Shaped the Postcolonial World* (Oxford: Peter Lang, 2017).

10 Boehmer et al., Introduction to *Global Histories*, 2.

11 Ibid.

12 Ibid., 3.

13 This caveat is indebted to Boehmer et al., Introduction to *Global Histories*, 4.

14 Ibid., 5–7.

not our central focus.[15] Detailed discussion of Ellison and 'globalization' in its post-1990 'world market' sense belongs to another, different book.

Global Ralph Ellison: Aesthetics and Politics Beyond US Borders brings together eleven scholars working in six different countries across four different continents. Its first part, 'The World in Ellison: Migratory Intertexts', extends prior scholarship by drawing on hitherto undiscussed archival evidence about the novelist's use of both classic literature and numerous other academic disciplines in which he was so widely read. The four chapters therein explore in detail the way Ellison thinks and writes elements of his own work at once *through*, *with* and (sometimes) *against* sources as various as the expatriate American Henry James (Sam Halliday), the British classicist Jane Ellen Harrison (Bryan Crable); the Roman poet Ovid (Tessa Roynon), and the Russian novelist Fyodor Dostoevsky (Stephen Rachman). Together these chapters demonstrate that the world's intellectual and cultural resources are equal in significance to its history and politics in their role as fundamental enablers of, or key comparative catalysts to, Ellison's conceptions of African American experience and of the many implications of Americanness. The new discoveries in the archive, particularly in the copies of the books that Ellison himself actually read and annotated, have thus to a large extent revealed the significant global dimensions of his thinking and of his oeuvre.[16]

The second part of this volume, meanwhile, 'Ellison in the World: Translations and Receptions', focuses on the translation history of *Invisible Man*, engaging both the linguistic and cultural-political senses of that word, 'translation'. These chapters explore the complex and often contradictory ways in which the novel has been read in the specific and always shifting contexts of apartheid and post-apartheid South Africa (Aretha Phiri); the USSR and post-Soviet Russia (Olga Panova); East and West Germany prior to reunification (Christa Buschendorf and Nicole Lindenberg); and post-World War II Japan (Michio Arimitsu and Raphaël

15 See Aretha Phiri's and Olga Panova's chapters (Chapters 5 and 6) in this volume.

16 For the full catalogue of Ralph Ellison's personal library, housed in the Library of Congress, see 'The Ralph Ellison Collection, 1937–2010', <https://findingaids.loc.gov/exist_collections/ead3pdf/rbc/2016/rb016001.pdf>, accessed 1 July 2020.

Lambert). This new direction in Ellison studies, while it cannot of course be comprehensive (and does not seek to be), unambiguously demonstrates the significance of *Invisible Man* in a range of non-US narratives of national identity and racial formation, and hence to processes of political and cultural coercion, complicity and/or resistance in those various settings. Both in its individual case studies and as a whole, then, this volume shows that to liberate Ralph Ellison from the imposed confines of US borders is at once to illuminate and to complicate the always-fraught questions of protest, subversion and appropriation that animate our understandings of his life and work.

One factor in the critical focus on Ellison's 'Americanness' is indubitably the 1950s / Cold War era 'old American studies' perspective of the many canonical Ellison scholars who for so long dominated the field. And not coincidentally, of course, Ellison's own presentation of both himself and his work, in letters, interviews and essays over the decades, is itself deeply invested in the many and often-conflicting meanings of 'America'. His claims to 'Americanness' lie at the core of his nuanced self-fashioning during the 1950s–1970s, including his careful self-positioning in relation to both the Civil Rights Movement and the Black Arts Movement. Yet while the word 'American' may well be the adjective that recurs most frequently across his *Collected Essays*, as Brent Hayes Edwards and countless others have argued, 'American' as Ellison uses it is by no means a stable or uncomplex term.[17] Potentially at least, there is a notable slippage between the intentions of Ellison's self-descriptions, and the effects of many critics' re-inscription of that self-positioning. In asserting his 'Americanness' across the decades of the 1940 to the 1990s Ellison, of course, meant many different things by the term, but one of these was an insistence that African Americans be properly recognized as Americans (and so a novel by an African American author be recognized as an American book); another, connected implication was in order to insist on and stake a claim to the as-yet-unrealized democratic vision of equality, freedom and individual opportunity in which the author staunchly believed. And so, as Lucas Morel and Timothy Parrish (among

17 See Edwards, 'Ralph Ellison and the Grain of Internationalism', 116–17.

others) have separately argued,[18] this novelist's claim to an American identity and American aesthetic can in itself be seen as a radical and resistant act. It was not necessarily the conservative endorsement of nationalism, American exceptionalism and concomitant (cultural) imperialism that our transnationally reattuned ears might detect in the easy reification of Ellison's Americanness that characterizes some quarters of the critical field.

Another factor in the scholarly reluctance, in some quarters, to consider Ellison's work in global contexts may be the perceived scarcity of international settings in both this author's biography and his literary work. The reality, of course, is that although (unlike Richard Wright or James Baldwin) Ellison never relocated on a long-term basis to Europe, he travelled widely in the 1950s in particular, and throughout his life he maintained a deep interest and investment in global cultures and issues. Beyond the always-and-already transnational nature of the African American folklore and music in which this author was immersed, the training in classical music that he received both at high school and at the Tuskegee Institute must have been one of his first encounters with an international culture. His subversive deployment of Beethoven's Fifth Symphony in *Invisible Man*, however, is rarely if ever documented as a 'transnational moment' or an 'international allusion' by critics. Similarly, while there are many invaluable studies of the novelist's allusiveness to non-American literature – for example, to the Greek and Roman classics, to Dante, to James Joyce, to the nineteenth-century Russian novelists, to Wole Soyinka or to Derek Walcott – again, critics rarely emphasize or examine the transnationalism itself of this intertextuality.[19] Indeed, one conscious

18 See Lucas E. Morel, ed., *Ralph Ellison and the Raft of Hope: A Political Companion to* Invisible Man (Lexington: University Press of Kentucky, 2004); Timothy Parrish, *Ralph Ellison and the Genius of America* (Amherst: University of Massachusetts Press, 2012).

19 On Ellison and the Greek and Roman classics, see Patrice Rankine, *Ulysses in Black: Ralph Ellison, Classicism and African American Literature* (Madison: University of Wisconsin Press, 2006); Justine McConnell, 'Invisible Odysseus: A Homeric Hero in Ralph Ellison's *Invisible Man*', in Lydia Langerwerf and Cressida Ryan, eds, *Zero to Hero, Hero to Zero: In Search of the Classical Hero* (Newcastle upon Tyne: Cambridge Scholars Press, 2010), 161–82; and Tessa Roynon, *The Classical Tradition in Modern American Fiction* (Edinburgh: Edinburgh University Press, 2021); on Ellison and

aim of our volume, in including chapters on Ellison's engagement with Jane Ellen Harrison and with Ovid, is to reframe his classical allusiveness as part of his 'worldliness'.[20] The comparative contexts that our first four chapters provide for each other are key to our reframing of Ellison's referentiality, and undergird our thesis that that the extra-national reach of his reading must be properly recognized as part of his life story.

Furthermore, with a few notable exceptions – including Marzioli and Edwards, of course – critics have not been especially well attuned to Ellison's interest in international affairs. For example, it is commonplace to use the anecdote about Ellison copying out Hemingway's *New York Times* pieces on the Spanish Civil War (while in Ohio during the winter of 1937–8) to emphasize his interest in Hemingway, but not to explore his interest in Spanish politics.[21] And even though both Lawrence Jackson and Arnold Rampersad devote several pages of their respective biographies to documenting Ellison's role, from 1942 to 1943, as Managing Editor at the

---

Dante, see Robert Butler, 'Dante's *Inferno* and Ellison's *Invisible Man*: A Study in Literary Continuity', *CLA Journal* 28/1 (1984), 54–77; on Ellison and Joyce, see Marc C. Conner, 'Father Abraham: Ellison's Agon with the Fathers in *Three Days before the Shooting …*', in Marc C. Conner and Lucas E. Morel, eds, *The New Territory: Ralph Ellison and the Twenty-First Century* (Jackson: University Press of Mississippi, 2016), 167–93; on Ellison and Dostoevsky, see Joseph Frank, 'Ralph Ellison and Dostoevsky', in Joseph Frank, ed., *Through the Russian Prism: Essays on Literature and Culture* (Princeton, NJ: Princeton University Press, 1990), 34–48; on Ellison and Allende, see Deborah Cohn, 'To See or Not to See: Invisibility, Clairvoyance, and Re-visions of History in *Invisible Man* and *La casa de los espíritus*', *Comparative Literature Studies* 33/4 (1996), 372–95; on Ellison and Soyinka, see Patrice Rankine, '"Black Is, Black Ain't": Classical Reception and Nothingness in Ralph Ellison, Wole Soyinka and Derek Walcott', *Revue de Littérature Comparée* 344/4 (2012), 457–74.

20 See Daniel Orrells, Gurminder Bhambra and Tessa Roynon, eds, *African Athena: New Agendas* (Oxford: Oxford University Press, 2011), for the argument that classical culture is 'pre-national' (16). Both prior to and, since the conference, 'Classics and/as World Literature', directed by Edith Hall at Kings College London in June 2016, many scholars have fruitfully considered classical literature as a key element of global literary culture.

21 See, for example, John F. Callahan, Introduction to *Flying Home and Other Stories* (London: Penguin, 2016), xvi–xvii.

short-lived magazine, *Negro Quarterly*, each biographer homes in on the articles therein that most pertain to the American national scene.[22] Edwards does usefully parse the internationalism of Ellison's own editorials in this publication; Williams attests to the fact that 'the comparative approach to race relations was particularly evident' in this journal as a whole; and Jackson, in an interesting turn of phrase, rightly summarizes that its 'cries for black rights, understood within a broad international context of Asian and African anticolonial movements', were 'bordering on the seditious'.[23] Yet, although beyond the scope of our own study here, there is surely a need for further and more detailed scholarly analysis of the transnational, anti-colonial and anti-racist nature of much of this journal's contents, which include, for example, 'Some Aspects of the Color Problem in Cuba', by Romula Lachantañere; 'India and the People's War' and 'The Crisis in India' both by Kumar Goshal; and 'Africa Against the Axis' by John Pittman.[24]

It was in 1943, soon after the *Negro Quarterly* folded, that Ellison himself went abroad for the first time, as a sea cook in the Merchant Marine. His ensuing travels in Europe included his being stationed in Swansea (in South Wales), an experience that precipitated his sense of identification with Welsh nationalists that he immortalizes in the short story of 1944, 'In a Strange Country', and of connectedness over national borders that he dramatizes in 'A Storm of Blizzard Proportions'.[25] Despite Williams's nuanced essay on Ellison's relationship with Wales, and Edwards's invocation of both this formative cultural encounter and of the gesturing towards Haitian history in another short story, 'Mister Toussan',[26] the prevailing understanding of Ellison's stories pays little heed to their transnationalism.

22 See Lawrence Jackson, *Ralph Ellison: Emergence of Genius* (New York: Wiley and Sons, 2002), 253–81; Arnold Rampersad, *Ralph Ellison* (New York: Vintage, 2008), 162–5.

23 Edwards, 'Ralph Ellison and the Grain of Internationalism', 118, 125; Williams, '"If We Only Had Some of What They Have": Ralph Ellison in Wales', 41; Jackson, *Ralph Ellison: Emergence of Genius*, 265–6.

24 See *Negro Quarterly* 1/2 (1942) and *Negro Quarterly* 1/3 (1942).

25 See Rampersad, *Ralph Ellison*, 170–1. Marc Conner also discusses Ellison's time in Wales in the Afterword to this volume.

26 Williams, '"If We Only Had Some of What They Have": Ralph Ellison in Wales'; Edwards, 'Ralph Ellison and the Grain of Internationalism'.

Instead, they are predominantly read as uniformly articulating, in Callahan's words in his introduction to the *Flying Home* anthology, 'Ellison's discovery of *his* American theme', and as pointing to his 'remarkably consistent vision of American identity over the fifty-five years of his writing life'.[27] Without question, Ellison emerges in these stories as an insightful chronicler of many dimensions of American and African American experience, but in that chronicling he is also profoundly conscious of America's global identity. And this consciousness only increases during the post-World War II era that was characterized both by that nation's problematic global dominance and by his own assured success as a novelist.

It is now widely accepted that the author's engagement with black internationalism in *Invisible Man* is more complex than the erstwhile conventional wisdom, rooted in the negative depiction of Ras the Destroyer, has allowed. And it was of course the worldwide success of this novel that propelled Ellison himself fully into the international sphere. As Chapters 6, 7 and 8 in this book testify (and as Jacqueline Covo began to explore in her 1974 assessment of the French, German and Italian critical reception of the novel),[28] numerous translations and foreign editions of the novel followed on from the Norwegian version that, first off the blocks, appeared in 1953. And, as Covo documents, the novel was reviewed not just across Europe but also in Southern Rhodesia (now Zimbabwe); Australia, New Zealand and India. As the contributors to the second part of *Global Ralph Ellison* attest, the many fascinating notes and letters in 'Foreign Rights and Translations' file on *Invisible Man* in the Library of Congress indicate both Fanny and Ralph Ellison's clear investment in and commitment to the many non-American incarnations of *Invisible Man*.[29] While we leave the bibliographic task of publishing a coherent catalogue of these translations and foreign editions to future scholars, the 'Ellison in the World'

27 Callahan, Introduction to *Flying Home and Other Stories*, xxi (italics in original), xxxii.

28 Jacqueline Covo, *The Blinking Eye: Ralph Waldo Emerson and His American, French, German and Italian Critics* (Metuchen, NJ: Scarecrow Press, 1974).

29 See the Ralph Ellison papers in the Library of Congress: I.153 ('Foreign Rights and Translations 1952–78'); I.154 ('Foreign Rights and Translations 1980–89') and II.66 ('Foreign Rights and Translations 1989–95').

section of this volume initiates the retrieval of this novel's transnational histories from their current place in the shadows of the extant biographical and critical record.

Following hot on the heels of his globetrotting novel, from 1954 onwards Ellison undertook a series of overseas trips to which scholars are only now beginning to pay focused attention.[30] As Buschendorf and Lindenberg discuss in Chapter 7 of this volume, he travelled to Austria and several times to West Germany; he also lived for two years in Rome and visited nearly every other major Italian city; he went at least three times to Paris; and also visited the Netherlands, London and Madrid. He became something of a regular at PEN International conferences, attending those held in London in 1956; Japan (as Arimitsu and Lambert discuss in Chapter 8 here) in 1957, which was a trip that also took him to Hong Kong and Pakistan; and in Frankfurt in 1959. The very fact of his participation in PEN and in the 1957 World Congress for Cultural Freedom in Mexico City speaks to the politically engaged international dimensions of his perspectives and position.[31] Yet it is curious that while biographer Rampersad dutifully notes all these trips and encounters, he is at far greater pains to emphasize Ellison's self-distancing from Africa and African resistance movements in the late 1950s and early 1960s – a subject returned to by Phiri in Chapter 5 here – than he is to interpret the international travels that Ellison did undertake as in any way important or formative. In fact, in a strange parenthetical paragraph, Rampersad instead infers great significance from where (and how) Ralph Ellison did *not* go: 'He never visited Africa. His brief trip to Mexico marked his only time in Latin America. In fact, Ralph and Fanny never once paid for a visit or vacation outside the United States'.[32]

If we conversely understand Ellison from the late 1950s onwards as someone profoundly shaped by the global mobility that he enjoyed during those few years, it comes as no surprise that the manuscripts that make up *Three Days Before the Shooting …* (2010) reflect, in the words of Welborn McIntyre,

30 See, for example, Marzioli, 'Ralph Ellison's Exception Diaspora'; also Sara Marzioli, 'Snapshots of the Eternal City: Ralph Ellison in Rome', *Modernism/Modernity* 24/4 (2017), 447–66.

31 See Marzioli, 'Ralph Ellison's Exception Diaspora'.

32 Rampersad, *Ralph Ellison*, 366.

the narrator of Book I, the recognition that 'the world is of a sad, complex whole'.[33] McIntyre remembers his wartime days in France, a peacetime visit to Salzburg, and an incident when socializing with the international intellectual elite in Rome. While he reflects on his friendship with a French writer named Vannec (whose name is inspired by Malraux),[34] his racist colleague McGowan makes dismissive reference to the freedom struggles of 'Nehru, Nasser, and the Mau Maus' from his comfortable seat in a Washington DC club.[35]

As the vast task of interpreting and analysing *Three Days* has only just begun, it is perhaps inevitable that the important first collection of scholarly essays on this work, *The New Territory*, only briefly treats the transnational dimensions of the work. While its introduction cites Posnock's declaration of Ellison's relevance to our 'global, transnational age', this volume does not itself unequivocally claim the new Ellisonian territory as global.[36] For example, while Eric Sundquist explores Ellison's interweaving of West African, African American and Graeco-Roman myths about flying in 'Hickman in Washington DC', and while Conner takes our understanding of Ellison's engagement with Joyce in significant new directions, no explicit claim is made in that volume for the transnationalism of *Three Days* as a whole.[37] While we do begin that process here – especially in the chapters by myself (Tessa Roynon) and by Stephen Rachman, on the influence, on the unfinished

33 Ralph Ellison, *Three Days before the Shooting …* (New York: Modern Library, 2011), 85.

34 For a discussion of the name 'Vannec' and Malraux in *Three Days*, see Benji De La Piedra, 'Ellison's White Liberal Rhinehart: The Negro American Core of Book I of *Three Days before the Shooting …*', *Literature of the Americas* 5 (2018), 132–50.

35 Ellison, *Three Days before the Shooting …*, 55; for discussion of this sentence, see Edwards, 'Ralph Ellison and the Grain of Internationalism', 129. In Chapter 7 in this volume, Christa Buschendorf and Nicole Lindenberg discuss the relationship between Ellison's travels in Germany and his representation of German towns in the unfinished novel.

36 Marc C. Conner and Lucas E. Morel, Introduction to *The New Territory: Ralph Ellison and the Twenty-First Century* (Jackson: University Press of Mississippi, 2016), 4.

37 Eric Sundquist, 'Ralph Ellison in His Labyrinth', in Marc C. Conner and Lucas E. Morel, eds, *The New Territory: Ralph Ellison and the Twenty-First Century* (Jackson: University Press of Mississippi, 2016), 117–41; Conner, 'Ellison's Agon with the Fathers in *Three Days before the Shooting …*', 177–86.

novel, of Ovid and of Dostoevsky, respectively – this important task is one that we hope future scholars will continue. Among the many new analyses that these manuscripts still demand, for example, it could certainly be argued that Hickman's prolonged encounter with Native American culture and traditions, manifest in his lengthy exchanges with the character of Love New in the 'Hickman in Georgia and Oklahoma' section, have their place in post-colonial and globalized understandings of this work and this author. They epitomize just one of the many ways in which Ellison, in this text, ventures beyond the parameters of United States identity.

Although Parts I and II of *Global Ralph Ellison* differ significantly (and consciously so) in both their subject matter and their methodology – the first four chapters focus on the literary and intellectual forces that shaped Ellison's creativity, while the last four chapters examine how his published writing shaped and was received by the worlds in which it appeared – they do have much in common beyond their globality. Each chapter in this volume tells a previously untold story: the story of a complex and multifaceted encounter either between Ellison and a specific intellectual ancestor, or between Ellison and his many worldwide readers. The nature of these encounters, moreover, is often counter-intuitive. Ellison's relationship with Henry James, for example, or his reception in apartheid and post-apartheid South Africa, have dimensions to them which challenge many of our first and too-easily-made assumptions.

These chapters are also striking for the insights they contain that are not exclusively about Ellison. From thinking about how he read Jane Ellen Harrison or Ovid or Dostoevsky, we discover more about those figures too, as well as about the often almost intangible processes of reading and intellectual formation in general. Through focusing on how Soviet critics or, in a very different way, contemporary novelists such as Ōe Kenzaburō (from Japan) have responded to Ellison, and have to some extent harnessed him to their own agendas, we see just how subjective and motivated literary reception invariably is. These chapters reveal the power and influence that individual translators, publishers and scholars exert in the shaping of whole cultures and political mindsets. The glimpses into how African American literature was conceptualized behind the Iron Curtain – in East Germany or the USSR in the 1950s and 1960s – reconnects 'Western' readers with black American novelists such as John O. Killens (1916–87), who was contemporaneous with Ellison and was paid significant attention in those regions at that time, but whose name is seldom heard within the US academy of today.

Lastly, all eight chapters in this volume are remarkable for their use of the archive. The respective studies of Ellison's engagement with Jane Ellen Harrison, Ovid, Dostoevsky and Henry James all make significant use of the 'Ralph Ellison Collection' in the Library of Congress – the treasure trove that is the author's personal book collection. The authors of these chapters posit provocative new connections between texts, and focus in detail on specific passages that were important to Ellison, often bringing to light annotations that scholars have never discussed until now. For the chapters in Part II, contributors have made extensive use of material in the 'Foreign Rights and Translations' folders in the Ralph Ellison papers, and have conducted extraordinary detective work in tracking down translated editions of *Invisible Man* and in early reviews of the novel in long-buried newspapers and journals in their respective locales. The authors of these chapters have proved beyond doubt this text's impact as a 'world novel', through seeking out and contacting figures who played a significant role in the trajectories they have reconstructed. Communication and correspondence – whether in the form of the magisterial *Selected Letters of Ralph Ellison* (whose timely arrival has been so useful to our project),[38] or of relevant letters by Ellison that remain unpublished, or of letters by would-be translators and enthusiastic readers and scholars from around the globe to Ellison, or of letters to and from Fanny Ellison both to family members and to publishers and agents, or of recent e-mails between the authors of these chapters and the key players in their research (both students and professors) – are one of the most important resources on which this volume draws.

'The World in Ellison: Migratory Intertexts', Part I of *Global Ralph Ellison*, begins with Sam Halliday's study of Ellison's ambivalent relationship with Henry James. It focuses in particular on how aspects of the 'international' or expatriate James paradoxically helped the African American author to explore many dimensions of Americanness. Using letters, notes

38 *The Selected Letters of Ralph Ellison*, eds, John F. Callahan and Marc C. Conner (New York: Random House, 2019).

and marginalia alongside the published record, and examining Ellison's responses to James alongside those of Baldwin and Wright, Halliday argues that all three black writers found paradigms for their explorations of racial exclusion and a sense of exile through the white, expatriate nineteenth-century writer's perspectives on Europe.

Next, in Chapter 2, Bryan Crable explores Ellison's debt to the writings of the well-known 'Cambridge Ritualist', Jane Ellen Harrison, and in particular to her work *Themis*, which first appeared in 1912. Crable shows that Harrison's scholarship on archaic Greek culture played a key role in Ellison's thinking about racial identity, race relations and race conflict in the USA, and was a significant influence on *Invisible Man*. This chapter goes on to argue that Harrison's conceptualizations of sacrifice and of sacrament, in particular, crucially informed the novelist's approach to American race ritual, and may even have played a role in his struggle to complete his second fictional work.

In the third chapter, I (Tessa Roynon) home in on another dimension of European and classical culture that was formative for Ellison: that of the Roman poet, Ovid, and in particular the mock-epic epic, the *Metamorphoses*, which Ovid composed in around 8 CE. Through a focus on the thematics of change in both *Invisible Man* and *Three Days before the Shooting …*, I first discuss the ways in which a generalized 'Ovidian dynamic', concerned with chaos and transformation, informs Ellison's oeuvre-wide explorations of instability and transition. I then analyse how the over-reaching Ovidian heroes Icarus and Phaethon not only resonate significantly in the 'Hickman in Washington DC' section of *Three Days …*, but also how in so doing they are integral to this text's interest in the connectedness of Africa and ancient Greece and Rome. Lastly, I argue that in that same section of the unfinished novel Ellison invokes both Ovid's famous sculptor, Pygmalion, and the ill-fated huntsman, Actaeon, in his explorations of the power and limitations of the artistic figure – whether this be jazzman, preacher or novelist.

And in the fourth and final chapter on Ellison's transnational intellectual formation, Stephen Rachman makes extensive use of the archive to demonstrate the hitherto unacknowledged breadth, depth and complexity of Ellison's research into and engagement with the fictional works and aesthetic theories of Dostoevsky. In a reassessment that greatly extends the conventional wisdom about this literary pairing, Rachman sheds light on the role of Dostoevsky in Ellison's relationship with Richard Wright, and the connections between Ellison's thinking about nineteenth-century Russian culture and his theories of blues, jazz and other vernacular forms of African American culture. Rachman also locates the origins of several of the scenarios in *Thee Days before the Shooting* ... in Dostoevsky's texts.

This volume's Part II, 'Ellison in the World', constitutes a deliberate new departure from the chapters that precede it. In the first of this quartet of ground-breaking chapters, Aretha Phiri maps out the complex and often conflicted reception of both *Invisible Man* and its author in the South Africa of the apartheid and post-apartheid eras. Beginning with a nuanced consideration of Ellison's sometimes vexed relationship to black politics in general, and African politics in particular, Phiri goes on to delineate how the iconic novel has in turn been banned, fêted, misappropriated, rejected and identified with in numerous different contexts over the turbulent decades of the 1950s to the present. In a closing section on 'teaching and studying *Invisible Man* in post-apartheid contexts', Phiri draws illuminating conclusions from her research among contemporary students and academics about the ways the novel's problematizing of identity politics may or may not speak to the contested issues of race, gender and the decolonizing of the curriculum in South Africa today.

Addressing very different but no less fraught (and still-evolving) political contexts, in Chapter 6 Olga Panova charts the 'complex fate' of *Invisible Man*, and of the status and reputation of Ellison, in both the USSR and post-Soviet Russia. Panova considers Ellison's paradoxical status of an 'invisible classic' – almost unknown to the common Russian reader (due to the fact that *Invisible Man* as a whole still remains untranslated into Russian), but very well known to Russian scholars specializing in American literature. This chapter illuminates the fascinating ways in which interpretations of *Invisible Man* are refashioned according to the fluctuating climate of the Cold War and its aftermath. Delineating a trajectory of the scattered and fragmentary translation of sections of the Ellisonian oeuvre, it excavates significant archival material, for example, about an unauthorized Ukrainian translation of the 'Battle Royal' published in 1977. The chapter ends on an upbeat note with the news that Olga Panova herself is currently under contract to complete the first full-length translation of Ellison's 1952 novel into Russian.

In Chapter 7, Christa Buschendorf and Nicole Lindenberg shed further light on our understanding of the reception of Ellison in Europe during the Cold War through their comparison of the widely differing responses to the man and his work in East and West Germany. They begin with a discussion of the merits and shortcomings of the 1954 German translation of *Invisible Man* by Georg Goyert, and by analysing the significance of Ellison's visit to Austria in that same year, where he participated in the Salzburg Seminar. They also document the Ellisons' various travels in West Germany during the course of the 1950s. Focusing primarily on the trajectory of scholarly work on *Invisible Man* in journals, monographs and literary histories in the then-new field of American studies, the authors show that while in West Germany Ellison is praised for his aesthetics and his humanism, in East Germany he is criticized and even overlooked for his (perceived) lack of progressive and overt political thinking.

Michio Arimitsu and Raphaël Lambert's analysis of the evolving responses to Ellison and to African American literature as a whole in post-World War II Japan constitutes the eighth and final chapter in this volume. This chapter argues that Hashimoto Fukuo's 1958 translation of *Invisible Man* played a significant role in the increasing visibility and relevance of black American literature for the national reading public. Going on to discuss the significance of the thirteen-volume anthology of African American literature, *Kokujin bungaku zenshū* [*The Complete Works of Black Literature*], that appeared in the early 1960s and that featured Hashimoto's full translation of Ellison's text, Arimitsu and Lambert reflect on the part played by the Ellisonian concepts of invisibility and diversity on mid-to-late twentieth-century conceptions of racial identity in Japan. They illuminate the novel's importance to future Nobel Prizewinner Ōe Kenzaburō, among many other leading intellectuals of the postwar era.

In bringing this volume to a close, Marc Conner, in his Afterword, observes that the themes of chaos, suffering, racial injustice and transformative potential in Ellison's work speak to the precise moment in which we are completing our work on this publication: to the summer of 2020, when the Covid-19 pandemic and the global anti-racist protests precipitated by the brutal murder of George Floyd continue to dominate world headlines. Ellison's work indubitably has a capacity to speak to the most pressing international crises of our times: the disruptive reverberations of *Invisible Man* in German author Jenny Erpenbeck's 2015 novel *Go, Went, Gone* [*Gehen, Ging, Gegangen*], about the refugee situation in contemporary Germany, is just one further example of this phenomenon.

In both theorizing and exemplifying the 'global Ralph Ellison' in this volume as a whole, we should remember that to Ellison himself (as Conner implies in his Afterword), the concept of 'the world' meant very different things at different times. As Crable has noted, in 1945 Ellison wrote to Kenneth Burke that he 'would like to write simply as an American, or even better, a citizen of the world', but that his identity as a 'Negro American' made such a purportedly 'universal' stance impossible, as it would require him to 'throw away the racial … emphasis'.[39] Yet in 1963, in his famous essay 'The World and the Jug', the author implicitly claims that 'the world' is as much the black American's as it is anyone else's, and resists the 'jug' of 'segregation' into which Irving Howe wishes to contain him and his work.[40] The infinitely variable concept of the 'global Ralph Ellison' is an ongoing field of inquiry in which much work remains to be done: on the relationship between contemporary experimental African writers (such as the self-avowed Ellison fan, Teju Cole) and Ellison, for example, or in excavating the currently still-buried stories of the reception of Ellison in the Caribbean, in Latin America, or in China. Yet despite the complexities, contradictions and occlusions that the vast perspective of the transnational Ralph Ellison involves, the resistant *potential* of his work, when seen through this lens, is possibly one of its few certainties.

39 Bryan Crable, *Ralph Ellison and Kenneth Burke: At the Roots of the Racial Divide* (Charlottesville: University of Virginia Press, 2012), 64.

40 Ralph Ellison, 'The World and the Jug', in John F. Callahan, ed., *The Collected Essays of Ralph Ellison* (New York: Modern Library, 1995), 163–4.

Bibliography

Arac, Jonathan, 'Global and Babel: Language and Planet in American Literature', in Wai Chee Dimock and Lawrence Buell, eds, *Shades of the Planet: American Literature as World Literature* (Princeton, NJ: Princeton University Press, 2007), 19–38.

——, 'Toward a Critical Genealogy of the U.S. Discourse of Identity: *Invisible Man* after Fifty Years', *boundary 2* 30/2 (2003), 195–216.

Boehmer, Elleke, Rouven Kunstmann, Priyasha Mukhopadhyay and Asha Rogers, eds, *The Global Histories of Books: Methods and Practices* (London: Palgrave Macmillan, 2017).

Burton, Antoinette and Isabel Hofmeyr, eds, *Ten Books that Shaped the British Empire: Creating an Imperial Commons* (Durham, NC: Duke University Press, 2014).

Butler, Robert, 'Dante's *Inferno* and Ellison's *Invisible Man*: A Study in Literary Continuity', *CLA Journal* 28/1 (1984), 54–77.

Callahan, John F., 'Introduction' to *Flying Home and Other Stories* (London: Penguin, 2016), ix–xxxiii.

Cohn, Deborah, 'To See or Not to See: Invisibility, Clairvoyance, and Re-visions of History in *Invisible Man* and *La casa de los espíritus*', *Comparative Literature Studies* 33/4 (1996), 372–95.

Conner, Marc C., 'Father Abraham: Ellison's Agon with the Fathers in *Three Days before the Shooting …*', in Marc C. Conner and Lucas E. Morel, eds, *The New Territory: Ralph Ellison and the Twenty-First Century* (Jackson: University Press of Mississippi, 2016), 167–93.

—— and Lucas E. Morel, eds, *The New Territory: Ralph Ellison and the Twenty-First Century* (Jackson: University Press of Mississippi, 2016), 3–38.

Covo, Jacqueline, *The Blinking Eye: Ralph Waldo Ellison and His American, French, German and Italian Critics* (Metuchen, NJ: Scarecrow Press, 1974).

Crable, Bryan, *Ralph Ellison and Kenneth Burke: At the Roots of the Racial Divide* (Charlottesville: University of Virginia Press, 2012).

Davies, Dominic, Erica Lombard and Benjamin Mountford, eds, *Fighting Words: Fifteen Books that Shaped the Postcolonial World* (Oxford: Peter Lang, 2017).

De La Piedra, Benji, 'Ellison's White Liberal Rhinehart: The Negro American Core of Book I of *Three Days before the Shooting …*', *Literature of the Americas* 5 (2018), 132–50.

Dimock, Wai Chee and Lawrence Buell, eds, *Shades of the Planet: American Literature as World Literature* (Princeton, NJ: Princeton University Press, 2007).

Edwards, Brent Hayes, *The Practice of Diaspora: Literature, Translation and the Rise of Black Internationalism* (Cambridge, MA: Harvard University Press, 2003).
——, 'Ralph Ellison and the Grain of Internationalism', in Brian T. Edwards and Dilip Parameshwar Gaonkar, eds, *Globalizing American Studies* (Chicago: Chicago University Press, 2010), 115–34.
Edwards, Brian T. and Dilip Parameshwar Gaonkar, eds, *Globalizing American Studies* (Chicago: Chicago University Press, 2010).
Ellison, Ralph, *Invisible Man* (New York: Vintage, 1995).
——, *The Selected Letters of Ralph Ellison*, eds, John F. Callahan and Marc C. Conner (New York: Random House, 2019).
——, *Three Days before the Shooting …* (New York: Modern Library, 2011).
——, 'The World and the Jug', in John F. Callahan, ed., *The Collected Essays of Ralph Ellison* (New York: Modern Library, 2003), 155–88.
'Foreign Rights and Translations, 1952–78', Library of Congress, Ralph Ellison papers I.153.
'Foreign Rights and Translations, 1980–89', Library of Congress, Ralph Ellison papers I.154.
'Foreign Rights and Translations, 1989–95', Library of Congress, Ralph Ellison papers II.66.
Frank, Joseph, 'Ralph Ellison and Dostoevsky', in *Through the Russian Prism: Essays on Literature and Culture* (Princeton, NJ: Princeton University Press, 1990), 34–48.
Giles, Paul, *The Global Remapping of American Literature* (Princeton, NJ: Princeton University Press, 2011).
Gilroy, Paul, *The Black Atlantic: Modernity and Double Consciousness* (London: Verso, 1993).
Kelley, Robin D. G., *Freedom Dreams: The Black Radical Imagination* (Boston, MA: Beacon Press, 2002).
Makalani, Minkah, *In the Cause of Freedom: Radical Black Internationalism from Harlem to London, 1917–39* (Chapel Hill: University of North Carolina Press, 2011).
Marzioli, Sara, 'Ralph Ellison's Exceptional Diaspora: The View from Rome', *Atlantic Studies* 9/4 (2012), 447–66.
——, 'Snapshots of the Eternal City: Ralph Ellison in Rome', *Modernism/Modernity* 24/4 (2017), 829–39.
McConnell, Justine, 'Invisible Odysseus: A Homeric Hero in Ralph Ellison's *Invisible Man*', in Lydia Langerwerf and Cressida Ryan, eds, *Zero to Hero, Hero to Zero: In Search of the Classical Hero* (Newcastle upon Tyne: Cambridge Scholars Press, 2010), 161–82.

Morel, Lucas E., ed., *Ralph Ellison and the Raft of Hope: A Political Companion to* Invisible Man (Lexington: University Press of Kentucky, 2004).
Negro Quarterly 1/2 (1942).
Negro Quarterly 1/3 (1942).
Orrells, Daniel, Gurminder Bhambra and Tessa Roynon, eds, *African Athena: New Agendas* (Oxford: Oxford University Press, 2011).
Parrish, Timothy, *Ralph Ellison and the Genius of America* (Amherst: University of Massachusetts Press, 2012).
'The Ralph Ellison Collection, 1937–2010', <https://findingaids.loc.gov/exist_collections/ead3pdf/rbc/2016/rb016001.pdf>, accessed 1 July 2020.
Rampersad, Arnold, *Ralph Ellison: A Biography* (New York: Vintage, 2008).
Rankine, Patrice, '"Black Is, Black Ain't": Classical Reception and Nothingness in Ralph Ellison, Wole Soyinka and Derek Walcott', *Revue de Littérature Comparée* 344/4 (2012), 457–74.
——, *Ulysses in Black: Ralph Ellison, Classicism, and African American Literature* (Madison: University of Wisconsin Press, 2006).
Rogers, Gayle, 'American Modernisms in the World', in Joshua Miller, ed., *The Cambridge Companion to the American Modernist Novel* (Cambridge, UK: Cambridge University Press, 2015), 227–44.
Roynon, Tessa, *The Classical Tradition in Modern American Fiction* (Edinburgh: Edinburgh University Press, 2021).
Sundquist, Eric, 'Ralph Ellison in His Labyrinth', in Marc C. Conner and Lucas E. Morel, eds, *The New Territory: Ralph Ellison and the Twenty-First Century* (Jackson: University Press of Mississippi, 2016), 117–41.
Tyrrell, Ian, 'Reflections on the Transnational Turn in United States History: Theory and Practice', *Journal of Global History* 4/3 (2009), 453–74.
Umoren, Imaobong, *Race Women Internationalists: Activist-Intellectuals and Global Freedom Struggles* (Oakland: University of California Press, 2018).
Williams, Daniel, '"If We Only Had Some of What They Have": Ralph Ellison in Wales', *Comparative American Studies: An International Journal* 4/1 (2006), 25–48.

PART I

The World in Ellison: Migratory Intertexts

SAM HALLIDAY

1 Ralph Ellison and the Divergent African American Claims on Henry James

ABSTRACT:
Ralph Ellison was a devotee of Henry James, whom he regarded as a key theorist and practitioner of the novel in America. But he also chafed against aspects of James's work, under the influence of critics who thought James negligent of America itself. In this chapter, I consider how these competing impulses contribute to Ellison's appraisal of James, focusing on the latter's status as an 'American abroad'. To do this, the chapter reads that appraisal alongside responses to James by two of Ellison's African American contemporaries, Richard Wright and James Baldwin. All three writers felt that James's most important lessons for them, as Americans, paradoxically, came via his relationship to Europe. In that relationship, they found models for their own examinations of racial exile and exclusion.

Ralph Ellison's regard for Henry James was deep and unconcealed. He makes James central to his vision of the novel in essays such as 'The Novel as a Function of American Democracy' (1967), and often mentions James in interviews and letters. Yet the seeds of this regard within James's work, and the intellectual and political consequences of them for Ellison's own, remain largely unexplored. In this chapter, I explore them in relation to a claim that James himself may well have been surprised by. This is the claim that Ellison takes James's 'international theme' and bends it to the services of domestic, if not parochial concerns. The transatlantic topics of the former's work are revised or repurposed as 'national' topics in the latter's. Cosmopolitanism is transcoded as citizenship. In this respect, the most salient terms of Ellison's relation to James are to be found not in those interviews and letters, where Ellison refers to James directly (or rather, not *only* in those), but in 'Some Questions and Some Answers' (1958), a text of his post-*Invisible Man* fame where Ellison focuses on political themes pertaining to the United States and its relation to the wider world. Here, Ellison observes that 'the United States is an international country' and that it is disposed as such to 'intra-national conflicts'.[1] Relations that elsewhere inhere *between* countries here exist *within* one. In the United States, the sort of international dynamics that fascinated James recur inside (as well as between) regions, states, towns and cities. It is in echo of the 'inter' in the 'intra' that Ellison puts James to use.

The conflicts of most concern to Ellison inside the United States, meanwhile, revolve primarily around race. In his conception of American history, the experience of African Americans, and their generally adversarial relations with white, Euro-Americans, especially, are pivotal. Take four phases of this history that he addresses piecemeal, if not systematically, at points throughout his work: the Middle Passage, which brought slaves from Africa to the Americas from the early seventeenth to the early nineteenth centuries, and was crucial in its creation of a people identified (and, in Ellison's lifetime, identifying *as*) 'Negroes'; the American Revolution, of 1776, which withheld citizenship from that people, even in the act of creating it for others; the Civil War, of 1861–5, which belatedly bestowed citizenship on African Americans by bringing defeat to the slaveholding South; and the Great Migration, of the early 1900s, whereby huge numbers of African Americans transported themselves from the South to the industrial and urban north.[2] The Civil War aside, James's work may seem to have precious little to say about these things. And yet, for African Americans like Ellison, what it *does* say resonates powerfully with them, and with their own, otherwise distinct concerns with racial marginality, exile, incomprehension and discrimination.[3] Accordingly, this chapter

1 Ralph Ellison, 'Some Questions and Some Answers', in John F. Callahan, ed., *The Collected Essays of Ralph Ellison* (New York: Modern Library, 1995), 299–300.

2 On the Great Migration, see, above all, Lawrence R. Rodgers, *Canaan Bound: The African American Great Migration Novel* (Urbana: University of Illinois Press, 1997). For Ellison on the Middle Passage, and its relation to the term 'Negro,' see his 'Some Questions and Some Answers', 291. Ellison's references to the War of Independence and Civil War are discussed below.

3 And not just African *Americans*: for a riveting account of how and why James appealed to the Afro-Caribbean British intellectual Stuart Hall, see Hall, with Bill Schwarz, *Familiar Stranger: A Life between Two Islands* (London: Allen Lane, 2017), 215–17.

examines Ellison alongside two fellow African American novelists drawn to James for similar reasons, and whose regard for James thus holds up a powerful light to Ellison's own: Richard Wright and James Baldwin. Like Ellison, Wright and Baldwin co-opted elements of James's work for their respective analyses of cultural disparity and dislocation. Like James, they both made residences abroad, including stays in a European city whose literary representation James helped shape: Paris. All three devoured James's self-reflexive commentaries on technique and form.

Ellison and Wright, however, also treated James with ambivalence at times, scorning him for being overly enamoured of the European milieu in which he moved. In a letter to fellow novelist Albert Murray of 1956, for instance, Ellison writes of being impressed by two aristocrats he has met in London but adds that, notwithstanding this, he is 'not about to do a Henry James'.[4] In 1951, Wright insisted to an interviewer, similarly, that despite long residence abroad, his writing was not 'going in the Henry James direction'.[5] Both authors thus disclaimed a drift from patriotic virtue they sense their interlocutors will suspect. They dissociated themselves from James in this context to acknowledge his reputation for maintaining this drift to an egregious degree. Bound up with this reputation was a belief that James held few lessons for later writers, other than the negative one of showing how little good came of turning attention from the homeland. And this, above all, is what Ellison and Wright were determined to avoid. As we shall see, Ellison's conception of the novel, especially, demanded of its writers a kind of principled autochthony. Wright's comments in his 1951 interview broadly align him with this conception. And though Baldwin arrived at significantly different views – as we shall also see, he disagreed with Wright about what he called 'the meaning of Europe for an American Negro', especially – he too maintained that an American writer's paramount responsibility was to be an *American* writer, with all that that

4 Ralph Ellison, Letter to Albert Murray, 15 September 1956, in *Trading Twelves: The Selected Letters of Ralph Ellison and Albert Murray*, eds, Albert Murray and John F. Callahan (New York: Vintage, 2001), 143–44.

5 Allan Temko, 'An Interview with Expatriate Richard Wright in Paris', in Keneth Kinnamon and Michel Fabre, eds, *Conversations with Richard Wright* (Jackson: University of Mississippi, 1993), 153.

entails. A major thesis of this chapter is that the pressures exerted by this responsibility determine the lumpy shapes into which the three writers' ideas about James were sometimes forced.

To delineate these shapes, I both augment existing scholarship and highlight facets of the 'Jamesian' Ellison this scholarship has overlooked. As Michael Nowlin has recently observed, Baldwin's debt to James has often been recognized by scholars, though the same debt has more rarely considered by scholars of the other two writers – and where it has, has more rarely still been taken as an occasion for sustained investigation.[6] But as Nowlin goes on to show, James plays a significant role not only in the genealogy of Ellison, Wright and Baldwin's respective oeuvres but also in their relations with each other. In this chapter, I echo Nowlin's work, while paying more attention than he does to the nexus of national, transnational and intra-national James helps Ellison, Baldwin and Wright negotiate. To do this, I look at the published works of all four writers, as well as Ellison's unpublished documents: like several other writers in the present volume, I attend especially to his personal library and its marginalia. In the first and longest section of this chapter, I look in detail at Ellison's references to James, and show that, scattered though these are, they form a definite conceptual pattern. In two shorter sections, I consider variations on that pattern: in the second part, by comparing Ellison to Wright and Baldwin; in the third, returning to 'The Novel as a Function of American Democracy' and other texts that posit a nationally focused and race-responsive James.

'Complex Fate': The Jamesian Inheritance

What is an 'American'? In one of the fragmentary drafts of autobiography he wrote in the 1980s, Ellison answers this question by recalling how he

6 Michael Nowlin, 'Henry James and the Making of Modern African American Literature', *The Henry James Review* 39/3 (2018), 282–92.

arrived at this identity himself.[7] Rather than being one from birth, or having the status bestowed on one by governmental fiat (of the sort that may make one a US citizen, say, as in legal immigration), he argues, one becomes an American via a more protracted and possibly more arduous 'process of self-transformation'.[8] In his own case, this has involved moving to New York City as a young man, originally from Oklahoma, in the US's southwest, a move Ellison aligns broadly with the growth and maturation of the United States. For ever since the War of Independence, he argues, those processes have drawn the multitudinous and the singular, the regional and supra-regional, together. Thus the author's habituation in New York:

> I was becoming neither an abstract 'ex-southwesterner' nor a sophisticated 'New Yorker', but an individual variation upon a national type which after two hundred years of grappling with its racial, religious, and geographical diversity is still in the process of achieving a full measure of self-consciousness: A product of that democratic hope, uncertainty and turbulence in the mind and heart which identifies 'the American'.[9]

The couplet with which this recollection culminates is an allusion to Henry James's *The American* (1877, rev. 1907). At this novel's start, James introduces his protagonist by stating that '[a]n observer with anything of an eye for national types would have had no difficulty in determining' the character's 'origin', and would indeed appreciate the 'almost ideal completeness with which' the protagonist 'fill[s] out the national mould'.[10] Americanness for James, then, as for Ellison, is synonymous with 'type' – a term extending simultaneously in two directions along an axis that connects the individual, at one end, with the 'nation', at the other. To be *an* American is to possess attributes regarded as definitive of *the* American,

7 On these drafts, and their relation to Ellison's late work generally, see Marc C. Conner, '"Leaving the Territory": Ralph Ellison's Backward Glance', in Maria DiBattista and Emily O. Wittman, eds, *Modernism and Autobiography* (Cambridge, UK: Cambridge University Press, 2014), 113–26.

8 Ralph Ellison, Memoirs, Library of Congress, Ralph Ellison papers II:46, folder 6.

9 Ibid.

10 Henry James, *The American* (Boston, MA: Houghton Mifflin, 1877), 6.

as a category or genre. Though formally opposed, the typified and the typical are not so much antitheses as expressions and concomitants of each other. When Ellison invokes 'the American' in his autobiography, therefore, he is doing more than drawing attention to the fact that James uses the same couplet as a title for his novel; implicitly, he is also affirming the premise on which that title rests. According to this premise, nations are the 'mould' of nationals, and though the two authors differ in their respective accounts of what the typical American consists of (outward appearances in the case of James, inward 'mind and heart' in that of Ellison) both agree that this individual is founded in the nation, as in a forge or crucible.

The *prima facie* aptitude of James's title notwithstanding, there is however something slightly odd about Ellison's identification of his arrival in New York with *The American*, specifically. For James's text is not one set in the great American metropolis, or any other American location, but rather the French capital, Paris. Indeed, it is fundamentally a book about French culture's revelation, so to speak, of Americanness as such. In his Preface to the New York edition of the novel, James recalls how this theme presented itself to him as the story of a 'compatriot', confronting an 'aristocratic society', and its decidedly non-American exemplars, in 'another country'.[11] In the margins of his copy of this Preface, Ellison glosses this summary with the phrase, 'the clash of cultural values'.[12] And in doing so, he articulates a simple but momentous point – that for Americanness to emerge, here and in James's imaginary more broadly, it must be placed into contact, and indeed antagonism, with other national, transnational and quasi-national cultural formations. Elsewhere in his Preface, James recalls composing his novel in Paris, and credits that city's ambience with having helped to make his 'conception' of the novel 'concrete'.[13] The book's

11 Henry James, *The Art of the Novel: Critical Prefaces* (New York: Charles Scribner's Sons, 1937), 21–2.

12 Ellison's annotation is on page 21 of his copy of James's text. For a full list of books that Ellison owned, now held by Library of Congress, see 'The Ralph Ellison Collection, 1937–2010', <https://findingaids.loc.gov/exist_collections/ead3pdf/rbc/2016/rb016001.pdf>, accessed 1 July 2020.

13 James, *The Art of the Novel*, 23.

protagonist, that 'typ[ical]' American, is also said (again, in the Preface) to act under the 'strong contagion of the place'.[14] A foreign capital thus helps bring 'national' traits, for James and his character, to their full expression. For Ellison to fully identify with James's American in his autobiography, the New York he arrives in must have 'foreign' features too.

And this is what Ellison's autobiography goes on to suggest. To paraphrase a claim made in the present essay's introduction, an 'international' site in James's text is repurposed as a 'national' one in Ellison's. Concomitantly, Ellison's text proceeds to invoke James directly, not so much as author of *The American* (or any other designated text) but someone who, *as* an American, wrote this, and other books – in Europe. For just as Ellison recalls his habituation to New York under the sign of 'the American,' he also evokes James as an exemplary American abroad. Being a stranger in this city, Ellison thus recalls, was like traversing it 'without a map, Baedeker or Henry James'.[15] No less than Paris in the case of James's titular American, New York functions in Ellison's own as a locus of cultural and social as well as topographical and geographical estrangement. Were Ellison to have explored the city *with* a map, Baedeker or James, therefore, he would have done so equipped with those resources usually used by travellers to habituate themselves to *bona fide* foreign places: a 'map' to mitigate that topographical and geographical estrangement; a Baedeker to help navigate cultural and social coordinates, and so on.[16] James's appearance in Ellison's tripartite list thus serves to invest him with something of the other items in that list's authority and function: like the map and the Baedeker, his texts can be relied on to accurately portray the places they purport to, being firmly grounded in investigative nous and discerning observation. That

14 Ibid., 24.

15 Ralph Ellison, Memoirs, Library of Congress, Ralph Ellison papers II:46, folder 6. This passage appears in published form in Ellison's 'An 'Extravagance of Laughter' (1986), in *The Collected Essays of Ralph Ellison*, ed., John F. Callahan (New York: Modern Library, 1995), 632.

16 A 'Baedeker' is, of course, one of a series of travel guides widely used by travellers in the early twentieth century. See Suzanne Hobson, ' "Looking All Lost towards a Cook's Guide for Beauty": The Art of Literature and the Lessons of the Guidebook in Modernist Writing', *Studies in Travel Writing* 19/1 (2015), 30–47.

Ellison can suggest this without further gloss testifies to the currency that the idea of James, as 'an American abroad', had gained by the time that he was writing. If James is preeminently a novelist of 'the American' as type, he also thus embodies an important variation on that type: the émigré or expatriate, who, having left the homeland, writes *back*, to a readership including compatriots who may follow in his or her wake; a cicerone or tour guide to these compatriots; a guide to the initiate; a mentor to the ingénue.

This is the James that so offended cultural critics of the kind Ellison and Wright have at the back if not the forefront of their minds when they disclaim identification with James in the 1950s. The offence took hold during the first decades of the twentieth century, for a variety of overlapping reasons, combining aesthetic judgements with an aversion to James's manifest or imputed politics. (It is especially noteworthy in this context that James took up British citizenship, in 1915; proximately, in protest at the United States's refusal to take up arms on the British side in the First World War, but more generally, contemporaries and later commentators felt, as a meta-political declaration of translated loyalties.) An exemplary text in this respect is Vernon Parrington's *Main Currents of American Thought* (1927), a copy of which Ellison had in his library. Here, James is said to embody all that is *wrong* with exchanging the transatlantic for the national:

> He suffered the common fate of the *déraciné*; wandering between worlds, he found a home nowhere. It is not well for the artist to turn cosmopolitan, for the flavor of the fruit comes from the soil and sunshine of the native fields.[17]

As the Roaring Twenties gave way to the Great Depression, class-based objections were grafted on to deprecations like this, especially in the Leftist circles in which Ellison moved. As Ellison recalled decades later, those responsible for the journal *New Masses* were especially hostile: 'They felt that Henry James was a decadent snob who had nothing to teach a writer from the lower classes'.[18] According to this view, James's expatriatism and a

17 Vernon Parrington, *Main Currents of American Thought*, 3 vols (New York: Harcourt, Brace and Co., 1927), Vol. 3, 240.

18 Ralph Ellison, '"A Very Stern Discipline"' (1967), in John F. Callahan, ed., *The Collected Essays of Ralph Ellison* (New York: Modern Library, 1995), 746.

lofty disregard for social injustice were two sides of a single coin. This view makes explicit a prescription hinted at by Parrington: artists should be as fruit pickers in fields. Needless to say – Ellison does *not* say it, though he leaves room open to surmise that he may have heard it said – a concomitant of these views is an assumption that James especially had nothing to teach a writer from the lower classes who was black.

Already by the 1930s, though, James's reputation was recovering. As Ellison goes on to state: 'I was studying James', despite the *New Masses*'s interdictions.[19] A pioneering work in this respect is Joseph Warren Beach's *The Method of Henry James* (1918), which Ellison seems to have read on Wright's recommendation.[20] Though mainly lauding James as a technician, this study takes time to do so on 'national' (if not nationalist) grounds as well: James 'may not be as American as Mark Twain or Benjamin Franklin', Beach contends, 'but he is American as Emerson and Thoreau and Hawthorne are'.[21] Thus another text Ellison had a copy of in his library, a 1934 special issue of the journal *Hound and Horn* wherein Edmund Wilson and others present James as a misunderstood patriot and victim of insensitive misreading. '[I]n spite of the popular assumption founded on his expatriatism', Wilson writes, 'it is America' which ultimately receives benediction in James's work; moreover, '[i]n his shy circumlocutory way, he was genuinely democratic'.[22] The *style* of James's work has skewed perceptions of its substance. To such defenders, James is not just a good writer who happened to be an American; it is his ultimate success as an American – despite the many years abroad, the 'international theme' and so on – that makes his writing good.

Given all this, what did aspiring African American writers hope to get out of James? One answer is sheer technical know-how, as expressed above all in the series of Prefaces that James wrote for the New York Edition of

19 Ibid.

20 See Ralph Ellison, 'Hidden Name and Complex Fate' (1964), in John F. Callahan, ed., *The Collected Essays of Ralph Ellison* (New York: Modern Library, 1995), 204.

21 Joseph Warren Beach, *The Method of Henry James* (New Haven, CT: Yale University Press, 1918), 144.

22 Edmund Wilson, 'The Ambiguity of Henry James', *Hound and Horn* 7/3 (1934), 405.

his work (1907–9). This is Nowlin's explanation of why James appealed to Wright and Ellison, particularly: witness Wright's 'How Bigger Was Born' (1940) (which Ellison calls a 'Jamesian' preface to *Native Son* (1940)), and Ellison's own 'Introduction to the Thirtieth Anniversary Edition of *Invisible Man*' (1982).[23] Both of these are conspicuously (though not explicitly) indebted to James's example for their urbane self-consciousness and now-that-I-have-written-this, here-is-how-I-did-so retrospection. One can add two further bits of circumstantial evidence to this case: first, the fact that Ellison's 'Introduction' paraphrases a sentence from an essay by the critic R. P. Blackmur on James's Prefaces (I will address this sentence and its paraphrase directly in a moment); second, the fact that Beach's *The Method of Henry James*, the aforementioned text that Ellison seems to have read at Wright's behest, had an important hand in the later uptake of the Prefaces as a writer's *vade mecum*, and pitches itself as their propaedeutic.

There is another answer to this question, too, of manifest and indeed pivotal importance in Ellison's case, given his frequent appeals to the famous utterance by James it turns upon. This utterance contends: 'It's a complex fate, being an American, and one of the responsibilities it entails is fighting against a superstitious valuation of Europe'.[24] A predilection for Europe, in other words, is an integral but potentially pernicious component of American culture. Americanness itself is both disposition and awareness of that disposition: it is indeed the admixture of these things that makes one's 'fate' as an American 'complex'. Complexity and self-consciousness go hand in hand. And for Ellison, self-consciousness as such – notwithstanding superstitious valuation of Europe in this instance –is an American's most signal virtue.[25] Hence the way that in the very passage of his autobiography

23 Nowlin, 'Henry James and the Making of Modern African American Literature', 282. Ellison calls 'How Bigger was Born' 'Jamesian' in 'The World and the Jug', in *The Collected Essays of Ralph Ellison*, ed., John F. Callahan (New York: Modern Library, 1995), 167.

24 *Henry James: Selected Letters*, ed., Leon Edel (Cambridge, MA: Belknap Press, 1987), 93.

25 In addition to his statements to this effect considered further below, see Ellison's 'Address to the Harvard College Alumni, Class of 1949' (1974), in John F. Callahan, ed., *The Collected Essays of Ralph Ellison* (New York: Modern Library, 1995), 419–30; especially 429.

James appears in, as we have seen above, Ellison implicitly characterizes himself, no less than his nation, as 'still in the process of achieving a full measure of self-consciousness' upon arrival in New York. His arrival intimates the filling of this measure: the mix of familiar and strange he encounters in the city, the sort of experience from which self-consciousness will spring.

It is only once all the foregoing has been taken into account that one can understand the range and nuance of the role – or *roles* – that James plays, when invoked explicitly, in Ellison's published works. For Ellison's James is several, not always easily reconciled things, which tend to be distributed across disparate locations without connecting commentary. One location is the aforementioned 'Introduction to the Thirtieth Anniversary Edition of *Invisible Man*', in which James plays what initially seems a straightforwardly 'heroic' role, as paragon or master. But here there is a twist, as Ellison lifts the master's lesson for pocketing within his own curriculum. At issue here is 'Afro-American fiction,' whose protagonists prior to Ellison's own are said to have lacked 'intellectual depth':

> Too often [these protagonists are] figures caught up in the most intense forms of social struggle, subject to the most extreme forms of the human predicament, yet seldom able to articulate the issues which tortured them. Not that many worthy individuals aren't in fact inarticulate, but that there were, and are, enough exceptions in real life to provide the perceptive novelist with models. And even if they did not exist it would be necessary, both in the interest of fictional expressiveness and as examples of human possibility, to invent them. Henry James had taught us much with his hyperconscious, 'Super subtle fry', characters who embodied in their own cultured, upper-class way the American virtues of conscience and consciousness.[26]

James provides a 'model' that Ellison adapts to his distinct if not contrasting purpose: the depiction of embattled, black Americans, rather than 'cultured, upper-class' (and, as a matter of fact, white) ones. If James can have 'super subtle fry' in his works, Ellison can have them in his. The curiously roundabout account of verisimilitude proffered in this connection – according to Ellison, 'real-life' counterparts to his 'fry' *do* exist, but

26 Ralph Ellison, 'Introduction to the Thirtieth Anniversary Edition of *Invisible Man*' (1981), in John F. Callahan, ed., *The Collected Essays of Ralph Ellison* (New York: Modern Library, 1995), 485–6.

the legitimate representation of them in fiction does not depend on their so-doing – further extends this parallel, under cover of that paraphrase from Blackmur's essay on the New York Edition Prefaces touched upon above. For in the Ellison text just quoted, the sentence that states, 'And even if they did not exist it would be necessary [...] to invent them', is in fact a crib of one in Blackmur's that reads: '[James] defended his "super-subtle fry" in one way or another a dozen times, on the ground that if they did not exist they ought to, because they represented, if only by an imaginative irony, what life was capable of at its finest'.[27] In this account, James did not so much seek to copy life as set *it* an example. The evident appeal of this idea to Ellison – his sentence more or less directly transcribes Blackmur's, after all – thus evinces a more general yen for James the *idealist*, rather than James the meticulous recorder of realities. Hence the shift across the paragraph just quoted from 'human predicament' to 'human possibility'.

This leads us to another of Ellison's references to James's term for 'hyperconscious' individuals, 'super subtle fry'. And in so doing, it also leads us to differentiate those 'human' qualities with which James can be wholly identified from more particularly *national* ones, with which, for Ellison, ultimately, James cannot. In 'Society, Morality and the Novel' (1957), Ellison writes that in a democracy, one must depend upon each citizen, 'whoever he is and from whatever class and racial group, to attain the finest perception of human value, to become as consciously aware of life, say, as any of Henry James's "super-subtle fry" '.[28] At first, it seems that here, again, James is cast in a 'heroic' role, insofar as he is aligned with American political arrangements and their corresponding virtues. But here again also, there is a twist – this time, not so much in the use to which James is put than in the judgement passed upon him. For notwithstanding the frequency of

27 R. P. Blackmur, 'Introduction', in Henry James, ed., *The Art of the Novel: Critical Prefaces* (New York: Charles Scribner's Sons, 1937), xxv. Blackmur hyphenates 'super-subtle' even though Ellison himself does not. Blackmur's essay also appears in the issue of *Hound and Horn* cited in footnote 22 above.

28 Ralph Ellison, 'Society, Morality and the Novel' (1957), in John F. Callahan, ed., *The Collected Essays of Ralph Ellison* (New York: Modern Library, 1995), 726. Here, Ellison hyphenates 'super-subtle', whereas he does not do so in the introduction to *Invisible Man*.

his appeals to James's couplet, 'complex fate', noted above, Ellison comes to find James's analysis of that fate superficial. As he explains elsewhere in 'Society, Morality and the Novel': 'Being an American, wrote Henry James, is a complex fate, but perhaps far more troublesome than the necessity of guarding against a superstitious overvaluation [sic] of Europe is the problem of dealing with the omnipresent American ideal'.[29] Complexity does not inhere in relations to elsewhere; rather, it inheres in home. James has traced complexity to the wrong source. And in an essay named partly in tribute to James's couplet, 'Hidden Name and Complex Fate' (1964), Ellison underscores this point, aligning 'conscience' with 'consciousness' in the manner of the later 'Thirtieth Anniversary' preface: he writes of the 'burden of conscience and consciousness which Americans inherit as one of the results of the revolutionary circumstances of their national beginnings'.[30] Conscience and consciousness are quintessential to Americans; America is quintessentially complex.

So strong are Ellison's feelings on this point that his attitude towards James can become distinctly critical. On such occasions, James is cast not in a heroic but a kind of naysaying, 'unbeliever', role, as the denier of American complexity. A key text in this respect is *Hawthorne* (1879), James's study of Nathaniel Hawthorne, which is a major source for connoisseurs of James's insights into fiction writing but also for Parrington-esque dismay at his (putative) slighting of his homeland and correspondingly exorbitant regard for Europe. In this study, James highlights Hawthorne's declaration – made, not coincidentally, in the context of his own transatlantic sojourning – that a lack of 'picturesque and gloomy wrong' makes the United States uncongenial to writers of 'romance[s]'.[31] As James glosses:

> It takes so many things, as Hawthorne must have felt later in life, when he made the acquaintance of the denser, richer, warmer, European spectacle – it takes such an accumulation of history and custom, such a complexity of manners and types, to form a fund of suggestion for the novelist.[32]

29 Ellison, 'Society, Morality and the Novel', 706.

30 Ellison, 'Hidden Name and Complex Fate', 206.

31 James here quotes Hawthorne's Preface to *The Marble Faun* (1860); see James, *Hawthorne* (New York: Harper and Bros, 1879), 41.

32 James, *Hawthorne*, 42.

'[C]omplexity,' in this view, is what fiction writers most require but what the United States of Hawthorne's day could *not* provide. When Ellison relays this point in 'Society, Morality and the Novel', the bitter dish it represents is sugared – or served up in the forlorn hope that it *can* be sugared – with a claim that James 'base[s] his remarks' not on the actual condition of American society in Hawthorne's time but the 'thinness' of the 'notebooks' that Hawthorne wrote in response to them.[33] But even Ellison himself has no real faith in this palliation. He knows as well as any other reader of *Hawthorne* that 'Hawthorne' in that book is a largely a proxy or surrogate for James himself.

However much the younger author may resent James for this, he stifles this resentment – at this point, in print. But in an unpublished passage, seemingly excised from 'Society, Morality and the Novel', Ellison reveals what he really thinks of James's pejorative characterization of the authors' mutual homeland (the quotation that follows reproduces the crossings-out and note-to-self interrogation points of Ellison's typescript):

> His mistake lay in his assumption that [Europe] was the only type of society which offered complexity. What lay about him here in America was a society in which not class offered the novelist the most exciting clues to the nature of social reality but national cultural groupings, ways and customs brought from many European and other backgrounds and all whirling in a fluid, terrifically ~~speeded up~~ accelerated tempo of American change. James [...] found American reality too much for him and chose to deal with it at ? removed
>
> ?Great novels were the result and it is not our purpose to quarrel with him but only to point out the confusion as to the nature of American society and thus the American? which still causes us trouble, [...][34]

'American reality' was 'just too much' for James – who fled to Europe, in consequence, where everything was safer, more orderly, and *slower* (we can sense Ellison thinking as he is writing this, meanwhile: 'at least

33 Ellison, 'Society, Morality and the Novel', 722.

34 Ralph Ellison, Speeches and Letters, 1960–1993, Library of Congress, Ralph Ellison papers II:68, folder 4. This transcript is archived in a folder devoted to otherwise undated materials from 1990 to 1993. But in its substantive content, it seems much more likely to represent drafting of Ellison's 1957 essay, originally delivered as a lecture.

American reality is not too much for *me*!'). Insofar as this is not simply a personal failing on James's part, it represents a kind of a category error: a 'mistak[ing]' of one particular instance of complexity for the thing itself. Thus, the fine gradations of 'class' and attendant social forms for which Europe is famous find correlatives (though James could not perceive them as such) in the interplay of 'national cultural groupings' in the United States. The 'intra-national' dynamics of those states recapitulate the international ones of Europe: Ellison's critique of *Hawthorne* thus intimates the arguments of 'Some Questions and Some Answers', as presented in the introduction to this chapter. European 'complexity' is reprised in America by other means. For all his achievements as a writer (he wrote 'Great novels', after all), James's 'confus[ion]' about the nature of American reality makes his contributions to the interpretation of that reality irreducibly oblique.

To sum up: according to Ellison, James ably embodies American self-consciousness, but at the cost of dissociating it from American complexity, the actual ground (for Americans) of self-consciousness itself. James is an indispensable resource for aspiring novelists but someone whose slightly crooked sense of all this requires him to be twisted back upon himself. We will now see how, given all this, Ellison takes what he considers valuable in James and twists it to his examination of 'race' in the United States. This will in turn lead us to consider how Baldwin also does this, in his endeavour to explain how intra-national, racial conflicts in the United States are inflected by expatriatism. But it leads us first to Wright, the writer who encouraged Ellison's interest in James, and whose own analysis of race in the United States led to a no less freighted if ultimately more affirmative encounter with James's *Hawthorne*.

'Just How Complex This Fate Is': Ellison with Wright and Baldwin

The locus of Wright's most explicit engagement with *Hawthorne* is 'How Bigger was Born', the aforementioned 'Jamesian' Preface to *Native Son*. Here, Wright tries both to acknowledge the validity of James and

Hawthorne's criticisms of America and to expose the obsolescence of these criticisms in the light of twentieth-century events. On the one hand, this involves contending that the two were entitled to point out lacunae in the social fabric of their own day. On the other, it means insisting this fabric has since become – and to some extent, already was – much thicker than their respective estimates allowed, for reasons centring upon 'the Negro':

> Henry James and Hawthorne complained bitterly about the bleakness and flatness of the American scene. But I think that if they were alive, they'd feel at home in modern America. [...] [W]e do have in the Negro the embodiment of a past tragic enough to appease the spiritual hunger of even a James; and we have in the oppression of the Negro a shadow athwart our national life dense and heaving enough to satisfy even the gloomy broodings of a Hawthorne.[35]

What the first hand gives, the second takes away. Thus, while James and Hawthorne cannot be faulted for failing to foresee how a whole range of factors (among which we might adduce everything from the end of the Civil War and failure of Reconstruction, after Hawthorne's lifetime, to the outbreak of the Great Depression, after James's) have culminated in twentieth-century African Americans' 'oppression', they *can* be faulted for ignoring the underlying causes of this, already evident in their own days. The Negro's 'past', after all, was James and Hawthorne's present. Could these authors not, therefore, have paid rather more attention to this in their own works?

This, at least, is a question asked by Ellison of Hawthorne, specifically, in 'Society, Morality and the Novel'. Here, indeed, Ellison doubles down, observing of his predecessor that if Hawthorne was really interested in historic 'wrong[s]', he might have done more to investigate the roots of slavery, not to mention Colonial-era 'crime against the Indians'.[36] This line of attack notwithstanding, it is notable that, having pioneered it, Wright moves towards rapprochement with James's study. And in so doing, he effects a remarkable adaptation of that book's analysis to the circumstances of his own life. In *Black Boy* (1945), Wright interleaves the events of his

35 Richard Wright, *Native Son, and* 'How Bigger was Born' (New York: HarperPerennial, 1993), 540.

36 Ellison, 'Society, Morality and the Novel', 719.

impoverished childhood in Mississippi with more general reflections on black experience in early twentieth-century America. He mounts that experience in a very wide frame of reference. And to this end, Wright enters into his most intense but also *least* explicit engagement with *Hawthorne* – so discreet, indeed, that were it not for Ellison's drawing of attention to it (in a manner to be detailed shortly), it is possible that otherwise discerning readers may not recognize it as such at all. In a pivotal passage of the book, James's lament for the inhospitality faced by American novelists of the preceding century acts as a kind of shadow-text underneath Wright's commentary on all that twentieth-century 'Negroes' needed from America but could not find there:

> Whenever I thought of the essential bleakness of black life in America, I knew that Negroes had never been allowed to catch the full spirit of Western civilization, that they lived somehow in it but not of it. And when I brooded on the cultural barrenness of black life, I wondered if clean, positive tenderness, love, honor, loyalty, and the capacity to remember were native with man.[37]

'[B]lack life' is the confounded, stymied and truncated equivalent of white life: like Europe as experienced by Hawthorne in later years (according to James), the latter is much 'denser, richer, [and] warmer' than its comparator. To be clear, this is not because Wright thinks black people are constitutionally incapable of 'love, honor, loyalty', and so on – as Ellison puts it, 'far from implying that Negroes have no capacity for culture', this passage represents the 'strongest affirmation' possible that they possess it – but because he thinks 'Negroes' perforce endure conditions in which these things cannot prosper.[38] These conditions, meanwhile, are identical with and yet distinct from those of other Americans: in this way, Negroes are 'in' 'Western civilization' but 'not of it'. Thus too, in this passage, *Black Boy* echoes while also tweaking James's model, aligning 'black/white' and 'America/Europe', without conflating them. Hawthorne could leave America in search of things it lacked; African Americans are stuck

37 Richard Wright, *Black Boy (American Hunger)* (New York: HarperPerennial, 1993), 43.

38 Ralph Ellison, 'Richard Wright's Blues', in John F. Callahan, ed., *The Collected Essays of Ralph Ellison* (New York: Modern Library, 1995), 143.

there amid things they cannot have. New England novelists and hard time Mississippians are analogous: this does not mean they are the *same*.

How did Ellison respond to this? As we have seen, he moves to head off accusations of chauvinism against Wright, vis-à-vis African Americans, by claiming that *Black Boy*'s commentary on 'barrenness' is an expression not of doubt in blacks' capacity for culture but faith in it. This claim forms part of 'Richard Wright's Blues' (1945), the high-water mark of Ellison's regard for Wright, and a wide-ranging exploration of other affinities between them, grounded in their shared witnessing of and participation in the Great Migration. But in 'The World and the Jug' (1963–4), Ellison's stance shifts, partly in response to Irving Howe's championing of Wright's *Native Son* (which involves negative comparison with *Invisible Man*), partly because of Wright's decision to leave the United States for France, and partly because Wright's whole approach to African American culture in *Black Boy* now strikes him as wrong-headed. This later essay is, in turn, partly a response to Howe, and partly a riposte to Wright, targeting especially what Nowlin calls Wright's 'cultural destitution thesis'.[39] Like 'Richard Wright's Blues', 'The World and the Jug' quotes *Black Boy*'s refashioning of *Hawthorne*. This time though, it does so to dilate upon Wright's 'literariness': it is here, then, that Ellison reveals to those discerning readers who might otherwise overlook it that the relevant passage represents Wright's 'paraphrase of those items of a high civilization which were absent from American life during Hawthorne's day'.[40] But whereas, in the earlier essay, Ellison quotes this passage to acclaim it, he now decries it. The passage as excerpted in 'The World and the Jug' is succeeded by two questions: 'Must I be condemned because my sense of Negro life was quite different? Or because for me keeping faith would never allow me to even raise such a question about any segment of humanity?'[41] Clearly, the answer solicited is 'no'; of course Ellison should not be 'condemned' for believing that 'Negro life' is more diverse, stimulating, nurturing, and simply fun than Wright allows. In its expression, rather than suppression of 'humanity', this life has indeed made possible the emergence of no less cultured and discriminating an individual

39 Nowlin, 'Henry James and the Making of Modern African American Literature', 288.

40 Ibid., 167.

41 Ibid., 166.

than Wright himself.[42] In short, this 'life' is not like the America portrayed in *Hawthorne* at all. And by affecting that it is it, Wright has committed what we now know Ellison regards as the cardinal Jamesian sin – that of 'dissociat[ing] himself from the complexity' of his homeland.[43] Small wonder, then, that Wright followed James in quitting America for Europe; in this respect, the offending passage of *Black Boy*, while it predates Wright's actual departure for France, represents 'the beginning of Wright's exile'.[44]

And so, we are returned to Ellison's autobiographical writings of the 1980s, and the account of his arrival in New York therein. As we have seen, Ellison views this arrival though the lens of James's *The American*, and its portrayal of an American abroad. In 'An Extravagance of Laughter' (1985), he couples this lens with another, focused upon a claim that far from being 'barren', African American culture is in fact abundantly fertile, not least in its provision of resources for young or otherwise callow individuals venturing into the white-dominated world. Here, then, is a more fully fledged elaboration of what we might call, *pace* Nowlin, Ellison's 'cultural enrichment' thesis, and a belated attempt to clinch his argument with Wright. And given *Hawthorne*'s repudiation as a source, a different Jamesian text is called upon to help Ellison articulate that thesis – the one we have now seen Ellison invoke repeatedly, wherein James defines the American's 'complex fate': 'Just as Henry James felt it prudent to warn Americans against a "superstitious valuation of Europe", Negro folklore with its array of survival strategies warned against over-evaluation of white pretentions.'[45]

This 'folklore' is equivalent to the democratic, republican and supra-regional consciousness that (ideally) steels Americans against the allure of the Old World. For 'Negro[es]', read James's 'typical' American; for 'white pretensions', read the wiles and decadence of Belle Époque French aristocrats. African Americans confront – and prosper – in the white world just as Americans confront, and prosper, within Europe.

All this leads us, finally, to Baldwin. In his writing, the decision to leave America for Europe is both an imperative, born of racism, and a

42 Ibid., 167.

43 Ibid.

44 Ibid., 166.

45 Ellison, 'An Extravagance of Laugher', 646.

displacement, which does nothing to address the ultimate causes or consequences of that racism. A programmatic statement of this case is made in 'The Discovery of What it Means to be an American' (1959), wherein a now-familiar Jamesian aperçu again appears: '"It is a complex fate to be an American", Henry James observed, and the principal discovery an American writer makes in Europe is just how complex this fate is'.[46] But whereas James conceived this fate, above all, in terms of ambivalent feelings about cultural prestige, Baldwin does so in terms of ancestral lineage and historic place of origin – the fundamentals, so to speak, of fate itself. Although travel may promise escape from all these things, it instead precipitates a head-on confrontation with them. Thus:

> the day to which [the travelling writer's] entire sojourn has been tending. It is the day he realizes that there are no untroubled countries in this fearfully troubled world; that if he has been preparing himself for anything in Europe he has been preparing himself – for America. In short, the freedom that the American writer finds in Europe brings him, full circle, back to himself, with the responsibility for his development where it always was: in his own hands.[47]

'[T]rouble' is a planetary affliction, not a uniquely American one. And though the American's fate is indeed 'complex', the truth is that there are no *un*-complex fates, or nations, in this world: like unhappy families in Tolstoy, each nation is complex in its own way. The paradoxical consequence of leaving one's country to escape its particular form of trouble is to find oneself all the more thoroughly immersed in the minutiae *of* that trouble. In the case of the United States this means, among other things, the transmutation, rather than transcendence, of many Old World problems in the New World, and the continued immiseration of whole populations whose ancestors were brought as slaves from Africa. As Baldwin reports in a related essay: '"You can take the child out of the country," my elders were fond of saying, "but you can't take the country out of the

46 James Baldwin, 'The Discovery of What It Means to Be an American', in *Collected Essays* (New York: Library of America, 1998), 137.

47 Ibid., 141.

child"'.[48] His country's troubles are *in* Baldwin, not just his birthplace. This birthplace must nonetheless be left, if these two things are to be teased apart. Accordingly, Baldwin concludes: 'I found myself, willy-nilly, alchemized into an American the moment I touched French soil'.[49]

To choose self-designated 'exile', then, as Wright did, cannot, for Baldwin, lead to successful negotiation of one's status as both American and black. Wright's (putative) conviction that it could, Baldwin suggests, is rooted in a naïve or fanciful idea of Europe. Thus an essay written after Wright's death, wherein Baldwin recalls: 'The meaning of Europe for an American Negro was one of the things about which Richard Wright and I disagreed most vehemently'.[50] In particular, Baldwin continues, the pair disputed Wright's habitual reference to Paris as a 'city of refuge'.[51] This biblical designation (the phrase denotes a type of Levite settlement in ancient Israel) was used, as both authors surely knew, as the title of an important short story by African American writer Rudolph Fisher, published in 1925.[52] Here, the titular 'refuge' is Harlem, in New York City, the most famous destination for blacks leaving the American South in the Great Migration. Subsequent African American writers paid homage to this story; Ellison is one of them, in his depiction of a subway journey made by the narrator of *Invisible Man*, from Lower Manhattan to Harlem, upon arrival in New York. So, too, is Baldwin – though his homage to Fisher's story is also a critical revision, reimagining this journey not as a route to 'refuge' but as a descent into the abyss.[53] In *Another Country* (1962), Rufus Scott takes the subway uptown from Greenwich Village, thinking that he will alight in Harlem, but then travelling further, to get off near the George

48 James Baldwin, 'A Fly in the Buttermilk' (1958), in *Collected Essays* (New York: Library of America, 1998), 187.

49 Ibid., 187.

50 James Baldwin, 'Alas, Poor Richard' (1961), in *Collected Essays* (New York: Library of America, 1998), 249.

51 Ibid.

52 Rudolph Fisher, 'The City of Refuge', in John McCluskey Jr, ed., *The City of Refuge: The Collected Stories of Rudolph Fisher* (Columbia: University of Missouri Press, 1987), 3–16.

53 Fisher's story is, of course, not uncritical of the idea of 'refuge' in its own right: its title is intentionally ironic.

Washington Bridge – which he then jumps off to his death. This bridge, named in honour of the 'father of [Rufus's] country', is thus the ultimate destination of all Rufus's journeying, not only in New York but also in that country of which *Another Country* as a whole is an anatomy.[54] This, then, is Baldwin's commentary on what America has done to men like Rufus: the way that Revolutionary ideals connoted by the name, 'George Washington', have failed him; the fact that there is no satisfactory home for him either in Harlem or in the bohemian, multi-ethnic, international and relatively 'liberal' enclave of Greenwich Village. As Baldwin put it in an interview, New York is 'one of the loneliest places in the world'.[55] To one of its native residents in *Another Country*, it is a place of 'exile'.[56]

All of which is to say that *Another Country* is, in its own way, thoroughly Jamesian in inspiration. It is fitting, then, that Baldwin selects a text by James as an epigraph to his novel – though significantly this text concerns neither New York (in which both men were born), nor America in general, but Americans abroad, and their milieu. This epigraph is taken from one of those Prefaces to the New York Edition of James's work so admired by Ellison and Wright, and concerns the London-centred novella 'Lady Barbarina' (1884). Here, James observes, vis-à-vis those Americans abroad:

> They strike one, above all, as giving no account of themselves in any terms already consecrated by human use; to this inarticulate state they probably form, collectively, the most unprecedented of monuments; abysmal the mystery of what they think, what they feel, what they want, what they suppose themselves to be saying.[57]

By contrast to Ellison's prodigiously 'self-conscious' Americans, James's are 'monuments' of self-oblivion. For James himself, there is thus a split between the writer's consciousness, which can perceive this, and a more commonplace American one, which (by definition) cannot. Insofar as

54 James Baldwin, *Another Country* (Harmondsworth: Penguin, 1990), 92.

55 James Mossman, 'Race, Hate, Sex, and Colour: A Conversation with James Baldwin and Colin MacInnes', in Fred L. Stanley and Louis H. Pratt, eds, *Conversations with James Baldwin* (Jackson: University of Mississippi Press, 1989), 49.

56 Baldwin, *Another Country*, 311.

57 James, *The Art of the Novel*, 209; Baldwin, *Another Country*, unnumbered page.

their displacement from America is responsible for this self-oblivion, James's characters resemble Parrington's *déraciné*. But Baldwin's characters are not displaced abroad, and their 'abysmal' state cannot therefore be attributed to expatriatism.

Baldwin's use of James's 'Lady Barbarina' Preface thus not only confounds Parrington's critique but also turns the screw on James himself, precisely by identifying *déraciné*-like failings with Americans *at home*. If *Another Country*'s New Yorkers are in an 'abysmal' state, then, this must be owing to reasons rooted in New York itself; it must be because Baldwin sees them as analogues of James's characters in their spiritual and moral situations, rather than their socio-economic and geo-spatial ones. The point being made by Baldwin's identification of the characters in 'Lady Barbarina' with *Another Country*'s is that their rootedness is tantamount to deracination; that their autochthony is concomitant with spiritual displacement; that their knowledge of their city is quite at odds with their knowledge of themselves and of each other. *Pace* Ellison's repurposing of James, Baldwin believes that the lack of such knowledge is typically 'American', not 'super subtle fry'-like 'consciousness' and 'conscience'. James himself, in this view, is both an exception to and keen observer of this, paradoxically, because by leaving America, he gains analytic purchase on it: thus his function as a role model to Baldwin in 'The Discovery of What it Means to be an American', where he represents the 'good' American abroad. In *Another Country*, it falls to Eric play a complementary role. As an actor, Eric represents the artist; in his sexual generosity, he represents the transfiguring, redemptive power of love. Upon returning from abroad – where he has sojourned to his benefit – New York appears to him as 'strange', like some 'exotic city of the East'.[58] There are reasons to think of Eric as a surrogate for both James and Baldwin. As he records in a note upon his novel's final page, Baldwin completed *Another Country* while living in Istanbul.

58 Baldwin, *Another Country*, 227.

Ellison in 'Henry James's Word Pile'

Another Country thus completes an arc connecting James's work (or certain features of it) with that of Ellison, Wright and Baldwin, via the three African American writers' shared concerns. As such, the novel grants an opportunity to sum up these writers' divergent claims on James's work. Ellison's hypothetical claim might be encapsulated in an imagined sentence: 'I discovered New York in the same way James's expatriates discovered Europe, and in doing so, became self-conscious in a manner consonant with James's conception of the "complex fate"'. Wright's corresponding sentence might read: 'As a child, I felt bereft in America, and left accordingly, for reasons intimated by James's *Hawthorne*'. And in Baldwin's case, a corresponding sentence might contend: 'Americans are utterly un-self-aware, as James explained of Americans abroad, and now that I have been abroad, like James himself, I understand just how and why'. In all these imaginary sentences, the experience of race is an implicit rather than explicit theme, despite its emphatic and pervasive presence in all three writers' oeuvres otherwise. I have cast the sentences this way to stress the element of lateral thinking involved in moulding James's work around that theme itself. For make no mistake: James shows scant regard for African Americans in his work. As Ellison puts it in a letter to John Kouwenhoven, of 1987, James leaves African Americans 'out of his portrayal of American life'.[59] Nonetheless, Ellison continues: James '<u>did</u> provide clues that help me tell my stories'.[60] Though James might not have done it himself, what he *did* do helps Ellison see how the experiences and concerns of black Americans might be represented fictionally. In the remainder of this essay, I consider two ways in which, according to Ellison, James did this. The first of these involves James's *The Bostonians* (1886); the second, the more elemental qualities of James's style.

59 Ralph Ellison, Letter to John Kouwenhoven, 30 October 1987, in John F. Callahan and Marc C. Conner, eds, *The Selected Letters of Ralph Ellison* (New York: Random House, 2019), 937.

60 Ibid., 937 (underlining in original).

The case for *The Bostonians* is made in 'The Novel as a Function of American Democracy' (1967), wherein, as stated at the start of this chapter, James is made central to Ellison's vision of the novel as a form. Here, Ellison also sets out his demand that the novelist embody (as I also put it the start of this chapter) a kind of principled autochthony, fusing patriotism with aesthetics. Insofar as James investigates the 'complex fate', he fits this bill quite well. But insofar as his novels tend to be dominated by the 'international theme', as we have seen, he fits it badly, tackling America and Americanness obliquely, rather than head-on. All these factors enter into Ellison's enthusiasm for *The Bostonians*, perhaps the one full-length novel he *could* have used to show James as author of the sort of novel he most admired. This text is set after the Reconstruction and the Civil War, and dramatizes what would now be called the culture wars integral to both episodes, as waged by representatives of North and South who lock horns over values, beliefs, sensibilities and lovers. The crux of the historic dispute between North and South is, of course, slavery – the aftermath of which, in turn, forms the crux of Ellison's claim that *The Bostonians* is significant to African Americans.

In his commentary on the novel, Ellison begins by acknowledging now-familiar criticisms of James, which he then deflates with a striking and unusual depiction of James as a shy but steadfast keeper of the flame ignited by the 'good' side in the Civil War:

> By the time I began to write, Henry James was considered a snob, an upper-class expatriate who in New York and around Boston had fallen into some sort of decadent hot-house in which his head became much too large for his body. His sensibility was considered too delicate to interest anyone who was a real man concerned with things of the world as they existed. It was forgotten, though, that James came on the scene at a time when abolitionists were coming in and out of his father's house, and that he was part of a period in which there was great intellectual, religious, and civil rights ferment.[61]

61 Ralph Ellison, 'The Novel as a Function of American Democracy', in John F. Callahan, ed., *The Collected Essays of Ralph Ellison* (New York: Modern Library, 1995), 763.

In its concern with the affairs of its own day, *The Bostonians* is thus, paradoxically, a text of James's significantly earlier youth: a time when the struggle against slavery was not belated and senescent (as its tributaries appear in *The Bostonians*) but urgent and heroic. Though it may not be immediately evident, the novel's mainspring is solicitude for the disenfranchised – including black Americans – sorely lacking in the nation it depicts. The waning of this solicitude has brought the United States to a 'moment of crisis', a fact that James is well qualified to diagnose, given the circumstances of his youth.[62] And though Ellison does not raise the matter here, it is notable that this youth coincides with an epoch James evokes in *Hawthorne*. In his own copy of that book (now housed in the Library of Congress), Ellison underlines a passage in which James states that 'the most beautiful productions of the American mind' of that period 'were thoroughly local and national'.[63] Rather than narrow and parochial, James means that such 'productions' were vital and original. Here, then, is evidence of a 'nativist' or least nation-centred James – the sort of James that 'The Novel as a Function of American Democracy' presents as responsible for *The Bostonians*.

In his underlining of this book, then, we see again, the workings of that process whereby Ellison, like Wright and Baldwin, constructs a James best suited to his needs. This is not the only or 'definitive' James, but it is a *usable* one (to recall Van Wyck Brooks's phrase about the past) – both reflective and directive of the turns of Ellison's thought more generally.[64] It remains to be seen how Ellison considered James to be influenced by African Americans, and himself to be influenced in turn by James not just as a thinker but also as a stylist. In several letters of the 1980s, Ellison entertains the view that James absorbed (and then, in his prose, reproduced) African American speech, albeit in an ad hoc and inadvertent way. One such letter is addressed to Henry Louis Gates Jr, and forms a kind of footnote to Ellison's pioneering essays and other writing of the 1950s,

62 Ibid., 763.

63 Henry James, *Hawthorne* (1879; Garden City, NJ: Doubleday and Co., n.d.), 77 (underlining in original).

64 The *locus classicus* for this phrase is Van Wyck Brooks, 'On Creating a Usable Past', *The Dial* 64 (1918), 337–41.

wherein it is affirmed that much putatively 'white' American culture is suffused by a hidden or disavowed 'black' presence. Here, Ellison couches his claim via two antebellum-era vernacular tropes: the use of the singular noun 'Mose' to designate African Americans as a group (a favoured mannerism of Ellison's, as readers of his letters to Albert Murray will know); and the racial slur, 'nigger in the woodpile'. Crucially, Ellison tweaks the latter, substituting one of its terms to make his referent more clearly verbal. Thus, his claim: 'ole Mose is hiding in Henry James' word-pile'; that is, beneath the glossy canopy of James's 'upper class', ornate, elaborate and even 'snob[bish]' prose style lie African American (and, as such, working-class, demotic and so on) roots.[65] The thrust of this claim is of course entirely honorific: insofar as it assumes that James *has* roots, it again contributes to the revisionary defence of James, according to which James is more *engagé* than he looks, that we have explored above. And if this means that on a certain frequency, James spoke for African Americans like Ellison, the converse may also be true: Ellison may speak for – or with, or under the influence of – James. In another letter of the 1980s, to the James scholar R. W. B. Lewis, Ellison writes that James is 'hidden in the stuff of my writing much as the figures from Saint-Gaudens' sculpture were hidden in the lowly vat of plasticine'.[66] The 'decadent' expatriate with a head 'much too large for his body' is thus at work in Ellison's own word-pile. For both authors, this is indeed a complex fate.

65 Ralph Ellison, Letter to Henry Louis Gates Jr, 2 February 1984, in *The Selected Letters of Ralph* Ellison, eds, John F. Callahan and Marc C. Conner (New York: Random House, 2019), 824.

66 Ralph Ellison, Letter to R. W. B. Lewis, July [sic] 1991, in *The Selected Letters of Ralph Ellison*, eds, John F. Callahan and Marc C. Conner (New York: Random House, 2019), 974.

Bibliography

Baldwin, James, 'Alas, Poor Richard', in *Collected Essays* (New York: Library of America, 1998), 247–68.

——, *Another Country* (Harmondsworth: Penguin, 1990).

——, 'The Discovery of What It Means to Be an American', in *Collected Essays* (New York: Library of America, 1998), 137–42.

——, 'A Fly in the Buttermilk', in *Collected Essays* (New York: Library of America, 1998), 187–96.

Beach, Joseph Warren, *The Method of Henry James* (New Haven, CT: Yale University Press, 1918).

Blackmur, R. P., 'Introduction', in Henry James, ed., *The Art of the Novel: Critical Prefaces* (New York: Charles Scribner's Sons, 1937), xix–xxxix.

Brooks, Van Wyck, 'On Creating a Usable Past', *The Dial* 64 (1918), 337–41.

Conner, Marc C., '"Leaving the Territory": Ralph Ellison's Backward Glance', in Maria DiBattista and Emily O. Wittman, eds, *Modernism and Autobiography* (Cambridge, UK: Cambridge University Press, 2014), 113–26.

Ellison, Ralph, 'Address to the Harvard College Alumni, Class of 1949', in John F. Callahan, ed., *The Collected Essays of Ralph Ellison* (New York: Modern Library, 1995), 419–30.

——, 'An Extravagance of Laughter', in John F. Callahan, ed., *The Collected Essays of Ralph Ellison* (New York: Modern Library, 1995), 617–62.

——, 'Hidden Name and Complex Fate', in John F. Callahan, ed., *The Collected Essays of Ralph Ellison* (New York: Modern Library, 1995), 189–209.

——, 'Introduction to the Thirtieth Anniversary Edition of *Invisible Man*', in John F. Callahan, ed., *The Collected Essays of Ralph Ellison* (New York: Modern Library, 1995), 473–89.

——, Letter to Albert Murray, 15 September 1956, in *Trading Twelves: The Selected Letters of Ralph Ellison and Albert Murray*, eds Albert Murray and John F. Callahan (New York: Vintage, 2001), 142–6.

——, Letter to Henry Louis Gates Jr, 2 February 1984, in *The Selected Letters of Ralph Ellison*, eds, John F. Callahan and Marc C. Conner (New York: Random House, 2019), 822–4.

——, Letter to John Kouwenhoven, 30 October 1987, in *The Selected Letters of Ralph Ellison*, eds, John F. Callahan and Marc C. Conner (New York: Random House, 2019), 935–9.

——, Letter to R. W. B. Lewis, July [sic], 1991, in *The Selected Letters of Ralph Ellison*, eds, John F. Callahan and Marc C. Conner (New York: Random House, 2019), 973–4.

——, Memoirs, Library of Congress, Ralph Ellison papers II:46, folder 6.

——, 'The Novel as a Function of American Democracy', in John F. Callahan, ed., *The Collected Essays of Ralph Ellison* (New York: The Modern Library, 1995), 759–69.

——, 'Richard Wright's Blues', in John F. Callahan, ed., *The Collected Essays of Ralph Ellison* (New York: Modern Library, 1995), 128–44.

——, *The Selected Letters of Ralph Ellison*, eds, John F. Callahan and Marc C. Conner (New York: Random House, 2019).

——, 'Society, Morality and the Novel', in John F. Callahan, ed., *The Collected Essays of Ralph Ellison* (New York: Modern Library, 1995), 698–729.

——, 'Some Questions and Some Answers', in John F. Callahan, ed., *The Collected Essays of Ralph Ellison* (New York: Modern Library, 1995), 291–301.

——, Speeches and Letters, 1960–1993, Library of Congress, Ralph Ellison papers II:68, folder 4.

——, '"A Very Stern Discipline"', in John F. Callahan, ed., *The Collected Essays of Ralph Ellison* (New York: Modern Library, 1995), 730–58.

——, 'The World and the Jug', in John F. Callahan, ed., *The Collected Essays of Ralph Ellison* (New York: Modern Library, 1995), 155–88.

Fisher, Rudolf, 'The City of Refuge', in John McCluskey Jr, ed., *The City of Refuge: The Collected Stories of Rudolph Fisher* (Columbia: University of Missouri Press, 1987), 3–16.

Hall, Stuart with Bill Schwarz, *Familiar Stranger: A Life Between Two Islands* (London: Allen Lane, 2017).

Hobson, Suzanne, *The American* (Boston, MA: Houghton Mifflin, 1877).

——, *The Art of the Novel: Critical Prefaces* (New York: Charles Scribner's Sons, 1937).

——, *Hawthorne* (New York: Harper and Bros, 1879).

——, *Henry James: Selected Letters*, ed., Leon Edel (Cambridge, MA: Belknap Press, 1987).

——, '"Looking All Lost towards a Cook's Guide for Beauty": The Art of Literature and the Lessons of the Guidebook in Modernist Writing', *Studies in Travel Writing* 19/1 (2015), 30–47.

Mossman, James, 'Race, Hate, Sex, and Colour: A Conversation with James Baldwin and Colin MacInnes', in Fred L. Stanley and Louis H. Pratt, eds, *Conversations with James Baldwin* (Jackson: University of Mississippi Press, 1989), 46–58.

Nowlin, Michael, 'Henry James and the Making of Modern African American Literature', *The Henry James Review* 39/3 (2018), 282–92.

Parrington, Vernon, *Main Currents of American Thought*, 3 vols (New York: Harcourt, Brace and Co., 1927).

'The Ralph Ellison Collection, (1937–2010)', <https://findingaids.loc.gov/exist_collections/ead3pdf/rbc/2016/rb016001.pdf>, accessed 1 July 2020.

Rodgers, Lawrence R., *Canaan Bound: The African American Great Migration Novel* (Urbana: University of Illinois Press, 1997).

Temko, Allan, 'An Interview with Expatriate Richard Wright in Paris', in Keneth Kinnamon and Michel Fabre, eds, *Conversations with Richard Wright* (Jackson: University of Mississippi Press, 1993), 151–3.

Wilson, Edmund, 'The Ambiguity of Henry James', *Hound and Horn* 7/3 (1934), 385–406.

Wright, Richard, *Black Boy (American Hunger)* (New York: HarperPerennial, 1993).

——, *Native Son, and 'How Bigger Was Born'* (New York: HarperPerennial, 1993).

BRYAN CRABLE

2 Ellison's Appropriation of Jane Ellen Harrison's *Themis*: From Sacrifice to Sacrament

ABSTRACT:
Although scholars have typically emphasized Ralph Ellison's debt to Lord Raglan's *The Hero*, this chapter argues that Ellison's perspective on American life was actually more indebted to another Cambridge Ritualist, Jane Ellen Harrison. In short, this British classicist, studying archaic Greek culture, gave Ellison the insight necessary to unpack a distinctly American issue: that nation's 'racial divide'. This chapter advances this argument through a careful consideration of archival evidence, from Ellison's papers and library, indicating the impact of Harrison's *Themis* on Ellison's thought. The chapter concludes by returning to Harrison's arguments about the nature of archaic Greek culture, and Ellison's appropriation of them; Harrison's careful delineation of sacrifice and sacrament, I contend, not only gives us greater insight into Ellison's approach to American race ritual, but also (more speculatively) helps explain the trajectory of his career, including his struggle to complete and publish a second novel.

One of the most distinctive qualities of Ralph Ellison's work is its unabashed *Americanness*. His brilliant engagement with American culture – and its attendant racial hierarchy – makes him, as Timothy Parrish contends, not only one of 'the great American novelists', but also, and more broadly, 'a theorist of American possibility'.[1] Indeed, as Lucas Morel convincingly demonstrates, Ellison's fiction and nonfiction are best read as deliberate attempts to intervene in American culture; Ellison 'believed his writings would help America, as Martin Luther King, Jr put it, "Be true to what [it] said on paper" '.[2] Yet, paradoxically,

1 Timothy Parrish, *Ralph Ellison and the Genius of America* (Amherst: University of Massachusetts Press, 2012), x, ix.

2 Lucas E. Morel, 'Ralph Ellison's American Democratic Individualism', in Lucas E. Morel, ed., *Ralph Ellison and the Raft of Hope* (Lexington: University Press of Kentucky, 2004), 59.

as this chapter indicates, Ellison arrived at this perspective on American life through an appropriation of a very *non*-American source: British classicist Jane Ellen Harrison.[3]

Although the subject of ritual has long been associated with Ellison, the story of Ellison's engagement with Harrison, I contend, has not been fully told. As a result, I seek – with the other contributors to this volume – to contribute to the broadening of our conversations about Ellison's life and work, by placing his American meditations in a global context. Over the course of this chapter, I illuminate the ways in which this British classicist, studying archaic Greek culture, provoked Ellison to explore the ritual nature of the American racial divide – and thereby to complement his studies of black identity with a detailed examination of *whiteness*.

In what follows, I flesh out this argument by introducing the Cambridge Ritualists and tracing the history of Ellison's engagement with their work – focusing special attention on Harrison. Next, I use archival evidence, from Ellison's papers and personal library, to indicate the evolving influence Harrison's *Themis* exerted on *Invisible Man* (2010). Finally, the chapter concludes by returning to Harrison's arguments about the nature of archaic Greek culture and Ellison's appropriation of them; a more careful delineation of sacrifice and sacrament, I contend, sheds important insight on Ellison's work on his first novel, his nonfiction, and the ultimately unfinished *Three Days before the Shooting …* (2010). Reading Harrison into Ellison thus gives us greater insight into his approach to ritual, but also (more speculatively) helps explain the trajectory of his career, including his struggle to complete a second novel. I will first, though, contextualize this argument within the extant literature, highlighting the surprising lack of attention given to Harrison by Ellisonians.

3 My essay on the Cambridge Ritualists, forthcoming in Paul Devlin, ed., *Ralph Ellison in Context* (Cambridge, UK: Cambridge University Press), draws on a small proportion of the material in this chapter.

Ellison and Ritual

As this brief introduction implies, I am not the first to highlight the role of myth and ritual within Ellison's work. Patrice Rankine, for example, grounds his excellent *Ulysses in Black* in the contention that 'black classicism can in fact be part of a radical cultural identity', defending Ellison from those who would find his work apolitical, unconcerned with racial violence.[4] In fact, Rankine contends, we should arrive at the *opposite* conclusion: 'Rather than a symptom of his escapism or his literary or political conservatism, Ellison's mastery of myth and ritual brought him to uncommon positions on such pressing concerns for blacks living in the twentieth century as lynching'.[5] Barbara Foley, similarly, argues that 'Western mythology supplied not a way out from blackness, but general patterns by which to connect the "indignant consciousness" produced by capitalist racism with the thread of rebellion running throughout the history of class society'.[6] Although more interested in questions of leadership and democracy than Rankine or Foley, Parrish locates myth and ritual in Ellison's appraisal of the struggles and successes of Martin Luther King, Jr and the Civil Rights Movement: 'Writing within a historical context in which the emergence of an authentic black heroic leader seemed impossible, Ellison looked to myth to redeem the seeming nihilism of his historical moment'.[7]

Taking their lead from Ellison himself – such as his comment that Amiri Baraka 'could learn much from the Cambridge School's discoveries of the connection between poetry, drama and ritual'[8] – these scholars have traced Ellison's interest in myth and ritual to his study of the Cambridge

4 Patrice D. Rankine, *Ulysses in Black: Ralph Ellison, Classicism, and African American Literature* (Madison: University of Wisconsin Press, 2006), 42.

5 Ibid., 14–15.

6 Barbara Foley, *Wrestling with the Left: The Making of Ralph Ellison's* Invisible Man (Durham, NC: Duke University Press, 2010), 87.

7 Parrish, *Ralph Ellison and the Genius of America*, 189.

8 Ralph Ellison, 'Blues People', in John F. Callahan, ed., *The Collected Essays of Ralph Ellison* (New York: Modern Library, 1995), 287.

Ritualists. As Robert Segal explains, this label refers to 'a group of classicists all but one of whom were affiliated with Cambridge', whose defining works appeared during the first decades of the twentieth century.[9] Although, as Mary Beard notes, the 'Cambridge Ritualists' is not a name that these British classicists applied to themselves,[10] it has since become scholarly shorthand for the writings produced by Jane Ellen Harrison, Gilbert Murray, F. M. Cornford and A. B. Cook, emphasizing:

> an anthropological and comparativist rather than a philological and particularistic approach to Greek myth, ritual, and religion. The Ritualists argue that ancient Greeks were far closer to primitives than had been assumed – indeed, were much more like primitives than like moderns.[11]

Yet, despite the equation of this school of thought with Harrison, Murray, Cornford and Cook, the secondary literature on Ellison and the Ritualists has largely focused its attention on a text *influenced*, but not *written*, by these authors: Lord Raglan's *The Hero* (first published in 1936).[12] Rankine's study of Ellison's classicism, for example, is based entirely upon Raglan and James Frazer, the latter identified by Rankine as the source of Raglan's (and thus Ellison's) studies of mythic heroism.[13] Similarly, Parrish's treatment of Ellison, King and the Civil Rights Movement draws its inspiration from *The Hero*,[14] though Parrish notes Ellison's use of Gilbert Murray in the

9 Robert A. Segal, 'Series Editor's Foreword', in Robert Ackerman, ed., *The Myth and Ritual School: J. G. Frazer and The Cambridge Ritualists* (New York: Routledge, 1991), viii.

10 Mary Beard, *The Invention of Jane Harrison* (Cambridge, MA: Harvard University Press, 2000), 113.

11 Segal, 'Series Editor's Foreword', ix.

12 As will be discussed later in this chapter, Foley is something of an exception to this rule, since she draws attention to Raglan and to other members of the Cambridge School. Yet, as I will argue, Foley's emphasis on leftist politics leads her to misreadings of Jane Harrison and, as a consequence, Ellison.

13 Rankine, *Ulysses in Black*, 122–3, 125–6. Frazer is typically (though rather inaccurately) credited as the founder of the Cambridge School (e.g., Segal, 'Series Editor's Foreword', viii).

14 Parrish, *Ralph Ellison and the Genius of America*, 155, 170, 174, 181, 189–91, 205, 210.

essay, 'Tell It Like It Is, Baby'.[15] In large part, these scholars simply echo Ellison's own statements regarding the importance of Raglan's book – and his relative silence regarding other authors associated with the Cambridge School. Following the publication of *Invisible Man*, Ellison regularly credited *The Hero* with helping spark the opening passages of his novel. In 'The Art of Fiction', for example, he recalled to interviewers that:

> on a farm in Vermont where I was reading *The Hero* by Lord Raglan and speculating on the nature of Negro leadership in the United States, I wrote the first paragraph of *Invisible Man*, and was soon involved in the struggle of creating the novel.[16]

Given Ellison's repetition of this story in interviews and essays spanning several decades, it is understandable that scholars would take him at his word – and thereby equate his study of the Ritualists with Raglan's volume.[17]

I contend that these assumptions about Ellison's classicism are at least somewhat in need of correction. Although this places me in the awkward position of challenging Ellison's own identification of his influences, I would suggest that we profit by shifting our focus away from Raglan, and towards someone who, in my view, was *at least as* important to Ellison's studies of myth and ritual: Jane Ellen Harrison. By attending to Harrison, and

15 Ibid., 155–6; cf. Ralph Ellison, '"Tell It Like It Is, Baby"', in John F. Callahan, ed., *The Collected Essays of Ralph Ellison* (New York: Modern Library, 1995), 30, 46.

16 Ralph Ellison, 'The Art of Fiction: An Interview', in John F. Callahan, ed., *The Collected Essays of Ralph Ellison* (New York: Modern Library, 1995), 218. See also Ralph Ellison, 'On Initiation Rites and Power: A Lecture at West Point', in John F. Callahan, ed., *The Collected Essays of Ralph Ellison* (New York: Modern Library, 1995), 523–4; Ralph Ellison, 'That Same Pain, that Same Pleasure: An Interview', in John F. Callahan, ed., *The Collected Essays of Ralph Ellison* (New York: Modern Library, 1995), 76.

17 For an attempt to trace the exact nature of Ellison's encounter with Raglan, see Bryan Crable, '"Who Invents Rituals?": Ralph Ellison Reads Lord Raglan', *Literature of the Americas* 5 (2018), 27–42. Although published prior to the current volume, this essay was generated by the research for the presentation I delivered on Ellison and Harrison at The International Ralph Ellison Symposium, held at the University of Oxford in September 2017. My presentation at this Symposium was also, of course, my first attempt at the argument presented here.

reading Ellison *through* her, I argue that we thereby generate new insight into Ellison's perspective on race in America. Further, a focus on Harrison (rather than Raglan), I contend, also offers us a new angle on the evolution of Ellison's work – from his first novel, through his nonfiction, to the sprawling, posthumously published work, *Three Days before the Shooting* .... I suggest that these works collectively testify to the Harrisonian themes that troubled Ellison's studies of black America and black leadership – leading him to increasingly turn towards the ritual nature of white supremacy. In order to arrive at this conclusion, however, we must begin by tracing Ellison's introduction to this British scholar's work on archaic Greece.

Encountering Jane Harrison

Jane Harrison has long since lost her preeminent position in classical studies, and in other branches of the humanities[18] – and even those readers of Ellison who know her name (and her status as one of the earliest and foremost British female classicists) are likely not conversant with her writings. This despite the fact that, as Beard points out:

> the basic message of her work – that somewhere underneath the calm, shining, rational exterior of the classical world is a mass of weird, seething irrationality – is a tenet that almost everyone working in the history of Greek culture would now take for granted.[19]

18 Although there has been a small Harrison revival of sorts over the last two decades, it has largely been confined to feminist attempts to reclaim a forgotten forerunner, and has not translated into more mainstream scholarly interest. See, for example, Shelley Arlen, '"For Love of an Idea": Jane Ellen Harrison, Heretic and Humanist', *Women's History Review* 5/2 (1996), 165; Shelley Arlen, review of Annabel Robinson, *The Life and Work of Jane Ellen Harrison* (Oxford: Oxford University Press, 2002), in *English Literature in Transition, 1880–1920*, 47/3 (2004), 343; Sandra J. Peacock, 'An Awful Warmth about Her Heart: The Personal in Jane Harrison's Ideas on Religion', in William M. Calder III, ed., *The Cambridge Ritualists Reconsidered* (Atlanta, GA: Scholars Press, 1991), 184.

19 Beard, *The Invention of Jane Harrison*, 7.

Indeed, Rankine and Parrish conspicuously omit her from their discussions of Ellison's classicism, though she has been hailed as the pre-eminent Cambridge Ritualist, the *sine qua non* of the group: 'Although Gilbert Murray's and Francis Cornford's studies have traditionally been cited as the important work of the Ritualists, Jane Harrison actually stood at the center of the circle'.[20] Thomas Africa likens her to 'a Minoan goddess', calling her 'the presiding spirit of the Cambridge Ritualists',[21] while Robert Ackerman's book *The Myth and Ritual School* convincingly portrays Harrison as the key to unlocking the Cambridge School's insights: 'Of the Ritualists Gilbert Murray was (and is) clearly the best known, particularly to nonclassicists; nevertheless, I maintain that Jane Harrison was the center of the group'.[22] Ackerman claims that her books provided the Cambridge School's 'theoretical foundations',[23] identifying Harrison's *Themis: A Study of the Social Origins of Greek Religion* as 'the most important work of all'.[24]

Significantly, although these are relatively recent assessments of Harrison's import, they echo the source of Ellison's original exposure to the Cambridge Ritualists: his close friend, Stanley Edgar Hyman. For example, in his most famous book, *The Armed Vision* (first published in 1948), Hyman underscored the pivotal scholarly contribution made by Harrison: '*Themis* [...] constituted a kind of collective manifesto of what is known as the Cambridge school of classical scholarship, which completely revolutionized the study of Greek art and thought by turning on it the knowledge and theories of comparative anthropology'.[25] Hyman reaffirmed

20 Sandra J. Peacock, *Jane Ellen Harrison: The Mask and the Self* (New Haven, CT: Yale University Press, 1988), 2.

21 Thomas W. Africa, 'Aunt Glegg among the Dons, or Taking Jane Harrison at Her Word', in William M. Calder III, ed., *The Cambridge Ritualists Reconsidered* (Atlanta, GA: Scholars Press, 1991), 22.

22 Robert Ackerman, *The Myth and Ritual School: J. G. Frazer and The Cambridge Ritualists* (New York: Routledge, 1991), xiv.

23 Ibid., xiv.

24 Ibid., 123.

25 Stanley Edgar Hyman, *The Armed Vision: A Study in the Methods of Modern Literary Criticism* (New York: Vintage Books, 1955), 16.

this position seven years later, in an essay on the Ritualists that identifies the 'watershed year' for the Cambridge School as 1912, 'when Harrison published *Themis*, a full and brilliant exposition of the chthonic origins of Greek mythology'.[26] According to Hyman, Harrison's book provided the catalyst and foundation for the entire Ritualist perspective: 'With the appearance of *Themis*, a powerful general statement of the theory buttressed by a prodigy of scholarship in several complicated areas of Greek culture, a "Cambridge" or "ritual" approach generally became available'.[27] When *Themis* was reissued in 1962, Hyman added a deeply personal reflection to these scholarly assessments, calling it: 'A book that changed my life – there are times when I think it is the most revolutionary book of the twentieth century'.[28] Indeed, Hyman saw Harrison to be the foremost of the Ritualists; he certainly depicted her as more intellectually important than Raglan, whom he characterized as less an innovator than the writer who 'most effectively popularized' the Ritualists' views.[29]

Since Hyman introduced Ellison to the Cambridge School, it would seem to follow that these opinions would have been passed on to his friend as well; happily, we need not rely on speculation regarding this point. Not only do we know that Ellison read the treatments of the Cambridge School written by Hyman[30] – and thereby saw the value that his friend placed on Harrison's contribution to the Ritualists – but also that they specifically discussed Harrison's work.[31] For example, in a letter dated 19 October

26 Stanley Edgar Hyman, 'The Ritual View of Myth and the Mythic', *Journal of American Folklore* 68/270 (1955), 463.

27 Ibid., 464.

28 Stanley Edgar Hyman, 'Leaping for Goodly Themis', in Stanley Edgar Hyman, ed., *Standards: A Chronicle of Books for Our Time* (New York: Horizon Press, 1966), 103.

29 Stanley Edgar Hyman, 'Some Bankrupt Treasuries', *The Kenyon Review* 10/3 (1948), 498 n.2; see also Hyman, *The Armed Vision*, 124–5.

30 See, for example, Ralph Ellison, Letter to Stanley Hyman, 15 June 1948, Library of Congress, Stanley Edgar Hyman papers 6, folder 30; Ralph Ellison, Letter to Stanley Hyman, 27 April 1955, Library of Congress, Stanley Edgar Hyman papers 6, folder 30.

31 Interestingly, there is no record in the correspondence or archives of their discussing Raglan, though I have no doubt they had face-to-face conversations regarding *The Hero*.

1945, Hyman wrote Ellison of his enthusiasm for his friend's now-classic essay 'Richard Wright's Blues'. Yet, Hyman also provided Harrisonian criticism of it:

> Several of your points, I think, lead into something that you didn't mention, although you probably know it. Jane Harrison, in *Ancient Art and Ritual*, and some other people, point out that the savage has a very thin and meager individual personality, limited emotions, that most of his personality and full emotional expression is only possible collectively, in tribal ritual.[32]

After sketching out this objection in more detail, Hyman promised that, when Ellison lectured to Bennington later that month, the two would talk more about this point.

A few months later, a note to Hyman suggested that Ellison had spent time thinking about Harrison's emphasis upon 'tribal ritual':

> Fanny and I were out in the ocean with some friends last weekend and caught some bass. I have observed the passion with which some fellows pursue fish and can see traces of those rituals which Jane Harrison explores in *From Ritual to Romance*.[33]

Ellison here misidentifies Harrison as the author of this text, actually written by Jessie Weston; yet, Weston's volume is so heavily (and explicitly) indebted to Harrison that his conflation is, in some ways, quite excusable.[34] Ellison's real education in Harrison's thought began in early 1950, though, when Hyman gave him a copy of *Themis*. The gift was surely intended to assist in Ellison's work on *Invisible Man*, then still in process, but Harrison's influence on Ellison's thinking lingered beyond the publication of his first novel. Note, for example, Ellison's invocation of Harrison in the brilliant 1964 essay, 'If the Twain Shall Meet':

32 Ralph Ellison, Letter to Stanley Hyman, 19 October 1945, Library of Congress, Stanley Edgar Hyman papers, 6, folder 30.

33 Ralph Ellison, Letter to Stanley Hyman, 20 June 1946, in *The Selected Letters of Ralph Ellison*, eds, John F. Callahan and Marc C. Conner (New York: Random House, 2019), 216.

34 See, for example, Stanley Edgar Hyman, 'Jessie Weston and the Forest of Broceliande', in Phoebe Pettingell, ed., *The Critic's Credentials* (New York: Atheneum, 1978), 290–1.

> while the myths and mysteries that form the Southern mystique are *irrational* and even *primitive*, they are nevertheless real [...]. Like all mysteries and their attendant myths, they imply – as Jane Harrison teaches us in *Themis*, her study of ancient Greek religion – a rite. And rites are *actions*, the goal of which is the manipulation of power – in primitive religions magical power, in the South (and in the North) political power.[35]

Although this is the sole *explicit* reference to Harrison in Ellison's published work (at least as far as I can determine), it is significant that we have evidence of Ellison engaging, directly or through Hyman, at least two different works by Harrison: *Ancient Art & Ritual* and *Themis* (the latter identified by Hyman as the keystone text of the Cambridge School), together with Weston's *From Ritual to Romance*, itself inspired by Harrison. Further, we see Ellison discussing Harrison's work over the course of nearly twenty years, suggesting that he studied it more closely than one might imagine, given his repeated invocation of Raglan. Indeed, I believe that there is an argument to be made that Ellison was at least as influenced by Harrison as Raglan – and in ways that were more consequential for the arc of his career. Such a conclusion requires that we engage the archival evidence preserved in the Library of Congress, in Ellison's papers and his personal library.

Finding *Themis* in *Invisible Man*

Readers of this volume are likely to be familiar with Ellison's story, recited earlier, about the role of Raglan's *The Hero* in the birth of *Invisible Man*. Archival materials confirm it to a certain extent, since there is a first edition of *The Hero* in Ellison's preserved library, which contains some scattered annotations in pencil. Yet, by contrast, there are three Harrison volumes in the Library of Congress 'Ralph Ellison Collection': *Prolegomena to the*

35 Ralph Ellison, 'If the Twain Shall Meet', in John F. Callahan, ed., *The Collected Essays of Ralph Ellison* (New York: Modern Library, 1995), 572.

Study of Greek Religion, *Ancient Art & Ritual* and *Themis*.[36] Although the first two are unmarked (apart from Ellison's signature), *Themis* bears an inscription: below Ellison's signature, he wrote 'Gift from Stanley Hyman March 17, 1950'. Moreover, this text is marked three different ways: black ink (consistent with the date and signature), pencil and green ink. This indicates that Ellison carefully read the text, and on multiple occasions, not just once, as with the Raglan.[37]

In addition, there are no specific references to Raglan or his book in any of the folders containing notes or notebooks from Ellison's years of work on *Invisible Man* – though in an ultimately deleted portion of the novel, the character LeRoy has a copy of Raglan's volume on his shelf.[38] This absence is jarring, given Ellison's repeated invocation of Raglan when describing his novel's origin, and is intensified by the presence of archival materials that focus specifically on Harrison's book. Multiple folders of notes for *Invisible Man* include passages copied directly out of *Themis* (some handwritten, some typed), while several other folders include explicit references to it.

Indeed, in three of these folders of notes, Ellison quoted the same long passage from 'Excursus on the Ritual Forms Preserved in Greek Tragedy' – a section of *Themis* written by Gilbert Murray that appears as an appendix to Harrison's chapter on the hero. This passage identifies the pattern of events characteristic of Greek tragedy that, Murray argues, originated in archaic ritual practice. In this sequence, the '*Agon* or Contest' is followed by: 'A *Pathos* [...] generally a ritual or sacrificial death', which, since it

36 For the full catalogue of Ellison's personal library, see 'The Ralph Ellison Collection, (1937–2010)', <https://findingaids.loc.gov/exist_collections/ead3pdf/rbc/2016/rb016001.pdf>, accessed 22 May 2020.

37 Most of the annotations are in black ink, corresponding to the signature and inscription, and thus probably date from early 1950; yet, the fact that Ellison returned to the text multiple times is, I think, quite significant – especially since this is clearly not the case with *The Hero*.

38 Foley, *Wrestling with the Left*, 228. The mention of Raglan in drafts is not consistent, however; in one set of notes for the novel, Ellison lists LeRoy's books as including 'Greek myths' and 'works on anthropology', as well as Freud, Darwin and Marx, but includes no mention of Raglan (Ralph Ellison, Notes, 1942–1950, Library of Congress, Ralph Ellison papers I:152, folder 2).

'seems seldom or never to be actually performed under the eyes of the audience [...] is announced by a messenger'.[39] Following this announcement, 'A *Threnos* or Lamentation [...] a clash of contrary emotions' is followed by: 'An *Anagnorisis* – discovery or recognition' of a '*Theophany*', which entails 'Resurrection or Apotheosis [...] Epiphany in glory'.[40] In addition to copying out these passages in full, Ellison even added his own title: 'Stages of Tragic Ritual'.[41]

While labouring over *Invisible Man*, Ellison did more than faithfully copy this portion of *Themis*. His notes also draw on this sequence at several other points – especially the second ritual stage, '*Pathos*'. Murray's explanation of the term provides several examples familiar to the reader of Greek myth and tragedy: 'a ritual or sacrificial death, in which Adonis or Attis is slain by the tabu [sic] animal, the Pharmakos stoned, Osiris, Dionysus, Pentheus, Orpheus, Hippolytus torn to pieces (σπαραγμος)'.[42] This Greek word, *sparagmos*, Ellison often rendered in its English equivalent: *dismemberment*. In this Anglicized translation, the term can be found throughout Ellison's working notes on the novel, as well as early drafts.

For example, at the end of a series of typed reflections on his protagonist, Ellison wrote, 'IVM [Invisible Man] is the hero as delinquent. Old Mary and [the] group think they celebrate a resurrection, when he is still undergoing dismemberment'.[43] Within another page of notes outlining the narrator's arrival at Mary Rambo's rooming house, Ellison commented, 'He starts going to pieces almost immediately. Thus he dreams that his personality is being dismembered'.[44] In the margins of an outline of the last portion of the book, Ellison similarly mused that 'his mythomania is an adoption of other personalities and equals slaying of fisher king, a

39 Jane Ellen Harrison, *Themis: A Study of the Social Origins of Greek Religion* (Cambridge, UK: Cambridge University Press, 1927), 343.

40 Harrison, *Themis*, 343–4.

41 Ralph Ellison, Notes, 1942–1950, Library of Congress, Ralph Ellison papers I:152, folder 1.

42 Harrison, *Themis*, 343.

43 Ralph Ellison, Notes, 1942–1950, Library of Congress, Ralph Ellison papers I:151, folder 10.

44 Ibid.

dismemberment'.[45] Yet, interestingly, the author applied this same terminology to another character within his developing novel. In several points throughout the notes, Ellison identified LeRoy as the one who 'realizes the isolation implicit in his role of the dedicated' – which leads to his dismemberment, and the discovery of his hands and legs by other characters in Mary's rooming house.[46] Ellison described LeRoy as 'several things: Hero and scapegoat. Drowned sailor. Promise of racial success and leadership. The good man cut off in youth, in springtime of life'.[47]

Such parallels lead Foley to suggest that the ultimately excised LeRoy is the 'avatar of the dying king or god described by Frazer, Raglan, and the Cambridge School',[48] as well as 'the man who would function as the invisible man's absent double'.[49] Indeed, Foley's study of drafts of *Invisible Man* leads her – alone among Ellisonians – to recognize his use of Harrison's *Themis*. She points to the Ritualists' emphasis on the 'murdered, tortured, and dismembered god', their focus on 'the sacrificial function of this "year-daimon" in rituals of initiation, purification, and rebirth that symbolically enacted the group's attempts to gain the favor of the gods'.[50] Reflecting her book's project, however, Foley describes Harrison as 'a feminist and Fabian socialist', and thereby reads *Themis* as a study of 'primitive communalist Greek society'.[51] Further, for Foley, this suggests the political nature of the dismembered god; the parallel between 'Hercules, Dionysus, and Prometheus on the one hand, and Denmark Vesey, John Henry, and Joe Louis on the other' stems from the fact that all are 'heroes reflecting the needs of the "broad" masses of humanity and willing, when necessary, to sacrifice themselves in service to these needs'.[52] As a result, Foley concludes,

45 Ralph Ellison, Notes, 1942–1950, Library of Congress, Ralph Ellison papers I:152, folder 4.

46 Ralph Ellison, Notes, 1942–1950, Library of Congress, Ralph Ellison papers I:151, folder 7. See also Foley, *Wrestling with the Left*, 223–4, 271, 398 n.58.

47 Ralph Ellison, Notes, 1942–1950, Library of Congress, Ralph Ellison papers I:152, folder 3.

48 Foley, *Wrestling with the Left*, 223.

49 Ibid., 220.

50 Ibid., 84.

51 Ibid., 85.

52 Ibid., 87.

'Gathering ideas from sources as diverse as Harrison and Thomson, Wright and Malraux, the young Ellison sought out models of Promethean rebellion [...]. He was pursuing the red line of heroic history'.[53] Although Foley's reading of Ellison is compelling at times, I believe her commitments lead her to misread Harrison, and, moreover, she fails to recognize the evolution of Ellison's engagement with *Themis*; indeed, we can see evidence for both points through a closer examination of Ellison's notes and notebooks.

Within these archival materials, we see that Ellison drew upon Murray's stages of tragic ritual when drafting a letter to *LIFE* regarding coverage of Babe Ruth's funeral. After noting Ruth's battle with cancer as '*Agon/ Pathos*', Ellison sketched the remainder of the ritual: 'Press plays role of messenger bringing message of death. Body lies in state at stadium which was followed by a Threnos or lamentation [...]. And this is followed by Ruth's resurrection and apotheosis'.[54] Since Ruth's funeral took place in August 1948,[55] Ellison had clearly read this material prior to receiving his own copy of *Themis* from Hyman – but that should not lead us to thereby assume that he had carefully studied Harrison's book prior to this point, or, even, that he had even read the entire text. Indeed, if we look more carefully at Ellison's notebooks, we see that several of his extended quotations related to Murray's stages of tragic ritual come not from *Themis*, but from secondary sources discussing it – such as Robert Graves's *The White Goddess*,[56] Francis Fergusson's *The Idea of a Theater*,[57] and an essay on *Themis*

53 Ibid., 88.

54 Ralph Ellison, Notes, 1942–1950, Library of Congress, Ralph Ellison papers I:151, folder 9. Here Ellison misspelled 'threnos', but, as elsewhere in this chapter, I have silently corrected minor typos.

55 Leigh Montville, *The Big Bam: The Life and Times of Babe Ruth* (New York: Broadway Books, 2006), 366.

56 Ralph Ellison, Notes, 1942–1950, Library of Congress, Ralph Ellison papers I:152, folder 7.

57 Ralph Ellison, Notes, 1942–1950, Library of Congress, Ralph Ellison papers I:151, folder 10. For example, what Foley identifies as one of the 'long passages from Harrison and Murray [...] copied out in his notes and notebooks' is actually from Fergusson (Foley, *Wrestling with the Left*, 86).

by John Middleton Murry.[58] Since Graves's text was published in 1948 and Fergusson's in 1949 – while Ellison's annotated copy of *Themis* is dated 1950 – it appears Ellison encountered Gilbert Murray's discussion of tragic ritual from these other sources, and only later from Harrison's volume.

Such an interpretation of Ellison's encounter with *Themis* is supported by what we know of the evolution of *Invisible Man*. After the protagonist's first words, 'I am an invisible man', announced themselves to him, Ellison used the work of Kenneth Burke to structure his developing narrative:

> I wished to take advantage of Burke's observation that tragic heroes often follow a rhythmic development from a moment of purpose (the beginning) through 'passion' (the middle or 'agon' or complication) to a moment [of] 'perception' (the ending) in which he gleans some meaning from his experience.[59]

Ellison had begun to focus on these terms as indicating 'the nature of tragic rhythm' in the summer of 1947, something, he noted, that was a 'neat enough packaging for a profound commodity' that it would surely 'make a publisher smack his lips'.[60] Ellison thereafter adopted Burke's framework to summarize his view of human existence, and organize his protagonist's journey towards insight:

> Life, in that man is born into a world beyond his control, is tragic. Man sets out with one purpose which inevitably throws him into conflict with the hidden laws of the universe and from this springs his passion and his agony and the reward of passion and agony, if carried far enough, is a tiny bit of perception.[61]

58 Ralph Ellison, Notes, 1942–1950, Library of Congress, Ralph Ellison papers I:152, folder 1.

59 Ralph Ellison, Notes, 1942–1950, Library of Congress, Ralph Ellison papers I:152, folder 7. For more on this point, see Bryan Crable, *Ralph Ellison and Kenneth Burke: At the Roots of the Racial Divide* (Charlottesville: University of Virginia Press, 2012), 81–3.

60 Ralph Ellison, Letter to Stanley Hyman, 17 June 1947, in *The Selected Letters of Ralph Ellison*, eds, John F. Callahan and Marc C. Conner (New York: Random House, 2019), 226.

61 Ralph Ellison, Notes, 1942–1950, Library of Congress, Ralph Ellison papers I:152, folder 2.

Initially, therefore, Ellison seems to have looked to Murray's stages of tragic ritual solely as a way to strengthen this tripartite structure – deepening the tragic rhythm of his book through a greater attention to its ritual components. At several places in his notebooks, we thus see Ellison integrating Murray's stages into Burke's triad. For example, on a page of notes quoting Murray's stages of tragic ritual, Ellison emphasized Murray's numbering system: '1. Agon; 2. Pathos; 3. Messenger; 4. Threnos; 5. Anagnoris; 6. Theophany'. At the bottom of the page, Ellison added a handwritten note, identifying the first stage with purpose, the second with passion and the third with perception.[62] He did the same in another set of notes – the only difference is that the appended note on purpose, passion and perception was typed, not handwritten.[63] Elsewhere in the notebooks, Ellison sketched a slightly different synthesis of these terms; he equated purpose with 'agon = combat', passion with 'sparagmos, dismemberment' and perception with 'recognition scene, messenger, epiphany'.[64]

Taken in isolation – out of its context within the volume as a whole – Murray's stages of tragic ritual, yoked to Burke's triad of terms, would seem, as Foley suggests, to provide an excellent framework for organizing the story of his heroic narrator. Yet, although Ellison initially drew on Harrison's text in order to strengthen the Burkean structure of his novel, I contend that his studies of the text took him in a quite unexpected direction. Once he had taken the opportunity to study the entirety of *Themis*, Ellison recognized that Harrison's text was challenging his perspective on the nature of the hero, and on the nature of ritual; it led him to focus less on the hero than on the *community*, less on sacrifice than on *sacrament*. In short, the more time Ellison spent with his copy of Harrison's book, the more that he moved beyond the stages of ritual that had initially drawn him to the work – and the more he was drawn to the parallels between archaic Greek ritual and twentieth-century American culture. As a result, I see *Themis*

62 Ralph Ellison, Notes, 1942–1950, Library of Congress, Ralph Ellison papers I:151, folder 10.

63 Ralph Ellison, Notes, 1942–1950, Library of Congress, Ralph Ellison papers I:152, folder 1.

64 Ralph Ellison, Notes, 1942–1950, Library of Congress, Ralph Ellison papers I:152, folder 2.

as an important Ellisonian source, one that directed Ellison's attention in unique ways. It even, I suggest, troubled his focus on black leadership, and deepened his interest in the ritual nature of American white supremacy. *Themis*, consequently, helps us understand how the project of *Invisible Man* evolved into *Three Days before the Shooting . . .*, and also prompted some of Ellison's most important nonfiction. In order to arrive at this conclusion, we must more closely examine the arguments offered within *Themis*, to place the stages of tragic ritual back within their original context.

Ritual as Pre-theological and Sacramental

For readers like Hyman, the significance of *Themis* lies in its skilful explication and defence of the Cambridge position on myth and ritual: 'The primary meaning of myth in religion is just the same as in early literature; it is the spoken correlative of the acted rite, the thing done'.[65] For Harrison, we do as much damage to a myth by understanding it as aetiological, as an 'origins story', as we do by equating it with falsehood. Instead, myth and ritual must both be understood as potent, and inseparable, for they are part and parcel of the same religious practice: 'As man is a speaking as well as a motor animal, any complete human ceremony usually contains both elements, speech and action'.[66] In the religious practice characteristic of the archaic Greek community, in other words, a successful ceremony required the proper performance of both word (myth) and deed (ritual).

Yet, we must be cautious, as even this brief summary could lead us to think of the Homeric epic, the tales of trials undergone by ancient Greek heroes, or the rites enacted or violated by heroic figures in honour of the Olympian deities. Harrison argues vehemently against mistaking the kind of ritual she is tracing for those found in Homer and Hesiod – or in any of the stories regarding the Olympian gods and heroes. The Greeks who generated these heroic tales, Harrison contends, are much more *our* contemporaries

65 Harrison, *Themis*, 328.

66 Ibid., 329.

than exemplary of their archaic predecessors. As she suggests, we must learn instead to think in non-theological (or, better, pre-theological) religious terms: 'If then we would understand religion, we must get behind theology, behind, for the Greeks, the figures of the Olympians'.[67] Since, she says – in a passage marked by Ellison – the Olympians 'stand for articulate consciousness', we need to dig beneath them, searching for prior experiences of 'emotion, union, indivisibility', even the 'sub-conscious'.[68]

Understanding this earlier, 'sub-conscious' form of religious practice, Harrison continues, requires us to suspend our assumptions regarding not only the nature of religion, but also of community, heroism and the divine. When discussing archaic Greece, Harrison writes, we typically impose contemporary assumptions upon a radically distinct form of human life – for example, we consistently, but incorrectly, presume the existence of individuals and individual identities. She insists, instead, that this was a much later development in human history:

> Man in the totemistic stage rarely sets himself as an individual over against his tribe; he rarely sets himself as man over against the world around him. He has not yet captured his individual or his human soul, not yet drawn a circle around his separate self.[69]

We must therefore reject the temptation to impose our own distinction between subject and object, individual and environment, upon these communities; Harrison is excavating a form of social life without individuals, absent any tension between individual and collective, and prior to a rigorous division between human being and surrounding world. For Harrison, there are several important implications that follow from this starting point. First, we must accept a religious practice without gods: 'The very idea of a god [...] belongs to a later stage of epistemology, a stage in which man stands off from his own imagination, looks

67 Harrison, *Themis*, 490. Here, I would argue, is one point where Foley's reading of Harrison goes astray; though she at times seems to recognize the 'pre-Olympian' nature of Harrison's argument, Foley fails to think consistently about religious practice without deities or selves – and thus does not move beyond the hero as individual (Foley, *Wrestling with the Left*, 84–5, 257).

68 Harrison, *Themis*, xvii; see also 475–7.

69 Ibid., 121; see also 475.

at it, takes an attitude towards it, sees it as *object*'.[70] If there is no division between the individual and her environment, subject and object, then religion is not a means of connecting human beings to the gods; 'The ritual act', she stresses, 'is prior to the divinity'.[71]

Yet, there is another implication that follows from this conception of religious practice – one with important Ellisonian dimensions. Just as we cannot picture archaic ritual as involving gods, the same is true of the hero. Given the lack of distinction between subject and object, self and other, in this form of ritual activity there can also be no naming of a distinct person, no tracing of the life (however embellished) of a historical individual. As a result, Harrison emphasizes that we should not be thinking about *the hero*, a distinct individual who performs ritual acts, but instead the *hero-function* necessary for a successful communal ritual:

> The 'Hero' is not a dead man with a known name and history commemorated by funeral games. His title stands not for a personality, but for an office, defined by its functions and capable of being filled by a series of representatives.[72]

This passage caught Ellison's attention – he heavily marked and underlined it. He recognized that her text was asking him to think about ritual without gods, without individual selves, and, indeed, without a hero.

In order to avoid misleading terminology, in *Themis* Harrison therefore does not refer to 'the hero', the contemporary, individualistic concept, but rather to the *hero-function*; for this, she introduces the Greek term *daimon*. Although we are accustomed (as with Socrates) to thinking of the *daimon* as a spirit, Harrison argues that the term itself is difficult to translate; it is less an individual spirit than a communal role, a manifestation of the group 'who wears the mask and absorbs the ritual' and 'represents the permanent life of the group'.[73] Ellison marked a passage where Harrison explains this point further: 'The *daimon* proper [...] was a collective representation expressing not a personality so much as a function'.[74] In this context, then,

70 Harrison, *Themis*, 127 (italics in original).

71 Ibid., 29.

72 Ibid., 259.

73 Ibid., xiv.

74 Ibid., 315.

ritual is not a representation or celebration of an individual hero, nor is it a pattern of acts taken by an individual in devotion to a god – since neither self nor deity existed at this point. Instead, *Themis* describes ritual as a collective enactment (accompanied by the proper words, the myth), centred on the *daimon*, that does essential communal work. Within such ritual practice, the hero was not the one who took action, but the one who served as the focal point, even the *object*, of the rite. This is why Harrison describes the hero, the *daimon*, not as an actor, but as a *function*, as an 'office' – a role that could be filled by anyone. As a result, Harrison focuses not on an individual, *the* hero, but instead upon the community – the ones *for whom* the ritual does work, the ones for whom the hero-function is necessary.

Given this shift in emphasis, from the individual to the community, Harrison argues that archaic ritual is best described as the collective manipulation of the manifest power of the universe, via the office of the *daimon*. This conception of power derives from the communal nature of this form of social life, which emphasizes emotion and interconnection, not rationality and division: 'Intellectually the group is weak [...]. Emotionally the group is strong'.[75] Central to ritual, then, is what Harrison terms *mana*, the 'force or power which seems [...] uncanny, something which arrests [...] attention and rouses [...] a feeling of awe'.[76] In a passage marked by Ellison, Harrison argues that:

> It is not the fear of the individual savage that begets religion, it is fear felt together, fear emphasized, qualified, by a sort of social sanction. Moreover fear does not quite express the emotion felt. It is rather awe, and awe contains in it the element of wonder as well as fear.[77]

Harrison thus contends that religious practice originated with the collective need to grapple with *mana*, the power of the universe dwarfing that of the community. It is the need to protect the group from the overwhelming, terrible and awe-inspiring, forces of the ever-changing,

75 Ibid., 43.

76 Ibid., 66; see also 68.

77 Ibid., 64.

dynamic world that spawned the ritual office, the hero-function, the *daimon*.[78]

Religious practice, correspondingly, was *not* a matter of sacrifice – not in our contemporary sense – nor was it represented by the familiar figure of the scapegoat, burdened with sin and driven from the community. This is a limited, even distorted conception of archaic religious practice. According to Harrison, the characteristic form of religious activity in this period was instead the sacrament: 'Sacrifice is but a specialized form of sacrament [...] sacrament is the more primitive'.[79] Moreover, since, as Harrison reminds us, 'sanctity does not always issue in sacramental sacrifice',[80] we should not read the presence of death in sacramental ritual too literally. Sacramental rites actually took a number of forms – including totemistic consumption, as well as the ceremonies whereby the *daimon* is killed, dismembered, and subsequently reborn. She thus emphasizes not the act of sacrifice, but the communal summoning and focusing of power in the *daimon* through word and deed, designed to accomplish the sharing of *mana* by the group.[81] The vital point is that, in sacrament, the *daimon* 'was full of mana, was intensely sacred, because he is himself a [...] spirit of generation, even of immortality'.[82]

As a result, Harrison argues that, within sacramental ritual, the *daimon* 'dies as an individual and revives as an eternally recurrent functionary' – a transformation that need not require a literal death.[83] By assuming the requisite office, a member of the group is reborn as *daimon*, enabling the collective to live on. This explains the *daimon*'s death-that-is-not, the drama of rebirth, as well as its communal function; the *daimon*, as a 'spirit of generation, even of immortality' effectively renews the world, assures the passing of one year to the next, and thereby preserves the 'permanent life of the group'.[84] Thus, by collectively carrying out the ritual and speaking the

78 Ibid., 65.
79 Ibid., 134.
80 Ibid., 270–1.
81 Ibid., 134, 138.
82 Ibid., 271.
83 Ibid., 323.
84 Ibid., xiv.

proper words, by focusing and distributing *mana* through the sacralizing of the *daimon*, the group's existence is reaffirmed, fixed, made permanent against the ravages of natural events, the forces that produce change and challenge the group's identity – against, in a word, *chaos*.

A Harrisonian Fault Line Emerges

As noted earlier, it appears that Ellison initially drew on Murray's portion of *Themis* as a stand-alone framework, a complement to Burke's purpose, passion and perception. Yet elsewhere in the notebooks, we see Ellison placing this tragic ritual back within the context of Harrison's discussion of sacrament. In short, I argue, he began to focus not simply upon his narrator's journey to perception, but also upon the hero-function played by black Americans. In a typed note, for example, Ellison described his narrator as 'set aside and dedicated for leadership and thus for sacrifice and "dismemberment"'.[85] This directly echoes the language Harrison uses to discuss the nature of ritual: 'The bull [to be sacrificed] has been solemnly designated, set apart'.[86] Yet, as Ellison recognized, this is not truly a comment on the one to be sacrificed; this passage discussing 'the bull's function as a fertility *daemon*'[87] is more properly a reflection on the archaic Greek community – those for whom the hero-function, the *daimon*, is necessary.

It is clear that this Harrisonian point was one that increasingly drew Ellison's interest. At times, in his thinking about *Invisible Man*, we see Ellison considering his narrator's function for the black community, reflecting tension between the author's initial interest in the question of black leadership and his reading of *Themis*. One note described the narrator's arrival at Mary's in strikingly Harrisonian terms:

85 Ralph Ellison, Notes, 1942–1950, Library of Congress, Ralph Ellison papers I:151, folder 6.

86 Harrison, *Themis*, 152.

87 Ibid., 151.

> Ritually they load upon him their hopes and fears, and it is when thinking about this that ivm [Invisible Man] becomes strongly aware of his role and fights against the unwanted responsibility. He wants to lead, act, in his *own* interest, solely.[88]

Yet, later in this same folder of notes, Ellison admitted that this description is insufficient, since his protagonist has been 'dedicated by the whites *and* Negroes'.[89] Ellison therefore amended his description of the sacramental role played by his 'dedicated and set aside' narrator; this character still experiences the 'guilt arising from his sense of being dedicated for leadership', but, Ellison added, 'There is also [the] irony of his being dedicated also by whites, who fail to realize that by making him [the] object of sacrifice, they also covertly name him as leader, one stronger than they'.[90]

Ellison pointed to this duality of ritual function in a typescript entitled 'Working Notes for INVISIBLE MAN'. There, a page of 'More Notes' reads:

> The Invisible man [sic] discusses guilt arising out of his growing awareness that he is one set aside and dedicated for leadership and thus for sacrifice and 'dismemberment'. And this is a matter which is further confused for him because he realizes that he has also been set aside by the whites, who ironically fail to realize that by making him [an] object of sacrifice, they also covertly name [him] as their leader, one who is stronger than they.[91]

In this shift – from considering the narrator's role for the black community to his role for whites – we see a clear resonance with Harrison's text. After all, by being 'designated', she writes, the bull 'is sacred now, charged with the *mana* of the coming year, and his nurture is a matter of scrupulous religion'.[92] As she indicates, the collective ritual endows the *daimon* with the power of renewal and rebirth – which makes the *daimon* a deeply charged figure for the community, a figure of power, of fear and

88 Ralph Ellison, Notes, 1942–1950, Library of Congress, Ralph Ellison papers I:151, folder 10.

89 Ibid. Emphasis added.

90 Ibid.

91 Ralph Ellison, Notes, 1942–1950, Library of Congress, Ralph Ellison papers I:151, folder 6.

92 Harrison, *Themis*, 152.

awe combined. Although Harrison was describing archaic Greece, for Ellison, this explained a great deal about American life.

Noting, for example, that 'tragic patterns are revealed in the trivial', Ellison scribbled a list of popular carnival games with ritual significance: 'Throwing darts at Negro woman (picture)'; 'throwing "balls" at live Negro man'; and 'Hit the Nigger baby'.[93] As with these white 'pastimes', throughout the notebooks, we see Ellison reflect upon on the emotional or symbolic 'charge' that black Americans have in the white imagination – their ritual function, in Harrison's sense, for the white community. For example, a handwritten, unfinished note suggests that 'the lynching mood is not created by the stereotype, but by an inner sense of awe'.[94] At a different point, Ellison returns to this mixture of fear and awe, noting that, since 'whites are obsessed with [the] "Negro Problem" and cancer', it is even possible that 'they associate the two together in their subconscious'.[95]

Yet, this reflection on the ritual office occupied by black Americans is best seen, in Ellison's preparations for the novel, in the ultimately excised character Treadwell, the white man who brought the news of LeRoy's death to Mary's boarders. Within the notebooks, Ellison uses Treadwell as a vehicle for presenting a Harrisonian view of the white community, and its sacramental relationship to black Americans. Note, for example, that Treadwell describes LeRoy to the narrator as 'my friend – no, more than that – my brother', but then confesses that this closeness has an underside: 'With him I felt free, and yet I feared it – feared LeRoy'.[96] In an extended passage, Treadwell tries to explain this emotional charge to the narrator:

> We're trained to hate you, to suppress you. It's our major discipline, like that of a State Church, or serving a turn in the army or entering the service of a king. And so thorough is the deception that everything else we're trained to suppress becomes

93 Ralph Ellison, Notes, 1942–1950, Library of Congress, Ralph Ellison papers I:151, folder 6.

94 Ralph Ellison, Notes, 1942–1950, Library of Congress, Ralph Ellison papers I:151, folder 7.

95 Ralph Ellison, Notes, 1942–1950, Library of Congress, Ralph Ellison papers I:152, folder 4.

96 Ralph Ellison, Notes, 1942–1950, Library of Congress, Ralph Ellison papers I:152, folder 7.

> mixed up with it – hate for father, for mother, for brother, sex impulses, 'unclean' thoughts – everything becomes mixed up with the thought of suppressing you. So that it's hard to change our minds about anything without thoughts of you rushing into our minds.[97]

Though a book is required to unpack these passages properly, here I would note simply that they indicate an emerging emphasis within Ellison's work on *Invisible Man*, one that disturbed his focus on the question of black leadership, and on the narrator's quest for perception. To put it bluntly, as these archival materials indicate, we do not exhaust Ellison's treatment of myth and ritual by analysing the heroic nature of black American leadership, in his time or in ours. Just as vital an Ellisonian theme, I submit, is the nature of white supremacy and its materialization in the American public sphere – through its vital, sacramental rituals focused on the black body.

Ellison himself points us in this direction, in one of his later reflections on the writing of *Invisible Man*. Although he typically identified the question of black leadership as the genesis of his novel, 'On Initiation Rites and Power' rephrased the point: 'I was very much involved with the question of just why our Negro leadership was never able to enforce its will. Just what was there about the *structure of American society* that prevented Negroes from throwing up effective leaders?'[98] Here Ellison posed a question not about black leaders, but about the conditions under which they operate – a question that, I believe, his appropriation of Harrison led him to articulate in terms of the ritual importance of blackness for white Americans.

As Ellison recognized, black Americans, in Harrison's sense, have been accorded a sacred role in a communal rite designed to wrest permanence from the chaotic forces of change, thereby spreading *mana* through the group. Within white consciousness, black Americans are indeed heroic, but in the sense of the *daimon* – they serve a key role in ritually renewing the stability of white supremacy. Within *Invisible Man*, I believe that this point troubled Ellison's desire to trace the narrator's 'quest for the knowledge of

97 Ibid.

98 Ellison, 'On Initiation Rites and Power: A Lecture at West Point', 525 (italics added).

who he is'.[99] Although 'the hero' might provide material for such a project, Harrison's hero-function could not – since the *daimon*'s purpose is to assume an office for a community, to ritually ensure its permanence. As *daimon*, in short, the narrator would not be the subject, but the *object* of ritual action. As a result, Ellison appears to have streamlined his engagement with the ritual nature of whiteness in his first novel, dropping (among other things) the character of Treadwell along with LeRoy, and re-placing emphasis on the purpose, passion and perception of his narrator.

At the same time, Ellison did not abandon this thematic focus altogether. On the contrary, it reemerged in much of his nonfiction – where we see him interrogate precisely the ritual function of blackness for white Americans. We can thus read Harrisonian elements in myriad places within Ellison's post-1950 work: his tracing of the essential, vital blackness at the heart of whiteness; of whites' association of blackness with chaos; of the investment of sacred power in the black body (inspiring fear and awe); of the ritual mask that black Americans are forced to wear within the white public sphere; of the spectacular consumption of black Americans by whites – and, of course, the rituals of violence that are also central to the shoring up of white consciousness and the protection of the white-dominated public sphere. Here, of course, we think of Ellison's essays such as 'Twentieth Century Fiction and the Black Mask of Humanity'[100] or 'Change the Joke and Slip the Yoke',[101] but these thematics are no less present in his second novel, posthumously published as *Three Days before the Shooting ...*. In this case, however, I suggest that Ellison's reading of Harrison did more than trouble his focus – it, in some respects, appears to have generated a fault line in the project, one that he was not fully able to reconcile.

Whereas Treadwell was rather easily excised from *Invisible Man*, Welborn McIntyre – 'the white newspaper reporter in whose voice Ellison

99 Ralph Ellison, Notes, 1942–1950, Library of Congress, Ralph Ellison papers I:152, folder 2.

100 Ralph Ellison, 'Twentieth-Century Fiction and the Black Mask of Humanity', in John F. Callahan, ed., *The Collected Essays of Ralph Ellison* (New York: Modern Library, 1995), 81–99.

101 Ralph Ellison, 'Change the Joke and Slip the Yoke', in John F. Callahan, ed., *The Collected Essays of Ralph Ellison* (New York: Modern Library, 1995), 110–12.

wrote the only first-person narration in the entire novel' – proved much more troublesome in *Three Days* ….[102] As Bradley notes, despite decades of work on the project, Ellison 'seemed uninterested or unable to compose the handful of textual bridges that might have connected his disparate manuscripts in a cohesive narrative'.[103] Yet, a Harrisonian reading of the second novel suggests another possible explanation. We can see Ellison as fundamentally indecisive regarding the novel's project: would it be a focus, as with the first novel, on the perspective of a tragic figure seeking broadened consciousness (say, Bliss/Sunraider or Hickman), or would it instead interrogate whiteness and its attendant sacraments, the community for whom black Americans perform a vital office? This fault line, I suggest, haunts the book: although in many respects the plot revolves around the triad of Bliss/Sunraider, Hickman and Severen, Book I instead offers extended treatment of the troubled consciousness of white Americans, through the vehicle of McIntyre's memories and reflections on the assassination attempt on the Senator.

Throughout this portion of the novel, we see McIntyre wrestle with the ritual role that black Americans play in his imagination – their role as ritual bulwarks against chaos. Note, for example, the many moments that underscore McIntyre's fraught relationship to black characters, including (but not limited to) his unprovoked violence directed against Hickman in the hospital, his fascination with Lee Willie Minifees's actions, his repressed affair with Laura, his uneasy relationship to his white colleague McGowan, and his feverish dream about the lawn jockey.[104] McIntyre's struggle against chaos, which seems to threaten whenever black Americans deviate from his

102 John F. Callahan and Adam Bradley, 'General Introduction', in Ralph Ellison, ed., *Three Days before the Shooting* … (New York: Modern Library, 2010), xvii. Although offering a different interpretation of McIntyre than that advanced here, Benji De La Piedra makes a compelling (and refreshing) case for the centrality of McIntyre, and his whiteness, to Ellison's second novel. See Benji De La Piedra, 'Ellison's White Liberal Rhinehart: The Negro American Core of Book I of *Three Days before the Shooting* …', *Literature of the Americas* 5 (2018), 132–50.

103 Adam Bradley, *Ralph Ellison in Progress* (New Haven, CT: Yale University Press, 2010), 36–7.

104 See Ellison, *Three Days before the Shooting* …, 48, 53, 61, 72, 108–11, 116, 124, 128–31, 137, 178–94, 219, 229.

expectations, similarly recurs throughout this first portion of the novel.[105] Ellison saw McIntyre as vital to the novel, since 'Ellison seems to have revised each of the files in the McIntyre sequence in the waning months' of his life.[106] Yet, McIntyre's voice and direct perspective disappears after Book I; Ellison turns afterwards to the viewpoints and actions of Bliss/Sunraider and Hickman. I suggest this is not merely Ellison's decision to shift character or point of view, but to further complicate the novel's portrait of American culture – to, in a sense, explore the duality he had earlier abandoned, of black leadership and its ritual context, of black American as hero and as *daimon*.

This is why, I would suggest, we see one of the novel's central episodes – the death of Jessie Rockmore – told from two different perspectives, Hickman's and McIntyre's.[107] Although both episodes include a passing reference to the other,[108] and though McIntyre's version 'appears to be the last portion of the novel that Ellison saved to disk before his death',[109] these episodes remain largely unreconciled in the extant narrative. Just as significant, I believe, we also find Ellison presenting the same encounter with Cliofus through two different eyes, McIntyre's and Hickman's.[110] These portions of the second novel could be read as Ellison's indecision on how best to synthesize these characters and episodes; indeed, as his editors note, these dimensions of the novel 'challenge his readers to imagine potentialities of order and expression in the manuscript he left unrealized'.[111] In part, though, I believe that what we see in this novel is the logical outcome of Ellison's decision to retain, and equally emphasize, these twin themes, black leadership and the (white) context within which it must emerge. I would speculate that what Ellison likely envisioned as a grand synthesis

105 See ibid., 98, 135, 162, 172, 174, 219.

106 Ibid., 927.

107 For two versions of McIntyre's perspective on these events, see ibid., 139–74, 927–68; for two versions of Hickman's visit to Rockmore's, see ibid., 435–55, 611–60.

108 Ibid., 174, 613.

109 Ibid., 927.

110 For McIntyre's interview with Cliofus, see ibid., 1073–84; for Hickman's encounter with Cliofus in the nightclub, see ibid., 865–83.

111 Ellison, *Three Days before the Shooting ...*, 498.

evolved instead into a bifurcation – the deepening of a duality of emphasis into a fault line that could not be easily sealed, and thus a novel that could not be easily completed, despite decades of diligent work.

Though Ellison may have never fully reconciled these two emphases, his work does, I maintain, provide us with powerful theoretical resources for combating the continuing presence of American white supremacy. How, liberal pundits ask, can white supremacy endure, despite all the political and legal changes of the last century, and the birth of new generations increasingly removed from slavery, Reconstruction, Jim Crow and the Civil Rights Era? The answer, Ellison's writings suggest, lies in Harrison's text; the rituals central to whiteness perennially ensure its renewal, protect it against a changing historical and social context. White consciousness, like the white public sphere, is rendered permanent through the sacramental investment of the black body – and if this has not changed since Ellison was writing, it is because neither have the myths and rituals of race traced by Ellison's fiction and nonfiction.

I will close by simply noting that the entire ritual process traced by Harrison rests upon the figure of 'Themis', whose name is often (inaccurately) translated as 'Right'. Characteristically, Harrison cautions us against this view, since 'Themis was before the particular shapes of gods; she is not religion, but she is the stuff of which religion is made'.[112] Harrison therefore redefines 'Themis' as 'Social Order', the group's conception of proper conduct only later personified as an individual goddess: 'She is the force that brings and binds men together, she is "herd instinct", the collective conscience, the social sanction'.[113] Harrison ends her book by noting that the motivation for sacramental ritual lies in the conflation of this social order with that of the natural world – the 'pathetic conviction that moral goodness and material prosperity go together', and that human beings 'can magically affect for good nature's ordered going'.[114] Observing the dictates of 'Themis', or the proper enactment of communal ritual, is thought to ensure preservation of the natural order, and halt the descent into chaos. Yet, here

112 Harrison, *Themis*, 485.

113 Ibid., 485.

114 Ibid., 531.

I picture Ellison wryly embracing the traditional translation, since it allows us to glimpse an American 'Themis', the motive lurking behind our own tragic rituals: 'If you're black, stay back; if you're brown, stick around; if you're white, you're right'.[115]

Bibliography

Ackerman, Robert, *The Myth and Ritual School: J. G. Frazer and the Cambridge Ritualists* (New York: Routledge, 1991).

Africa, Thomas W., 'Aunt Glegg among the Dons, or Taking Jane Harrison at Her Word', in William M. Calder III, ed., *The Cambridge Ritualists Reconsidered* (Atlanta, GA: Scholars Press, 1991), 21–35.

Arlen, Shelley, '"For Love of an Idea": Jane Ellen Harrison, Heretic and Humanist', *Women's History Review* 5/2 (1996), 165–90.

——, review of Annabel Robinson, *The Life and Work of Jane Ellen Harrison* (Oxford: Oxford University Press, 2002), in *English Literature in Transition, 1880–1920*, 47/3 (2004), 342–46.

Beard, Mary, *The Invention of Jane Harrison* (Cambridge, MA: Harvard University Press, 2000).

Bradley, Adam, *Ralph Ellison in Progress: From* Invisible Man *to* Three Days before the Shooting … (New Haven, CT: Yale University Press, 2010).

Callahan, John F. and Adam Bradley, 'General Introduction', in Ralph Ellison, ed., *Three Days before the Shooting* … (New York: Modern Library, 2010), xv–xxix.

Crable, Bryan, *Ralph Ellison and Kenneth Burke: At the Roots of the Racial Divide* (Charlottesville: University of Virginia Press, 2012).

——, '"Who Invents Rituals?": Ralph Ellison Reads Lord Raglan', *Literature of the Americas* 5 (2018), 27–42. DOI: 10.22455/2541-7894-2018-5-27-42. <http://litda.ru/images/2018-5/LDA-2018-5_27-42_Crable.pdf>, accessed 8 July 2020.

De La Piedra, Benji, 'Ellison's White Liberal Rhinehart: The Negro American Core of Book I of *Three Days before the Shooting* …', *Literature of the Americas* 5 (2018), 132–50. DOI: 10.22455/2541-7894-2018-5–132–150. <http://litda.ru/images/2018-5/LDA-2018-5_132-150_De-la-Piedra.pdf>, accessed 8 July 2020.

115 Ellison, 'The Art of Fiction', 215.

Ellison, Ralph, 'The Art of Fiction: An Interview', in John F. Callahan, ed., *The Collected Essays of Ralph Ellison* (New York: Modern Library, 1995), 210–24.

——, 'Blues People', in John F. Callahan, ed., *The Collected Essays of Ralph Ellison* (New York: Modern Library, 1995), 278–87.

——, 'Change the Joke and Slip the Yoke', in John F. Callahan, ed., *The Collected Essays of Ralph Ellison* (New York: Modern Library, 1995), 100–12.

——, 'On Initiation Rites and Power: A Lecture at West Point', in John F. Callahan, ed., *The Collected Essays of Ralph Ellison* (New York: Modern Library, 1995), 520–41.

——, Letter to Stanley Hyman, 19 October 1945, Library of Congress, Stanley Edgar Hyman papers 6, folder 30.

——, Letter to Stanley Hyman, 20 June 1946, in *The Selected Letters of Ralph Ellison*, eds, John F. Callahan and Marc C. Conner (New York: Random House, 2019), 216–17.

——, Letter to Stanley Hyman, 17 June 1947, in *The Selected Letters of Ralph Ellison*, eds, John F. Callahan and Marc C. Conner (New York: Random House, 2019), 225–6.

——, Letter to Stanley Hyman, 15 June 1948, Library of Congress, Stanley Edgar Hyman papers 6, folder 30.

——, Letter to Stanley Hyman, 27 April 1955, Library of Congress, Stanley Edgar Hyman papers 6, folder 30.

——, Notes, 1942–1950, Library of Congress, Ralph Ellison papers I:151, folder 6.

——, Notes, 1942–1950, Library of Congress, Ralph Ellison papers I:151, folder 7.

——, Notes, 1942–1950, Library of Congress, Ralph Ellison papers I:151, folder 9.

——, Notes, 1942–1950, Library of Congress, Ralph Ellison papers I:151, folder 10.

——, Notes, 1942–1950, Library of Congress, Ralph Ellison papers I:152, folder 1.

——, Notes, 1942–1950, Library of Congress, Ralph Ellison papers I:152, folder 2.

——, Notes, 1942–1950, Library of Congress, Ralph Ellison papers I:152, folder 3.

——, Notes, 1942–1950, Library of Congress, Ralph Ellison papers I:152, folder 4.

——, Notes, 1942–1950, Library of Congress, Ralph Ellison papers I:152, folder 7.

——, 'That Same Pain, that Same Pleasure: An Interview', in John F. Callahan, ed., *The Collected Essays of Ralph Ellison* (New York: Modern Library, 1995), 63–80.

——, *The Selected Letters of Ralph Ellison*, eds, John F. Callahan and Marc C. Conner (New York: Random House, 2019).

——, '"Tell It Like It Is, Baby"', in John F. Callahan, ed., *The Collected Essays of Ralph Ellison* (New York: Modern Library, 1995), 29–46.

——, *Three Days before the Shooting …* (New York: Modern Library, 2010).

——, 'If the Twain Shall Meet', in John F. Callahan, ed., *The Collected Essays of Ralph Ellison* (New York: Modern Library, 1995), 563–76.

——, 'Twentieth-Century Fiction and the Black Mask of Humanity', in John F. Callahan, ed., *The Collected Essays of Ralph Ellison* (New York: Modern Library, 1995), 81–99.

Foley, Barbara, *Wrestling with the Left: The Making of Ralph Ellison's* Invisible Man (Durham: Duke University Press, 2010).

Harrison, Jane Ellen, *Themis: A Study of the Social Origins of Greek Religion, with an Excursus on the Ritual Forms Preserved in Greek Tragedy by Professor Gilbert Murray and a Chapter on the Origin of the Olympic Games by Mr. F. M. Cornford* (Cambridge, UK: Cambridge University Press, 1927).

Hyman, Stanley Edgar, *The Armed Vision: A Study in the Methods of Modern Literary Criticism* (New York: Vintage Books, 1955).

——, 'Jessie Weston and the Forest of Broceliande', in Phoebe Pettingell, ed., *The Critic's Credentials* (New York: Atheneum, 1978), 284–97.

——, 'Leaping for Goodly Themis', in Stanley Edgar Hyman, ed., *Standards: A Chronicle of Books for Our Time* (New York: Horizon Press, 1966), 103–7.

——, 'The Ritual View of Myth and the Mythic', *Journal of American Folklore* 68/270 (1955), 462–72.

——, 'Some Bankrupt Treasuries', *The Kenyon Review* 10/3 (1948), 484–500.

Montville, Leigh, *The Big Bam: The Life and Times of Babe Ruth* (New York: Broadway Books, 2006).

Morel, Lucas E., 'Ralph Ellison's American Democratic Individualism', in Lucas E. Morel, ed., *Ralph Ellison and the Raft of Hope* (Lexington: University Press of Kentucky, 2004), 58–90.

Parrish, Timothy, *Ralph Ellison and the Genius of America* (Amherst: University of Massachusetts Press, 2012).

Peacock, Sandra J., 'An Awful Warmth about Her Heart: The Personal in Jane Harrison's Ideas on Religion', in William M. Calder III, ed., *The Cambridge Ritualists Reconsidered* (Atlanta, GA: Scholars Press, 1991), 167–84.

——, *Jane Ellen Harrison: The Mask and the Self* (New Haven, CT: Yale University Press, 1988).

'The Ralph Ellison Collection, (1937–2010)', finding aid, <https://findingaids.loc.gov/exist_collections/ead3pdf/rbc/2016/rb016001.pdf>, accessed 22 May 2020.

Rankine, Patrice D., *Ulysses in Black: Ralph Ellison, Classicism, and African American Literature* (Madison: University of Wisconsin Press, 2006).

Segal, Robert A., 'Series Editor's Foreword', in Robert Ackerman, ed., *The Myth and Ritual School: J. G. Frazer and the Cambridge Ritualists* (New York: Routledge, 1991), vii–x.

TESSA ROYNON

3 Ralph Ellison and the *Metamorphoses* of Ovid: Transformative Allusions

ABSTRACT:
This chapter explores Ellison's little-discussed engagement with the Roman poet Ovid, in particular with his mock-epic epic, the *Metamorphoses*, composed in around 8 CE. Through a focus on the thematics of change in both *Invisible Man* and *Three Days before the Shooting* …, the chapter explores how a generalized 'Ovidian dynamic', concerned with chaos and transformation, informs Ellison's oeuvre-wide explorations of instability and transition. Next, it demonstrates that the over-reaching Ovidian heroes Icarus and Phaethon not only resonate significantly in the 'Hickman in Washington DC' section of *Three Days*, but are also integral to this text's interest in the connectedness of Africa with ancient Greece and Rome. Lastly, it argues that in this same section of the unfinished novel Ellison invokes both Ovid's famous sculptor, Pygmalion, and the ill-fated huntsman, Actaeon, in his explorations of the power and limitations of the artistic figure – whether this be jazzman, preacher or novelist.

Alonzo Hickman, the 'jazzman-turned-preacher' protagonist of *Three Days before the Shooting* … (2010), memorably describes ' "history" ' as a 'shifty hall of mirrors'.[1] This rich metaphor epitomizes Ellison's concern, throughout his fiction and nonfiction, with the interplay between aesthetic representation, the fluidity of individual identity and experience, and a rapidly changing America that has yet to address the racial injustices and violence characterizing both its past and its present. There

1 Ralph Ellison, *Three Days before the Shooting* … (New York: Modern Library, 2010), 526, 579.
I wish to thank Marc Conner and Raphaël Lambert for their reading of this chapter in draft form, and for their moral support through the challenges of 2019–20. The material in this chapter draws on a proportion of my discussion of Ralph Ellison in my sole-authored study, *The Classical Tradition in Modern American Fiction* (Edinburgh: Edinburgh University Press, 2021).

is a wealth of preexisting scholarship on this author's indebtedness to an eclectic range of literature, intellectual thought and cultural forms in his articulation of these themes. This chapter, in turn, breaks new critical ground by arguing that Ovid's *Metamorphoses* – the Latin epic exploring the concepts of transformation and shapeshifting that Ovid completed in 8 CE – is a defining presence in the Ellisonian oeuvre.

While scholars such as Rankine (2006) and Cook and Tatum (2010) have explored this writer's extensive engagement with Homer's *Odyssey*, and while there are several discussions of the tragic structures and impulses in his work, critics have overlooked the extent to which Ovid's poem resonates throughout Ellison's central thematics of chaos, transition and metamorphosis.[2] Through a focus on the thematics of change in both *Invisible Man* (1952) and *Three Days*, and a close analysis of the ways in which several key figures from the *Metamorphoses* – namely Phaethon, Pygmalion, Daedalus and Actaeon – resonate in the second novel, this chapter illuminates the widespread significance of Ovid's multivalent presences in these texts.

This Ovidian intertextuality – arguably to a greater extent than many other dimensions of Ellison's allusiveness to Greek and Roman tradition – is testament to the transnationalism of his own intellectual formation and literary engagement. Indeed, given Ovid's thematic preoccupation in the *Metamorphoses* with the permeability of borders, the Latin poet is an ideal 'resource' for any author interested in the arbitrariness of national boundaries, and so in a global perspective. Ovid's radical presence in more recent world fiction, such as Junot Díaz's *Brief Wondrous Life of Oscar Wao* (2007), Jhumpa Lahiri's *Unaccustomed Earth* (2008) and Jenny Erpenbeck's *Go, Went, Gone* [*Gehen, Ging, Gegangen*] (2015), resonates with his particular relevance to Ellison's extra-national concerns. Specifically, this novelist's dialogue with Ovid's tales of Phaethon and of Pygmalion enable him to recast the world: as one in which African and European traditions are more

2 See, for example, Marc C. Conner, 'Father Abraham: Ellison's Agon with the Fathers in *Three Days before the Shooting …*', in Marc C. Conner and Lucas E. Morel, eds, *The New Territory: Ralph Ellison and the Twenty-First Century* (Jackson: University Press of Mississippi, 2016), 167–93; or Grant Shreve, 'Ralph Ellison's *Three Days before the Shooting …* and the Implicit Morality of Form', in *The New Territory*, 218–44.

closely intertwined than is usually recognized, and as one in which the artist might exert a truly transformative power on flawed national mythology.

The fact that Ellison never mentions either Ovid or his poem by name anywhere in the published record may explain the critical silence about this literary relationship. It is also true that among the many thousands of books in this author's personal library – which include many Greek and Latin works in translation – no copy of the *Metamorphoses* exists.[3] Yet Ellison encountered Ovid through his reading of Dante, Shakespeare and Melville, and of Eliot, Joyce and Faulkner, as well as through the numerous volumes of psychology, sociology, anthropology, ancient history and literary criticism that he devoured over the decades. Although the novelist studied four years of Latin at his high school, Ovid appears in his biographical record for the first time (and the only explicit time, moreover) when he discovered *The Waste Land* in the Tuskegee library in 1935, and became fascinated with the sources in Eliot's footnotes.[4] Looking back on those days in his 'Hidden Name and Complex Fate' address of 1964, Ellison describes his undergraduate preoccupation with the 'references' in *The Waste Land* as 'the beginning of [his] conscious education in literature'.[5] Biographer Lawrence Jackson notes that Eliot's poem inspired the student Ellison 'to revive his dusty Latin skills [...] in order to understand a generous Ovid quote'; indulging in some Ovidian idiom of his own, Jackson observes that the young man was 'ripe for transformation at the hands of Eliot's masterpiece'.[6] The biographer perhaps took his cue here from Ellison's observation, in a lecture of 1969, that his reading in the books that Eliot referenced in *The Waste Land* had been 'the beginning

3 For a discussion of the classical works in Ellison's library, and his reading in this field, see Chapter 4 in Tessa Roynon, *The Classical Tradition in Modern American Fiction* (Edinburgh: Edinburgh University Press, 2021).

4 See Lawrence Jackson, *Ralph Ellison: Emergence of Genius* (New York: Wiley and Sons, 2002), 151–3.

5 Ralph Ellison, 'Hidden Name and Complex Fate', in John F. Callahan, ed., *The Collected Essays of Ralph Ellison* (New York: Modern Library, 2003), 189–209.

6 Jackson, *Emergence of Genius*, 152, 151.

of [his] transformation (or shall we say, metamorphosis) from a would-be composer into some sort of novelist'.[7]

While *The Waste Land*'s unifying force is the figure of Tiresias – and it is s/he who is the subject of the 'generous quote' in Eliot's footnotes – Ellison encountered numerous other Ovidian protagonists through his voracious reading both in modernist literature and in the classical sources and classically derived scholarship on which so many of his fellow modernists drew. In James Joyce, of course, he encountered not just the name 'Stephen Dedalus', but also the epigraphic deployment of the Daedalus myth in *Portrait of the Artist*; he would also have discovered allusions to the *Metamorphoses* in texts as unalike as the *Cantos* of Ezra Pound and the plays of George Bernard Shaw.[8] The novelist would have become immersed in Ovidian mythology through the archetypes of Freud; through the anthropologists of the Cambridge School such as Jane Ellen Harrison and Gilbert Murray, and through the insistently global perspectives of comparative mythologists such as Lord Raglan, Paul Radin, Otto Rank and Joseph Campbell.[9] He was also fascinated by authors who did not make explicit use of the *Metamorphoses*, but were nonetheless preoccupied by the idea of metamorphosis. These include Kafka, of course, but also and more significantly (for Ellison) the very different Malraux, whose predilection

7 Ralph Ellison, 'On Initiation Rites and Power: A Lecture at West Point', in John F. Callahan, ed., *The Collected Essays of Ralph Ellison* (New York: Modern Library, 2003), 525.

8 Scholarship on Ellison's debt to Joyce includes Robert N. List, *Dedalus in Harlem: The Joyce–Ellison Connection* (Washington, DC: University Press of America, 1982); Patrice Rankine, *Ulysses in Black: Ralph Ellison, Classicism, and African American Literature* (2006), and Conner, 'Father Abraham'. None of these, however, discusses these authors' engagement with Ovid in any detail. Both extant biographies of Ellison – Jackson (2002) and Rampersad (2008) – give detailed accounts of Ellison's voracious reading.

9 Ellison owned works by all of these thinkers. For the full catalogue of his personal library, which is held at the Library of Congress, Washington, DC, see 'The Ralph Ellison Collection', <https://findingaids.loc.gov/exist_collections/ead3pdf/rbc/2016/rb016001.pdf>, accessed 6 April 2020. On Ellison and the Cambridge School see Bryan Crable's essay, 'Ellison's Appropriation of Jane Ellen Harrison's *Themis*', which is Chapter 1 in this volume.

for the concept Ralph even references, via the Malrauxian-named character of M. Vannec, in *Three Days*.[10] Thinkers who were concerned with the idea of transformation continued to fascinate him even in the eighth decade of his life: he highlighted many passages in his 1981 translation of Bakhtin's *Dialogic Imagination* (1975), for example – a work which includes a significant discussion of the differences between 'metamorphosis' as conceptualized by Hesiod and Ovid.[11]

In the first part of this chapter, I demonstrate that Ellison's sense of the simultaneously inevitable, desirable and dangerous state of change or flux – one in which both the modern individual and modern society exist – is informed by the aesthetic-political phenomenon that I term the 'Ovidian dynamic'.[12] That is to say, it deploys to its own racially resistant ends the prevalent mid-twentieth-century understanding of the *Metamorphoses* as a manifesto for personal and political transformation and reinvention, and for the radical potential inherent in modernity's always shifting sands. My discussion builds on Adam Bradley's exposition of Ellison's original intention to expand, in his second novel, the character and concept of *Invisible Man's* infinitely shapeshifting and versatile Rinehart. As Bradley notes, Ellison (in his 'Change the Joke ...' essay) calls 'Rhinehart' (sic) 'an American virtuoso of identity who thrives on chaos and quick change'.[13]

10 See Ellison, *Three Days*, 87. On Ellison, Malraux and the name 'Vannec', see Benji De La Piedra, 'Ellison's White Liberal Rinehart: The Negro American Core of Book I of *Three Days before the Shooting* ...', *Literature of the Americas* 5 (2018), 132–50.

11 See M. M. Bakhtin, *The Dialogic Imagination: Four Essays*, ed., Michael Holquist, trans. Caryl Emerson and Michael Holquist (Austin: University of Texas Press, 1981), 114. Ellison dated his personal copy of this work by Bakhtin with the year '1986'.

12 For my initial conceptualization of the 'Ovidian dynamic' and its significance in modern American fiction, see Tessa Roynon, 'Ovid, Race and Identity in E. L. Doctorow's *Ragtime* (1975) and Jeffrey Eugenides's *Middlesex* (2002)', *International Journal of the Classical Tradition* 26/4 (2019), 377–96.

13 Ralph Ellison, 'Change the Joke and Slip the Yoke', in John F. Callahan, ed., *The Collected Essays of Ralph Ellison* (New York: Modern Library, 2003), 110; quoted in Adam Bradley, *Ralph Ellison in Progress: From* Invisible Man *to* Three Days before the Shooting ... (New Haven, CT: Yale University Press, 2010), 132.

In this first section I demonstrate the debt to Ovid inherent in Ellison's near-ubiquitous deployment of the concepts of 'transformation' and 'metamorphosis' in his portrayal of the many new identities assumed by both the invisible man and by Bliss/Sunraider, and of the ongoing evolution of Alonzo Hickman. I show that Ellison employs these same terms – sometimes enthusiastically and sometimes sceptically – to articulate the unstable worlds that all these characters must navigate.

The many continuities and discontinuities between the invisible man's quest for a viable black manhood and the wanderings of the multifaceted Odysseus has led critics to understand Ellison's widespread and multifaceted engagement with Proteus, the infinitely shapeshifting sea god, exclusively in its Homeric context.[14] Yet Proteus is of course a figure who epitomizes the thematic concerns of Ovid's epic, and within that text, the poet observes directly to that god, 'Some there are, [...] whose form has been once changed and remained in its new state. To others, the power is given to assume many forms, as to thee, Proteus, dweller in the earth-embracing sea.'[15] In the second part of this chapter, I discuss affinities between Ellison's central characters and two Ovidian heroes who change only 'once': Icarus, who famously flew too close to the sun, and who features significantly in both *Invisible Man* in the 'Hickman in Washington DC' section of the second novel; and Phaethon, who crashes the chariot of the sun, and is a highly significant archetypal presence in Part I of *Three Days*. These two figures have in common a paternally influenced over-reaching ambition that leads in each case to a catastrophic downfall, and each of these myths enables the novelist to challenge received wisdom about the separateness of Greek and Roman tradition from Africa.

In my chapter's third part I again focus on the 'Hickman in Washington DC' section of *Three Days*, turning now to its association between Hickman and three key Ovidian artist figures. The first two of these are Deucalion and Pygmalion, who separately resonate in the preacher's contemplation of

14 See, for example, Patrice Rankine, *Ulysses in Black*; or the chapter on Ellison (Chapter 5) in William Cook and James Tatum, *African American Writers and Classical Tradition* (Chicago, IL: University of Chicago Press, 2010).

15 Ovid, *Metamorphoses*, 2 vols, trans. Frank Justus Miller, rev. G. P. Goold (Cambridge, MA: Harvard University Press, 2004), VIII.730–1.

the statue of Abraham Lincoln, just as the *Metamorphoses* as a whole resonates in the contemplation on the same assassinated president in Ellison's important essay, 'Tell It Like It Is, Baby' (1965). The third is Daedalus, with whom Hickman is allied when he contemplates the tapestry depicting the fall of Icarus in the Longview Hotel. Through these moments of highly motivated ekphrasis, the author reflects on the role of the artist – whether jazz musician, novelist or preacher – in the incipient days of the Civil Rights Movement, and so in a nation on the cusp of seismic change. As I go on to explore, such passages demonstrate the centrality of Ovid to the thinking and feeling at the very core of Ellison's complex and multilayered representations of American experience.

Cultures and Identities in Flux

In 1945, as World War II was drawing to its close, the German classical scholar Hermann Fränkel published a monograph entitled *Ovid, A Poet between Two Worlds*. Fränkel's conception of the Latin poet's role in articulating an era of transition does much to explain the appeal of the *Metamorphoses* to Ellison.[16] Ovid composed his epic during the first decade of the first century CE, which in ancient Rome involved the development of the formidable force of Augustan imperial rule, and so constituted the completion of the transition from the republican system. Ellison's *Invisible Man* and *Three Days*, meanwhile, together map out the turbulent post-Reconstruction decades of Jim Crow laws in America's South. They address the phenomenon of black migration to and urbanization in the north, and the bumpy transition from racial segregation to desegregation as the Civil Rights Movement both gained momentum

16 See for, example, Fränkel's observation: 'No doubt in some ways Ovid's writings mark the beginning decline of Antiquity; should they not also contain elements indicating the emergence of a new world?' (Hermann Fränkel, *Ovid, A Poet between Two Worlds* (Berkeley: University of California Press, 1945)), 3. See also ibid., 82.

and generated entrenched and violent resistance. The constant tension between fluid evolution/revolution and stable intelligible form that is inherent in Ovidian tales – in their descriptions both of the physical world and of individual characters' trajectories – informs Ellison's depictions of both his nation and of individuals such as the invisible man, Rinehart, Bliss/Sunraider and Hickman, as each seeks a stable identity in changing times.

The *Metamorphoses* opens with Ovid's version of the creation myth, the formation of the world from 'chaos', which is a 'rough, unordered mass of things' in which 'no form of things remained the same', and 'all objects were at odds'.[17] It is impossible to miss Ellison's near-obsession with chaos, and with what he has called 'the chaos of America'; it is something of a refrain throughout his essays, interviews and letters as well as his fiction.[18] In the epilogue to *Invisible Man*, moreover, the narrator ponders his grandfather's perspective on the principles that the American founders 'had dreamed into being out of the chaos and the darkness of the feudal past'.[19] The invisible man also encounters the 'real chaos' that lies at the heart of the north's freedom of possibility, before proceeding to witness it embodied in the Harlem riots.[20] *Three Days*, meanwhile – which Ellison described in a 1972 interview as a study of 'the ruptured and chaotic memory of the national consciousness',[21] is punctuated with invocations of chaos by its various narrators and focalized protagonists. Reporter Welborn McIntyre's memories fuse with the assassination attempt on the senator by assuming 'chaotic life';[22] he describes the elevator incident as 'chaos', and in the transition from chapters 12 to 13 he uses the word twice in two paragraphs, first thankful that 'chaos had been eliminated' from society,

17 Ovid, *Metamorphoses*, I.5–30.

18 Ralph Ellison, 'Alain Locke', in John F. Callahan, ed., *The Collected Essays of Ralph Ellison* (New York: Modern Library, 2003), 449. For further Ellisonian invocations of chaos, see Maryemma Graham and Amritjit Singh, eds, *Conversations with Ralph Ellison* (Jackson: University Press of Mississippi, 1995), 26, 72, 97, 125.

19 Ralph Ellison, *Invisible Man* (New York: Vintage, 1995), 574.

20 Ibid., 499.

21 Graham and Singh, *Conversations*, 215.

22 Ellison, *Three Days*, 13.

but then fearing 'more chaos to come'.[23] In his thunderous speech to the Senate, Bliss/Sunraider declaims that America is 'a nation conditioned to ring out the chaos of history';[24] later, in his hospital bed, he recollects his rhetoric about the 'hero's task' being 'to face the universal chaos in the name of human freedom and to win!'.[25] While there are, of course, numerous momentous invocations of chaos within Greek and Roman literature, it is the *Metamorphoses*'s interest in the relationship between chaos and change that makes Ovid a particularly significant influence on Ellison.

When Bliss/Sunraider re-preaches Eatmore's fire sermon, he quotes Shakespeare's Ovidian-inflected passage in *The Tempest* (on which Eliot also riffs in *The Waste Land*), about the sea-changes wrought by death: '*Full fathom five thy father lies*'.[26] The unifying conception in *Three Days*, that (as Hickman puts it), 'change, [...] endless change, is the name of this American game!',[27] recalls Ovid's articulation of the doctrine of Pythagoras in *Metamorphoses* Book XV, which expresses the thematic core of that poem: 'there is nothing in the world that keeps its form; all things are in a state of flux, and everything is brought into being with a changing nature'.[28] This vision resonates both in Ellison's fiction and nonfiction. In his 1948 essay 'Harlem is Nowhere', for example, the novelist writes of, the psychological malaise affecting that locale, that 'American Negroes are caught in a vast process of change'; that it is 'a world so fluid and shifting that often within the mind the real and the unreal merge'; and that the institutions of his own 'slum-shocked culture' are 'caught in a process of chaotic change'.[29] Three years earlier, in his 1945 'working notes' for *Invisible Man*, he writes

23 Ibid., 174–5.

24 Ibid., 240.

25 Ibid., 264.

26 Ibid., 305 (italics in original).

27 Ibid., 587.

28 Ovid, *Metamorphoses* XV.177–9. Compare here Ellison's discussion of the 'swift change of American society' in 'Living with Music', in *The Collected Essays of Ralph Ellison*, ed. John F. Callahan (New York: Modern Library, 2003), 236; and his description of 'this country, which reinvents itself every ten days', in Graham and Singh, *Conversations*, 214.

29 Ralph Ellison, 'Harlem Is Nowhere', in John F. Callahan, ed., *The Collected Essays of Ralph Ellison* (New York: Modern Library, 2003), 321, 322, 325.

that 'invisibility' for the black man 'springs from a great formlessness of Negro life wherein all values are in flux'.[30] Such notes anticipate the invisible man's perception, when wearing Rinehartian dark glasses, of the street scene's 'merging fluidity of forms'.[31] This narrator's observation, a few pages later, that 'the world seemed to flow before [his] eyes' is similarly resonant of the unstable fluidity of the Ovidian world.[32] The cinematic quality of these scenes – in which the invisible man moves through the city's streets – accords with the affinities between Ovid's writing and technologies of the moving image that many twentieth-century writers have perceived.[33] And the filmic potential of a rapidly changing and unstable society is of course made explicit in *Three Days*. This occurs both figuratively, for example when McIntyre, after hitting his head, describes the faces of the people in the Harlem bar, that 'suddenly flowed, liquid and loose' in a scene that resembles 'a motion picture', and literally, in Bliss/Sunraider's memories of his brief career as a corrupt and incompetent 'Mister Movie-man'.[34] The reels of that character's Civil War film not coincidentally constitute 'a jumble of scenes' in which 'all images ran' (of course!) 'to chaos'.[35]

In the invisible man's realization that 'coming North' involves confronting a world in which 'all boundaries' are 'down',[36] Ellison examines the full implications of the individual's freedom to shape his or her own identity. This defining ideal of modern America is something that the narrator struggles in vain to achieve until this novel's ironic end. As Ellison wrote in his 'working notes' to the novel, the rapidity of urbanization 'throws up personalities as fluid and changeable as molten metal rendered iridescent from

30 Ralph Ellison, 'Working Notes for *Invisible Man*', in John F. Callahan, ed., *The Collected Essays of Ralph Ellison* (New York: Modern Library, 2003), 343.

31 Ellison, *Invisible Man*, 491.

32 Ibid., 499.

33 On Ovid and cinema, see, for example, Martin M. Winkler, *Ovid on Screen: A Montage of Attractions* (Cambridge, UK: Cambridge University Press, 2020).

34 Ellison, *Three Days*, 123, 277.

35 Ibid., 279. See also Nicole Lindenberg, "'What if Movie Is Bliss's Own Life?": The Symbolic Violence of the Movie in Ralph Ellison's Unfinished Second Novel, *Three Days before the Shooting …*', *Literature of the Americas* 5 (2018), 116–31.

36 Ellison, *Invisible Man*, 499.

the effect of cooling air'.[37] His protagonist ultimately 'turned away' from the 'possibilities posed by Rinehart's multiple personalities', suddenly finding the idea that 'you could actually make yourself anew' to be 'frightening'.[38] Yet until this point, his trajectory or *Bildung* has been defined by a series of new identities that he has embraced enthusiastically each time, and by a positive conception of the potential for self-transformation inherent in early twentieth-century American culture. There is a dramatic irony in his sincere deployment of the discourse of metamorphosis as he documents his changing fortunes to the reader. On first arriving in New York City, for example, he notes the 'change that was coming over him', and that he has been 'subtly changed';[39] in his exuberant and motivating speech to the crowd about the 'dispossession' he tells his listeners that '*something strange and miraculous and transforming is taking place in me right now*'.[40]

Through the disparity between the invisible man's hopeful convictions and the bleak realities of repeated rejection and failure, Ellison implicitly undercuts Alain Locke's optimistic discourse of Ovidian transformation in his introductory essay to *The New Negro* anthology of 1925. Locke, therein contemplating the new phenomenon of African American urban life centred on Harlem, declares that the Negro had undergone a 'metamorphosis', and that a 'transformed and transforming psychology permeates the masses'.[41] Ellison's sceptical perspective on this euphoria anticipates Joe Trace's lament in Toni Morrison's *Jazz* (1992); in that novel, Joe rejects such an outlook altogether, declaring that he'd 'changed once too often'.[42] To no avail, he ruefully implies, he had 'been a New Negro all [his] life'.[43] Yet Ellison's stance towards the idea of black self-reinvention is more one of conflictedness than of outright rejection. In *Invisible Man*, when Tod Clifton muses on the three African American boys he identifies

37 Ellison, 'Working Notes', 343.

38 Ellison, *Invisible Man*, 499.

39 Ibid., 178.

40 Ibid., 345 (italics in original).

41 Alain Locke, 'Introduction: The New Negro', in Alain Locke, ed., *The New Negro: Voices of the Harlem Renaissance* (New York: Simon and Schuster), 3, 12.

42 Toni Morrison, *Jazz* (New York: Vintage, 2004), 129.

43 Ibid., 129.

as recent arrivals to New York from the South, he notes that they 'speak a jived-up transitional language' and imagines that they 'think transitional thoughts'.[44] Here, the trademark Ellisonian excitement about that moment of 'change in the making', as it were, is manifest.

As Adam Bradley observes, Ellison's plans for the character that was to become Bliss/Sunraider in *Three Days* (as documented in the 'Opus II' notebook) indicate that while the 'rootlessness' of *Invisible Man*'s Rinehart was 'a form of freedom', this new protagonist is 'an individual trapped by his own racial indeterminacy, his protean ability to shift shades as well as shapes'.[45] The prototypes of both Odysseus and the Yoruban Eshu-Elegba (or the Haitian Legba) are often invoked by critics to describe this kind of trickster figure who, for better or worse, changes not only his name but also his racial identity and race politics.[46] In his development from preaching protégé through film-maker to white supremacist statesman, Bliss/Sunraider certainly diverges in once-unimaginable ways from the path that Hickman had imagined for him. It is striking that Ovid's observation about Proteus – that 'now men saw thee as a youth, now as a lion'[47] – echoes almost uncannily in Hickman's musings that his 'little boy preacher' whom he had 'cast as a hero and symbol in the order of Christ' went on 'to become an insatiable lion in Washington'.[48]

Hickman, meanwhile, devotes equal energy to musing on his own self-transformations. He recalls that it was through his encounter with Bliss's biological mother, at the time of his birth, that he 'started to change' from being a 'wild and reckless' musician into his new identity as a preacher.[49] He charts his transition from being a jazz trombonist to becoming one of 'god's trombones' (in other words, a preacher) with an

44 Ellison, *Invisible Man*, 441.

45 Bradley, *Ralph Ellison in Progress*, 134; see also De La Piedra, 'Ellison's White Liberal Rhinehart', 134.

46 See for example Eric Sundquist, 'Ralph Ellison in His Labyrinth', in Marc C. Conner and Lucas E. Morel, eds, *The New Territory: Ralph Ellison and the Twenty-First Century* (Jackson: University Press of Mississippi, 2016), 129–31.

47 Ovid, *Metamorphoses* VIII.732.

48 Ellison, *Three Days*, 527, 529.

49 Ibid., 464–6.

attention to the physical process of the change that is reminiscent of descriptions of changing forms in the *Metamorphoses*. 'My trombone mouthpiece had grown to my lips', Hickman recalls, 'and my good right arm changed into a slide'.[50]

In relation to each and every one of these excavations of the Ovidian resonances in Ellison's fictional explorations of societal and individual change, classicist Herman Fränkel's analysis of the *Metamorphoses* as a whole is invaluable. It makes that poem's appeal to this particular novelist almost self-evident. Fränkel writes that the theme of metamorphosis gave Ovid 'ample scope for the displaying of the phenomena of insecure and fleeting identity, of a self divided in itself or spilling over into another self'.[51] Ovid's epic would appear to be fundamental, in complex and various ways, to Hickman's conviction in this text – one that expresses a recurring preoccupation of the Ellisonian oeuvre – that 'men change and have wills and wear masks'.[52]

Ovidian Traces in Ellison's High-Flying Heroes

In his incarnation as Senator Sunraider, *Three Days*'s Bliss unambiguously articulates a mythical conception both of the American people and of himself. In the sonorous speech that he is delivering in the Senate when he is shot, he compares his audience to 'great birds', declaiming that 'it is in our nature to soar', and that 'by following the courses mapped through the adventurous efforts of our fathers we affirm and revitalize their awesome vision'.[53] As Eric Sundquist points out, the myth of Daedalus and Icarus (as told by Ovid in Book VIII of the *Metamorphoses*) resonates in these words, anticipating Hickman's meditation on the 'Fall of Icarus' tapestry in 'Hickman in Washington DC'.[54] While Ellison laments the

50 Ibid., 471.

51 Hermann Fränkel, *Ovid, A Poet between Two Worlds*, 99.

52 Ellison, *Three Days*, 421.

53 Ibid., 238.

54 Sundquist, 'Ralph Ellison in His Labyrinth', 133–5.

tendency of white writers such as Fitzgerald to restrict the role of black characters to that of a mute 'witness' to the fall of an Icarian protagonist,[55] in both *Invisible Man* and *Three Days* he identifies his own protagonists with that ill-fated hero. As Conner has observed, Ellison's concern in his second novel with the 'flights and falls [...] of questing figures' is an important part of his indebtedness to James Joyce, in whose fiction Icarus-inflected paradigms of flight and flying are a recurring preoccupation.[56] And while the myth of Icarus resonates in the dangerous but necessary 'plunge' outside of history undergone by both Tod Clifton and the narrator in Ellison's *Invisible Man*, it is also a significant presence in his early short stories such as 'Mister Toussan', 'That I Had the Wings' and 'Flying Home'.[57]

One prior literary deployment of the myth that may well have influenced Ellison is in Dante's *Divine Comedy*: Dante (whose work Ellison owned in four different editions) makes numerous references to Icarus's unhappy end. The Italian poet's drawing of a parallel between Icarus and a different but equally ill-fated Ovidian hero, Phaethon, might in turn have alerted Ellison to the resonances with his own concerns of this second, equally over-ambitious mythical figure.[58] As Ovid tells us, it is purportedly thanks to the global fire that burns when Phaethon crashes the chariot belonging to his father, the Sun, that 'the Aethiops turned black'.[59] In Ellison's exploration of the shifting nature of racial identity throughout *Three Days* as a whole, the myth of Phaethon functions as a powerful intertext thanks to its status as a kind of fantastical 'Just So' story or speculative tale about

55 Ralph Ellison, 'The Little Man at Chehaw Station', in John F. Callahan, ed., *The Collected Essays of Ralph Ellison* (New York: Modern Library, 2003), 503.

56 Conner, 'Father Abraham', 175.

57 In *Invisible Man* the narrator dreams of 'the self that flew without wings and plunged from great heights' (Ellison, *Invisible Man*, 380). For further Icarian echoes in this novel, see ibid., 435, 438, 447.

58 Dante's several references to Phaethon may well have suggested the myth to Ellison. Notably, in *Inferno* XVII.106–111, Dante compares Virgil's fear of flying to that of both Phaethon and Icarus at the moment of their downward plunges back to earth. See <https://digitaldante.columbia.edu/dante/divine-comedy/inferno/inferno-17>, accessed 7 April 2020.

59 Ovid, *Metamorphoses* II.236.

how African people's skin became black. Yet the myth's resonances within *Three Days* go much further than that: they also speak to that text's key themes of anxiety about paternity, and of catastrophic downfall from a great height.[60]

In Ovid's unusually long and psychologically detailed tale, Phaethon is anxious about whether the Sun (here called Phoebus) is really his father, and asks that Phoebus allow him to drive the chariot that pulls the sun as a proof of his paternity. Fearful of and already grieving the anticipated catastrophe, Phoebus expresses 'fatherly anxiety' and 'a father's cares', but reluctantly agrees.[61] Phaethon is at first delighted to be entrusted with the magnificent chariot, every splendid feature of which Ovid describes in painstaking detail. When soaring through 'the top of heaven', however, disaster soon strikes: the horses run wild, Phaethon cannot control them, and the chariot goes off course before 'plunging headlong down' into the earth. The ensuing worldwide conflagration is described over sixty lines of the poem. When Jupiter at last ends the chaos, by striking Phaethon dead with a thunderbolt, the youth's body follows the scorched and scattered 'fragments of the wrecked chariot'. It is 'hurled headlong and falls with a long trail from the sky'. 'Though he greatly failed', his epitaph reads, he 'more greatly dared'.[62]

In its themes of an ultimately doomed relationship between a father and a son; of filial insecurity and paternal grieving; of a young man overreaching himself; of a flight that ends catastrophically for the whole world as well as for these protagonists; and in its preoccupation with darkness and light, the Phaethon myth possibly surpasses the Icarus/Daedalus myth in speaking to the central themes of *Three Days*. It clearly symbolizes Ellison's novel-wide concern with 'an array of absent fathers' and, again, with the 'flights and falls of [...] questing figures'.[63] Its aptness very possibly explains why tropes of both the chariot and the fire recur, in various forms, throughout Ellison's depictions of both Bliss/Sunraider and Lee Willie Minifees, and of the combustible political background of their lives.

60 On paternity in *Three Days*, see Conner, 'Father Abraham'.

61 Ovid, *Metamorphoses* II.91–2, 94.

62 Ovid, *Metamorphoses* II.179–228.

63 Conner, 'Father Abraham', 167; 175.

Bliss himself appears oblivious to the Phaethon-inflected irony of his discourse during his speech in the Senate, as well as to that of his acquired name, 'Sunraider'. Yet Ellison punctuates his account of Bliss/Sunraider's consciousness, as well as others' perceptions of him, with vignettes and symbolic objects that contribute to the power of this myth as a kind of theme tune accompanying this character's life. In Book I, McIntyre's own narrative consciousness in turn develops the mythical dimensions of Bliss/Sunraider's life by bestowing great significance on various events that explicitly involve the senator, as well as on those that implicitly reflect on his life and times. Minifees's burning of his Cadillac is the most obvious of these, but the focus on the elevator 'car' that appears to be out of control, gliding and plunging,[64] and the 'unforeseen combustibility of the sports car at Le Mans',[65] also bring Phaethon to mind. In this first book, McIntyre's own mythologizing tendencies are clearly on display in his depictions of a protagonist who, the narrator claims, 'lived with fire and with ice, with sun and with lightning'.[66]

In Book II, meanwhile, Ellison's exploration of Bliss/Sunraider's and Hickman's present and past itself intensifies the dialogue with the myth of the son of the Sun. The senator's rhetorical flourish about 'the darkness in lightness and the lightness in darkness' is made only too real by Severen's shooting of the chandelier, which the fallen senator perceives as 'a watery distortion of crystal light, a light which seemed to descend and settle him within a ring of liquid fire'.[67] If these words are reminiscent of the lengthy description of the conflagration caused by Phaethon's misguided ambition in Book II of the *Metamorphoses*, then Bliss's preaching of a sermon by 'John. P. Eatmore' is even more so.[68] This 'fire sermon' of course alludes to a vast range of texts – from *The Waste Land* to the preaching on hell in *Portrait of the Artist* and to Milton's chaos in *Paradise Lost*.[69] But, while

64 Ellison, *Three Days*, 28–9.

65 Ibid., 73.

66 Ibid., 30.

67 Ibid., 241, 246.

68 Ibid., 302.

69 On the 'fire sermon' in *Three Days*, see Paul Devlin, 'A Literary Archaeology of Reverend Hickman's Juneteenth Sermon in Ralph Ellison's Second Novel', *Literature of the Americas* 5 (2018), 116–31.

Sundquist compares Sunraider to Prometheus at this point, the line from the sermon that he quotes – 'for man was beseeching the Lord for warmth when it was the *sun* itself he coveted' – brings Phaethon to mind just as much as the fire-stealing Titan.[70] The sermonic account of man's 'headlong plunge, in hectic heathen flight' in the 'volcanic fire', and of humanity's 'charred flesh',[71] echoes Ovid's long description of burning volcanic mountains, of the Earth's singed hair and ashy eyes, and of Phaethon's burning face as he falls. Bliss/Sunraider's sickbed hallucinations (or memories?) of his 'flying' from a train on which he was hobo-ing, recalls Phaethon's fate just as much as Icarus's in its preoccupation with the sun and sunlight.[72] And his befuddled recollection of a car that flies, the '*mirage-like image of black metal agleam with chrome*' that he watched '*floating away*', once more suggests the airborne chariot of the Sun.[73]

Just before Bliss/Sunraider is shot, he raises a laugh in the Senate by referring to the 'wildest black man behind the wheel of a Cadillac'.[74] Although he dismisses it as a comic trifle here, his sickbed hallucination of the flying car perhaps indicates how Minifees's burning of his convertible Cadillac has disturbed and now haunts the Senator more than he has been prepared to admit. Yet it is striking that critics to date have paid very little attention to the Cadillac-burning incident: in *The New Territory*, for example, which contains five detailed analyses of *Three Days*, there is only one passing reference to Minifees.[75] This episode's lack of appeal or interest to scholars is possibly due to the fact that it is already highly interpreted (if not over-interpreted) within the text by several characters. Yet in McIntyre's telling us that the scene was 'unbelievably wild' and that

70 Ellison, *Three Days*, 305 (italics in original); Sundquist, 'Ralph Ellison in His Labyrinth', 134.

71 *Three Days*, 305–6, 309.

72 Ibid., 308–9.

73 Ibid., 411 (italics in original).

74 Ibid., 243.

75 This reference occurs in Timothy Parrish, 'Ralph Ellison's *Three Days*: The Aesthetics of Political Change', in Marc C. Conner and Lucas E. Morel, eds, *The New Territory: Ralph Ellison and the Twenty-First Century* (Jackson: University Press of Mississippi, 2016), 212.

the immolation was 'a crude and most portentous gesture';[76] in the racist McGowan's later assertion that the 'nigra' was 'trying to politicize the Cadillac';[77] and in Minifees's own declaration that he had burnt his car 'to answer that half-assed senator',[78] there is a linguistic flatness or obviousness that obscures as much as it reveals. My contention is that to read the act of Cadillac-burning in relation to the Ovidian myth that reverberates within it, and to interpret Minifees himself as a kind of 'anti-Phaethon', is to understand more fully the political significance of this event.

Speaking with McIntyre in the psychiatric ward, Minifees refers to his incendiary action as his 'Sunraider riff'.[79] We might also understand it as his 'Phaethon riff', as Ellison creates a connection, or rather an associative disconnection, between Phaethon's ill-fated driving of the chariot of the sun and Minifees's burning of his car. McIntyre's reference to the 'gleaming' white Cadillac as a 'shining chariot'[80] is echoed by Ellison in a 1976 interview, in which, in attesting to the significance of elegance in black culture, he cites 'the way the dedicated worshipper of the Cadillac sits at the steering wheel of his chariot'.[81] Ovid's detailed description of the beautiful gold and silver mechanics of Phoebus's chariot resonate in the 'gleam' of Minifees's vehicle, and Ellison further emphasizes the classical and archetypal elements of the scene through Sunraider's broadcasted insults about the 'neopagan comfort' of Cadillacs, and the 'fiery metamorphosis of the white machine' once it has been set alight.[82] McIntyre's description of the spectacle of the 'flaming convertible' being 'distorted by heat' constitutes that same Ovidian eye for the physical process of transition or transformation that Ellison so often displays.[83] Minifees's assertion that the Senator's insults made him feel that his 'brain was on fire' – although driving the Cadillac had entailed that 'good old familiar feeling of flying'[84] – compels

76 Ellison, *Three Days*, 46, 47.
77 Ibid., 59.
78 Ibid., 223.
79 Ibid., 222.
80 Ibid., 37.
81 Graham and Singh, *Conversations*, 329.
82 Ellison, *Three Days*, 47, 39.
83 Ibid., 40, 39.
84 Ibid., 43, 42.

us to think further about what the relationship between this black man and Phaethon; or between this black man and Bliss/Sunraider-as-Phaethon, might mean.

Ovid's tale of Phaethon is about both a son's anxiety that his father proves his paternity, and about that son's desire to impress and to equal his father in greatness and prowess. Perhaps Minifees's burning of his own 'shining chariot',[85] then, his ultimate rejection or inversion of Phaethon's heroic aspiration and catastrophic downfall, is also a rejection of the white patriarchal power that Senator Sunraider and American dominant culture symbolize. In his committee session remarks on the Cadillac that had so angered Minifees, the Senator mocks African American 'desire' for wealth and power, asking whether they want 'a jet plane on every Harlem rooftop?'.[86] This particular black American man, however, rejects both the power of white men and the chance to equal their purported greatness and prowess, by destroying what those white men have made desirable. While disaster and destruction strike Phaethon because he loses control, inadvertently wreaks havoc, and is laid low by Jupiter's thunderbolt, Minifees conversely asserts control, deliberately creates havoc, and does not wait for some omnipotent force's weaponry to bring him down. Even though Minifees has to 'hit [him]self' to 'hurt' Sunraider,[87] and even though he is subsequently institutionalized by the powers that be, he is left with his autonomy and self-determination intact.

Understanding Bliss/Sunraider as a neo-Phaethon and Minifees as an anti-Phaethon has one further important implication. If the fire caused by Phaethon led to the 'Aethiopians' becoming black-skinned, then Minifees's subversion of the Phaethon role is also a subversion of this idea; Ellison thus rejects the idea of the primacy and priority of white people in power. In her 1998 novel, *Paradise*, Toni Morrison 'out-Ovids Ovid' by inverting the Phaethon myth to suggest the 'original world' is one built 'on the sand waves of the lonely Sahara',[88] and hence asserts the 'original' dark-toned skin

85 Ibid., 37.
86 Ibid., 47.
87 Ibid., 224.
88 Toni Morrison, *Paradise* (London: Vintage, 229; 233).

of the human race.[89] Ellison's mythical resonances in the Minifees episode anticipate that move. They can be read as a subtle 'black classicist' intertextuality that roots the origins of human existence in Africa, and that thereby asserts not black equality with whites, but black priority.[90]

Interestingly, Sundquist illuminates the way that Ellison inflects the Icarus story with a radical black politics, too: the critic elucidates the way Ellison interweaves the Icarian flying myth with the 'Ibo Landing story', which in its folkloric survival about enslaved Africans flying out of the sea back to Africa has been central within African American resistance.[91] Sundquist implies that Ellison's preoccupation with flight and flying in many of his earlier short stories and in *Invisible Man* may be associated as much with West African and African American folkloric tradition about flights as they can with the Daedalus/Icarus myth. His point sits well alongside my own about the ways in which Ellison, in Books I and II of *Three Days*, exploits the Greek, Roman and African interconnections inherent in Ovid's myth of Phaethon.

Ovidian Artist Figures in *Three Days*

While Ellison's novelistic engagement (through Phaethon) with what I term the 'Africannness of classicism' may contribute to shifting perceptions of intellectual and cultural history,[92] and so may ultimately influence

89 For further discussion see Tessa Roynon, *Toni Morrison and the Classical Tradition: Transforming American Culture* (Cambridge, UK: Cambridge University Press, 2013), 169–75.

90 For further discussion of *Three Days* and black classicism, see the chapter on Ellison (Chapter 4) in Tessa Roynon, *The Classical Tradition in Modern American Fiction* (Edinburgh: Edinburgh University Press, 2021).

91 See Ellison, *Three Days*, 598–9; and Sundquist, 'Ralph Ellison in His Labyrinth', 132–5.

92 See Tessa Roynon, 'The Africanness of Classicism in the Work of Toni Morrison', in Daniel Orrells, Gurminder Bhambra and Tessa Roynon, eds, *African Athena: New Agendas* (Oxford: Oxford University Press, 2011), 381–98.

political reality, the point of the Icarus story as Ovid depicts it (and as artists such as Ellison reinvoke it) is that, on one level, the fate of Icarus influences absolutely nothing. As depicted in Bruegel's painting, 'Landscape with the Fall of Icarus', and in poems such as those by William Carlos Williams ('Landscape with the Fall of Icarus') and W. H. Auden ('Musée des Beaux Arts'), this is a tale that illuminates human unawareness of and indifference to the suffering of others. Unlike Phaethon, whose fall sets the world on fire and thus has a lasting, ubiquitous impact, Icarus simply sinks without trace. Ellison's widespread use of the myth can therefore be understood as a questioning of the indifference of humanity at large to the plight of black Americans during centuries of racial injustice and racially motivated violence.

The efforts of Daedalus as artist/engineer, as the creator of Icarus's problematic wings, might also be said to end in erasure and obliviousness. Yet there is a paradox here, in that non-mythical – or historical – artists' response to this story about the futility of human endeavour, of course, makes an impact in itself. Questions about the function of the artist and the possibilities for art are a preoccupation of Ellison's work,[93] and Ovid's *Metamorphoses* provides him with a range of archetypal artist figures that are invaluable to his exploration of these themes. Ovid's own preoccupation with dilemmas about the role of the artist and the power (or impotence) of artistry informs Ellison's second novel in important ways,[94] particularly in the computer sequence written in 1982: 'Hickman in Washington DC'. Here Ellison makes significant reference not just to Daedalus but also to the figures of Deucalion and Pygmalion. Ultimately, through Hickman's meditations on the power and the limitations of storytelling, of music, of

93 In 'The World and the Jug', Ellison wonders 'how much of his life the [Negro] individual writer is able to transform into art'. Ralph Ellison, 'The World and the Jug', in John F. Callahan, ed., *The Collected Essays of Ralph Ellison* (New York: Modern Library, 2003), 159.

94 For an overview of the artist figures in the *Metamorphoses*, see Donald Lateiner, 'Mythic and Non-Mythic Artists in Ovid's *Metamorphoses*', *Ramus* 13/1 (1984), 1–30. Lateiner categorizes Ovid's treatment of this subject into 'Paradigms of Creation'; 'The Failures of Art'; 'The Inadequacies of Art'; 'Flawed Triumphs' (Arachne and Daedalus) and 'The Perfect Artist' (Pygmalion).

the visual arts and of preaching to narrate the past, account for the present and shape the future, Ellison constructs a metafiction that reflects on his own role as novelist. In so doing – as well as in the self-scrutiny that characterizes his essay, 'Tell It Like It Is, Baby' – he picks up on and develops continuing Ovid's own self-reflexivity in the *Metamorphoses*.

In 'Hickman in Washington DC', the stunning view that Hickman takes in from the Lincoln Memorial steps is freighted both with painful history and ambiguous promise. In Hickman's appreciation of the cherry blossom, the 'majestic and white' Jefferson Memorial, and 'the far distant dome of the Capitol',[95] the tone is for a brief moment one of genuine idyllic pastoral. Yet in Hickman's mind, this serenity is soon complicated by his perception of a near-postmodern fluidity, instability and meta-awareness: 'Reflected in its pool Lincoln's marble-clad memorial rippled and swayed, and the reflections of visitors arrayed on its steps were bobbing and weaving in the breeze-ruffled water like figures in a dream sequence from a historical movie'.[96] As Hickman meditates on the statue of Lincoln itself – on the implications of its 'great sculptural form' and the 'voiceless eloquence of impermeable stone'[97] – he believes for a moment that he is witnessing a remarkable transformation. 'The stone seemed to come alive', Ellison writes, 'The great chest appearing to heave as though stirred at last by the aura of acts unfinished and promises unkept which he and his flock brought into its presence'.[98]

The novelist here implicitly associates Hickman with two artists, in Ovid's *Metamorphoses*, who have the power to change stone or sculpture into living humanity. The first of these is Deucalion, who appears in Book I as a key player in the Ovidian creation myth. Together with Pyrrha, Deucalion is ordered by Themis to recreate human beings (after their destruction in the flood) by throwing stones, which 'lose their hardness and stiffness', initially resembling the 'statues just begun out of marble' before being 'changed to flesh'.[99] The second is Pygmalion, the Cypriot sculptor whom

95 Ellison, *Three Days*, 579.
96 Ibid., 578.
97 Ibid., 575, 574.
98 Ibid., 576.
99 Ovid, *Metamorphoses* I.401–8.

Ellison invokes explicitly, with reference to Sippy Brown, in the 'Georgia and Oklahoma' section of *Three Days*.[100] Ovid's Pygmalion famously creates a statue of a woman that is so realistic that it appears to be 'living', and so beautiful that he loves and prays to marry it. Venus grants his prayer by bringing the statue to life.[101] Through re-casting these Ovidian tropes of vivified stone in an imagined and momentary revivification of Abraham Lincoln, the novelist of course seeks to revivify Lincoln's vision of racial justice and equality. Ellison longs to restore those ideals both to the incipient Civil Rights era in which Hickman visits DC, but also to the racially fraught Reaganite era (the 1980s) in which the writer is now revising his work. Crucially, however, the Ovidian echoes also reinscribe the significance of Hickman himself, as a powerfully generative artist figure akin to Deucalion and Pygmalion, one whose creative thinking and passionate faith may well transform the troubled, apparently set-in-stone racial conservatism characterizing the American culture he inhabits.

Ellison's essay 'Tell It Like It Is, Baby' – begun in 1956 and completed in 1965 – shares with 'Hickman in Washington DC' some strikingly Ovid-inflected perspectives on the American nineteenth century. This essay's tragic conception of Lincoln's life, death and legacy are accompanied by a palpable engagement with the Roman poet's structuring principle of metamorphosis.[102] For example, while in *Three Days* Hickman believes the statue of Lincoln is coming to life, Ellison notes in the essay that in being transported through his dream back to that president's assassination, it was 'as though a book of nineteenth-century photographs had erupted into vivid life'.[103] While witnessing the desecration of Lincoln's corpse, the

100 See Ellison, *Three Days*, 699, where Ellison describes Sippy as affecting a 'Pygmalion–Falstaff feat of transformation' on Bliss/Sunraider.

101 See Ovid, *Metamorphoses* X.250ff.

102 Ellison implicitly draws attention to the original political contexts of Ovid's poem, and their parallels with the present day through repeated references to his own location in Rome: to the 'Roman dark', 'the hushed Roman night' and the 'the bright Roman day' (Ralph Ellison, '"Tell It Like It Is, Baby"', in John F. Callahan, ed., *The Collected Essays of Ralph Ellison* (New York: Modern Library, 2003), 32, 44).

103 Ibid., 34.

essayist expects to be changed, himself, into a beast with 'hairy paws',[104] and he describes the post-desecrated dead body of the president as 'the Happy Hooligan transformation'.[105] In the essay, Ellison only finds consolation and the restoration of order through remembering a scene from a film in which actor Charles Laughton recites the Gettysburg Address: in this re-iteration Lincoln's words are 'transformed into a most resonant image of the American's post-Civil War imperative of conscience and consciousness achieved'.[106] Within *Three Days*, meanwhile, it is arguably Hickman's encounter with the temporarily re-vivified statue of Lincoln that transforms that memorial into a similar 'resonant image of the American's post-Civil War imperative of conscience and consciousness achieved'. For the African American author, the creator who makes sense of the chaos – the Deucalion-like or Pygmalion-like artist figure himself (always a 'he', in Ellison's case) – is every bit as significant as his creation. This conviction is evident in the illuminating reflection on his own creative process with which he brings 'Tell It Like It Is, Baby' to a close: past and present 'collide within his interior life', he writes, 'either to be jumbled in the chaos of dream, or brought to ordered significance through the forms and techniques of his art'.[107]

Ellison's claim that he heard a 'nightingale' during his sleep-disturbed but productive 'Roman night' brings not just Keats's famous ode to mind, but also the mythical Philomel (or Philomela), whom Eliot references in *The Waste Land*, and who in Ovid's *Metamorphoses* articulates the profound chaos of her trauma as a victim of rape and bodily mutilation through weaving a tapestry.[108] It is perhaps Philomel's 'web', as Ovid describes it,[109] as well as the powerful painting depicting her in Eliot's poem, that inspires the ekphrasis on the tapestry in the 'Fall' section of *Three Days*.[110] Here, in the lounge of the Longview Hotel, the eponymous character meditates on

104 Ibid., 38.

105 Ibid., 40.

106 Ibid., 45.

107 Ibid., 46. Ellison uses the central Ovidian term even to describe his own authorial formation, when he describes his 'odd metamorphosis as a writer' (ibid., 29).

108 See T. S. Eliot, *The Waste Land*, in T. S. Eliot, *The Waste Land and Other Poems* (London: Faber, 2010), l. 99–106.

109 Ovid, *Metamorphoses* VI.576.

110 See Ellison, *Three Days*, 591–600.

the enormous wall-hanging or tapestry in which Bruegel's 'Landscape with the Fall of Icarus' is bordered by 'miniature portraits' of heroic American 'inventors and scientists', along with numerous technological inventions.[111] Equal in significance to the Bliss/Sunraider-as-Icarus dynamic here is the concomitant construction of Hickman, the father figure, as Daedalus: as the artist-engineer who created both the Cretan labyrinth and the wings that enabled both his son and himself to fly. Resonating within Hickman's meditation on the woven version of the Bruegel is not just Joyce's invocation of Daedalus in Stephen's obviously allusive surname, but also the Irish author's epigraph to *Portrait of the Artist*, where he quotes (in Latin) Ovid's account of how Daedalus, hating his exile in Crete, 'sets his mind at work among unknown arts'.[112] For both this 'Fall' episode and the 'Hickman in Washington DC' section as a whole might well be understood as Hickman's portrait of himself as an artist, as a young man and also as an ageing man. He ruminates on the way he has shaped Bliss/Sunraider's life ('we cast him as a hero'),[113] but also embarks on long autobiographical reflections on his past as both a jazz trombonist and as a preacher, contemplating the transformative, generative and regenerative powers of both of those arts.

While Joyce uses the wonderfully ambiguous term, 'artificer', to denote the composite of God, his father and Daedalus whom he addresses at the end of *Portrait*,[114] Ellison on first glance appears less sceptical than Joyce about the Pygmalion-like or Daedalus-like artistic powers that he attributes to Hickman, to Bliss/Sunraider, and of course to himself as novelist. For the most part he appears less ambivalent and less prone to irony than is Joyce about the positive effects of artistry, and hence about the noble or heroic role of the artist. Having said which, there are certainly traces of Joycean scepticism in the later novelist's exploration of these themes: while Joyce's artist uses the verb 'to forge', fraught with connotations about deceit and trickery, when he sets out to 'forge' his artistic creations 'in the smithy of

111 Ibid., 598.

112 Ovid, *Metamorphoses* VIII.188.

113 Ellison, *Three Days*, 527.

114 James Joyce, *A Portrait of the Artist as a Young Man*, in *The Essential James Joyce* (London: Grafton, 1989), 365.

[his] soul',[115] Hickman conceives of his tour of the National Mall as a passage through 'the shifty hall of mirrors called "history" '.[116] Ellison's choice of the word 'shifty' (instead of 'shifting') here preserves a Joycean attention to the potential deceitfulness or trickeries inherent in representational and narrative endeavours.

In addition, by associating Hickman with one further figure from Ovid's *Metamorphoses*, Ellison introduces a new, albeit still implicit, anxiety about the role played by the artist. This figure is Actaeon, the young hunter who in Ovid's poem accidentally intrudes on the goddess Diana bathing in a woodland grove. To punish him for seeing her naked, the goddess transforms Actaeon into a stag that is devoured by its own hounds.[117] Perhaps influenced again by T. S. Eliot, whose notes to *The Waste Land* reference a seventeenth-century poet's allusion to the myth of Diana and Actaeon, or by Joseph Campbell, who in the first volume of his *Masks of God* tetralogy includes a lengthy discussion of the same myth, Ellison draws an implicit analogy between Hickman and Actaeon, and thereby introduces the idea of the artist as a problematic voyeur. In the '[McMillen]' section of 'Hickman in Washington DC', when Hickman and Deacon Wilhite are intruding into Jessie Rockmore's hallway in their search for Bliss/Sunraider, the novelist describes Hickman seeing a man in the mirror. Realising that it is a reflection of himself, 'he saw the prongs of two set of deer antlers that appeared to sprout [...] from the sides of his own hatted head'.[118] Here there are clear echoes of Ovid's description of the Actaeon-as-stag, who espies his own new shape and antlers reflected 'in a clear pool'.[119] While in the *Metamorphoses* Diana effects this brutal transformation upon Actaeon because he has voyeuristically gazed at her private bathing, Hickman observes that it is his 'inner self' that has 'found his [own] act of trespassing so outrageous as to materialize and charge its bodily flesh with violating all laws of privacy'.[120] Through the representation of Hickman as an Actaeon-like voyeur in his

115 Ibid., 365.
116 Ellison, *Three Days*, 579.
117 See Ovid, *Metamorphoses* III.165–252.
118 Ellison, *Three Days*, 615.
119 Ovid, *Metamorphoses* III.200.
120 Ellison, *Three Days*, 615.

pursuit of Sunraider; as an observer; and as a detective-like figure attempting to make sense of all that he perceives, Ellison both questions the ethics of artistic quest and observation, and simultaneously suggests that the artist is a vulnerable and embattled figure. In so doing he expresses an anxiety about the role of the artist that is reminiscent of James Joyce's work, but that is quite uncharacteristic of the Ellisonian outlook as a whole.

In illuminating the ways in which Ovid's *Metamorphoses* informs Ellison's thematics of individual and social transformation, underpins his explorations of over-ambitious heroic action, and shapes his consideration of the role of the artist, this essay has shown that the Roman poet is fundamental to the Ellisonian worldview and its inseparable aesthetic. The 'Ovidian dynamic' resonates not just in the mythical archetypes – those embodying a range of transformations – which Ellison encountered through his reading. It is also integral to his creative process, in that like an improvising musician, he transforms his reading into new material. 'Through the *act* of reading', Ellison declared in 1964, 'I had become acquainted with other possible selves, freer, more courageous, [...] even wise'.[121] The uses to which he put his reading in and about Ovid's *Metamorphoses* testify to the way his autodidacticism made him into a novelist.

It must be acknowledged that the unboundaried nature of the manuscripts that constitute *Three Days before the Shooting ...* – the numerous retellings of the same event, the multiple drafts, and the sense of the infinite changeability of the protagonists – to some extent testify to the drawbacks of an Ovidian-inflected conception of limitless transformation. The influence on Ellison of Joseph Campbell in this respect, who in *The Masks of God* created an endlessly proliferating comparative mythology defined by innumerable connections between archetypes from global cultural traditions, and by infinite potential for transitions, can be seen as somewhat problematic. Campbell's work perhaps suggested to Ellison an overabundance of narrative and symbolic possibilities that was ultimately reductive or counterproductive, a boundlessness of the kind that Rinehart himself, in

121 Ralph Ellison, 'Introduction' to *Shadow and Act*, in *The Collected Essays of Ralph Ellison*, ed., John F. Callahan (New York: Modern Library, 2003), 57 (italics in original).

Invisible Man, turns away from.[122] Yet in attending to the myriad uses to which Ellison puts the *Metamorphoses* in his oeuvre, we witness his modernist aesthetic processes at their sophisticated best. As do the jazzmen's 'jam sessions' so fondly recalled by Hickman, Ellison's allusiveness bears witness to his 'skill at revealing old forms in the new and the new forms in the old'.[123] As it does in T. S. Eliot's *Waste Land*, in Ellison's hands the old, 'remembered art' of Ovid becomes a new, remembered art.[124]

Bibliography

Bakhtin, M. M., *The Dialogic Imagination: Four Essays*, ed., Michael Holquist, trans. Caryl Emerson and Michael Holquist (Austin: University of Texas Press, 1981).

Bradley, Adam, *Ralph Ellison in Progress: From* Invisible Man *to* Three Days before the Shooting … (New Haven, CT: Yale University Press, 2010).

Conner, Marc C., 'Father Abraham: Ellison's Agon with the Fathers in *Three Days before the Shooting …*', in Marc C. Conner and Lucas E. Morel, eds, *The New Territory: Ralph Ellison and the Twenty-First Century* (Jackson: University Press of Mississippi, 2016), 167–93.

Cook, William and James Tatum, *African American Writers and Classical Tradition* (Chicago: University of Chicago Press, 2010).

Dante, *Inferno*, <https://digitaldante.columbia.edu/dante/divine-comedy/inferno>, accessed 5 June 2020.

De La Piedra, Benji, 'White Liberal Rinehart: The Negro American Core of Book I of *Three Days before the Shooting …*', *Literature of the Americas* 5 (2018), 132–50.

Devlin, Paul, 'A Literary Archaeology of Reverend Hickman's Juneteenth Sermon in Ralph Ellison's Second Novel', *Literature of the Americas* 5 (2018), 116–31.

Eliot, T. S., *The Waste Land and Other Poems* (London: Faber, 2010).

122 See Ellison, *Invisible Man*, 499. Compare Bradley, *Ralph Ellison in Progress*, 125–6: 'The novel itself would take on the Protean cast of its first protagonist. […] It may finally be that Bliss is too freighted with myth and symbolism; perhaps he stood for so much that Ellison could no longer endow him with life'.

123 Ellison, *Three Days*, 637.

124 Ellison, '"Tell It Like It Is, Baby"', 45.

Ellison, Ralph, 'Alain Locke', in John F. Callahan, ed., *The Collected Essays of Ralph Ellison* (New York: Modern Library, 2003), 443–52.

——, 'Change the Joke and Slip the Yoke', in John F. Callahan, ed., *The Collected Essays of Ralph Ellison* (New York: Modern Library, 2003), 100–112.

——, 'Harlem is Nowhere', in John F. Callahan, ed., *The Collected Essays of Ralph Ellison* (New York: Modern Library, 2003), 320–7.

——, 'Hidden Name and Complex Fate', in John F. Callahan, ed., *The Collected Essays of Ralph Ellison* (New York: Modern Library, 2003), 189–209.

——, 'On Initiation Rites and Power: A Lecture at West Point', in John F. Callahan, ed., *The Collected Essays of Ralph Ellison* (New York: Modern Library, 2003), 524.

——, 'Introduction' to *Shadow and Act*, in *The Collected Essays of Ralph Ellison*, ed., John F. Callahan (New York: Modern Library, 2003), 49–62.

——, *Invisible Man* (New York: Vintage, 1995).

——, 'The Little Man at Chehaw Station', in John F. Callahan, ed., *The Collected Essays of Ralph Ellison* (New York: Modern Library, 2003), 493–523.

——, 'Living with Music', in John F. Callahan, ed., *The Collected Essays of Ralph Ellison* (New York: Modern Library, 2003), 227–36.

——, '"Tell It Like It Is, Baby"', in John F. Callahan, ed., *The Collected Essays of Ralph Ellison* (New York: Modern Library, 2003), 27–46.

——, 'Working Notes for *Invisible Man*', in John F. Callahan, ed., *The Collected Essays of Ralph Ellison* (New York: Modern Library, 2003), 341–50.

——, 'The World and the Jug', in John F. Callahan, ed., *The Collected Essays of Ralph Ellison* (New York: Modern Library, 2003), 155–88.

Fränkel, Hermann. *Ovid: A Poet between Two Worlds* (Berkeley and Los Angeles: University of California Press, 1945).

Graham, Maryemma and Amritjit Singh, eds, *Conversations with Ralph Ellison* (Jackson: University Press of Mississippi, 1995).

Jackson, Lawrence, *Ralph Ellison: Emergence of Genius* (New York: Wiley and Sons, 2002).

Joyce, James, *A Portrait of the Artist as a Young Man*, in *The Essential James Joyce* (London: Grafton, 1989), 175–366.

Lateiner, Donald, 'Mythic and Non-Mythic Artists in Ovid's *Metamorphoses*', *Ramus* 13/1 (1984), 1–30.

Lindenberg, Nicole, "'What if Movie Is Bliss's Own Life?": The Symbolic Violence of the Movie in Ralph Ellison's Unfinished Second Novel, *Three Days before the Shooting …*', *Literature of the Americas* 5 (2018), 116–31.

List, Robert N., *Dedalus in Harlem: The Joyce–Ellison Connection* (Washington, DC: University Press of America, 1982).

Locke, Alain, 'The New Negro', in Alain Locke, ed., *The New Negro: Voices of the Harlem Renaissance* (New York: Simon and Schuster 1997), 3–18.

Ovid, *Metamorphoses*, 2 vols, trans. Frank Justus Miller, rev. G. P. Goold (Cambridge, MA: Harvard University Press, 2004).

Parrish, Timothy, 'Ralph Ellison's *Three Days*: The Aesthetics of Political Change', in Marc C. Conner and Lucas E. Morel, eds, *The New Territory: Ralph Ellison and the Twenty-First Century* (Jackson: University Press of Mississippi, 2016), 194–217.

Ralph Ellison Collection, <https://findingaids.loc.gov/exist_collections/ead3pdf/rbc/2016/rb016001.pdf>, accessed 5 June 2020.

Rampersad, Arnold, *Ralph Ellison* (New York: Vintage, 2008).

Rankine, Patrice, *Ulysses in Black: Ralph Ellison, Classicism, and African American Literature* (Madison: University of Wisconsin Press, 2006).

Roynon, Tessa, 'The Africanness of Classicism in the Work of Toni Morrison', in Daniel Orrells, Gurminder K. Bhambra and Tessa Roynon, eds, *African Athena: New Agendas* (Oxford: Oxford University Press, 2011), 381–98.

——, *The Classical Tradition in Modern American Fiction* (Edinburgh: Edinburgh University Press, 2021).

——, 'Ovid, Race and Identity in E. L. Doctorow's *Ragtime* (1975) and Jeffrey Eugenides's *Middlesex* (2002)', *International Journal of the Classical Tradition* 26/4 (2019), 377–96.

——, *Toni Morrison and the Classical Tradition: Transforming American Culture* (Cambridge, UK: Cambridge University Press, 2013).

Shreve, Grant, 'Ralph Ellison's *Three Days before the Shooting* … and the Implicit Morality of Form', in Marc C. Conner and Lucas E. Morel, eds, *The New Territory: Ralph Ellison and the Twenty-First Century* (Jackson: University Press of Mississippi, 2016), 218–42.

Sundquist, Eric, 'Ralph Ellison in His Labyrinth', in Marc C. Conner and Lucas E. Morel, eds, *The New Territory: Ralph Ellison and the Twenty-First Century* (Jackson: University Press of Mississippi, 2016), 117–41.

Winkler, Martin M., *Ovid on Screen: A Montage of Attractions* (Cambridge, UK: Cambridge University Press, 2020).

STEPHEN RACHMAN

4 Ellison and Dostoevsky: A Critical Reassessment of the Aesthetics and Politics

ABSTRACT:
After an overview of the well-known aspects of Ralph Ellison's interest in and connections to the works and literary ideas of the Russian novelist Fyodor Dostoevsky, this chapter reveals the hitherto unknown depths of Ellison's research into and usage of the works and aesthetic theories of the Russian writer as he applied them to American and African American literary and social contexts. Making use of archival materials and Ellison's personal library, which includes numerous works by and about Dostoevsky, this reassessment addresses the role of the Russian classics, and in particular, of Dostoevsky, in Ellison's intellectual formation, the role that Dostoevsky played in Ellison's literary relationship with Richard Wright; the ways that Ellison's interests in the blues, jazz and other folk and vernacular forms of African American culture were filtered through his analysis of nineteenth-century Russian culture; and the Dostoevskyan origins of a number of fictional scenarios that would find their way into *Three Days before the Shooting* ….

To the best of my knowledge, Ralph Ellison first encountered the works of Fyodor Dostoevsky in the winter quarter of 1936 at the Tuskegee Institute, when he took a course in English from Morteza Drexel Sprague.[1] The novel was *Crime and Punishment* and it reportedly made a deep impression on him, though not as deep at the time as, perhaps, Thomas Hardy's *Jude the Obscure*. But whereas the Hardy novel struck Ellison with visceral force in that moment, Dostoevsky would penetrate deeply into Ellison's creative and critical activity. It would be Dostoevsky that Ellison, in 'The World and the Jug', would choose as one of his literary 'ancestors' – the only nineteenth-century author he would claim. It would be the Russian novelist's works that would provide the literary templates, the cultural, aesthetic and theoretical

1 Arnold Rampersad, *Ralph Ellison* (New York: Alfred A. Knopf, 2007), 76.

tools that he would return to time and again as he sought to apply Dostoevskyan literary models to questions of race, nationality and culture in American contexts.[2]

In the extant literary criticism, while observations about Dostoevsky's influence on Ralph Ellison have become commonplace, discussions very rarely involve specificity or substantial detail. This chapter provides a critical reassessment of the complex and multifaceted question of 'Ellison and Dostoevsky' in light of the wealth of posthumous materials left behind by Ellison (including *Three Days before the Shooting* … (2010)) and in light of insufficiently consulted archival materials, such as the Library of Congress catalogue of Ellison's personal library (which includes numerous works not only by Dostoevsky but also about him).[3] The results of that reassessment are striking in three particular ways that are addressed here. First, the role of the Russian classics, and in particular, of Dostoevsky, in Ellison's intellectual formation and political/aesthetic credos are much deeper and more sustained than has been previously known, such that it requires a revaluation of the scope and nature of the pluralistic literary traditions to which he was committed. Second, in light of the intensity of Ellison's investment in Dostoevsky, the role that the Russian writer played in Ellison's literary relationship with Richard Wright, who also had a literary stake in Dostoevsky, indicates that Ellison's interests in the blues, jazz, and other folk and vernacular forms of African American culture were filtered through his analysis of nineteenth-century Russian culture. Thirdly, a survey of his marginalia, left behind in his personal library, reveals the origins of a number of fictional scenarios that would find their way into *Three Days before the Shooting* …. In addition, materials that did not make it into the final drafts of the unfinished magnum opus derive directly from in his intense studies of Dostoevsky.

2 Ralph Ellison, 'The World and the Jug', in John F. Callahan, ed., *The Collected Essays of Ralph Ellison* (New York: Modern Library, 1995), 185.

3 For the full catalogue of Ralph Ellison's personal library, which is held at the Library of Congress, Washington, DC, see 'The Ralph Ellison Collection, (1937–2010)', <https://findingaids.loc.gov/exist_collections/ead3pdf/rbc/2016/rb016001.pdf>, accessed 22 May 2020.

Ellison's 1936 encounter with *Crime and Punishment* (which was first published in 1866) would be the beginning of a lifelong study, an aesthetic, political and cultural preoccupation with Russian literature. As Kenneth Warren has noted, Ellison has been viewed through opposing guises – as transracial social theorist and 'a race man', as seemingly sympathetic to Black Nationalism and opposed to it, as a high literary theorist and vernacular folk artist – and a great deal of criticism has striven to understand the multifaceted and at times contradictory potentials of his work in terms of the vicissitudes of American democracy and racial politics.[4] What remains more obscure is the degree to which Ellison's racial-political-literary positions are connected with his investment in Dostoevsky as much more than a white, European, canonical authority, but rather as an aesthetic model and a model of how literature might catalyse ideological and social change. As Ellison deepened his study of Dostoevsky through the crucial germinative years of his literary apprenticeship, the Russian novelist would become a touchstone in Ellison's literary conversations with crucial figures in his development, notably Richard Wright and Kenneth Burke. This literary connection would have a crucial impact on *Invisible Man* (1952) but even more deeply on Ellison's long and elusive career in the wake of his landmark novel. Through his study, teaching, critical commentary and the long works-in-progress that would posthumously appear as *Juneteenth* (1999) and *Three Days before the Shooting …* (2010), Ellison never stopped turning to Dostoevsky as both a roadmap and a test of his literary and cultural ideas.

Most of the literature touching upon this Russo–African–American literary nexus deals with the development of *Invisible Man*, and rightly so. Dostoevsky enters the standard list of Ellison's literary 'relatives' and 'ancestors' together with Hemingway, Malraux, Joyce, Eliot, Melville, Wright, Henry James – and one comes across this list in almost every critical study on Ellison. The seminal studies that pay special attention to the connection for the most part concentrate on obvious or suggested parallels in ideas, imagery, characters, clear or vague reminiscences and allusions.[5] A set of

4 Kenneth Warren, *So Black and Blue: Ralph Ellison and the Occasion of Criticism* (Chicago, IL: University of Chicago Press, 2003), 18–20.

5 These include (in order of publication): Robert A Bone, *The Negro Novel in America* (New Haven, CT: Yale University Press, 1958); William Goede, 'On Lower Frequencies: The Buried Men in Wright and Ellison', *Modem Fiction Studies* 15

canonical citations from a handful of Ellison's nonfictional texts – interviews, essays ('The World and the Jug', 'The Art of Fiction', 'The Black Mask of Humanity') and reviews in which he refers to Dostoevsky – tend to comprise the basis for these parallels. Furthermore, in the studies devoted to Ellison–Wright and Ellison–Sartre/Camus connections, a Dostoevskyan context has also been established.[6]

'After Dostoyevsky You Don't Need Kafka': Literary Ancestry, Alienation and Literary Pluralism

The parallels between Dostoevsky's underground man and Ellison's invisible man have been striking and apparent to readers and critics alike since the novel's first publication. Wright Morris, writing for the *New York Times Book Review* in 1952, admired the protagonist's basement hole with its precisely astonishing 1,369 bare, burning filament lightbulbs with power filched from the Monopolated Light & Power company's grid. 'A fine Dostoevskyan touch', Morris observed, adding that, 'In his *Notes from the Underground* Dostoevsky says: "We are discussing things seriously: but if you won't deign to give me your attention, I will drop your acquaintance. I can retreat into my underground hole."'[7] In this early review, Morris points out not only the patent spatial similarity between the underground of the Russian novel with that in Ellison's Harlem, but also the attitudinal dialectic between author and reader implied by

(1969), 483–92; Earl A. Cash, 'The Narrators in *Invisible Man* and *Notes from the Underground*: Brothers in Spirit', *CLA Journal* 16/4 (1973), 505–7; Joseph Frank, 'Ralph Ellison and a Literary "Ancestor": Dostoevski', in Kimberly W. Benston, ed., *Speaking for You: The Vision of Ralph Ellison* (Washington, DC: Howard University Press, 1987), 231–44.

6 See, for example, Esther M. Jackson, 'The American Negro and the Image of the Absurd', *Phylon* 23/4 (1962), 359–71.

7 Wright Morris, 'The World Below: *Invisible Man*. by Ralph Ellison. 439 pp. New York: Random House. $3.50', *New York Times* (13 April 1952).

the underground man which Ellison also adapted for his own purposes. Dostoevsky's underground man understands that his implied reader holds a position of cultural superiority and must 'deign' or condescend to give his words attention, but he still retains an alienated majesty in the face of such condescension: he can 'drop' the acquaintance of any such readers who refuse to take him seriously.

In the preface to the thirtieth anniversary edition of *Invisible Man*, Ellison reflected upon the connection between his narrator and Dostoevsky's. As his narrator-protagonist evolved in his imagination, Ellison made a series of strategic recognitions that would inform the aesthetics, politics and social dynamics of the novel:[8]

> It now appeared that this voice of invisibility issued from deep within our complex American underground. So how crazy-logical that I should finally locate its owner living – and oh, so garrulously – in an abandoned cellar. [...] I was already having enough difficulty trying to avoid writing what might turn out to be nothing more than another novel of racial protest instead of the dramatic study in comparative humanity which I felt any worthwhile novel should be, and the voice appeared to be leading me precisely in that direction.[9]

The first recognition was that this voice that would guide his novel emanated from a speaker who, while socially invisible, derives from 'our complex American underground' – Ellison's figuration of African American communities reflected through an imaginative lens – 'the inner-outer, subjective-objective process of the developing fiction, [...] its pied rind

8 Ellison's retrospective account of the development of *Invisible Man* is admittedly streamlined. He mentions that the process was 'far more disjointed than I make it sound'. Ralph Ellison, *Invisible Man* (New York: Random House,1982), xvii. Scholars such as Arnold Rampersad (in *Ralph Ellison*) and Barbara Foley (*Wrestling with the Left: The Making of Ralph Ellison's* Invisible Man, Durham, NC: Duke University Press, 2011) have demonstrated ways in which Ellison's aesthetic disposition often covered over his connections with the Left, both the Communist Party and the aesthetic debates surrounding Leftist fiction. The role that Dostoevsky plays in this element of Ellison's literary-political thought will be addressed in the second section of this essay.

9 Ralph Ellison, *Invisible Man*, 30th Anniversary Edition (New York: Random House, 1982), xvii.

and surreal heart', as he would evocatively add.[10] This created a tension in his conception of the novel. Given the history of racial oppression in the United States in the years from the end of Reconstruction to the beginnings of the Civil Rights era, that is to say, the period that Ellison took to be the background for his novel, it is inevitable that such a voice issuing from a socially invisible character might naturally express itself in terms of racial protest. After all, the condition of social invisibility and the everyday content of the experience of African Americans would naturally contain a great deal in it that one might protest. Nevertheless, Ellison felt that the literary expression of racial protest was aesthetically insufficient. The literary ambition to avoid writing a mere protest novel, to avoid the fictionalization of sociological verities was part and parcel of Ellison's design. Indeed, with thirty years of hindsight, Ellison's descriptor for the social landscape – underground, as opposed to underclass, or other possible terms for the landscape of Jim Crow or *de facto* segregation in late nineteenth- and twentieth-century America – encoded within it a more capacious cultural and rhetorical fluidity open to the 'study of comparative humanity' that Ellison desired for his novel and to which he felt all novels worth their salt should aspire.

For Ellison, the consequences of this socio-literary choice between the novel of racial protest and the novel about race that dramatizes humanity in all its comparative complexity would be immense, pointing towards his break with Leftist politics, the resistance his writing would encounter in the 1960s, and most saliently here, a commitment to pluralistic literary and cultural models, of which Dostoevsky is the key representative. The voice he opted for was one that suggested a 'blues-toned laugher-at-wounds' that 'managed to emerge less angry than ironic' and that refused to exclude itself from its 'indictment of the human condition'.[11] This ironic texture of the voice of the Invisible Man allowed Ellison to recognize his incipient creation as a '"character" [...] in the dual meaning of the term'.[12] Ellison went on:

10 Ibid., xvii.

11 Ibid., xvii–xviii.

12 Ibid., xviii.

> I associated [this narrator], ever so distantly, with the narrator of Dostoevsky's *Notes from Underground*, and with that *I* began to structure the movement of my plot, while *he* began to merge with my more specialized concerns with fictional form and with certain problems arising out of the pluralistic literary tradition from which I spring.[13]

Ellison's italicization of '*I*' and '*he*' signifies – even in his retrospective assessment of the novel's creation – the importance that the distant association of Dostoevsky's underground man conferred upon his own craft. The italics dramatize a necessary aesthetic distance Dostoevsky provided for the plotting of *Invisible Man*, a curious division of labor in which Ellison's authorial self distributes the tasks of novel-writing. In a gesture that betokens a kind of mild psychosis familiar to many writers, Ellison's self – the *I* in his formulation – controlled the structure of the novel (its tripartite organization), while *he* (the narrator) dealt with the multicultural content of the novel, the high and low registers, the philosophical and the pool-room, the tragic and the comic. The ironic voice of his narrator, which in Dostoevsky's terms can drop those who do not deign to take him seriously and in Ellison's terms could see the tragic and the comic simultaneously, could depict the violent conditions of race in the United States, 'those ongoing conflicts, tragic and comic, that had claimed my group's energies since the abandonment of the Reconstruction' at the same time.[14] And it could do so in the service of a pluralistic global literature.

Dostoevsky allowed Ellison to envision an indigenous African American literature in global literary terms, a culturally plural novel of ideas in which a socially invisible body of color gives full-throated voice to an American alienation born of racial prejudice. As we can see from Ellison's own account of his creative activity, the main conduit of connection is literary. It was characterological with stylistic and formal properties and related to the shared aesthetic sensibility we have come to recognize as alienation, but with Ellison all forms of alienation are not interchangeable. Ellison's literary pluralism was bound up in Dostoevskyan alienation, not Kafkaesque alienation, not the alienation of Richard Wright, but a specific form which was simultaneously literary and sociological in a way

13 Ibid., xviii.
14 Ibid., xviii.

that corresponded to the American political and racial scene. For Ellison, this pluralism was fundamental to his social vision and his art and yet it retained a number of cultural tensions. The primary one had to do with what anthropologists have called the phonemic/phonetic divide, the importation of non-indigenous language and forms into cultural analysis.

For Ellison, underlying the example and problem of Dostoevsky lay one fundamental question: how could a nineteenth-century Russian novelist whose critique was directed at Russian cultural problems describe a literary and social model that was utterly relevant to the situation of the African American in the late nineteenth and early twentieth century? Joseph Frank, Dostoevsky's most authoritative English-language biographer, friend and one-time colleague of Ellison's at Rutgers in the 1960s, answered this question in ideological terms. Rather than the underground imagery, Frank argued that, 'Ellison's profound grasp of the dominating ideological implications of Dostoevsky's work' was central to 'his perception of its relevance to his own creative purposes; his perception, that is, of how he could use Dostoevsky's relation to the Russian culture of his time to express his own position [...] in relation to the dominating white culture'.[15]

What then did the complex American underground of Ellison's world share with Dostoevsky's underground? The first element consisted of a cultural homology. Dostoevsky's underground man labours under the domination of Western European influences, the utopian-inflected enlightened rationalism that he dissects. While wholly conversant with these Western influences, as he has been acculturated in St Petersburg's Europeanized climate, he expresses his alienation through an abiding sense that his own identity has been imposed upon him, and that these categorical impositions have made his human existence perverse, incompatible and, at times, impossible.

Where the underground man asserts a wilful perversity in the face of such cultural impositions, Ellison's invisible man discovers through a

15 Joseph Frank, 'On Ralph Ellison and a "Literary Ancestor": Dostoevsky', Library of Congress, Ralph Ellison papers I:48, folders 2 and 7. Frank published a version of this essay in *The New Criterion* but I have chosen to quote from the fuller manuscript that he sent to Ellison, and that is part of Ellison's papers in the Library of Congress.

series of disillusioning experiences (the humiliating battle royal, the duplicitous letter of recommendation from Dr Bledsoe and so on), that the ideologies of racism and white supremacy that impose various definitions on his identity implicitly or explicitly contravene his humanity. Just as the underground man shows the pitfalls and traps of the European ideologies that were attractive to the Russian intelligentsia of the mid-nineteenth century, the invisible man exposes the ways in which his education as part of if not exactly an intelligentsia, then an African American cultural elite, has been corrupted and denatured by the white supremacist ideology it seeks to countermand. Where Dostoevsky takes on the quasi-utopian socialism exemplified by Nikolay Gavrilovich Chernyshevsky's *What Is to Be Done?* (1863) and the materialism and utilitarian strains of political and social thought that had filtered into Russia during the 1840s, Ellison targets a strain of hypocritical assimilationist rhetoric found in the manicured precincts of the traditional black college as he experienced it and reported on it in the 1930s. As his protagonist explores other potentially liberating movements, he discovers more contradictions and tensions between ideology and his sense of his own identity. The race hatred underlying the Africanist rhetoric of Ras the Exhorter and the stoking of racial violence in the name of radical Leftist politics of 'the Brotherhood' end up contributing to, with staggering irony, the further social invisibility of Ellison's protagonist.

The cultural homology between nineteenth-century Russian elite prejudices and white supremacist elitism in the United States provided Ellison with another important literary framework to reposition and transvaluate African American culture. Dostoevsky recognized how elite Russian culture had rendered the Russian peasantry and its folk cultures effectively invisible. In his *The House of the Dead* (first published in 1862), a text that Ellison repeatedly mined, Dostoevsky admonishes his educated readership:

> You may be your whole life in daily relations with the peasant, forty years you may do business with him regularly as the day comes. [...] well, you'll never know what is at the bottom of the man's mind or heart. You may think you know something about him, but it is all optical illusion, nothing more. My readers will charge me with exaggeration, but I am convinced I am quite right. I don't go on theory or book-reading in this; in my case the realities of life have given me only too ample

> time and opportunity for reviewing and correcting my theoretic convictions, which, as to this, are now fixed.[16]

An inability of elites to recognize the cultural integrity and complexity of Russian peasant culture underlies Dostoevsky's point, and this type of Dostoevskyan insight into the ways in which one stratum of society might be wholly ignorant of another despite apparent proximity became more than a motif in *Invisible Man*. For Ellison, it became an article of social faith and a talking point as he tried to persuade others to rethink American culture and its problems. In Ellison's thinking, the way a genuine pluralism was obscured by ideological blindness was one of the problems of American life. For example, a 1963 speech on the challenges of US education, especially for young African American students, expresses the tension between competing visions of America, one pluralistic, the other monolithic.

> The American scene is a diversified one, and the society which gives it its character is a pluralistic society – or at least it is supposed to be. Ideally it is, but we seem to insist, on the other hand, that this society is *not* pluralistic. We have been speaking as though it were *not* made up of diversified cultures but was in fact one monolithic culture. And one which is perfect, the best of all possible cultures, with the best of all people affirming its perfection.
>
> Well, if this were true there would be no point in our being here. But we are here, and since we are, let us try to see American society in all of its diversity.[17]

In this lecture, Ellison adapts Dostoevsky's point in a generalized way: belief in American exceptionalism and utopian tendencies to believe the nation had attained an ideal society obscures the reality of American cultural diversity; *pluribus* obscured by *unum*.

Working from a sense that American educational strategies privileged elite white forms of cultural values in a way that ignored the diverse cultural realities of African Americans (an argument that would anticipate

16 Fyodor Dostoevsky, *The House of the Dead; or, Prison Life in Siberia*, Project Gutenberg (1911), <http://www.gutenberg.org/files/37536/37536-h/37536-h.htm>, accessed 15 April 2020, 307.

17 Ralph Ellison, 'What These Children are Like', in John F. Callahan, ed., *The Collected Essays of Ralph Ellison* (New York: Modern Library, 1995), 542.

by several decades the controversies over cultural biases in standardized testing), Ellison posits, 'There is no such thing as a culturally deprived kid'.[18] Rather, Ellison argued, educational authorities persist in mistakenly ignoring what constitutes culture. He invokes culinary, musical and poetic examples from the black communities (chitterlings, jazz, verbal word-play), to demonstrate the indigenous vibrancy of the culture, reserving a special place for imaginative language. Tailoring one of his favourite dicta from Kenneth Burke for the occasion, Ellison urged his audience to think sociologically, asserting that 'language is equipment for living'.[19] As Bryan Crable observes, 'Burke's contention is that human beings symbolically equip themselves to engage their social and natural environment'.[20] Ellison follows this approach suggesting that, 'One uses the language which helps to preserve one's life', and that the pressure of survival in the United States has produced a rich vernacular tradition in African American communities that would be the envy of experimental and modern poets. Not dictionary knowledge, 'but within the bounds of their familiar environment and within the bounds of their rich oral culture', black youth 'possess a great virtuosity with the music and poetry of words'.[21]

As Dostoevsky sought in the 1860s to persuade his audience of the legitimacy of a folk and peasant culture that they could not readily perceive, Ellison sought to persuade his audience in the 1960s that black youth culture was vibrant and artful. The playful use of language was a reflection of its durability, its slang an expression of how utterly alive it was to its own social realities:

18 Ellison, 'What These Children Are Like', 543.

19 Ibid. See Kenneth Burke, 'Literature as Equipment for Living', in Stanley Edgar Hyman, ed., *Perspectives by Incongruity* (Bloomington: Indiana University Press, 1964), 100. Burke actually specified that 'literature', not language, should be thought of as equipment for living. However, Ellison wished to talk about the indigenous verbal wordplay that emerges in young African Americans and so strategically, broadened the point to language itself.

20 Bryan Crable, *Ralph Ellison and Kenneth Burke: At the Roots of the Racial Divide* (Charlottesville and London: University of Virginia Press, 2011), 93.

21 Ellison, 'What These Children Are Like', 544.

> The great body of Negro slang – that unorthodox language – exists precisely because Negroes need words which will communicate, which will designate the objects, processes, manners and subtleties of their urban experience with the least amount of distortion from the outside.[22]

What it lacked, in Ellison's eyes, was a mainstream culture to acknowledge its validity, and much like Dostoevsky, he was also sceptical that the educational establishment he was addressing would be responsive in a constructive way, so he closed his argument with a warning straight out of *Notes from Underground*: 'I don't know what intelligence is. But this I do know, both from life and from literature: whenever you reduce human life to two plus two equals four, the human element within the human animal says, "I don't give a damn" '.[23] The alienation of the American student was similar to that of his invisible man via the underground man, a reaction to a system – in this case educational – that neither acknowledged one's culture nor the realities to which it was most responsive. In expressing 'what these children are like', Ellison suggested that they are very much like Dostoevsky's underground man. Furthermore, he expressed this as a fundamental principal of what constitutes humanity and as an article of faith ('this I do know, both from life and literature'). We can presume that by life he meant what he had gathered from his own experience and we can now assume with confidence precisely what literature he had in mind: Dostoevsky.

As Dostoevsky argued that peasant life was fundamental to Russian experience, Ellison argued (in this lecture and in many other places) that

22 Ibid., 551.

23 Ibid., 551. In *Notes from Underground*, Dostoevsky has an extended and recurrent riff on the concept of 'two times two equals four'. The phrase appears twelve times in the text. In 'What these Children are Like', Ellison varies it with the expression 'two plus two', but the point is wholly in keeping with the attitude of the underground man. In the translation cited in this essay, a relevant instance reads, 'after all, two times two equals four is no longer life, gentlemen, but the beginning of death'. See Fyodor Dostoevsky, *Notes from Underground*, trans. Boris Jakim (Grand Rapids, MI; Cambridge, UK: William B. Erdmans Publishing Company, 2009), 31. In this way, Ellison interpolates the attitude of the underground man into the roots of disaffection in the African American student.

'Black' life and experience was fundamental to American experience (especially in his 1970 essay, 'What America Would be Like without Blacks').[24] Indigenous vernacular speech, spirituals, jazz, the blues, soul food and many others were all on Ellison's radar as artistic and cultural forms that were underappreciated by the larger society, indeed, not even recognized as 'culture', by many African Americans themselves. Only on a trip to France did he realize 'the obvious fact' that what he had just thought of as mere 'peasant food' was 'part of a high low-class cuisine'.[25] Through all of his examples runs a concern that American society and educational biases tend to blind its citizens to what counts as actually being culturally valuable and significant. As Ellison made himself a student of African American, and more generally, American folk and popular culture, he collected all he knew from his own experience and digested the works of popular cultural historians, such as Constance Rourke and Stanley Edgar Hyman. In a profound sense, the interests in indigenous folk arts, cultural valuation and American pluralism coalesced in a figuration that blended high and low and complemented that of the complex American underground: jazz. The pluralism of the United States lay in this territory for Ellison and informed his insistence that the culture and language were fundamentally 'all jazz-shaped', in the 'sudden turns, shocks and swift changes of pace' that mark it style. Almost paraphrasing Duke Ellington, Ellison asserts that 'the real secret of the game is to make life swing'.[26]

A robust critical literature has explored Ellison's thinking and politics about music – jazz in particular – especially concerned with charting the way it circulates around debates about Afrocentrist separatism or integrationist pluralism. With *Invisible Man*'s magisterial phonographic hearing of Louis Armstrong's '(What Did I Do to be So) Black and Blue' – its reefer-induced meditation on the blues and sorrow songs, its sermons on the blackness of blackness, invisibility sound and silence while the blood-red sloe gin glistens over the vanilla-white ice cream – Ellison has inspired

24 Ralph Ellison, 'What America Would be Like without Blacks', in John F. Callahan, ed., *The Collected Essays of Ralph Ellison* (New York: Modern Library, 1995), 577–84.

25 Ellison, 'What These Children Are Like', 544.

26 Ellison, 'What America Would Be Like without Blacks', 582.

many critics to theorize the problems of race, performance and music.[27] In Ellison's figuration of Armstrong, Fred Moten has observed, 'there is an instantiation of a kind of dialog between knowledge of in/visibility and the absence of that knowledge, between improvement and the vernacular'.[28] Following this line, Walton M. Muyumba argues that Ellison shaped 'his literary aesthetic out of the jazz aesthetic'.[29] Ellison's literary portraits of major jazz figures such as Armstrong, Charlie Christian, Jimmy Rushing and Charlie Parker have become occasions for complex social theorizing and a means to assess 'Ellison's stated commitments to individuality through masterful self-invention', in the words of Paul Allen Anderson, 'and [...] his idealizations of the "marvel of social organization"'.[30]

Here, too, however we also find Dostoevsky as a guide, not so much to the content of jazz, but to how it circulated in American culture. For example, in Ellison's sceptical portrait of Charlie Parker and the welter of legend and mythologization that materialized around the alto saxophonist in the post-war bebop era, he meditates on the contradictions in the character of 'Bird':

> He was given to extremes of sadism and masochism, capable of the most staggering excesses and the most exacting physical discipline and assertion of will. Indeed, one gets the image of such a character as Stavrogin in Dostoevsky's *The Possessed*, who while many things to many people seemed essentially devoid of a human center – except, and an important exception indeed, Parker was an artist who found his moments of sustained and meaningful integration through the reed and keys of the alto saxophone.[31]

27 Ralph Ellison, *Invisible Man* (New York: Random House, 1952), 8–14.

28 Fred Moten, *In the Break: The Aesthetics of the Black Radical Tradition* (Minneapolis: University of Minnesota Press, 2003), 70.

29 Walton Muyumba, *The Shadow and the Act: Black Intellectual Practice, Jazz Improvisation, and Philosophical Pragmatism* (Chicago, IL: University of Chicago Press, 2009), 151.

30 Paul Allen Anderson, 'Ralph Ellison's Music Lessons', in Ross Posnock, ed., *The Cambridge Companion to Ralph Ellison* (Cambridge, UK: Cambridge University Press, 2005), 83.

31 Ralph Ellison, 'On Bird, Bird-Watching and Jazz', in John F. Callahan, ed., *The Collected Essays of Ralph Ellison* (New York: Modern Library, 1995), 263–4.

Perhaps it is our habit of viewing indigenous art forms in native terms that has blinded us to the ways that Ellison continually turned to Dostoevsky for cultural analogues for the American artifacts that he held up for scrutiny. Bird-as-Stavrogin-with-an-art-form was Ellison's way of triangulating the paradoxes of Parker, who had come to be a darling of the Beatnik and 'white hipster' culture of the 1950s, capturing 'something of the discordancies, the yearning, romance and cunning of the age'.[32]

A marginal note in Ellison's personal copy of Mikhail M. Bakhtin's *Problems of Dostoevsky's Poetics* (1973) affords us a glimpse into the chain of cultural and mental associations that connect Ellison's assessment of Charlie Parker, jazz's functions in American society, and Dostoevsky. In the relevant passage, Bakhtin analysed Leonid Grossman's commentary on Dostoevsky's use of the elements of the adventure novel, especially those melodramatic ones in which social mixing occurs. In the margin Ellison scrawled a note in pencil, 'Jazz experiences [or experiments] broke down social hierarchy which was separate to an extent [B]ut not religious'.[33] While it is far from clear what Ellison's specific point was, it is striking how the social mixing points towards the contradictions of Parker and how constantly he turned his critical study of Dostoevsky in terms of plot and situation to think through the materials of his own American experience. Of course, Ellison had written the piece on Parker at least ten years prior to reading the Bakhtin, but what is salient is the way he used the Russian materials to confirm his own cultural hypotheses. What was jazz-shaped about America could be dramatized through Russian literary strategies.

In a study that Ellison read, re-read and in which he left numerous marginal comments, *Tolstoy or Dostoevsky: An Essay in the Old Criticism* (1959), George Steiner observes that 'the underground man is necessary to his betters. He is a reminder of mortality in moments of *hubris*, a buffoon who speaks the truth and a confidant who saps illusion'.[34] Ellison underscored this passage as confirmation of his own sense of the socio-literary

32 Ibid., 264.

33 M. M. Bakhtin, *Problems of Dostoevsky's Poetics*, trans. R. W. Rotsel (Ann Arbor: University of Michigan Press, 1973), 84.

34 George Steiner, *Tolstoy or Dostoevsky: An Essay in the Old Criticism* (New York: Alfred A. Knopf, 1959), 217.

purposes that Dostoevsky's invention serves. Ellison's social vision insisted that there must be comic as well as tragic elements to the American experience of people of color, and that the mode through which the alienated voice could express both of those elements could be found in the character of the underground man. An underscored passage in Ellison's copy of Mikhail M. Bakhtin's *Problems of Dostoevsky's Poetics* sums up the underlying nexus of ideology and voice that the underground and invisible men share: 'His thought is developed and constructed as the *thought of a person personally insulted by the world order*, personally debased by its blind inevitability'.[35]

Dostoevsky would enable Ellison's art and criticism in many ways, but the conjunction of ideology and voice in the way that Bakhtin expresses it provides us with a clearer sense of *Invisible Man*'s aesthetics of alienation and why Ellison would prefer this brand of alienation to Kafka's, as the epigraph to this essay has it, or any other literary models available to him. In a 1968 interview in which Ellison fielded a question about whether or not in the creation of *Invisible Man* he 'had borrowed at all from the Kafka idea of the alienation of the Jew in Europe?', he flatly rejected this proposition. 'No', he explained:

> I had enough alienation of my own to draw on ... The most direct treatment of alienation which I knew, and which in the very rhythm of the epilogue [to *Invisible Man*], was Dostoyevsky's *Notes from the Underground.* [...] After Dostoyevsky you don't need Kafka.[36]

In rejecting the notion of Kafka's influence, Ellison reminds us that not all brands of alienation are interchangeable. Note also that he foregrounds his own direct experience of alienation, the cultural texture and verbal specificity of its grievances that give shape to its ideological expression and its vocal register. It would be Dostoevsky's expression of mid-nineteenth-century Russian alienation – a world in which an intellectual elite devalued its indigenous folk and popular culture – that seemed

35 M. M. Bakhtin, *Problems of Dostoevsky's Poetics*, 198 (italics in original).

36 Maryemma Graham and Amritjit Singh, eds, *Conversations with Ralph Ellison* (Jackson: University Press of Mississippi, 1995), 137–8. Note this text uses the spelling 'Dostoyevsky' and inserts 'the' into *Notes from Underground.*

to align itself most closely with Ellison's experience of being black in America. Of this, he was certain. Several years before he would encounter Bakhtin, Ellison had arrived at an insight that anticipated the Bakhtinian one. His own experience of alienation meshed with Dostoevsky's – not Kafka's – and it would be Dostoevsky's models of discourse to which he would turn time and again for confirmation and authorization of his own literary practice in the forty-odd years following the publication and triumph of *Invisible Man*.

Ellison's Blues: Revisiting 'Richard Wright's Blues' in the Context of *The House of the Dead*

Many commentators have focused on how Ellison, in selecting his literary 'ancestors' in his rebuttal to Irving Howe in 'The World and the Jug', distanced himself from an Afrocentric or African American-centric literary lineage as well as the Marxist/Leftist politics of his formative years as a writer.[37] While these are important extrapolations, in choosing his ancestors Ellison's primary objective was to *not* choose Richard Wright, whom Howe had lumped him with, and from whom he felt a strong need to set himself apart. 'I respected Wright's work and I knew him', Ellison declared, 'but this is not to say that he "influenced" me as significantly as you assume'.[38] For this reason, Ellison here suggested that Wright was a literary 'relative', not a writer who he would choose to align himself with as an aesthetic influence but one he was connected with through experience and circumstance. Ellison insisted that what had brought him together with Wright in the first place was not their 'common racial identity' but rather, their shared interest in modernist literature, and, most saliently here, their shared interest in the writings of Dostoevsky and

37 See, for example: Rampersad, *Ralph Ellison*, 121; Barbara Foley, *Wrestling with the Left: The Making of Ralph Ellison's* Invisible Man (Durham, NC: Duke University Press, 2010), 69–70.

38 Ellison, 'The World and the Jug', 185.

other contemporary writers such as Ernest Hemingway, André Malraux and James Joyce.[39]

Indeed, Ellison was always touchy about matters of priority and influence. He felt that Wright had always underestimated his own (Ellison's) learning, philosophical depth and intellectual sophistication. 'It was important to Ralph', Ellison's biographer, Arnold Rampersad, noted, 'to point out that he had read Dostoyevsky before meeting Wright: "He assumed that I hadn't read any of … Dostoyevsky … I was somewhat chagrined by his apparent condescension" '.[40] It was not merely indignation at Wright's presumption of ignorance that made Ellison bristle. They had both been reading and exploring Dostoevsky and the modern writers since they first met in the 1930s. Ellison felt that he had a more profound grasp than did Wright of the models of cultural critique that Dostoevsky provided to a writer attempting to translate his African American experience into the modern novel.

Looking back on his relationship with Wright, Ellison suggested that the older writer's presumptive condescension limited the free exchange of literary ideas between the two writers. Ellison said that Wright's 'underestimation made for a certain irony in our relationship; because sometimes, thanks to my own reading and quite different experience, I was in a position to have suggestions for solving problems from which he might have benefited'.[41] Ellison certainly, as Rampersad and Foley have demonstrated, concealed and minimized his involvement with Communist Party and Leftist activities during the period of his friendship with Wright, and therefore we must speculate with care about anything he may have read back into that period. Nonetheless, while Ellison does not specify what problems he might have helped Wright solve, I think we may reasonably propose that some of those suggestions concern his reading of Dostoevsky

39 Ibid., 185. For a recent study of Ellison's relationship to modernist authors, see Marc Conner, 'Father Abraham: Ellison's Agon with the Fathers in *Three Days before the Shooting …*', in Marc C. Conner and Lucas E. Morel, eds, *The New Territory: Ralph Ellison and the Twenty-First Century* (Jackson: University Press of Mississippi, 2016), 167–93.

40 Rampersad, *Ralph Ellison*, 121. Rampersad chooses the spelling, 'Dostoyevsky'.

41 Graham and Singh, *Conversations*, 323.

and Ellison's developing theories of literature and culture. When discussing his involvement with the left and Wright in the 1960s, Ellison, in a fairly candid moment, remarked:

> I never wrote the official type of fiction. I wrote what might be called propaganda – having to do with the Negro struggle – but my fiction was always trying to be something else; something different even from Wright's fiction. I never accepted the ideology which the *New Masses* attempted to impose on writers. They hated Dostoyevsky, but I was studying Dostoyevsky.[42]

Ellison's nonfiction of these years might be seen as propaganda, even by his own estimation, but his fiction, with its different embrace of folk-art culture, high and low, tragic and comic, philosophical and commonplace – and its Dostoevskyan models – separated his ideological critique from that found in the *New Masses* and from the fiction of Wright. We should recall that, in the creation of *Invisible Man*, Ellison felt that Dostoevsky allowed him to address 'more specialized concerns with fictional form and [deal] with certain problems arising out of the pluralistic literary tradition from which I spring', and that it was precisely these ideas that he began developing in the mid-1940s.[43] It then becomes clearer how Dostoevsky shaped the way Ellison read Wright, and how he assessed Wright's literary, political and social positions.

Hiding in plain sight is the evidence of Ellison's 1945 *Antioch Review* essay on Wright's memoir, *Black Boy*, entitled 'Richard Wright's Blues'. Bryan Crable has pointed out the influences of Kenneth Burke on Ellison's defence of Richard Wright's *Black Boy*, and as we saw in our discussion of Ellison's lecture on education, where Burke is invoked Dostoevsky also appears.[44] Among its crucial recognitions, Ellison's essay proposes that *Black Boy*, 'as a psychological document of life under oppressive conditions [...] recalls *The House of the Dead*, Dostoevsky's profound study of the humanity

42 Ibid., 124.

43 Ellison, *Invisible Man*, 30th Anniversary Edition, xviii.

44 Crable, *Ralph Ellison and Kenneth Burke*, 55–8. Crable here shows how Ellison's defence of the aesthetic value of *Black Boy* relies on Burke's 'pentad of dramatism' from *A Grammar of Motives* (1945).

of Russian criminals'.[45] As noted above, *The House of the Dead* was a crucial text for *Invisible Man* and Ellison's growing cultural theories of literature.[46] While Ellison would use *The House of the Dead* in *Invisible Man* to shape the lineaments of the complex African American underground and the conditions of cultural blindness that would render it invisible for the Caucasian-American establishment, it was in in 'Richard Wright's Blues' that he gave his Dostoevskyan ideas their first full utterance.

The most suggestive and telling moment arrives towards the end of the essay where Ellison, drawing on the African American literary critic and composer Edward Bland, describes the psychological qualities of the 'pre-individualistic black community' depicted in *Black Boy*.[47] With Wright's journey from the Deep South to the urban north in mind, Ellison discusses the psycho-social consequences of asserting one's individuality in the South in African American communities. The costs of such individualistic assertions – a virtual necessity for literary artists such as Wright or Ellison – were often brutal, and typically enforced by the black family as a form of 'behavior control', experience having taught them 'that the whole group is punished for the actions of the single member'.[48] Explaining the source of Wright's alienation not as a distortion of the black South but as a natural consequence of his temperament under these social conditions, Ellison describes how deeply the suppression of the individual through physical and psychological discipline had penetrated African American life, even as an expression of parental concern and love:

> Even parental love is given a qualitative balance akin to 'sadism', and the extent of beatings and psychological maimings meted out by Southern Negro parents rivals *those described by the nineteenth-century Russian writers as characteristic of peasant life under the Czars*.[49]

45 Ralph Ellison, 'Richard Wright's Blues', in John F. Callahan, ed., *The Collected Essays of Ralph Ellison* (New York: Modern Library, 1995), 129.

46 Barbara Foley has shown how this Dostoevsky text figured in Ellison's early fiction, especially in connection with Wright. See Foley, *Wrestling with the Left*, 138–9, for her discussion of 'The Initiation'.

47 Ellison, 'Richard Wright's Blues', 140.

48 Ibid.

49 Ibid., 141 (italics added).

In an essay studded with thick ethnographic descriptions of the conditions in both the American South and and its urban north, this is the only moment in which the cultural comparison reaches for a Western cultural analogue far beyond its place and time. Notably, it is a reference to Czarist Russia and the Russian writers who describe peasant life with its beatings within the brutal bonds of filial love.[50] While Ellison doubtless had a number of Russian writers in mind, the descriptions of specific whippings and the general culture of beatings in *The House of the Dead* must have served as a guide. The merciless beatings of a peasant daughter, Akoulka Koudimovna,[51] would have made a strong impression on Ellison, or the case of Alexander Petrovich, a prisoner who Dostoevsky relates had survived a punishment of 4,000 lashings. Petrovich explains his incredible durability this way:

> 'I only laughed at them. Why? Because, when I was a youngster, I had grown up under the whip. Well, I am well, and alive now; but I have been beaten in the course of my life', he repeated, with a passive air, as he brought his story to an end.[52]

In this way, Dostoevsky served Ellison as a measuring stick by which to explain the roots of Wright's negative reactions to African American family life. Whereas the other literary figures invoked in the essay are used to point out how *Black Boy* functions in terms of the role of art in general (André Malraux) or to distinguish its focus from other modernist classics (James Joyce's *Stephen Hero*), Dostoevsky is invoked as a figure who informs the social conditions upon which Wright's 'sensibility was nourished'.[53] While Joyce is invoked as an aesthetic model for Wright, and Nehru is invoked as a political example articulating a way towards freedom, Dostoevsky is invoked as a social model and a cultural parallel.

As with *The House of the Dead*, 'Richard Wright's Blues' takes up the problem of cultural blindness. Ellison's ultimate defence of *Black Boy*

50 Ibid., 134, contains one brief allusion to the regression and degradation experienced by the 'cultured inmates of Nazi prisons', but that is undoubtedly related more to the revelations of current events in 1945 than to Ellison's research.

51 Dostoevsky, *The House of the Dead*, 253–4.

52 Ibid., 216.

53 Ibid., 133.

suggests that the book does not depict a distortion of African American life in the South, but rather a general cultural and ideological blindness to its essential cruelty and to the zeal with which it crushes the individual that would have the temerity to break away. 'Why then have Southern whites, who claim to "know" the Negro', Ellison asks, 'missed all this?':

> Simply because they, too, are armored against the horror and the cruelty. Either they deny the Negro's humanity and feel no cause to measure his actions against civilized norms; or they protect themselves from their guilt in the Negro's condition, and from their fear.[54]

For Ellison, *Black Boy* becomes an occasion to begin articulating the confrontation with invisibility and the ideological armor that creates it for both blacks and whites alike. The younger author's essay discusses folk life in the South on much the same terms as *The House of the Dead* does Russian peasant life. Just as the Russian elite does not see beneath its own stereotyped vision of the peasantry, the white Southern world misses much of what that it needs to know about black culture even as it claims to know it. Indeed, Ellison offers even more detail than Dostoevsky could offer about the psychology of social blindness, of why these phenomena cannot be seen.

'Richard Wright's Blues' concludes with an invocation of the complex American underground that would become Ellison's great literary project. Ellison comes to the verdict that Wright's 'most important achievement' was that he 'converted' the African American 'impulse toward self-annihilation and "going under-ground" into a will to confront the world'.[55] Through the terrain of Dostoevsky (which he to an extent shared with Wright in this period), Ellison had found a way to articulate his own literary project by way of a defence of Wright: to use the space of the underground to confront the world.

By conceiving of Wright's work as the conversion of impulses into a cohesive literary expression that confronts what the culture has concealed or denied, Ellison began to indicate the terms on which he would

54 Ibid., 141.

55 Ibid., 144.

convert the ideological currents and social realities of his world into the cultural-symbolic literary system of *Invisible Man*. The usage of the term 'impulse' in this formulation is crucial. In defining *Black Boy* as an impulse converted into a statement, Ellison forges an analogue to the blues themselves, which he had defined as 'an impulse to keep the painful details and episodes of brutal experience alive in one's aching consciousness [...] and to transcend it [...] by squeezing from it a near-tragic, near-comic lyricism'.[56] Ellison selected privileged cultural geographies (the Territory, the Underground) and forms, typically drawn from African American popular culture, through which to communicate the literary pluralism at the heart of his work. In *Invisible Man*, the jazz of Louis Armstrong travelling over the lower frequencies of the American airwaves created the terms on which what could not be seen might be heard and might, consequently, speak for you. In 'Richard Wright's Blues', the blues themselves are the privileged cultural 'folk-art form'.[57]

In *The House of the Dead*, Dostoevsky describes the prison songs and the comic and tragic songs found in the peasant culture of Siberia. At a certain moment after hearing a convict orchestra, he came to understand, 'perfectly, and for the first time, the remarkable boldness, the striking abandonment, which are expressed in our popular dance tunes, and our village songs'.[58] Much as Dostoevsky had done, Ellison would stage for his readers significant moments of listening, as in his famous use of Armstrong in *Invisible Man*, and in his essay on *Black Boy* in which he asserts a fundamental sense of the blues as an aesthetic form that emerges out of a direct kind of human experience. Through all the blindness and ambiguities with which the reception of a folk-art form might be fraught, these cultural forms contain within in them, as Emily Lordi suggests in a related context, 'the unrealized promise of a pluralistic democracy'.[59] The tension that the blues expresses in a folk form in this way parallels Ellison's sense of what the modern literary memoir can or should do.

56 Ibid., 129.

57 Ibid., 129.

58 Dostoevsky, *The House of the Dead*, 181–2.

59 Emily J. Lordi, *Black Resonance: Iconic Women Singers and African American Literature* (New Brunswick, NJ: Rutgers University Press, 2013), 66.

In their correspondence, Wright dismissed Ellison's analysis of the blues pertaining to his own work. In a letter to Ellison written in July 1945 he explained:

> I think I mentioned over the phone that I did not see the blues concept; I do see it, but only very slightly. And surely not enough to play such an important rule [role] as you assigned it. I'm not trying to carp over the fact that it was a Negro expression form. I simply did not see it. The relationship is too slight. Your psychoanalytic concepts, on the other hand, were damn well used. But the blues concept is not on their level, not at all.[60]

Wright's reaction indicates that he simply did not see the blues as fundamental to his own modes of expression or symbolic matrix. Rather, that was Ellison's imposition on his work: the former undergraduate musician had offered a musical motif as a form of critique and a sign that he viewed Wright's work and its potentials for symbolic cultural critique in a different way.

Ellison's response to Wright's rejection of the blues was equally telling. On 11 August 1945, he replied:

> I didn't expect you to agree with them at all. About the blues I have a lot more to say [...]. Briefly, Black Boy [sic] is positive politically because it faced a tough situation honestly [.] But in a formal artistic sense it is regressive. [...] I see it as being at once more basic (in that it is concerned only with fundamentals without illusions which is the essence of the blues attitude) than your previous work, and less broad, because you have inverted your idealism and put your humanism in storage for more stable times. When Richard Wright exhibits the blues attitude that is a profound criticism of the present political atmosphere and of his own previous writings – even though an incomplete one.[61]

In this reply, we see the fuller meaning of what Ellison hinted at in the published essay. The 'blues attitude' expresses a narrowing of the social canvas, a retreat from the 'Marxist optimism, humanism of Native Son

60 Richard Wright, Letter to Ralph Ellison, 25 July 1945, Library of Congress, Ralph Ellison papers I:76, folder 2.

61 Ralph Ellison, Letter to Richard Wright, 11 August 1945, Library of Congress, Ralph Ellison papers I.76, folder 2.

and Twelve Million Black Voices' [sic].[62] In Ellison's estimation, the inadequacy of Wright's position represents a literary-political retreat and it would require the literary machinery of *Invisible Man* to position the blues within a cultural matrix of other folk-art forms and political positions. As Paul Allen Anderson has suggested, the figure of Pete Wheatstraw with his upset apple cart symbolically represented this critique.[63] Ellison's formulation of the blues, its cultural significance, and what roles it might play in modern literature are connected to his growing convictions about the power of Dostoevsky's models, and he sought to operationalize the blues and other related forms in terms of Dostoevsky's poetics. This perspective was coming into view for him in 1945 and would find its expression in *Invisible Man*. It would also find expression in most of the writing he would do, both critically and fictionally, from that point on.

Ellison's Marginalia: Cultural Comparativism, the Dostoevskyan Genesis of *Three Days* and 'Cliofus and the Russian Novel'

The Library of Congress holdings of Ralph Ellison's personal library contain thirty-eight English-language volumes pertaining to Dostoevsky. Of these, twenty are primary sources and eighteen are secondary, either critical or biographical. The earliest of the primary materials are the Constance Garnett translations from the 1920s and the latest are a deluxe illustrated Franklin Library edition of Jessie Coulson's translation of *Crime and Punishment* from 1982. The earliest inscriptions in Ellison's hand date to 1942, *The Insulted and the Injured* and *The Gambler and Other Stories*, both Garnett translations. The earliest of the secondary materials is Boris Brasol's *The Mighty Three: Poushkin, Gogol, Dostoievsky. A Critical Trilogy* ([sic] 1936) and the latest is a personally inscribed copy of his friend

62 Ralph Ellison, Draft Letter to Richard Wright, 11 August 1945, Library of Congress, Ralph Ellison papers I.76, folder 2.

63 Anderson, 'Ralph Ellison's Music Lessons', 89–90.

Joseph Frank's *Dostoevsky: The Seeds of Revolt, 1821–1849* (1976). Many of the volumes have been annotated, underscored in pen and pencil, marked with yellow and orange highlighter, and peppered with marginalia; these extensive markings point to Ellison's scholarly, critical, pedagogical and fictive activities before and after the publication of *Invisible Man*. As a whole they indicate much more than literary ancestry, but rather a lifelong pursuit and touchstone for all of Ellison's career.

Reading over Ellison's shoulder in his studies of Dostoevsky affords a fascinating view of how he used that Russian novelist to filter a host of modern literary figures and concerns, welding together the nineteenth century with the twentieth. Through the scene of Ellison's reading of Dostoevsky, we can approach the scene of writing. Here, we see the American author as critic and literary artist, suturing the two activities together in a web of literary connection crucial to his art. For example, Ellison scholarship has long been aware of André Malraux's influence, especially *Man's Fate* (*La Condition Humaine*) and *The Psychology of Art*, and in connection with these works the function of art in the grandest terms and in revolutionary times has been the point of emphasis.[64] In a passage in Donald Fanger's *Dostoevsky and Romantic Realism: A Study of Dostoevsky in Relation to Balzac, Dickens, and Gogol* (1965) – which Ellison owned – we encounter a passage dealing with Dostoevsky's *A Raw Youth* (*The Adolescent*) and the concept of character. This passage is strikingly reminiscent of Ellison's discussion of character in his 1981 introduction to *Invisible Man*. Fanger discusses how Dostoevsky's characters do not delineate change *per se*, but rather oscillate with escalating intensity between polar extremes. Fanger concludes, 'He does not so much develop as progressively express this self-division and so advance to meet his tragic fate'.[65] Ellison underscored this passage in pencil and noted in the margin 'Malraux's too'. If our scholarship has tended to compartmentalize Ellison's influences, obtaining a single concept from a single author perhaps too

64 See, for example, Rampersad, *Ralph Ellison*, 119–20; Anderson, 'Ralph Ellison's Music Lessons', 84.

65 Donald Fanger, *Dostoevsky and Romantic Realism: A Study of Dostoevsky in Relation to Balzac, Dickens, and Gogol* (Cambridge, MA: Harvard University Press, 1965), 220.

neatly, then in his ongoing studies of Dostoevsky we see him synthesizing a series of literary connections and insights. From Invisible Man to Alonzo Hickman and Bliss/Severin (in *Three Days before the Shooting …*) we encounter Ellison creating precisely this kind of character, not one who goes through clear-cut transformation, but rather one who oscillates between poles, advancing towards his fate.

Similar connections can be made to the work of Ernest Hemingway, another author who is always mentioned as part of Ellison's pantheon but seldom in explicit connection with Dostoevsky. In Steiner's *Tolstoy or Dostoevsky*, there is an extended commentary on *The Idiot* in which that scholar details Dostoevsky's handling of the masochistic psychology of abjection and the way pride finds its 'most refined pleasures in self-damnation'.[66] In a pivotal scene in which Nastasya Filippovna taunts Prince Myshkin, Steiner admires the intuitive qualities of the dialogue, and Ellison underscored the observation that, 'in the rage of action the characters experience moments of total insight. Language itself is pouring out its secrets'. Ellison wrote in the margin by the dialogue Steiner quotes from *The Idiot*: 'Brett in The Sun Also Rises'.[67] And we encounter something similar in the American novelist's copy of Bakhtin's *Problems of Dostoevsky's Poetics*: a discussion of *The Gambler* is highlighted in which Bakhtin analyses how the 'Russians abroad' depicted therein constitute a '*carnival collective* which considers itself to be a certain degree outside the norms and order of ordinary life […] in an atmosphere of scandal'.[68] Once again in the margin appears: 'The Sun Also Rises'. A few pages later, on the margins of Bakhtin's commentary on carnivalization in *The Idiot* – a discussion of Prince Myshkin's inability to occupy a specific position in life and his ability to penetrate the lives others by remaining tangential to his own existence – Ellison wrote, 'Jake Barnes is somewhat akin to Myshkin'.[69] It is beyond the scope of this essay to demonstrate the specific ways that Ellison utilized this connection between *The Sun Also Rises* and Dostoevsky's *The Idiot* and *The Gambler*, but his ongoing reading and thinking *through*

66 Steiner, *Tolstoy or Dostoevsky*, 165.

67 Ibid., 165–6.

68 Bakhtin, *Problems of Dostoevsky's Poetics*, 143 (italics in original).

69 Ibid., 145.

Dostoevsky was indubitably definitive in his mapping and re-mapping of the terrain of modern literature.

Perhaps the most important insight that Ellison's annotations of Dostoevsky yield concerns the fundamental problem of the relationship between the nineteenth-century Russia depicted in Dostoevsky's works and the African American scene that Ellison wished to mine for his material. Ellison's literary pluralism depended on an ongoing comparatist approach, and Steiner's study was particularly valuable to him in this area. Dozens of passages comparing American literature and culture to that of Russia are marked or highlighted in Ellison's personal copy.[70] Steiner's contention (following Harry Levin) that, 'the psychological and material circumstances' that led to the developments in Russian literature 'were present also on the American scene, and it is through American eyes that some of them may be most clearly perceived', was precisely the kind of critical move that enabled Ellison's study of American literature and experience by way of Dostoevsky.[71] The marginal note on page 33 reveals not simply recognition, but Ellison's germinative critique. Where Steiner suggests that 'the uncertainties of taste' and style found in the authors of the American renaissance might be attributable to their having produced their works in 'relative isolation', Ellison adds to it: 'Not only this but a certain moral honesty was missing in most of the reading public'.[72] In this pithy comment we see the seeds of the moral argumentation for the novel Ellison would promote in his critical essays, notably in *Going to the Territory* (1986), where he explores the moral capacities and blindness of both the artist and the audience as they collaborate in creating a shared social vision.

Ellison's annotations in his copy of Steiner's monograph reveal a remarkable intensification of homologies between Russian situations found in Dostoevsky's novels and American conditions. Another example of marginal commentary in pen (on page 309 of *Tolstoy or Dostoevsky?*) reveals

70 See Steiner, *Tolstoy or Dostoevsky*?; pages 31 and 33 in Ellison's personal copy show two examples, one of his highlighting on page 31 (the use of the fluorescent yellow highlighter indicates that those passages were marked in the 1970s or 1980s), and there is marginal commentary in pen on page 33.

71 Ibid., 31.

72 Ibid., 33.

Ellison working through Steiner's analysis of a quasi-hallucinatory scene in *The Possessed* (also known as *The Devils* or *The Demons*) in which Marya Timofeyevna describes her single motherhood and its conclusion in infanticide: 'What I weep for most is that I had a baby and I never had a husband'.[73] This prompts Ellison's marginal ruminations on African American mothers:

> For negro mothers the question is: how many saviors, did you birth, abort, or have killed by the welfare or by being kicked in the stomach. Mothers----→This is an answer for Negro mothers[?] who are scorned for <u>not</u> having husbands.[74]

Dostoevsky's text becomes the point of departure for his working up a series of concerns touching on the complex of violence and shaming that African American single mothers might have faced. Even more remarkable still, this appears to be the origin of Maud's dream in Book II of *Three Days before the Shooting ...*.

Among Jessie Rockmore's lodgers, readers will recall Maud's impassioned recollection to Alonzo Hickman and Deacon Wilhite of her dream about having given birth to three children only to be dispossessed of them:

> Was I wrong ... I mean when my own folks scorned me and called me a bitch ... was I wrong when I said to those women who I thought were my good friends and had them turn against me: 'All right, all right now', I said, 'How many little saviors have y'all thrown into the garbage can or flushed down the toilet? How many of you women who're out here calling *me* a bitch have had a little savior to die because of your just wanting to live free off the Welfare? And how many of you have lost your chance to raise up a little black savior by being kicked in the belly by your evil boyfriends or no-good husbands?'[75]

In his re-staging of the scene from Dostoevsky's *The Possessed*, Ellison carefully structures the impact of Maud's monologue – which is an Americanized version of *skaz*, the Russian term for a narrative technique related to the spoken word in contradistinction to more literary or written styles of narration – so that the impact of the speech is registered

73 Quoted in ibid., 309.

74 Ibid., 309.

75 Ralph Ellison, *Three Days before the Shooting ...*, eds, John. F. Callahan and Adam Bradley (New York: Modern Library, 2010), 453.

dramatically. Moved and troubled by Maud's story, Hickman is forced to go beyond his stock repertoire of replies in order to answer her with some measure of honesty. He recognizes the ways in which Maud has exposed his own racial identity, calling it 'strong medicine' that makes 'everybody recall their own dreams and frustrations and guilt'.[76] In a book that was crafted episodically it seems that the connections and resonances between characters and narrative elements are achieved through instances of recognition and misrecognition. Dostoevsky appears to have served Ellison as the theoretical binding agent connecting these moments together.

This is by no means the only instance of Ellison using his critical investigations of Dostoevsky as material for the lifelong project that would become his unfinished novel. While reading Bakhtin's discussion of carnivalization of the nether world in *Problems of Dostoevsky's Poetics*, Ellison wrote the following marginal note on page 110: 'Bert Williams "Take Away those Pearly Gates"'.[77] Here he refers to 'O Death Where is Thy Sting?', a 1918 recording by the pioneering African American Vaudevillean and comedian, Bert Williams. In the relevant passage, Bakhtin discusses the social levelling and reversals that take place underground and in the underworld itself. 'In the representation of the nether world the carnival logic of "the world upside down" was often applied. In the nether world the emperor becomes slave, the slave – emperor, etc.'[78] In the Williams song, a parson's Sunday sermon describes a fiery hell filled with booze and sinful women and a parishioner objects to the sermon, saying he no longer cares about the 'pearly gates'.[79] This same association turns up in *Three Days*, in a scene (narrated by Jessie Blackmore's faithful retainer, McMillan) in which Blackmore, on the threshold of death, engages a white prostitute, Cordelia Duval:

> So Mister Jessie just looked at her awhile. Then he said, 'And have you been practicing your present profession long?'

76 Ibid., 452.

77 Bakhtin, *Problems of Dostoevsky's Poetics*, 110.

78 Ibid., 109–10.

79 Bert Williams, 'O Death Where Is Thy Sting?' Smithsonian Folkways Recordings (1981), n.p., <https://folkways.si.edu/bert-williams/o-death-where-is-thy-sting/american-popular-humor/track/smithsonian>, accessed 15 April 2020.

> And the lady said, 'Long enough to know all the tricks, Dad. You know any new ones? I think you're trying to insult me, Dad. I was in the Follies and I knew Flo Ziegfeld and Will Rogers and I knew that spook boy Bert Williams too. He was a great performer and real cute when took off his greasepaint. And wasn't he a riot when he walked around pecking in his rooster costume! 'Ah ain't evah done nothing to *no*body', he used to sing, and 'Take Away Those Pearly Gates' was another. We were all friends together and they were all sweet to me!'[80]

The prudent, abstemious Blackmore, sensing his end, has contrived a night of revelry while seated in his coffin, a night involving a case of whisky and the prostitute. Duval's scene culminates in a drunken dance in a garment of expired American currency. Just as a stranger enters unexpectedly, Rockmore dies upright in his coffin.

In this telescoping concatenated narrative which oscillates between blackness and whiteness alternate – a black narrator addressing a white reporter describes the vernacular voices of his boss, and a white female prostitute describes the songs of a black entertainer who performed in greasepaint – Ellison contrives from another Dostoevskyan gambit a scene in which a proliferation of Bakhtinian carnivalesque reversals ensues. The prostitute becomes queen, hell becomes heaven, an African American performer takes off his greasepaint and appears white, the white prostitute performs a dance in the manner of Josephine Baker, and the earthiest lowdown debauchery becomes the most elevated moment of humanity. As the scene plays out in its second version, in Book II, the pearly gates of the Bert Williams song become the White House Gates where Jessie Blackmore places himself in proper relationship to the president of the United States. The alienation and pluralism that had informed Ellison's cultural perspective from the gestation of *Invisible Man* find their expression in a carnival of reversal.

The final example I would like to address comes from the manuscripts in the Ralph Ellison papers in the Library of Congress. A folder of drafts (with a provisional title, 'Cliofus and the Russian Novel') that did not make it into *Three Days before the Shooting* ..., ones that date roughly to 1982, contain a story narrated by Cliofus, a character who appears in

80 Ralph Ellison, *Three Days before the Shooting* ..., 158–9.

the 'Hickman in Georgia & Oklahoma' section of *Three Days before the Shooting* .... Cliofus was raised together with Severin by Janey Glover and is gifted with extraordinary improvisational narrative powers; he is described by Ellison as 'word-drunk',[81] and by Callahan and Bradley as a 'teller of tall tales',[82] and in the published text he regales Hickman. In the episode in the draft manuscript, Cliofus describes his experience reading a 'Russian novel'. As with much of this late writing, it is framed in multiple ways as something that has been related to McIntyre, but the core of it is essentially retold in the more colloquial register of Cliofus's voice. Without mentioning the title of the work, it is made clear that Cliofus is reading *The Brothers Karamazov* and is attempting to make that novel correlate to his own community in a very direct set of correspondences:

> It was a story about some brothers who are disgusted with their father for being such a dog-butted Russian-style woman-chaser and money-waster. At first it was kind of confusing because it took place back in the 19th century and because I didn't know too much about Russians – but I got the chippy-chasing and money-wasting part right away. The one who was doing it was the boy's father who had been cashing in on some property which the sons had been left by their mothers – who were different women – and he'd been throwing it away on his whores. He was also a liquor-head and a kind of Bugs Bunny type liked to put everybody down and was notorious for chasing anything wearing skirts .... But what got things heated up was his trying to take a girl away from one of his own sons.[83]

In the various drafts, Ellison describes Cliofus – either in a dreaming or waking state – carrying out the central task of matching up scenes in the Dostoevsky with those in his Oklahoma community:

> So by looking at those Russians in light of folks I knew, and by asking myself who among us had done something similar to what those Russians were doing I realized there was nothing really new about families fighting over property, or about an old man chasing a chippy.[84]

81 Ellison, *Three Days*, 860.

82 John F. Callahan and Adam Bradley, 'General Introduction' to Ralph Ellison, *Three Days before the Shooting* ... (New York: Modern Library, 2010), xvii.

83 Ralph Ellison, 'Cliofus and the Russian Novel', MS, Library of Congress, Ralph Ellison papers I:117, folder 2.

84 Ibid.

As with all that Ellison writes, a complex narrative layering animates this central task: Cliofus's ruminations on matching up African American locals with their Russian counterparts is intercut with another plot about a local shooting, thereby connecting it to the main plot of *Three Days*. The cultural work of the episode, indeed the dreamwork of it (as part of this correlation takes place in a dream), is to imagine in vernacular terms the basis for Ellison's literary pluralism. The act of reading Dostoevsky and then processing that act in terms of one's own locality and experience gives rise to a commentary on cultural parallels.

In this way we return to that fundamental issue for Ellison that I address earlier in the first part of this chapter: the phonemic and phonetic distinction that fundamentally alters our perspective on Ellison's literary pluralism in just such a way that global literary study has promised. With this episode of Cliofus's attempt to assimilate *The Brothers Karamazov* into 'The Territory', so to speak, we see an example of the routes by which literary pluralism might arrive and instantiate itself in a vernacular culture. Ellison attempted to dramatize how one culture might serve as an analogue for another, no matter how very different the places and times might seem to be. As with all of his engagement with Dostoevsky, Ellison posits a strong homological connection between the Russian peasant experience of the nineteenth century and the African American experience in the twentieth. It appears that while he arrived at this homology very early on in his literary career, he never stopped attempting to verify, confirm and corroborate it. Indeed, it is not too much to say that Dostoevsky's work and the critical tradition it has engendered formed for Ellison a complex literary underground which we are only now beginning to uncover.

Bibliography

Anderson, Paul Allen, 'Ralph Ellison's Music Lessons', in Ross Posnock, ed., *The Cambridge Companion to Ralph Ellison* (Cambridge, UK: Cambridge University Press, 2005), 82–103.

Bakhtin, M. M. *Problems of Dostoevsky's Poetics*, trans. R. W. Rotsel (Ann Arbor: University of Michigan Press, 1973).

Bone, Robert A., *The Negro Novel in America* (New Haven, CT: Yale University Press, 1958).

Burke, Kenneth, 'Literature as Equipment for Living', in Stanley Edgar Hyman, ed., *Perspectives by Incongruity* (Bloomington: Indiana University Press, 1964), 100–9.

Callahan, John F. and Adam Bradley, 'General Introduction' to Ralph Ellison, *Three Days before the Shooting …* (New York: Modern Library, 2010), xv–xxix.

Cash, Earl A., 'The Narrators in *Invisible Man* and *Notes from the Underground*: Brothers in Spirit', *CLA Journal* 16/4 (1973), 505–7.

Conner, Marc. 'Father Abraham: Ellison's Agon with the Fathers *in Three Days before the Shooting …*', in Marc C. Conner and Lucas E. Morel, eds, *The New Territory: Ralph Ellison and the Twenty-First Century* (Jackson: University Press of Mississippi, 2016), 167–93.

Crable, Bryan, *Ralph Ellison and Kenneth Burke: At the Roots of the Racial Divide* (Charlottesville and London: University of Virginia Press, 2011).

Dostoevsky, Fyodor, *The House of the Dead; or, Prison Life in Siberia*, Project Gutenberg (1911): <http://www.gutenberg.org/files/37536/37536-h/37536-h.htm>, accessed 15 April 2020.

——, *Notes from Underground*, trans. Boris Jakim (Grand Rapids, MI and Cambridge, UK: William B. Erdmans Publishing Company, 2009).

——, 'On Bird, Bird-Watching and Jazz', in *The Collected Essays of Ralph Ellison*, ed., John F. Callahan (New York: Modern Library, 1995), 256–65.

——, 'Cliofus and the Russian Novel', MS, Library of Congress, Ralph Ellison papers I:117, folder 2.

——, *Invisible Man* (New York: Random House, 1952).

——, *Invisible Man*, 30th Anniversary Edition (New York: Random House, 1982).

——, *Juneteenth* (New York: Random House, 1999).

——, Letter to Richard Wright, 11 August 1945, Library of Congress, Ralph Ellison papers I:76, folder 2.

——, 'Richard Wright's Blues', in John F. Callahan, ed., *The Collected Essays of Ralph Ellison* (New York: Modern Library, 1995), 128–44.

——, *Three Days before the Shooting …*, (New York: Modern Library, 2010).

——, 'What America Would Be Like without Blacks', in John F. Callahan, ed., *The Collected Essays of Ralph Ellison* (New York: Modern Library, 1995), 577–84.

——, 'What These Children Are Like', in John F. Callahan, ed., *The Collected Essays of Ralph Ellison* (New York: Modern Library, 1995), 542–51.

——, 'The World and the Jug', in John F. Callahan, ed., *The Collected Essays of Ralph Ellison* (New York: Modern Library, 1995), 155–88.

Fanger, Donald, *Dostoevsky and Romantic Realism: A Study of Dostoevsky in Relation to Balzac, Dickens, and Gogol* (Cambridge, MA: Harvard University Press, 1965).

Foley, Barbara, *Wrestling with the Left: The Making of Ralph Ellison's* Invisible Man (Durham, NC: Duke University Press, 2010).

Frank, Joseph, 'On Ralph Ellison and a "Literary Ancestor": Dostoevsky', MS, Library of Congress, Ralph Ellison papers I:48, folder 2.

——, 'Ralph Ellison and a Literary "Ancestor": Dostoevski', in Kimberly W. Benston, ed., *Speaking for You: The Vision of Ralph Ellison* (Washington, DC: Howard University Press, 1987), 231–44.

Goede, William, 'On Lower Frequencies: The Buried Men in Wright and Ellison', *Modem Fiction Studies* 15 (1969), 483–92.

Graham, Maryemma and Amritjit Singh, eds, *Conversations with Ralph Ellison* (Jackson: University Press of Mississippi, 1995).

Jackson, Esther M., 'The American Negro and the Image of the Absurd', *Phylon* 23/ 4 (1962), 359–71.

Lordi, Emily J., *Black Resonance: Iconic Women Singers and African American Literature* (New Brunswick, NJ: Rutgers University Press, 2013).

Morris, Wright, 'The World Below: *Invisible Man.* by Ralph Ellison. 439 pp. New York: Random House. $3.50', *New York Times* (13 April 1952).

Moten, Fred, *In the Break: The Aesthetics of the Black Radical Tradition* (Minneapolis: University of Minnesota Press, 2003).

Muyumba, Walton M., *The Shadow and the Act: Black Intellectual Practice, Jazz Improvisation, and Philosophical Pragmatism* (Chicago: University of Chicago Press, 2009).

'The Ralph Ellison Collection, (1937–2010)', finding aid, <https://findingaids.loc.gov/exist_collections/ead3pdf/rbc/2016/rb016001.pdf>, accessed 22 May 2020.

Rampersad, Arnold, *Ralph Ellison* (New York: Alfred A. Knopf, 2007).

Steiner, George, *Tolstoy or Dostoevsky: An Essay in the Old Criticism* (New York: Alfred A. Knopf, 1959).

Warren, Kenneth, *So Black and Blue: Ralph Ellison and the Occasion of Criticism* (Chicago: University of Chicago Press, 2003).

Williams, Bert, 'O Death Where Is Thy Sting?' Smithsonian Folkways Recordings (1981), <https://folkways.si.edu/bert-williams/o-death-where-is-thy-sting/american-popular-humor/track/smithsonian>, accessed 15 April 2020.

Wright, John S., 'Ellison's Experimental Attitude and the Technologies of Illumination', in Ross Posnock, ed., *The Cambridge Companion to Ralph Ellison* (Cambridge, UK: Cambridge University Press, 2005), 157–71.

Wright, Richard, Letter to Ralph Ellison, 25 July 1945, Library of Congress, Ralph Ellison papers I:76, folder 2.

PART II

Ellison in the World: Translations and Receptions

ARETHA PHIRI

5 (In)visible Man: Tracing Ralph Ellison's Legacy to South Africa

ABSTRACT:
This chapter is concerned with Ralph Ellison's reception by and influence on Africa and Africans generally, and South Africa and South Africans in particular. Focusing on *Invisible Man*'s transnational, diasporic impulse and resonance, the chapter expands on predominantly Americanist readings of the author by tracing and exploring his legacy to Africa and specific relatedness to (apartheid and post-apartheid) South Africa. Arguing that receptions of Ellison in this context are frequently elusive, and often controversial, this chapter maintains that this novelist's critical and artistic problematization of identity politics, broadly understood, goes some way towards explaining his enduringly ambiguous and complicated status in the South African national (literary) consciousness in particular.

Published in 1952 and awarded the coveted National Book Award in 1953, *Invisible Man* was hailed a literary masterpiece. Ranked in the 100 best English-language novels in *Time* magazine and reprinted by Penguin as recently as 2014, it has cemented its place in the post-war American canon. Shaping, through an anonymous protagonist, a narrative about the quest for identity in the face of racial oppression and subjective erasure, *Invisible Man* apparently reflected the temper of a changing global political climate. This included burgeoning civil rights movements and simultaneous black nationalist politics in America, as well as growing global impatience with Western imperialism evident in a protracted Cold War (1947–91) and in Africa's liberatory, pan-Africanist decolonization movements from the 1950s onwards.

But where established Ellisonian scholarship is typically preoccupied with his contributions to the idea of America, this chapter is concerned with Ellison's reception by and influence on Africa and Africans generally, and South Africa and South Africans in particular. Robert Butler maintained, in 2016, that if we are to gain a fuller, more comprehensive knowledge of the author and his extraordinary novel, 'We need not only to build upon [the existing] large body of research and criticism but also step clear of it for a while and develop a fresh look at the book'.[1] Where John F. Callahan links *Invisible Man*'s 'embodiment of an open, responsive, literary text' formally to 'Ellison's commitment to an American improvisatory vernacular',[2] I am interested in its transnational, diasporic impulse and resonance, a significant factor often overlooked in (American) academic circles.[3] In order to expand on the many Americanist readings of the author in this way, this chapter takes up the challenge proffered by Butler by tracing Ellison's legacy to South Africa, a country that in its post-apartheid, post utopian moment continues, not unlike (black) America, its 'search for new systems of social organization and creative values'.[4] Exploring his specific relatedness to South Africa, the chapter argues that receptions of Ellison in this context are frequently elusive, and often controversial. In accordance with this reading, this chapter maintains that this novelist's critical and artistic problematization of identity politics, broadly understood, goes some way towards explaining his enduringly ambiguous and complicated status in the South African national (literary) consciousness in particular. In the analyses that follow, I first explore the ways in which Ellison both positioned himself and has been understood by scholars in relation to US-centred black nationalism, to Pan-Africanism and to African independence movements. Second, I map out the varied and often-conflicting receptions of Ellison's novel by literary critics, social commentators and political figures in South Africa from the 1950s to the present day, interweaving these with biographical details about the often-enigmatic and contradictory-seeming

1 Robert Butler, '*Invisible Man* and the Politics of Love', in Marc C. Conner and Lucas E. Morel, eds, *The New Territory: Ralph Ellison and the Twenty-First Century* (Jackson: University of Mississippi Press, 2016), 13.

2 John F Callahan, 'Frequencies of Eloquence: The Performance and Composition of *Invisible Man*', in Robert O'Meally, ed., *New Essays on Invisible Man* (New York: Cambridge University Press, 1988), 89.

3 Among exceptions here is Sara Marzioli's 'Ralph Ellison's Exceptional Diaspora: The View from Rome', *Atlantic Studies* 9/4 (2012), 447–66.

4 Larry Neal, 'Ellison's Zoot Suit', in John Hersey, ed., *Ralph Ellison: A Collection of Critical Essays* (Englewood Cliffs, NJ: Prentice-Hall, 1974), 63.

writer himself. And third, I draw on interviews that I have conducted with current or recent South Africa-based academics and students, in order to analyse the way *Invisible Man* has been taught, received and discussed in that country in recent decades.

Ellison's Complex Relationship to Black Politics

In order to make sense of the ostensibly divergent responses to Ellison and of his complicated position, it is important to decipher what underpins the ambivalence that has characterized his career and his place in the literary canon. For his intellectual literary contributions, Ellison received numerous endowments, was persistently courted – including internationally – as a nationally representative artist, and was awarded the highest honour of the Presidential Medal of Freedom in 1969. Indeed, a self-identified 'Negro' American writer concerned with enunciating a distinctive yet inclusive and influential culture, he was embraced by the literary establishment as an exemplar of a sophisticated aesthetic and discourse which, embedded in a (highbrow) modernist tradition, indicated his shift from a previously liberal, communist politics and aligned him with the literary elite.[5] At the same time, enhancing a chorus of established scholarship (such as Bellow 1952, Hyman 1964, Warren 1965 and Vogler 1970)[6] that lays claim to a better understanding of Ellison's ideology and legacy, Larry Neal's revised interpretation of *Invisible Man* (in 1970) – as a novel attempting 'to construct its own universe, based on

5 See Michael Nowlin, 'Ralph Ellison, James Baldwin, and the Liberal Imagination', *The Arizona Quarterly* 60/2 (2004), 117–40.

6 Saul Bellow, 'Man Underground', *Commentary* 13/6 (1952), 608–10; Stanley Edgar Hyman, 'Ralph Ellison in Our Time', *The New Leader* 47/22 (1964), 21–2; Robert Penn Warren, 'The Unity of Experience', *Commentary* 39/5 (1965), 91–6; Thomas A. Vogler, 'Invisible Man: Somebody's Protest Novel', *The Iowa Review* 1/2 (1970), 64–82.

its own imperatives' – maintained that 'all Black [American] creative artists owe Ellison a special gratitude'.[7]

Declarations such as that, 'At bottom, *Invisible Man* is a book for citizens, especially American citizens',[8] add to the sentiment that Ellison's 'extraordinary and arguably singular achievement as an American intellectual still goes unrecognized'.[9] As the introduction to this volume documents, many critics today continue to focus on the narrative of Ellison as a quintessentially, distinctly American writer concerned both with problematizing post-war American realism and illuminating its ideal promise of a 'cosmopolitan democracy'.[10] The recent collection of essays entitled *The New Territory: Ralph Ellison and the Twenty-First Century* (2016), in its consideration of the novelist in an ostensibly post-racial, post-black Obama era, is primarily concerned with the infinitely complex and visionary 'American character' of Ellisonian philosophy.[11]

Yet, for all the accumulated prestige and associated fervent critical commitment to an American ideal, this writer and his monumental novel have not escaped negative receptions, both during his lifetime and afterwards. Following Irving Howe's dismissal, in 1952, of *Invisible Man* as stylistically and thematically pretentious, and as atypical of black 'protest'

7 Larry Neal, 'Politics as Ritual: Ellison's Zoot Suit', *Black World* (1970), 50. Neal had, in a previous 1967 review, expressed his view that Ellison seemed 'awed by Western literary criticism and aesthetics' and did not 'attempt to move toward the development of a new Black aesthetic theory as other Black artists have done'. See Ernest Kaiser, 'A Critical Look at Ellison's Fiction and at Social and Literary Criticism by and about the Author', *Black World* 20 (December 1970), 83.

8 Lucas E. Morel, 'Ralph Ellison's Democratic Individualism', in Lucas E. Morel, ed., *Ralph Ellison and the Raft of Hope: A Political Companion to* Invisible Man (Lexington: University Press of Kentucky, 2004), 77.

9 Timothy Parrish, *Ralph Ellison and the Genius of America* (Iowa City: University of Iowa Press, 2012), 5.

10 Ross Posnock, 'Introduction', in Ross Posnock, ed., *The Cambridge Companion to Ralph Ellison* (Cambridge, UK: Cambridge University Press, 2005), 1.

11 Marc C. Conner and Lucas E. Morel, 'Introduction', in Conner and Morel, eds, *The New Territory: Ralph Ellison and the Twenty-First Century* (Jackson: University of Mississippi Press, 2016), 3.

writing,[12] some contemporaneous reviews of the novel denounced its (anti-Communist) contempt for and distortive representation of African Americans.[13] And years later, Ernest Kaiser's 1970 review for the *Black World* pronounced *Invisible Man* a 'contrived novel' that 'has nothing to do with the Black man's reality in America'.[14] Barbara Foley's recent examination in *Wrestling with the Left* (2010), meanwhile, which reads in this 'conflicted and contradictory text' the multiple 'traces of his struggle to repress then abolish the ghost of his leftist consciousness and conscience',[15] finally laments Ellison's ideological abandonment and literary excision of a radical, Marxist working-class consciousness. Her reading effectively resonates with biographer Arnold Rampersad's observation that Ellison's sense of place in the black world in particular was 'bedevil[led]'.[16] Rampersad posits that in a twentieth-century, global era of growing anti-racist, anti-colonial black consciousness, the novelist was apparently detached from and indifferent to the socio-political challenges of black America.

In his 2015 study, *African American Political Thought and American Culture*, Alex Zamalin maintains that the 'great irony was that Ellison himself could never fully embody the political and social democratic commitment his work had been trying to illustrate to Americans for almost half a century'.[17] Zamalin further observes that:

> For all his public lectures and speeches at prestigious universities from the 1950s through the 1960s, Ellison, unlike [James] Baldwin, joined very few Civil Rights marches and remained stubbornly loyal to President Lyndon Johnson even as the Vietnam War became increasingly unpopular. Ellison was embarrassingly antifeminist,

12 Irving Howe, 'Black Boys and Native Sons', in John Hersey, ed., *Ralph Ellison: A Collection of Critical Essays* (Englewood Cliffs, NJ: Prentice-Hall, 1974), 36–8.

13 See Kaiser, 'A Critical Look at Ellison's Fiction', 53–97.

14 Ibid., 81–4.

15 Barbara Foley, *Wrestling with the Left: The Making of Ralph Ellison's Invisible Man* (London: Duke University Press, 2010), 7.

16 Arnold Rampersad, *Ralph Ellison: A Biography* (New York: Alfred A. Knopf, 2007), 234.

17 Alex Zamalin, *African American Political Thought and American Culture: The Nation's Struggle for Racial Justice* (New York: Palgrave Macmillan, 2015), 70.

> sometimes even homophobic and, unlike one of his own mentors, Langston Hughes, selfishly refused to assist young black writers.[18]

While he was derided by several younger black writers as having 'sold out', and chided by many African American students as an 'Uncle Tom',[19] Toni Morrison's recollection in 2004 of her limited engagement with Ellison suggests her own sense of his elitism: 'My suspicion was that he considered himself an exception. He got to speak for us but he did not like to be identified with us'.[20] Growing increasingly disenchanted with a Harlem community of writers that included his initial mentors, Richard Wright and Langston Hughes,[21] Ellison certainly shied away from the 'easy rhetoric of black separatism or of racial chauvinism'.[22] While obviously cognizant of and concerned about American racial and socio-economic inequity, this type of criticism suggests that he was seen by many to have retreated to and found sanctuary in an apparently (self-)indulgent intellectual individualism.

In distancing himself from a radical black separatist politics, Ellison was explicitly derisive of the suppositions made therein of an African heritage. Hostile to black nationalist invocations of a 'mythical internationalism' which, fixated on African roots, ostensibly 'hindered the development of a national consciousness among American Negroes',[23] he was impatient with contemporaneous 'heady invocations of European, African and Asian backgrounds accompanied by chants of proclaiming the inviolability of ancestral blood'.[24] Foregrounding the civil rights and lived experiences of

18 Ibid., 79.

19 Kaiser, 'A Critical Look at Ellison's Fiction', 93–5 and Rampersad, *Ralph Ellison*, 440.

20 Rampersad, *Ralph Ellison*, 488.

21 See chapters 1 and 17 in Lawrence Jackson, *Ralph Ellison: Emergence of Genius* (Athens: University of Georgia Press, 2007).

22 Hollie West, 'Exploring the Life of a Not So Visible Man', in Maryemma Graham and Amritjit Singh, eds, *Conversations with Ralph Ellison* (Jackson: University of Mississippi Press, 1995), 239.

23 Foley, *Wrestling with the Left*, 51.

24 Ralph Ellison, 'Shadow and Act: Introduction', in John F. Callahan, ed., *The Collected Essays of Ralph Ellison* (New York: Modern Library, 2003), 59.

what he would have conceived of as 'Negro Americans', he was not unlike the iconic Martin Luther King Jr, who made similarly tempered, moderate political pronouncements during his career:

> The Negro is an American. [...] And I think he's got to face the fact that he is an American, his culture is basically American, and one becomes adjusted to this when he realizes what, what he is. [...] Our destiny is tied up with the destiny of America.[25]

This echoes another famous political figure, author and anti-slavery activist, Frederick Douglass, whose limited reflections on and even dismissal of any racial connection with Africa reflect an abolitionist stance that was premised on his commitment ante-and post-bellum to the 'full participation in American life for people of African descent'.[26] Aligned with a Negro American purpose, Ellison likewise viewed (attachments to) Africa as 'a geographical abstraction' to which he laid no claim.[27] Committed primarily to his (mixed) American heritage and to American concerns, he avoided any involvement in championing Africa's independence movements and is noted for disavowing any affiliation with African 'culture' other than the aesthetic one that is evidenced in his penchant for African art and sculpture.[28]

Indeed, despite a later occasion in which he attended a luncheon for the poet-president of Senegal, Leopold Senghor,[29] or when he joined a committee supporting the release from jail of Ghanaian novelist, Kofi

25 See Garance Franke-Ruta, 'Martin Luther King Jr's Amazing Interview with Robert Penn Warren', *The Atlantic* (26 August 2013), <https://www.theatlantic.com/politics/archive/2013/08/martin-luther-king-jrs-amazing-1964-interview-with-robert-penn-warren/279014>, accessed 10 October 2018.

26 See Daniel Kilbride, 'What Did Africa Mean to Frederick Douglass?' *Slavery & Abolition* 36/1 (2015), 42.

27 Ishmael Reed, Troupe Quincy and Steve Cannon, 'The Essential Ellison', in Maryemma Graham and Amritjit Singh eds, *Conversations with Ralph Ellison* (Jackson: University of Mississippi Press, 1995), 376.

28 See 'African Art 1970–1992', Library of Congress, Ralph Ellison papers, I:180, folder 3. This folder includes imagistic newspaper clippings on African art exhibited in American and European museums and galleries as well as articles on African influences on contemporary black American painting.

29 Rampersad, *Ralph Ellison*, 427.

Awoonor,[30] the consensus has been that Ellison gave no particular consideration to African affairs. Despite his role as Managing Editor of *Negro Quarterly* during 1942–3, a magazine that frequently exhibited internationalist concerns, he ignored requests for potential contributions to the Paris-based journal founded in 1947, *Présence Africaine*.[31] Noting Ellison's 'non-committal' attitude, in the mid-1950s, to Ghana's imminent independence, Rampersad concludes, 'On the whole, the African independence movement, thrilling to many blacks, failed to stir Ralph. While he was not for colonialism, he saw himself (as Wright saw himself) as first and foremost a Western intellectual'.[32]

In an interview published in *Phylon* in 1960, Harold Isaacs records how Ellison declined a state-sponsored visit to a newly independent Ghana in 1957: 'I had no interest in it, [...] no special emotional attachment to the place. I don't read much on Africa nowadays. It is just a part of the bigger world picture to me'.[33] Similarly, both in his encounters with Africans in the diaspora while he was a student at the Tuskegee Institute in the mid-1930s, and at the 1955 and 1957 African Writers conferences in Paris and Rome, Ellison expressed a strong sense of alienation that was not antagonistic but articulated his lack of 'cultural identification with them'.[34] His cynicism about a racialized African continuum is demonstrated not just in his satirical representation of a pan-Africanist black nationalism in *Invisible Man*'s controversial figure of Ras the Exhorter; nor merely in his refusal of an invitation by South African writer, Ezekiel Mphahlele (1919–2008) to an international writer's conference in Uganda in the 1960s.[35] Years later and despite helping to launch the 'Treasures of Ancient Nigeria' exhibition as part of his formal association with the Department of Primitive Art at the Metropolitan Museum in 1980, an 'over-committed' Ellison rejected an invitation by the Phelps Stokes Fund (which worked in Liberia, Ghana and South Africa, among other locations) to join a commission to

30 Ibid., 480.
31 Ibid., 234.
32 Ibid., 300.
33 Harold Isaacs, 'Five Writers and Their African Ancestors', *Phylon* 21/4 (1960), 317.
34 Ibid., 320.
35 Rampersad, *Ralph Ellison*, 386.

'publicize the plight of over four million refugees from war, oppression, or drought'.[36] Rampersad is persuaded by Harold Isaacs's view that the novelist appeared to give 'little or no thought at all of any African influence on his culture, past or present, or on himself';[37] Ellison apparently quipped to Isaacs that he found the African content of American Negro life 'more fanciful than actual'.[38]

Ellison and *Invisible Man* in South Africa: Shadow or Act?

As its year of publication was 1952, *Invisible Man* not unexpectedly resonated with a politically turbulent era in South Africa, one marked simultaneously by increasingly militant opposition to the apartheid government's draconian legislation and the accumulated temper of a politically conscientized and Americanized black urban culture. It is notable that, in his 1997 essay on the black literary journalism of the Sophiatown Generation – a 1950s movement that paralleled aesthetically the 1920s Harlem Renaissance and that comprised 'protest writing' by such prominent writers as Mphahlele, Peter Abrahams and Can Themba – scholar Neville Choonoo cites Ellison, alongside Richard Wright and James Baldwin, as a 'role model' to black South African writers and journalists.[39] Indeed, Paul Gready remarks specifically of Bloke Modisane's *Blame Me on History* (1963), a journalistic memoir of black (male) life under apartheid, that its preoccupation with 'the problems of identity and impression

36 Ibid., 522.

37 Isaacs, 'Five Writers and Their African Ancestors', 319; see also Rampersad, *Ralph Ellison*, 366.

38 Isaacs, 'Five Writers and Their African Ancestors', 322.

39 Neville Choonoo, 'The Sophiatown Generation: Black Literary Journalism during the 1950s', in Les Switzer, ed., *South Africa's Alternative Press: Voice of Protest and Resistance, 1880s–1960s* (Cambridge, UK: Cambridge University Press, 1997), 254–6.

management necessary in the "handling" of whites owes a considerable debt to Ellison's *The Invisible Man'* [sic].[40]

Equally instructive is the memoir of celebrated South African novelist, Nadine Gordimer (1923–2014): *Telling Times: Writing and Living: 1954–2008*. This documents the lifting, in the 1970s, of a long-standing ban on *Invisible Man* by the apartheid government's Customs and Post Office Acts. Likely to have been implemented in the early 1960s, this ban (as Gordimer explains) would have seen the publication categorized as 'undesirable' if any part of it was deemed:

> indecent or obscene or is offensive or harmful to public morals; is blasphemous or offensive to the religious convictions or feeling of any section of the inhabitants of the Republic; *brings any section of the inhabitants into ridicule or contempt; is harmful to the relations between any sections of the inhabitants*; is prejudicial to the safety of the State, the general welfare, or the peace and good order.[41]

Gordimer delineates further what may be considered indecent, obscene or offensive material. This is any publication that includes the portrayal of:

> murder, suicide, death, horror, fighting, brawling, ill-treatment, lawlessness, gangsterism, robbery, crime, the technique of crimes and criminals, tippling, drunkenness, trafficking in or addiction to drugs, smuggling, sexual intercourse, prostitution, promiscuity, white-slaving, licentiousness, lust, passionate love scenes, sexual assault, rape, sodomy, masochism, sadism, sexual bestiality, abortion, change of sex, night life, physical poses, nudity, scant or inadequate dress, divorce and marital infidelity, adultery, illegitimacy, *human or social deviation or degeneracy*, or any other similar or related phenomenon.[42]

This ridiculously exhaustive catalogue of misdemeanours speaks to the absurdity of (the reality of) apartheid South Africa and highlights how the banning of a novel as irreverent as *Invisible Man*, with its themes and

40 Paul Gready, 'The Sophiatown Writers of the Fifties: The Unreal Reality of Their World', *Journal of Southern African Studies* 16/1 (1990), 144.

41 Nadine Gordimer, *Telling Times: Writing and Living, 1954–2008* (London: Bloomsbury, 2011), 124–5 (italics in original).

42 Ibid., 124 (italics in original).

scenes not only of interracial sex, civil disobedience and protest against racial discrimination, but also of incest and public violence, was inevitable.

Yet in an article published in the *Liberator* in 1967 and provocatively entitled, 'Ralph Ellison: Shadow or Act?', celebrated South African poet, Keorapetse Kgositsile (1938–2018) gives a tempered reading of Ellison's relevance to the African nation(s). While lauding the artistic prowess of *Invisible Man*, he questions, in the particular context of a brutal South African apartheid regime, Ellison's specific relatedness to the 'peoples of Africa in our efforts to reshape that continent'.[43] This is significant because, as 'Africa became a prime metaphor through which African-Americans sought to self-define, and Kogistile represented the materiality of the continent', here was an Afrodiasporic Black Arts (and Black Power) proponent and committed pan-Africanist, publicly taking to task Ellison's apparent disassociation of art from (cultural and socio-)politics.[44]

Questioning his acclaimed individualism and observing his evident 'contradiction between social commitment for a writer and his commitment to style', Kgositsile muses that Ellison 'might very well be the "original" displaced man'.[45] At the official Proceedings of the Symposium on Contemporary African Literature and First African Literature Association Conference, which was held at the University of Texas in 1975 and which included contributions from other notable African scholars including Dennis Brutus, Chinua Achebe and Ali A. Mazrui, Kgositsile followed his initial query with an assertion that appears to allude again to Ellison. In a panel on 'Literature and Commitment in South Africa', he argues against the notion of apolitical creativity by maintaining that in:

> a situation of oppression, there are no choices beyond didactic writing; either you are a tool of oppression or an instrument of liberation. It's that simple. Every writer

43 Keorapetse Kgositsile, 'Ralph Ellison: Shadow or *Act*', *Liberator* 7/5 (1967), 11.

44 Uhuru Phalafala, 'A Song of Constant Beginnings', *Mail & Guardian* (12 January 2018), <https://mg.co.za/article/2018-01-12-00-a-song-of-constant-beginnings>, accessed 15 January 2018.

45 Kgositsile, 'Ralph Ellison: Shadow or Act?', 11.

> is committed to certain values, even if he attempts to create illusions, such as art for art's sake.[46]

Published in 1976 – the year of the momentous Soweto Uprising by black South African school children who opposed the introduction of Afrikaans as a formal medium of instruction and which resulted in the death of at least 176 people – Kgositsile's insistence in the Proceedings on the necessarily political character and social commitment of literature echoed the urgency of black socio-political existence under the apartheid regime. It also anticipated South Africa's series of 'states of emergency' in the 1980s. Indeed, in yet another scathing attack, published in *The Black Scholar* in 1986 and which recalls his scepticism about Ellison, Kgositsile excoriated those 'charlatans, pimps and prostitutes running around masquerading as artists … Their hideous masks must be yanked off by the artists with a sense of duty and a clear social vision'. He concludes: 'Creative energy is not locked in any tower, ivory or black … Outside of social life there is no culture, there is no art; and that is one of the major differences between man and beast'.[47] Interestingly, as if in broad conversation with Kgositsile, an article penned by noted African American historian Manning Marable, in a political column entitled, 'Along the Color Line', notes the United Nations Special Committee Against Apartheid's initiation of a cultural boycott against American artists who performed in South Africa from 1981 onwards. This was a boycott which aimed to prevent the provision of 'cultural legitimacy to a dictatorial [apartheid] regime'.[48] Where Marable observes liberal outrage at the censuring of American artists here, he argues that 'US consumers, Black and white, have a right to know whether the artists they support are in turn supporting fundamental, human rights issues'.[49]

46 Keorapetse Kgositsile, 'Panel on Literature and Commitment in South Africa', *Issue* 6/1 (1976), 35.

47 Keorapetse Kgositsile, 'Culture and Resistance in South Africa', *The Black Scholar* 17/4 (1986), 31.

48 Manning Marable, 'Along the Color Line: Targeting Artists Who Perform in S. Africa', *Los Angeles Sentinel* (18 April 1985), A7.

49 Ibid.

But at the other end of the spectrum, maintaining that there 'is no racial novel', and that, 'All literature marks the road through which we (civilization) have come and points the way we go', Ellison consistently defended his stance of a 'cosmopolitan intellectual[ism]',[50] which, while championing the ('Negro') American cause, was motivated by a universalist, non-racial ethics. In 1969, Ellison had himself offered an explanation for and defence of the mechanisms of the novel:

> I would think that implicitly the novel protests. It protests the agonies of growing up. It protests the problem of finding a way into a complex, intricately structured society in a way which could allow this particular man to behave in a manly way, and which would allow him to seize some instrumentalities of political power. That is where the protest is on one level. On another level, the protest lies in my trying to make a story out of these elements without falling into the clichés which have marked and marred most fiction about American Negros – that is, to write literature instead of political protest. Beyond this, I would say simply that in the very act of trying to create something, there is implicit protest against the way things are, a protest against man's vulnerability before the larger forces of society and the universe. [...] I think that [the novelist's] task is to present the human, to make it eloquent, and to provide some sense of transcendence over the given – that is, to make his protest meaningful, significant and eloquent of human value.[51]

His interpretation here of the inherently but *complexly* political character of art (as practice and aesthetic), one which is inextricably linked to and motivated by multifaceted human experiences and endeavours, reflects the existential underpinnings of Ellison's sophisticated, broader vision.

In terms of the channelling of his own energies, however, the novelist continued to be unwilling or unable to translate his sense of 'protest' into direct action, even against apartheid in South Africa. As his novel remained a proverbial thorn in the South African government's side, it is no surprise that campaigners, at the imminent demise of the apartheid regime in the 1980s, sought Ellison's explicit involvement in the anti-apartheid struggle. Bayard Rustin, a prominent civil rights and

50 Rampersad, *Ralph Ellison*, 279, 152.

51 Ralph Ellison, 'On Initiation Rites and Power: A Lecture at West Point', in John F. Callahan, ed., *The Collected Essays of Ralph Ellison* (New York: Modern Library, 2003), 544–5.

anti-apartheid activist, anticipated that Ellison would wholeheartedly participate as a 'US sponsor' to a programme entitled Project South Africa (PSA), devised by the A. Phillip Randolph Educational Fund and of which he was the chair. Concerned with promoting peaceful change in the country by offering material and moral support, this was in response to the organization's report of 1984 entitled, 'South Africa: Is Peaceful Change Possible?', and which outlines recommendations for a free, just and equitable, non-racial society.[52] After an investigatory trip to South Africa and in order to 'strengthen humanitarian groups working within South Africa for peaceful change', Rustin penned a letter to Ellison in April 1985 – now among Ellison's papers in the Library of Congress – in which he massaged the author's notoriety and prestige: 'We are interested in assembling a group of prestigious Americans in a variety of fields who are committed to social change and enhancing democratic values by peaceful means', he wrote. 'I believe you are one such person and hope that you are willing to join our group of sponsors'.[53] Ellison, however, declined the invitation. Attached to Rustin's letter, in the archive, is a handwritten note (most probably penned by Ellison's wife, Fanny) that reads: 'In sympathy with what is being done but he cannot join'. A further letter from Rustin to Fanny Ellison in 1986 suggests that continued efforts to persuade Ellison to actively avail himself to the anti-apartheid cause were futile.[54]

And yet, the story (as always) is complicated and multifaceted. Where he appeared outwardly indifferent to African politics, it is evident that Ellison was not in fact uninterested. A folder housed in the Manuscripts Division at the Library of Congress, entitled 'Africa 1943–89', evidences how his interest extended far beyond African art (and its influence on African American art and culture); it reveals, in a number of collected newspaper clippings and critical articles, a sustained intellectual curiosity with (pre- and post-independence) African politics and politicians generally and the

52 Bayard Rustin, Charles Bloomstein and Walter Naegle, *South Africa: Is Peaceful Change Possible?* (New York: New York Friends Group, 1984).

53 Rustin, Bayard, Letter to Ralph Ellison, 5 April 1985, Library of Congress, Ralph Ellison papers, I:35 folder 1.

54 Rustin, Bayard, Letter to Fanny Ellison, 10 July 1986, Library of Congress, Ralph Ellison papers, I.35 folder 1.

daily lived affairs of apartheid South Africa in particular.[55] Ellison's demonstration of a profound interest in the minutiae of political and politicized life here translates to *Invisible Man*'s attempt at and retention of 'a broad political focus on both race consciousness and national culture by redefining the terms of social reality'.[56] Indeed, in his portrayal of black male brutality in the Battle Royale scene, his depiction of intra-racial incest in the Trueblood episode, his representation of Dr Bledsoe's expedient dealings (and vice versa) with the white patron of his college, Mr Norton, it is evident that Ellison was concerned with evoking while simultaneously pushing the boundaries of historically conventional racial representations.

The novel's capacity for pushing boundaries perhaps explains the fact that, despite evidence of his disdain for overt political activism and apparent continued detachment from the politics of the African continent, Ellison's influence on and relevance to South Africa outlived the negative reactions to his apparently indifferent attitude. Interest in the novel and its implications extended far beyond the unbanning of *Invisible Man* and the official demise of the apartheid era. In the closing years of that regime, where it appears that a kind of black (Atlantic) futurism had taken hold even before the current Afrofuturist wave, Ellison's relevance is illustrated in a critical scholarship that has sought to establish a pointed link between *Invisible Man* and the country's socio-politics and literature. In 1989, writer and academic J. U. Jacobs published a comparative interpretation of the experiential manoeuvrings of Walter Serote's protagonist in his iconic novel, *To Every Birth Its Blood* (1981), with Invisible Man's improvisatory existential techniques. In his article, 'The Blues: An Afro-American Matrix for Black South African Writing', Jacobs makes cross-cultural musical connections between what he describes as Ellison's 'blues novel' and '[South] African jazz'.[57] And as early as 1999, in the heady, utopian years post-apartheid, Thomas J. Kitson's scholarly reading of Ellison's views on

55 'Africa 1943–1989', Library of Congress, Ralph Ellison papers, I:179, folder 4, and 'Africa 1953, 1959', Library of Congress, Ralph Ellison papers, I:OV 20, folder 1.

56 Thomas Schaub, 'Ellison's Masks and the Novel of Reality', in Robert O'Meally, ed., *New Essays on* Invisible Man (New York: Cambridge University Press, 1988), 123.

57 J. U. Jacobs, 'The Blues: An Afro-American Matrix for Black South African Writing', *English in Africa* 16/2 (1988), 15–16.

diasporic identity problematizes – in a different vein to Kgositsile's initial query in the 1960s – the author's relevance to the current needs for African and African American identity formation: it emphasizes Ellison's 'complex relationship with racial counter-discourses in the diaspora'.[58] In this way, Ellison anticipates in the present moment critical, academic contemplations of South Africa's enduringly fractious and complex race relations and identity politics.

It is Ellison's simultaneously insightful and disruptive, political and imaginative engagement with 'social reality' that has found favour with later generations of academics, artists and commentators. Aligned with the growth of 'black' science fiction from the African continent, Lisa Yaszek's 2005 interpretation of *Invisible Man* proposes that the novel can be read as foreshadowing current 'Afrofuturist thinking about the future of black history and culture'.[59] She maintains that Ellison be regarded as a proto-Afrofuturist writer whose novel's 'experimental prose style' and promulgation of a 'kind of technoscientific humanism, one that is not so much rooted in nostalgic myths of an idyllic, organic past as it is in the recognition of how technological change in the present' might 'pave the way for new and more egalitarian futures'.[60] She thus associates his work with contemporary Afrofuturism's necessary reclamation not just of the history of the past, but of a future history. This future-oriented, visionary outlook resonates with recent disruptive moves in contemporary literature by Africans in the diaspora, which, arguing against the delimiting ethnic imperatives that continue to plague African literary publishing and reception, excoriate the 'danger of a single story',[61] and rally

58 Thomas J. Kitson, 'Tempering Race and Nation: Recent Debates in Diaspora Identity', *Research in African Literatures* 30/2 (1999), 92.

59 Lisa Yaszek, 'An Afrofuturist Reading of Ralph Ellison's *Invisible Man*', *Rethinking History* 9/2–3 (2005), 297.

60 Ibid., 298, 304.

61 Chimamanda Ngozi Adichie, 'The Danger of a Single Story', Ted Talk (July 2009), <http://www.ted.com/talks/chimamanda_adichie_the_danger_of_a_single_story.html>, accessed 5 September 2016.

against 'literary pass-laws' that seek to restrict where 'African literature can go'.[62]

Grant Farred's provocatively entitled article of 2006, '"Shooting the white girl first": Race in Post-Apartheid South Africa', meanwhile references Toni Morrison's *Paradise* (1997) – a novel that unveils the violent failure of totalitarian, racialized communities. Farred thereby attests to the possibilities in South Africa of counter-discursive narratives. He highlights Ellison's deployment of a slippery, eponymous protagonist whose 'black body wages an epistemological campaign to refute its deficient representation, its enunciation as a lack, an absence, the Other, or an interrupted or suspended humanity', and thereby suggests that Ellison's hero might help the nation imagine a world in which 'the racialized body – the historically denigrated body – is not always read *a priori*, and interminably, as a deficit'.[63]

In a completely opposite kind of reception, in 2007 Ellison is strategically harnessed, alongside W. E. B. DuBois, to a more singular nationalist vision in the keynote address by the then Minister of Foreign Affairs, Dr Nkosazana Dlamini-Zuma, at the National Consultative Conference on the African Diaspora. Appropriating and quoting Ellison's own observations in his essay, 'Some Questions and Some Answers' – '[i]t is not culture which binds the people who are of partially African origin now scattered throughout the world, but an identity of passions'[64] – Dlamini-Zuma advocates, within the context of a pan-Africanist African Renaissance movement, a transatlantic utopian vision of Africa premised on the binding legacy of slavery.[65] Seemingly ignorant of Ellison's historic dismissal of what

62 Helon Habila, 'Tradition and the African Writer', *The Caine Prize for African Writing* (2014), <http://caineprizeblogspot.com/2014/06/what-is-african-literature-tradition.html>, accessed 10 September 2016.

63 Grant Farred, '"Shooting the White Girl First": Race in Post-Apartheid South Africa', in Kamari Maxine Clarke and Deborah A. Thomas, eds, *Globalization and Race: Transformations in the Cultural Production of Blackness* (Durham, NC: Duke University Press, 2006), 228.

64 Ralph Ellison, 'Some Questions and Some Answers', in John F. Callahan, ed., *The Collected Essays of Ralph Ellison* (New York: Modern Library, 2003), 293.

65 Nkosazana Dlamini-Zuma, 'Keynote Address by the Minister of Foreign Affairs of South Africa' (17 April 2007), <https://www.gov.za/n-dlamini-zuma-consultative-conference-african-diaspora>, accessed 10 January 2017.

he appeared to view as a limited and limiting diasporic connection, this is an intriguingly expedient inclusion here of the American author into an Africanist nationalist treatise that continues to permeate South African socio-political and socio-economic discourse.

In a far more nuanced appreciation, in 2013 the poet Phillippa Yaa de Villiers commended the 'brilliance of a writer who can take such a personal, psychological trauma' and 'spin' a story that reflects the 'hellish' intricacies of post-apartheid South Africa.[66] Similarly bemoaning that in recent times 'the turn to racial nationalism and essentialism has taken a more pronounced, ugly twist in a country always predisposed to racial sensitivities', in 2018 the commentator Saliem Fakir referred to *Invisible Man*'s ability to bring to the fore not just 'the many ways in which black experience can be invisible in the totality of whiteness'. In a contemporary moment of discursive national chauvinism which every day produces new forms of invisibility, the novel highlights that where 'race essentialism is the assertion of a new form of racial dominance in which the national project is assigned to a specific group and in which the presence and influence of other groups are systematically diluted', history inevitably 'repeats itself'.[67]

Decolonizing the Curriculum; Transforming South Africa: Teaching and Studying *Invisible Man* in Post-Apartheid Contexts

Aligned with the 2014 African American BlackLivesMatter movement's demand for equitable treatment by state institutions, South Africa's

66 Phillippa Yaa De Villiers, '*Invisible Man* by Ralph Ellison – A Review and Invitation', *Bookslive* (12 July 2013), <http://philyaa.bookslive.co.za/blog/2013/07/12/invisible-man-by-ralph-ellison-a-review-and-invitation>, accessed 18 January 2017.

67 Saliem Fakir, 'The Politics of Invisibility and Racial Dominance – A New Dawn of Racial Vulgarity', *Daily Maverick* (8 July 2018), <https://www.dailymaverick.co.za/opinionista/2018-07-08-the-politics-of-invisibility-and-racial-dominance-a-new-dawn-of-racial-vulgarity>, accessed 5 October 2018.

socio-historical transformation imperatives have seen the emergence of the RhodesMustFall and FeesMustFall movements of 2015.[68] The generic calls for socio-economic and socio-political redress include demands for equitable access to Higher Education and reflect its current 'decolonial', 'Africanist' turn, underlining here what Kirk B. Sides observes as the transatlantic 'terrain of a racialized global modernity'.[69] Tellingly, literary scholar Phil Ndlela's academic 'quest for an equitable education system in South Africa' through the prism of decolonial theory positions Ellison's novelistic achievement and essayistic forays alongside those of Afrocentric South African intellectual stalwarts and (militant) icons the likes of A. C. Jordan (1906–68) and Steve Biko (1946–77). Linking these (anti-apartheid) political actors to how Ralph Ellison 'addresses the question of the systematic exclusion of black people, and America's dogged refusal to recognise them', Ndlela accentuates the invariably transnational character of decolonial movements and undermines parochial readings of the current moment.[70]

Ndlela's comparative reading is not just stimulating; it is instructive of the extent of Ellison's resonance for and influence in the country. Discovering that *Invisible Man* has been and continues to be studied as part of the English Literature curriculum in institutions of Higher Learning in the country, I set out, as an Ellisonian scholar who teaches the text at my own institution, Rhodes University (located in Grahamstown/Makhanda, in the Eastern Cape, South Africa), to trace the historical and continued reception of Ellison in the South African educational landscape. In a series of email interviews conducted over 2018 and 2019 and with predominantly

68 Underlining demands for equitable access to institutions of Higher Learning in the country, the RhodesMustFall movement called for the removal of the colonialist commemorative statue of Cecil John Rhodes from the grounds of Cape Town University. Shortly thereafter, the FeesMustFall movement called for fee-free education for all university applicants.

69 Kirk B. Sides, 'Precedence and Warning: Global Apartheid and South Africa's Long Conversation on Race', *Safundi* 18/3 (2017), 224.

70 Phil Ndlela, 'He "Brightened the Corner": Decolonial A. C. Jordan and the Quest for an Equitable Education System in Apartheid South Africa', *Litnet* (12 April 2017), <https://www.litnet.co.za/brightened-corner-decolonial-ac-jordan-quest-equitable-education-system-apartheid-south-africa>, accessed 18 February 2017.

white female academics from a fairly representative sample of accredited institutions of Higher Learning,[71] I posed the following specific questions.

1. When did you start teaching *Invisible Man* and what was the reasoning behind the decision to teach the text in your department?
2. If no longer teaching it, how long did you teach the novel for? Is it still being taught?
3. Was *Invisible Man* taught to undergraduate or postgraduate students, i.e. at what level was the text taught? Was there a rationale behind this?
4. Could you give a rough indication of the student demographics in this regard, including race, ethnicity, gender, class etc.?
5. In your opinion, what was/is the reception of and response to the novel by your students?
6. As someone who teaches/ has taught Ralph Ellison, what do you think is his appeal to and what relevance does *Invisible Man* have for students in a South African setting?

The responses to my questions were intriguing. Rather remarkably, for example, the novel was taught generally to undergraduate, English One students at the University of KwaZulu Natal (UKZN) for five years from around 1975, in the historically Zulu heartland and what was later to become the political hub of the former president, Jacob Zuma. This was after *Invisible Man* had been unbanned, and a year before the infamous and bloody 1976 student uprisings aligned with a growing Black Consciousness movement. Due to restricted access to white institutions of higher learning for black students, these classes were overwhelmingly white and predominantly female, necessitating the strategic

71 This was by default rather than by design. Email interview requests were sent out to at least half of the accredited twenty-six public South African universities. Only six responses were garnered at the time of writing this article. Exceptions to the study's demographics included an email interview with Phillippa Yaa de Villiers and an email interview conducted with a student at the University of Pretoria whose research on *Invisible Man* was recommended by her lecturer. Apart from de Villiers, all interviewees preferred not to be named.

navigation of such a provocative text with the imminent demise of apartheid and the need thus for socio-political/socio-cultural and intellectual re-orientation.[72]

The lecturer involved in teaching *Invisible Man* here explains that, despite the violence on South African streets and the parallels invoked with a previous African American civil rights movement, the generalized focus was 'mostly on the formal properties of the text, rather than on the socio-political or psycho-social history that Ellison was representing'. She further explained that 'the mode of teaching in the 1970s did not really equip [students] to engage with the text in this way [...] and they really did not have the moral or imaginative experience needed' to engage with the novel in a meaningful way. Concurring with this teacher's view is the poet Phillippa Yaa de Villiers, who was a student under South Africa's educational system in the late 1970s herself, although she has not actually taught the book. Reading this interpretive depoliticization of literature as one of a series of South Africa's dehumanizing systems which would be recognizable to African Americans, she explains that *Invisible Man* 'was not taught in school because racist ideology's *raison d'être* is to nullify and deny the presence of an African mind, and to remove its evidence from language. Black [American] writing was systematically hidden from us'.[73]

Insulated pedagogically from black South African and global politics and everyday realities in this way, the accommodationist move employed by the apartheid government (right up to its imminent demise in the later 1980s) to promote in the curricula a continental post-colonial pedagogy is not surprising. Forced to restructure its syllabus radically to include more South African and African writing, this UKZN English department witnessed the eventual squeezing out of Ellison's and other notable African American texts. Specialized courses such as American Literature, offered at postgraduate level and which would include Ellison's text, only occurred from the 1990s onwards. This delay spelled, in the context of an emergent

72 At this time, in the latter 1970s and due to South Africa's racialized, segregationist legislation and practice, students from other 'minority' racial groups were admitted to white universities only in order to study subjects not available at designated black universities.

73 This correspondence formed part of an email interview conducted in 2019.

black administration, a missed opportunity for more critical, transnationally comparative and globally integrative teachings of blackness (and race) that might have simultaneously frustrated and undermined both white separatist and black nationalist politics and thinking.

Indeed, the UKZN lecturer, now retired, bemoans not having had the experience of teaching Ellison's novel more recently, 'in a time when the political and psycho-social relevance [of *Invisible Man*] would be more readily felt by South African readers'. She explains:

> Although black experience in the US does not translate directly to South Africa, "invisibility" is undoubtedly a symptom that people of this country are struggling to comprehend and to articulate – and to struggle with some white peoples' incomprehension of why it continues to be a legacy of apartheid so long after the legal side of the system was abolished.

Meanwhile, at the University of Fort Hare, a predominantly black institution in the Eastern Cape, *Invisible Man* has been studied since 2007 at Third Year level. Attesting to the University's standing as a key institution in the higher education of prominent African anti-colonial political figures and as their political preserve, *Invisible Man* is taught as part of the African Diaspora module that discusses post-colonial theory through an African American context.[74] Taught to a class of primarily isiXhosa female students, the lecturer here explains that although referencing 'a time frame and context with which they are unfamiliar', the novel offers them, in the spirit of the institution's historically transnational, pan-Africanist orientation, 'a broader perspective of race relations, responses to oppression, issues of black masculinity which remain significant in the minds of our students today'. This is clearly a rather different approach from the limited pedagogical perspective that had been adopted at UKZN.

The sense of immediacy registered here resonates with the experience of a lecturer teaching at the University of Pretoria, a previously white Afrikaans institution located in the Gauteng province. Admitting that

74 Established in 1916, Fort Hare's notable alumni include former African presidents, Seretse Khama (Botswana), Julius Nyerere (Tanzania), Kenneth Kaunda (Zambia) Nelson Mandela (South Africa), and Robert Mugabe (Zimbabwe).

she began teaching *Invisible Man* in 2015 in response to the FeesMustFall 'protests', she explained that the novel was included broadly in a Twentieth-Century Literature component which comprised sub-sections on Modernism and American literature as part of the Second Year English syllabus. Not unlike the UKZN lecturer above, she observes how the text is 'usefully read in the context of Western literary modernism'. But considering the current democratizing agendas of South African higher education and that she teaches a class of 600 middle-class students – comprised equally of black and white students at a 65/35 per cent ratio of women to men – she also notes how the omission of black writers in this course needed remedying. In this regard, she describes her students as generally 'excited, inspired and challenged' by Ellison's text. Echoing Yaszek's Afrofuturist reading of *Invisible Man* and highlighting the novel's attention to black vernacular idiom, expression, philosophy, song and oral performance – all of which powerfully make 'this history visible and concrete' – the lecturer elucidates:

> Apart from the issues it raises about black American experience, the novel is also stylistically exciting and intriguing. It is a puzzle which students enjoy putting together, one which is made up of a complex pattern of striking and suggestive motifs and metaphors. In addition the events that are described are shocking, jarring, unexpected and frequently violent. I would imagine that the students are attracted to the intensity of feeling that the novel articulates, particularly the rage of the protagonist and the violence of the events that occur. I would imagine that students respond to the powerful critique of white liberal patronage and the brutality of the system that the protagonist must negotiate.

That the affective, imaginative impact of the novel is translated into a critical, academic interrogation of contemporary South African socio-politics is demonstrated in the work of one of her Honours students, in 2015. This student developed a mini-dissertation that explores the similarities and differences between the concepts of black invisibility in Ellison's *Invisible Man* and the narratives that emerged across South African University campuses in response to the FeesMustFall movement.

This student explains her own experience of the novel and the findings of her research:

> I had never read a book quite like it before. *Invisible Man* deals with an environment where some young black students are battling to remove the shackles of generational poverty and subjugation. [...] Post-apartheid South Africa is still going through some of these issues and the conversations sparked by the text are definitely worth having in South Africa today. Some of the student narratives that emerged during the 2015 FeesMustFall protests expressed intense feelings of invisibility. This is an important theme in Ralph Ellison's text as well and there are important questions to be asked about how and why black students in institutions of higher learning feel unseen and unheard more than twenty years after 1994. Just as in *Invisible Man*, it is important for [...] South Africa to have conversations about the black experience across the landscape of this country and institutions of higher learning, because there exists a common thread of a particular black experience across completely different contexts, and feelings of invisibility remain intense across space and time. Everyone needs to ask themselves why this is the case and perhaps there could be solutions about what emerging from the 'underground' of self knowledge would look like.

Echoing the observations of the UKZN lecturer, the student's focus on the black experience and the structural and ideological failures of post-apartheid South Africa resonates with *Invisible Man*'s emphasis on pervasive and enduring black invisibility. But her abstruse, indefinite solutions to this historic impasse resonate also with the novel's own complicated plot and ambiguous ending. And in the mind of this student's lecturer, it is precisely the novel's critique of 'reconciliatory politics, black nationalism and class-based communism' that encourages her students to 'negotiate a tricky path between these [historical] positions'. The lecturer explains that it is its 'open and suggestive' resolution, its advocacy of 'a stance of flexibility and critical reflectiveness rather than subservience to a particular perspective', that renders *Invisible Man* so attractive to and relevant in a current political climate which, while seemingly more sophisticated in approach, is at risk of rehearsing the rigid ideologies and identitarian politics that dominated South Africa pre- and immediately post-apartheid.

Where this lecturer describes white students as 'enthralled', she is careful to highlight the particular 'congruence between the novel's concerns and the experience of many black South Africans'. While she admits that she is yet to be approached on *Invisible Man*'s critique of black nationalism – a critique that would surely provoke those in support of current black nationalist agendas that seek to empower predominantly black South Africans – she again echoes her own student and the UKZN lecturer. She observes that the 'notion of invisibility and the multifaceted way in which it is presented in the novel is hugely appealing and relevant [to the students]. In this sense, the novel speaks to the South African context in a powerful way'.[75] The poet de Villiers, who is currently lecturing in the Department of Creative Writing at Wits University, concurs with this assessment. She adds that 'the novel also captures various ways in which the black world refuses to see itself', and suggests that its complex approach reflects the complexity of human (socio-political and historical) life. Describing Ellison's writing as 'scarily honest' – 'so present it demands the reader's consciousness', she commends the way:

> it engages the individual in history, and not just any history, the history of change in a society. [...] The power of idiomatic writing [...] that is as redolent as this, is that it is able to capture contradictions, therefore offering the reader several points of view from which to engage a particular problem. It is intensely human, dealing with very abstract ideas in human terms.

Testament to its 'transformative' impulse, *Invisible Man* is taught at Rhodes University, the formerly British colonial, English-speaking institution in the Eastern Cape where I am employed.[76] While the novel's inclusion at Honours level in the Department of Literary Studies in English as part of the American Literature paper was scheduled for 2015, this was ironically abandoned due to the volatility of the FeesMustFall movement which, in its interruption of scheduled classes, prevented the text from actually being taught. Finally incorporated in 2017 as part of continued responses to pedagogical transformation imperatives, it has been taught to classes of predominantly middle-class students. Where the 2017 class comprised mostly black, female students, the 2018 class – also predominantly female – was more racially varied, made up of an almost proportionate

75 A growing black nationalist sentiment is revealed not least in the emergence of the working-class affiliated, communist-/socialist-leaning oppositional political group, Economic Freedom Fighters (EFF), led by the radical and controversial figure, Julius Malema.

76 Previously simply referred to as the English Department, the department has itself, since the FeesMustFall movement, undergone an appellative process of transformation including a purposeful name change to the Department of Literary Studies

number of white, black and Indian students. The 2019 class was comprised entirely of white male, white female and white transgender students.

Albeit interested in the novel's engagement with (American) race and class relations – a concern indubitably linked to the RhodesMustFall and FeesMustFall movements that influenced its inclusion in the curriculum in the first place – students of the 2017 and 2019 classes primarily expressed discomfort with the representation of women, black and white. Female characterization in the novel was criticized for endorsing stereotypical, one-dimensional portraits of womanhood: either highly sexualized, demonstrated in the narrator's sexual encounter with the tempestuous personality of Sybil, or overly maternal, evidenced in his dealings with the matriarchal persona of Mary Rambo. Interestingly, and recalling the invisible man's own bemused reaction to his topical reassignment while a member of the Brotherhood to the 'Woman Question', this afforded a necessarily (because atypically) feminist reading of *Invisible Man* that reflected and translated into a problematization of the marginalization of women's (and other genders') presences during both student-led movements.[77] In a number of oral presentations and written assignments that challenged the perceived androcentric character of the text and the period, the students here were able to realign a predominantly critical preoccupation with the novel's racial representations, national (American) and canonical, to include the consideration of women (and other genders) in global historic and contemporary transformation agendas.

Disorienting and compelling students to re-situate it into that nebulous category of 'world literature', *Invisible Man*'s formally and ideologically challenging character seemed to resonate with these students' generic sense of identitarian displacement. Although articulated differently, this linked these students with the concerns of the 2018 class with 'wokeness'

---

in English. Discussions around the changing of the name of the institution, Rhodes University, are ongoing.

77 See Vashna Jaganarth, 'South Africa: Student Movement Splinters as Patriarchy Muscles out Diversity', *The Conversation* (19 April 2016), <https://theconversation.com/south-africa-student-movement-splinters-as-patriarchy-muscles-out-diversity-57855>, accessed 12 September 2018.

and being 'woke'. The extent to which the phrase tended to permeate discussions around the (comparative, transnational) relevance of *Invisible Man* in a twenty-first-century context was interesting, but the ways in which it was also used to describe Ellison's personal lack of overt political involvement (in their eyes he was not 'woke') were remarkable. Rehearsing the controversy that has plagued readings of Ellison in this regard, the students here reiterated Kgositsile's (and a similar pan-Africanist) interpretation of the socio-political instrumentalism of literature.

With some (white) students pronouncing Ellison a 'sell out',[78] it was interesting to witness, notwithstanding the limited literary critical discourse underpinning these pronouncements, the impassioned responses his work continues to generate. More worrying, however, was the violence of this rhetoric which, equally upsetting to Ellison at the time, indicates the long and difficult road that South Africa continues to travel in its realization of a democratic and integrative, non-racial politics. The findings of a 2014 South African Reconciliation Barometer Report by the Institute for Justice and Reconciliation report that 'white South Africans indicate high levels of denial of past injustice, low levels of responsibility for past injustice, and low levels of support for redress' required by those who suffered from apartheid's implementation.[79] Conversely, current black South African impatience with the level and pace of restitution has culminated in a divisive, partisan discourse that, in its insistence on racial loyalty, is not unlike the internal (black on black) violence experienced during apartheid.[80] The recourse to such politically charged rhetoric by some of the students, then, reveals the ways in which, as Ellison was critically aware and took pains to

78 The term 'sell out' is loosely equivalent to the Zulu term 'impimpi' and has a particular resonance in South African political history, implying political informants of the apartheid police.

79 Kim Wale, 'Reflecting on Reconciliation: Lessons from the Past, Prospects for the Future', in The Institute for Justice and Reconciliation, *South African Reconciliation Barometer Survey: 2014 Report* (Compress, 2014), 29.

80 Reparatory initiatives have included the 1994 Truth and Reconciliation Commission (TRC), calls in 2011 for a reparative wealth tax on white South Africans for the socio-economic disabling of apartheid to black South Africans and, more recently, calls for the 'radical transformation' of 'white monopoly capital' which include debates around the expropriation of land without compensation.

highlight, the past is negatively reiterated in the present and delimits (the potential for) modern formations of subjectivity. It is telling in an epic novel which represents the disarray of (American) society and violence of social relations that the protagonist, who begins the novel with an indictment of society's refusal to 'see' him, finally retreats from society and finds solace (in the darkness) underground. This symbolic gesture reveals a 'transcendent impulse to undo all categories, all metonymies and reifications, and thrust the self beyond received patterns and relationships'.[81]

Encouragingly, however, the not unfamiliar myopic readings of some students, which sought to contain Ellison's creative politics, did not go unchallenged. Not only did the inevitably persistent politicization of the author and his work generate much robust discussion and impassioned debate, it inspired some students to interrogate the applicability, within the context of a transforming South Africa, of reading (Ellison's) race into (his) literature while simultaneously testing the efficacy of his (literary) democratic vision. Where students generally tended towards inconclusive arguments, in a comparative, intergenerational reading of Ellison's novel and Justin Simien's popular satirical television series 'Dear White People' (2014), one student suggested that *Invisible Man* was visionary in its complex navigation of (American) race relations. She argued that in its ability to 'provoke questions about how one should protest against everyday injustices', the novel anticipated in a contemporary global age the use of new technological 'mediums to explore the age-old issues of racism and black identity'. In this regard and recalling Yaszek's 'proto-Afrofuturist' reading of Ellison, where current readings of *Invisible Man* seek to make links between the novel and an ostensibly progressive Obama administration, this student was able to establish continued, extensive readings of the novel even under a regressively racialized Trump administration.

Indeed, perturbed by the racist and anti-immigrant sentiments that have pervaded that presidency in the USA, one student, as part of her seminar presentation in 2019, made a forceful and heartfelt argument for

81 Kimberly W. Benston, 'I Yam What I Am: The Topos of (Un)naming in Afro-American Literature', in Henry Louis Gates Jr, ed., *Black Literature and Literary Theory* (New York: Routledge, 1990), 151.

Invisible Man's continued resonance in and relevance to contemporary American race politics. It is a sentiment reiterated and expanded in the Masters thesis of a female student entitled, 'Navigating Blackness in the African Diaspora'. This study, offering a comparative, transnational and transcultural reading of blackness in Ellison's *Invisible Man*, Percival Everett's *Erasure* (2001), Zoë Wicomb's *Playing in the Light* (2006) and NoViolet Bulawayo's *We Need New Names* (2013), demonstrates Ellison's enduring universal relevance and applicability.

In his influential introductory essay to *Shadow and Act*, Ralph Ellison reveals his reluctance to 'interpret the world and all its devices in terms of race'. He explains the significance of his existentialist quest in *Invisible Man*:

> How, in other words, should I think of myself and my pluralistic sense of the world, how express my vision of the human predicament, without reducing it to a point which would render it sterile before that necessary and tragic—though enhancing—reduction which must occur before the fictive vision can come alive? It is quite possible that much potential fiction by Negro Americans fails precisely at this point: through the writers' refusal (often through provincialism or lack of courage or opportunism) to achieve a vision of life and resourcefulness of craft commensurate with the complexity of their actual situation. Too often they fear to leave the uneasy sanctuary of race to take their chances with the world of art.[82]

As evidenced here and above, Ellison did not perceive of art as separate from society but as intrinsically fundamental, in its irreducible multivalency, to enabling the critical revivification and extension of social traditions and values. In this way literature, for Ellison, provides a 'study in comparative humanity' that allows for 'a universal identification, while at the same time not violating the specificity of the particular experience and the particular character'.[83]

While Ellison would likely question, and perhaps even dismiss, the not unproblematic Africanist appropriations of and readings into his work, these transatlantic and intergenerational responses evidence the extent to which his influence on and relatedness broadly to the continent and to South Africa in particular persist. They testify to his enduring relevance.

82 Ralph Ellison, 'Shadow and Act: Introduction', 59.

83 Ralph Ellison, 'On Initiation Rites and Power', 538–9.

His embodied and artistic deployment of a sophisticated cosmopolitan intellectualism exposes not just the contradictions of racialism prevalent in the apartheid *and* post-apartheid eras; it responds to and complicates, in the backdrop of a resurgent pan-Africanism, growing demands in twenty-first-century South Africa for a transformed, 'Africanized' socio-political economy and ideology. In this regard, it is his commitment to exploring a complex, knotty existence, as well as his expansive, futuristic vision of (black) subjectivity that today reinforces Ellison's specific relevance to South Africa in its efforts to reshape itself and its place in the continent. His desire to express in his work and in his fiction a 'vision of the human predicament' appears fundamentally and eloquently to speak on many and on varied global frequencies.

Bibliography

Adichie, Chimamanda Ngozi, 'The Danger of a Single Story', Ted Talk (2009), <http://www.ted.com/talks/chimamanda_adichie_the_danger_of_a_single_story.html>, accessed 5 September 2016.

'Africa 1943–1989', Library of Congress, Ralph Ellison papers, I:179, folder 4.

'Africa 1953, 1959', Library of Congress, Ralph Ellison papers, I:OV 20, folder 1.

'African Art 1970–1992', Library of Congress, Ralph Ellison papers, I:180, folder 3.

Bellow, Saul, 'Man Underground', *Commentary* 13/6 (1952), 608–10.

Benston, Kimberly W., 'I Yam What I Am: The Topos of (Un) Naming in Afro-American Literature', in Henry Louis Gates Jr, ed., *Black Literature and Literary Theory* (New York: Routledge, 1990), 151–74.

Butler, Robert, '*Invisible Man* and the Politics of Love', in Marc C. Conner and Lucas E. Morel, eds, *The New Territory: Ralph Ellison and the Twenty-First Century* (Jackson: University of Mississippi Press, 2016), 39–54.

Callahan, John F., 'Frequencies of Eloquence: The Performance and Composition of *Invisible Man*', in Robert O'Meally, ed., *New Essays on* Invisible Man (New York: Cambridge University Press, 1988), 55–94.

Choonoo, Neville R, 'The Sophiatown Generation: Black Literary Journalism during the 1950s', in Les Switzer, ed., *South Africa's Alternative Press: Voice of Protest and Resistance, 1880s–1960s* (Cambridge, UK: Cambridge University Press, 1997), 252–65.

Conner, Marc C. and Lucas E. Morel, 'Introduction', in *The New Territory: Ralph Ellison and the Twenty-First Century* (Jackson: University of Mississippi Press, 2016), 3–38.

——, eds, *The New Territory: Ralph Ellison and the Twenty-First Century* (Jackson: University of Mississippi Press, 2016).

De Villiers, Phillippa Yaa, '*Invisible Man* by Ralph Ellison – A Review and Invitation', *Bookslive* (12 July 2013), <http://philyaa.bookslive.co.za/blog/2013/07/12/invisible-man-by-ralph-ellison-a-review-and-invitation>, accessed 18 January 2017.

Dlamini-Zuma, Nkosazana, 'Keynote Address by the Minister of Foreign Affairs of South Africa', (17 April 2007): <https://www.gov.za/n-dlamini-zuma-consultative-conference-african-diaspora>, accessed 10 January 2017.

Ellison, Ralph, 'The Art of Fiction: An Interview', in John F. Callahan, ed., *The Collected Essays of Ralph Ellison* (New York: Modern Library, 2003), 200–24.

——, 'On Initiation Rites and Power: A Lecture at West Point', in John F. Callahan, ed., *The Collected Essays of Ralph Ellison* (New York: Modern Library, 2003), 524–45.

——, *Invisible Man* (New York: Penguin, 1965).

——, 'The Little Man at the Chehaw Station', in John F. Callahan, ed., *The Collected Essays of Ralph Ellison* (New York: Modern Library, 2003), 493–523.

——, 'Shadow and Act: Introduction', in John F. Callahan, ed., *The Collected Essays of Ralph Ellison* (New York: Modern Library, 2003), 47–60.

——, 'Some Questions and Some Answers', in John F. Callahan, ed., *The Collected Essays of Ralph Ellison* (New York: Modern Library, 2003), 293.

Fakir, Saliem, 'The Politics of Invisibility and Racial Dominance – A New Dawn of Racial Vulgarity', *Daily Maverick* (8 July 2018): <https://www.dailymaverick.co.za/opinionista/2018-07-08-the-politics-of-invisibility-and-racial-dominance-a-new-dawn-of-racial-vulgarity>, accessed 5 October 2018.

Farred, Grant, '"Shooting the White Girl First": Race in Post-Apartheid South Africa', in Kamari Maxine Clarke and Deborah A. Thomas, eds, *Globalization and Race: Transformations in the Cultural Production of Blackness* (Durham, NC: Duke University Press, 2006), 226–46.

Foley, Barbara, *Wrestling with the Left: The Making of Ralph Ellison's Invisible Man* (Durham, NC: Duke University Press, 2010).

Franke-Ruta, Garance, 'Martin Luther King Jr's Amazing Interview with Robert Penn Warren', *The Atlantic* (26 August 2013): <https://www.theatlantic.com/politics/archive/2013/08/martin-luther-king-jrs-amazing-1964-interview-with-robert-penn-warren/279014>, accessed 10 October 2018.

Gordimer, Nadine, *Telling Times: Writing and Living, 1954–2008* (London: Bloomsbury, 2011).

Gready, Paul, 'The Sophiatown Writers of the Fifties: The Unreal Reality of Their World', *Journal of Southern African Studies* 16/1 (1990), 139–64.

Habila, Helon, 'Tradition and the African Writer', 'The Caine Prize for African Writing' (2014): <http://caineprizeblogspot.com/2014/06/what-is-african-literature-tradition.html>, accessed 10 September 2016.

Howe, Irving, 'Black Boys and Native Sons', in John Hersey, ed., *Ralph Ellison: A Collection of Critical Essays* (Englewood Cliffs, NJ: Prentice-Hall, 1974), 36–8.

Hyman, Stanley Edgar, 'Ralph Ellison in Our Time', *The New Leader* 47/22 (1964), 21–2.

Isaacs, Harold R., 'Five Writers and Their African Ancestors', *Phylon* 21/4 (1960), 317–36.

Jackson, Lawrence, *Ralph Ellison: Emergence of Genius* (Athens: University of Georgia Press, 2007).

Jacobs, J. U., 'The Blues: An Afro-American Matrix for Black South African Writing', *English in Africa* 16/2 (1988), 3–17.

Jaganarth, Vashna, 'South Africa: Student Movement Splinters as Patriarchy Muscles Out Diversity', *The Conversation* (19 April 2016): <https://theconversation.com/south-africa-student-movement-splinters-as-patriarchy-muscles-out-diversity-57855>, accessed 12 September 2018.

Kaiser, Ernest, 'A Critical Look at Ellison's Fiction and at Social and Literary Criticism by and about the Author', *Black World* (December 1970), 53–97.

Kilbride, Daniel, 'What Did Africa Mean to Frederick Douglass?' *Slavery & Abolition* 36/1 (2015), 40–62.

Kitson, Thomas J., 'Tempering Race and Nation: Recent Debates in Diaspora Identity', *Research in African Literatures* 30/2 (1999), 88–95.

Kgositsile, Keorapetse, 'Culture and Resistance in South Africa', *The Black Scholar* 17/4 (1986), 28–31.

——, 'Ralph Ellison: Shadow or Act?', *Liberator* 7/5 (1967), 11–12.

——, Dennis Brutus, Chinua Achebe and Ali A. Mazrui, 'Panel on Literature and Commitment in South Africa', *Issue* 6/1 (1976), 34–46.

Marable, William Manning, 'Along the Color Line: Targeting Artists Who Perform in S. Africa', *Los Angeles Sentinel* (18 April 1985), A7.

Marzioli, Sara, 'Ralph Ellison's Exceptional Diaspora: The View from Rome', *Atlantic Studies* 9/4 (2012), 447–66.

Morel, Lucas E., 'Ralph Ellison's Democratic Individualism', in Lucas E. Morel, ed., *Ralph Ellison and the Raft of Hope: A Political Companion to* Invisible Man (Lexington: University Press of Kentucky, 2004), 58–90.

Ndlela, Phil, 'He "Brightened the Corner": Decolonial A. C. Jordan and the Quest for an Equitable Education System in Apartheid South Africa', *Litnet* (12 April 2017): <https://www.litnet.co.za/brightened-corner-decolonial-ac-jordan-quest-equitable-education-system-apartheid-south-africa>, accessed 18 February 2017.

Neal, Larry, 'Ellison's Zoot Suit', in John Hersey, ed., *Ralph Ellison: A Collection of Critical Essays* (Englewood Cliffs, NJ: Prentice-Hall, 1974), 58–79.

O'Meally, Robert, 'Introduction', in Robert O'Meally, ed., *New Essays on* Invisible Man (New York: Cambridge University Press, 1988), 1–23.

Parrish, Timothy, *Ralph Ellison and the Genius of America* (Iowa City: University of Iowa Press, 2012).

Phalafala, Uhuru Portia, 'A Song of Constant Beginnings', *Mail & Guardian* (12 January 2018), <https://mg.co.za/article/2018-01-12-00-a-song-of-constant-beginnings>, accessed 15 January 2018.

Posnock, Ross, 'Introduction', in Ross Posnock, ed., *The Cambridge Companion to Ralph Ellison* (Cambridge, UK: Cambridge University Press, 2005), 1–10.

Rampersad, Arnold, *Ralph Ellison: A Biography* (New York: Alfred A Knopf, 2007).

Reed, Ishmael, Troupe Quincy and Steve Cannon, 'The Essential Ellison', in Maryemma Graham and Amritjit Singh, eds, *Conversations with Ralph Ellison* (Jackson: University of Mississippi Press, 1995), 343–77.

Rustin, Bayard, Letter to Fanny Ellison, 10 July 1986, Library of Congress, Ralph Ellison papers, I:35, folder 1.

——, Letter to Ralph Ellison, 5 April 1985, Library of Congress, Ralph Ellison papers, I:35, folder 1.

——, Charles Bloomstein and Walter Naegle, *South Africa: Is Peaceful Change Possible?* (New York: New York Friends Group, 1984).

Schaub, Thomas, 'Ellison's Masks and the Novel of Reality', in Robert O'Meally, ed., *New Essays on* Invisible Man (New York: Cambridge University Press, 1988), 123–56.

Sides, Kirk B., 'Precedence and Warning: Global Apartheid and South Africa's Long Conversation on Race', *Safundi* 18/3 (2017), 221–38.

Vogler, Thomas, A., 'Invisible Man: Somebody's Protest Novel', *The Iowa Review* 1/2 (1970), 64–82.

Wale, Kim, 'Reflecting on Reconciliation: Lessons from the Past, Prospects for the Future', *South African Reconciliation Barometer Report* (Cape Town, South Africa: Institute for Justice and Reconciliation, 2014), 1–45.

Warren, Robert Penn, 'The Unity of Experience', *Commentary* 39/5 (1965), 91–6.

West, Hollie, 'Exploring the Life of a Not So Visible Man', in Maryemma Graham and Amritjit Singh, eds, *Conversations with Ralph Ellison* (Jackson: University of Mississippi Press, 1995), 235–58.

Yaszek, Lisa, 'An Afrofuturist Reading of Ralph Ellison's *Invisible Man*', *Rethinking History* 9/2–3 (2005), 297–313.

Zamalin, Alex, *African American Political Thought and American Culture: The Nation's Struggle for Racial Justice* (New York: Palgrave Macmillan, 2015).

OLGA PANOVA

6 Ralph Ellison in the USSR and Post-Soviet Russia: 'Hidden Name and Complex Fate'

ABSTRACT:
The chapter examines the history and politics of the reception, translations, publishing and teaching of Ralph Ellison's works in the USSR and post-Soviet Russia. It considers Ellison's paradoxical status of an 'invisible classic' – almost unknown to the common Russian reader (due to the fact that *Invisible Man* still remains untranslated into Russian), but very well-known to the Russian scholars specializing in American literature. Tracing the complex dynamic of Ellison's image and reputation in the USSR /Russia since 1960s, when his novel was for the first time mentioned by Soviet literary critics, through the late Soviet decades and up to the present day, the chapter uses a variety of materials, including periodicals, archived documents, correspondence and memories.

Ralph Ellison's strange fate in Russia remains a mystery. So far, no exhaustive explanation has been given to a number of striking facts: Ellison's masterpiece *Invisible Man* (1952) is still untranslated into Russian, let alone most of his other fiction and his classic collection of essays, *Shadow and Act* (1964). There is not one scholarly book on Ellison, and the number of critical essays scarcely reaches half a dozen. It's as though there were a conspiracy of silence, trying to make Ralph Ellison an 'invisible writer' for the Russian reading public. And yet Ellison is not completely out of sight in the Russian academy: his status as a classic of the twentieth-century American literature is acknowledged, and references to his works are scattered in both Soviet and post-Soviet critical essays and books. Ellison remains in Russia (as he used also to be in the USSR) an enigmatic 'dark horse', and only the 'consecrated ones', i.e. the scholars of American literature, guard an apparently esoteric knowledge of his works. To inquire into the phenomenon of Ellison's invisibility in this country, and to have a closer look at his paradoxical status as a modern classic both famous and unknown, this chapter examines the characteristics of the Soviet and post-Soviet literary field, and the history and politics of translations, publishing, criticism and teaching of Ralph Ellison's works in the USSR and post-Soviet Russia. The analysis will focus on how these factors have shaped Ellison's image in the late Soviet and post-Soviet periods, and how Ellison in turn might or might not have spoken to those specific contexts.[1]

If we turn to the historical background and try to define the place African American literature occupied in the Soviet editorial policy, it becomes obvious that since the early 1920s the so-called 'Negro problem' was a key issue of the ideological and political struggle with 'capitalist America'. The 'Negro problem' was constantly the focus of the jeremiads against racial oppression in the USA that flooded the Soviet press. Political strivings, propaganda and ideological guidelines had a direct influence over Soviet cultural policy and cultural diplomacy, including Soviet–African American literary contacts, translations and publishing.

The politics of literary reputation also played an important role in the critical evaluation of African American writers. Soviet literary critics always strove to find a 'black genius' – a great proletarian or revolutionary writer who could be presented to the reading public as a spiritual leader of the Negro people in America and a true friend of the USSR. The first candidate happened to be Claude McKay, a delegate to the Fourth Congress of Comintern[2] in 1922, who spent half a year in the Soviet Union from 1922 to 1923. His reputation, however, underwent a drastic change at the turn of 1920s–1930s: he was labelled by Soviet critics as a 'lumpen-intellectual' and a 'petty bourgeois bohemian degenerate'.[3] In the early 1930s the role

1 The research carried out for the writing of this paper has been funded by the Russian Foundation for Basic Research (RFBR) through competitive research grant 'History of African American Literature, XVIII–XXth century', Re. No. 18-012-00241 A. My essay forthcoming in *Ralph Ellison in Context*, ed., Paul Devlin (Cambridge, UK: Cambridge University Press, 2020/21), draws on a small proportion of the material in this chapter.

2 The Communist International; also known as the Third International (1919–43).

3 See, for example, Boris Pesis, 'Towards Rear Guard', *Kniga i revoliutsiia* [*Book and Revolution*] 29–30 (1930), 16–18 (in Russian); Abel Startsev, 'To Harlem, to Harlem!', *Oktiabr'* [*October*] 4–5 (1931), 236 (in Russian). Throughout this essay, all translations from the Russian are my own unless otherwise stated. Citations for scholarship written in Russian will be given in English only from this point onwards.

of the 'greatest black genius', friend of the Soviet Union, was bestowed on Langston Hughes. Later, from 1938 onwards, it was bestowed upon Richard Wright, whose *Uncle Tom's Children* and *Native Son* were a sensational success in Russia. Besides his obvious literary talent, Wright also benefited from being a Communist Party member. His reputation soared so high in the USSR, that despite his so-called 'renegade' and 'deluded' behaviour in the mid-1940s – which included publication of 'I Tried to be a Communist' in the *Atlantic Monthly* (1944) and his departure from the Communist Party – in the 1960s he was again acknowledged as the greatest twentieth-century black American writer.[4]

James Baldwin and Ralph Ellison were usually described as the 'Negro authors of the new wave' in the Soviet literary criticism. They found themselves in the gigantic shadow of Richard Wright and were treated as his 'posterity', 'successors' and 'disciples'. Soviet critics didn't take into account Ellison's distancing of himself from Wright,[5] and paid no attention to the fact that Ellison (who was only six years younger than Wright) began his career in the late 1930s, or that Baldwin (who was ten years younger than Ellison) started in late 1940s, at the beginning of the Cold War. These critics failed to acknowledge that these three 'greatest black novelists' actually belonged to three different literary generations. They ignored Ellison's own belief that he stood closer to the generation of Richard Wright, who had entered the world of literature in the Red Thirties. Critics such as Barbara Foley, however, have argued that Ellison followed the path of that generation.[6] He, too, she asserts, was under the spell of the Leftist ideas for a while, and in the post-war period the logic of a 'Kronstadt rebel'[7] – that

4 For further discussion of the Soviet contacts and reception of McKay and Wright, see Olga Panova, 'Exotic Visitor: Claude McKay in the Soviet Union', *Literature of the Americas* 6 (2019), 220–56 (in Russian); Olga Panova, 'Richard Wright's Might-Have-Been Travel to the USSR', *Literature of the Americas* 3 (2017), 176–228 (in Russian).

5 Note, for example, Ellison's comment, 'No, Wright was no spiritual father of mine …', in his essay 'The World and the Jug', in Ralph Ellison, *Shadow and Act* (New York: Vintage 1995), 117.

6 Barbara Foley, *Wrestling with the Left: The Making of Ralph Ellison's* Invisible Man (Durham, NC: Duke University Press, 2010).

7 See Richard Crossman's 1949 anthology *The God that Failed*, especially Louis Fischer's concept of 'Kronstadt'.

of the former believer in Communism who then turned against it – led him to a revision of his attitudes.

Here we come to a preliminary hypothesis concerning at least one of the reasons why Ellison had been for so long ignored in the USSR: having made his debut in the Leftist press, he was too young to have distinguished himself as a 'great revolutionary black writer' before World War II. And unlike the author of *Native Son*, he didn't have an alibi that could have saved his reputation when his bitter caricature of the Communist Party appeared in 1952, at the peak of McCarthyism and the Cold War. Another interesting fact concerning Ellison's literary reputation is the mirror effect: while in the US during the promotional campaign for *Invisible Man* Random House did its best to obscure Ellison's quite radical views of the earlier period (which fueled indignation in the American Leftist press and contributed to the perception of Ellison's *hors de combat* position, as a politically disengaged artist), Soviet critics in the 1970s–1980s, on the other hand, tended to ignore the Brotherhood episode and to disguise Ellison's anti-communism. They emphasized the anti-racist focus of the novel, pushing forward such episodes as the Battle Royal, the prophetic dream of the letter ordering to 'keep this nigger boy running',[8] and the protagonist's speech in defence of the elderly black couple evicted from the apartment.

An Evolving Literary Reputation: A Survey of the Critical Reception of Ellison, 1960s–1980s

Soviet critics started to pay attention to Ralph Ellison and his works in the early 1960s – ten years after the publication of the *Invisible Man*. This lapse in time seems strange – but turned out to be beneficial for the writer and his masterpiece. From 1946 until the end of the 1950s, American literary studies in Russia were being used as a weapon in the Cold War. The anti-American propagandistic campaign launched in 1946, after

8 Ralph Ellison, *Invisible Man* (New York: Signet Books, 1953), 35.

Churchill's Fulton speech, reached its peak in 1949–1955. This escalation followed the 1949 Resolution of the Central Committee of the CP USSR that announced anti-Americanism to be a general Party line.[9] The critics had to demonstrate their ability to work in accordance with the ideological guidelines. Deming Brown, who was an eyewitness, describes the situation in the following way:

> Soviet spokesmen really shifted their attention to a newly identified adversary and directed against the United States the same bitter arsenal they had used against the Third Reich. The result was an appalling increment of misinterpretations and lies. [...] The only evident discipline behind the remarks of literary critics was a Party line that demanded universal condemnation of all American writing that was not clearly Communist in its orientation. For the critics had simply lost respect for, or at any rate had lost sight of, literary values.[10]

Here is a typical example of such 'criticism' of the late 1940s to early 1950s (actually a tirade of verbal abuse), from a prominent Soviet critic named Moris Mendelson (1904–82):

> A striking example of a writer who has succumbed to the influence of reactionary bourgeois ideology and distorted his talent is Richard Wright. [...] Wright, just like other American decadents, began to depict Negroes as absolutely dumb, idiotic people, unable to protest against the evil. [...] In his novella *The Man Who Lived Underground* published at the height of the war, Wright's decadence reaches maximum force. The hero of the novel is a Negro degenerate, blinded with irrational fear, who turns into a beast, crawls into the underground sewers and lives there surrounded with corpses and garbage. [...] Renegade Wright obviously tries to undermine any human belief in the possibility to destroy the wretched capitalist system.[11]

9 'Plan of activities directed at the strengthening of anti-American propaganda for the Union of the Soviet Writers of 1 April 1949', in D. G. Nadzhafov and Z. S. Belousova, eds, *Stalin and Cosmopolitanism. Documents of the Agitprop of the CP USSR Central Committee, 1945–1953* (Moscow: MFD Publ.; Materik Publ., 2005), 346–8 (in Russian).

10 Deming Brown, *Soviet Attitudes towards American Writing* (Princeton, NJ: Princeton University Press, 1962), 169.

11 Moris O. Mendelson, *Contemporary American Literature: A Public Lecture Held on 20 April 1947 in the Moscow Conference Hall* (Moscow: Pravda Publ., 1947), 22–3 (in Russian).

Ellison was lucky: this 'cup of poison' was taken from him during the first decade of the Cold War. An echo of that period, however, can still be heard in the first comments on his novel. In the 1962 companion to contemporary American literature published in the academic series,[12] Ellison's novel was mentioned by Anna A. Elistratova (1910–74), a highly reputed scholar of American and British literature, who started her career in the early 1930s. She devoted almost two pages of her twenty-page essay to *Invisible Man*:

> Ralph Ellison's novel *Invisible Man* (1947) [sic],[13] which made much noise some time ago, is an example of anti-realistic approach to the tragedy of young Americans who are just coming to life. [...] Ellison's book very convincingly and vividly shows humiliations and abuses Negro youngsters suffer in bourgeois America [...] At the same time the author obviously tends to undermine the idea of working class solidarity. The hero fails over and over again each time he tries to join civic-minded workers who are fighting for their rights. Describing his attempts Ellison uses grim, sinister, pretentious allegories that bring to mind reactionary lampoons by Orwell and suchlike scribblers. The hero feels a stranger everywhere – in the plant floor, at the trade-union meeting. [...] In his hysterical complacency and paranoia he worships the cult of the underground existence, praises his 'hole' where he hides away from the whole world, in his beastly spiteful loneliness following the path of all the reactionary imitators of Dostoevsky. He is invisible, because he is not a friend, a comrade, a citizen, he is just nothing, a void [...]. Ellison's book leaves a painful impression. [...] Spiteful, desperate, cynical, paranoid delirious denial, and wild frenetic individualism are characteristic of the crisis the American young generation is currently going through.[14]

This passage was seminal for the Soviet criticism of the 1960 to early 1970s: it defined the basic pattern for the interpretation of Ellison's novel. Critics used to praise the first episodes (up to the Liberty Paint Factory

12 This critical series dedicated to contemporary American literature launched in 1955 by A. M. Gorky Institute of World Literature (IWL) of the USSR Academy of Sciences was a remarkable Soviet project in American literary studies.

13 Elistratova misrecords the date of the novel's publication as 1947.

14 Anna A. Elistratova, 'Spiritual Crisis of the USA Young Generation in the American Novel', in Ivan I. Anisimov, Anna A. Elistratova, Roman M. Samarin and Georgiy P. Zlobin, eds, *Contemporary USA Literature* (Moscow: Academy of Sciences of the USSR Publ., 1962), 30–1 (in Russian).

episode) as anti-racist and realistic. At the same time, they criticized the second half, especially the Brotherhood part – a practice exemplified by Moris Mendelson, who resided in the United States from 1922 to 1931, entered the CP USA in 1922, and graduated from New York City College in 1926. Back in the USSR he became a professor of English and American literature, a research fellow in the Soviet Academy of Sciences, and (co) author of 16 books and about 200 essays on American literature. In his 1964 book devoted to the contemporary American novel, Mendelson marked Wright's and Dostoevsky's influence on Ellison, who tried 'to justify the right of an embittered individual to hide in a hole', and preached 'exasperated individualism'. Mendelson insists that it is because of Wright's influence that 'a young Negro writer, endowed with the power of observation and lyricism [...] tried to enter the world of literature singing hallelujah to renegadism'. This 'reactionary dogma', according to Mendelson, explains Ralph Ellison's (perceived) 'sterility' and long silence.[15]

Anna Elistratova, meanwhile, included the analysis of Ellison's novel in her essay on the 'spiritual crisis of the USA young generation' quoted above; for a decade or so Soviet critics used to consider Ellison against the backdrop of the youth movement of the 1960s, despite the fact that he was nearing the age of 40 when his novel was published, and obviously didn't, in the 1960s, feel like an 'angry young man'. Ellison and Baldwin were usually compared (and opposed) to the young black nationalists of the 1960s such as LeRoi Jones (Amiri Baraka), John O. Killens and William Melvin Kelly. Thus, for example, Ellison was mentioned during a roundtable discussion by 26-year-old Alexey M. Zverev (1939–2003), a would-be star of American literary studies in the 1970s–1980s who became famous for his seminal book, *Modernism in the USA Literature* (1979). At this roundtable discussion, which was organized by the extremely popular thick literary magazine *Inostrannaia Literatura* [*Foreign Literature*] at the end of 1965, Zverev's critical appraisal of *Invisible Man* was highly positive even when he spoke about the episodes of the novel that were usually subject to harsh criticism:

15 Mendelson, *Contemporary American Novel* (Moscow: Nauka Publ., 1964), 454–5 (In Russian).

> The hero doesn't know that his master is a snooper, informer of the bosses. [...] He comes to the trade-union meeting with the best intentions and tries to make friends with the workers, but they drive him out with indignation, and soon the boss throws him out of work. His third stage is his activity as an agitator of a half-mystical 'Brotherhood' (which hints of the Communist Party of the USA). Being very inexperienced, he provokes an outbreak of black racism and becomes an outcast hiding in the New York sewers, having lost any desire to move forward. The youngster gives up the idea to come to the surface, and becomes an invisible man [...] a new underground man of the twentieth century.[16]

Zverev finds much in common between Ellison and two more American writers closely connected with 1960s youth movement: J. D. Salinger and Jack Kerouac. Their heroes similarly reject the existing order of things, and their denial leads them to absolute loneliness. Zverev describes this type of character as 'metaphysical',[17] static and incompatible with the idea of change; the critic assumes that here is the reason for Ellison's long silence and Kerouac's self-repetition. This idea, common to both Mendelson and Zverev despite their generation gap, anticipates the criticism of the 1970s–1980s, when Ellison was treated as a writer heavily influenced by existentialism. As early as 1969, Alexander Muliarchik (b. 1938), a prolific critic and scholar, labelled Ellison's work with the key word 'alienation', which was constantly repeated in the next decade.[18]

Ellison also attracted the attention of Raisa Orlova (1918–89), a reputed critic and scholar of American literature, who having defended her doctorate in Gorky Institute started to work for *Inostrannaia Literatura* in 1958. In 1966 Orlova esteemed *Invisible Man* as a 'talented novel' and cited Ellison's essay 'Harlem is Nowhere';[19] later, in the 1970s, she several

16 'The Young People of the Sixties and Literature about Them. A Roundtable Discussion', *Inostrannaia Literatura* 12 (1965), 251–2 (in Russian).

17 Ibid., 251.

18 Alexander S. Muliarchik, 'Development Trends of the Postwar American Novel as Treated by the Literary Criticism of the USA', in Moris O. Mendelson, Alexander N. Nikoliukin and Roman M. Samarin, eds, *Contemporary Literary Criticism in the USA: Debates over American Literature* (Moscow: Nauka Publ., 1969), 296, 303 (in Russian).

19 Raisa D. Orlova, 'Voices of the Negro Revolution', *Voprosy literatury* [*Questions of Literature*] 1 (1966), 147, 151 (in Russian).

times referred to Ellison's fictional and nonfictional texts. Orlova's interest in Ellison's work was much more serious than one might conclude from her published works. In the draft version of her 1966 essay, 'Voices of Negro Revolution', there is a page-long fragment on the *Invisible Man* that was later cut, either by Orlova herself or by the editors, from the printed version:

> The Negro writer Ralph Ellison is among those who represent all America at the literary markets of other continents. He wrote the novel *Invisible Man*; its protagonist is a Negro, but his life symbolizes tragic alienation and loneliness in the big cities that causes millions of people of all races to suffer. [...]
>
> Ellison's novel is multidimensional. It's a realistic novel about a journey from childhood to manhood, from the South to the North. [...] However, besides these realistic motives, there is something incognizable, inexpressible, mystical, underlying the plot – a black abyss, the beginning and the end of the human existence. [...]
>
> The title of the novel is inexhaustible; it's a profound metaphor. Invisible Man is a Negro, but the metaphor is wider, more encompassing. It's a man of the twentieth century, rootless, unsteady, living in a vague, unreal world. It's a man whom the power of conformity tries to divest of his identity, of everything that is personal, unique, essential. The book and the hero symbolize an urge for harmony that, according to Ellison, can be found in the myth.[20]

This fragment demonstrates the striking difference between Orlova's analysis and the approach typical of the Soviet criticism in the 1960s.

In 1971, Orlova's disciple Tamara K. Senkevich from Tbilisi State Pedagogical Institute defended the first Soviet PhD dissertation on Ellison.[21]

20 Valeria N. Abrosimova, 'Raisa Orlova's *Bridges*: *Russian–American Literary Connections* Half a Century Later', *Literature of the Americas* 6 (2019), 377 (in Russian). Orlova's draft version of the essay quoted by Abrosimova is kept in Maria N. Orlova's personal archive, folios 69–71.

21 Tamara K. Senkevich, 'Problems of the Contemporary Negro Novel in the USA, 1940–1952, and *Invisible Man* by Ralph Ellison', PhD dissertation (Tbilisi, 1971) (in Russian). Senkevich also published two articles on Ellison in Georgian academic periodicals: 'On the Problem of Alienation in Ellison's Novel *Invisible Man*', *Scholarly Reports of the Academy of Sciences of the Georgian Soviet Socialist Republic* 58/2 (1970), 497–500 (in Russian with abstracts in English and Georgian); 'Ralph Ellison and His Novel *Invisible Man*', *Academic Papers of Tbilisi Pedagogical Institute of Foreign Languages* 11–12 (1972), 392–403 (in Russian).

Being a scholar from the national province of Georgia, in the Caucasus, she did things that were impossible in Moscow or Leningrad. In Brezhnev's USSR, Georgia was an important centre of African American literary studies, where Georgian scholars defended dissertations and published books and articles on Harlem Renaissance, Langston Hughes, Richard Wright, James Baldwin.[22] Although Orlova had had to erase the complimentary paragraph on Ellison from her published essay, her student praised *Invisible Man* as a masterpiece and as the foundational text for the post-war African American literature. Tamara Senkevich claimed that she was arguing against bourgeois critics who depicted Ellison's hero as an escapist, conformist, individualist and reactionary follower of Dostoevsky and existentialist dogma. In fact, however, she entered into controversy with the *maîtres* of the Soviet criticism that followed the propagandistic clichés of the 1940s to early 1960s. Senkevich insists that the narrator's escapism is his *tour de force* in his struggle with the wretched social system and that during his 'hibernation' he has made impressive intellectual and spiritual progress. She treats the Epilogue as optimistic and stresses the important role of folklore in the novel – which according to the Soviet methodological directives meant that the writer was sharing basic revolutionary and internationalist values embedded in 'folk spirit'.

Throughout the 1970s, the change for the better in the critical approach to Ellison is obvious. Soviet critics are briefly mentioning Ellison here and there, evaluating his creative work and his social and political attitudes in a very positive way. Alexander N. Nikoliukin (b. 1928), an eminent scholar, would-be co-author and co-editor of four companions to contemporary American literature, editor of several anthologies of American essays, and author of two classical books on the nineteenth-century Russian–American literary connections (1981, 1987), comments on the controversy between Ellison and the black militant writers of the 1960s, such as John O. Killens and LeRoi Jones, in the 1973 academic companion to contemporary American literature. He there defends Ellison from accusations of

22 In the early 1970s Ralph Ellison knew nothing about the interest in his work in Soviet Georgia; however, as the third part of this essay documents, ten years later he learned about the reception of his novel in the Caucasus.

Uncle Tomism and of commitment to the 'white bourgeois culture'.[23] In 1977, meanwhile, Alexey Zverev describes Ellison as a conservative, who joined the 'right-wing liberals, advocates of social compromise' of the older generation (such as John Steinbeck and James T. Farrell), making the reader understand that this attitude is much more attractive in comparison with the far-Left black radicalism.[24]

By this time, Richard Wright is no longer an unchallenged authority – in the 1970s the critics admit Ellison's and Baldwin's right to criticize their classic forebear. Alexander Muliarchik, for example, agrees that Wright's doctrine that reduces black fiction to the literature of protest 'was restrictive, and that Wright's characters were too primitive, behaving like beasts of prey chased by hunters'. He writes:

> Ellison and Baldwin insisted that Wright in fact supported the myth of the Negro as an inferior creature, and for good reason. The writers of the new wave … refused to follow Wright's principle, to be limited to the social dimension only and to view the Negro as an object of social struggle. They claim that the Negro is to be valued as an individual, a personality. Therefore these writers paid a special attention to the history of black people, their culture, myths, folklore, their peculiar psychology. […] They nevertheless didn't lose sight of the social aspect; on the contrary, it was deepened. The identity quest sharpened social conflicts generated by racism.[25]

Raisa Orlova treats the subject less radically: she insists that the differences between Wright and 'black authors of the new wave' are transient, while the continuity of the tradition is obvious:

> Wright also influenced Ralph Ellison. The very plot of his novel *Invisible Man* is an obvious echo of Wright's story *The Man Who Lived Underground*. Ellison's novel

23 Alexander N. Nikoliukin, 'The Topic of the Negro Protest', in Moris O. Mendelson and Alexander S. Muliarchik, eds, *The Main Currents of Contemporary American Literature* (Moscow: Nauka Publ., 1973), 218–19 (in Russian).

24 Alexey M. Zverev, 'Social Struggle of the 1960s and the Literature of the USA', in Alexander S. Muliarchik, ed., *American Literature and the Social and Political Struggle, 1960s–Early 1970s* (Moscow: Nauka Publ., 1977), 36 (in Russian).

25 Alexander S. Muliarchik, 'Youth Movement and the American Novel of the Early 1970s', in Alexander S. Muliarchik, ed., *American Literature and the Social and Political Struggle, 1960s–Early 1970s* (Moscow: Nauka publ., 1977), 64 (in Russian).

> affirms the rebellion of the individual to an even greater degree than Baldwin's publicistic utterances [sic]. Wright's disciples and heirs polemically distanced themselves from him. But in time many of these writers – Baldwin especially – recognized their affinity with Wright and began to accept ideas they had previously regarded as sociological illusions, as the 'naïve ideals of collectivism'.[26]

It is striking that, in this passage, 'the rebellion of an individual' (which a decade previously was a target of harsh criticism) is now, in McCarthyist America, treated as a sign of human dignity.[27] McCathyism is described by Soviet critics as a form of totalitarianism that silences the voice of nonconformists (i.e. the Left), so in the USSR praising 'American dissidents' became one of the key issues on the agenda. No doubt the sophisticated reader could also interpret these passages as an implicit criticism of the Soviet authoritarian regime. Muliarchik lauds Ellison's 'moral attitude that is in full accordance with the famous Faulkner's formula from his Nobel speech' (about humanity's heroic capacity to prevail), and argues that 'the fetish of alienation must not obscure the real relations between the artist and the society'.[28]

At the end of the decade, two contributors to the 1978 academic companion to American literature argued that Ellison's novel was realistic, its protagonist being a typical character of the 'gloomy 1950s', and having nothing in common with Kafkian abstractions and decadence. Tatiana L. Morozova stated, 'Ellison in his novel *Invisible Man* made an attempt to depict a typical hero of the time … to show disappointment in the struggle for the social progress which was characteristic of the McCarthy era'. She defined the novel as a picaresque, the protagonist as 'black Candide' gradually losing his illusions, and refused to condemn the hero's underground existence. She described his underground existence as the third way – neither

26 Raisa D. Orlova, 'Richard Wright: Writer and Prophet', in Maya Tugusheva, ed., *Twentieth-Century American Literature: A Soviet View*, trans. Ronald Vroon (Moscow: Progress Publishers, 1976), 406.

27 Alexander S. Muliarchik, 'Critical Realism in the Postwar American Novel', in Tugusheva, *Twentieth-Century American Literature: A Soviet View*, 112.

28 Alexander S. Muliarchik, 'The Writer and Contemporary America', in Alexander S. Muliarchik, ed., *American Literature and the Social and Political Struggle, 1960s–Early 1970s* (Moscow: Nauka Publ., 1977), 7, 15 (in Russian).

rebellion, nor conformity – which is, no doubt, a step beyond the rigid Soviet ideological frameworks of the previous decade.[29]

Sergei A. Chakovsky, a specialist in African American literary studies, goes even further: Ellison's novel is not 'the revolt against protest',[30] but 'the widening of the protest, its logical evolution to a new intellectual and aesthetic quality'.[31] Chakovsky was the first among Soviet critics who interpreted the Epilogue in full accordance with the text written by Ellison (instead of inventing another ideologically bound falsification):

> The invisible man is helpless against social injustice, but he is not broken – despite the ending which may seem pessimistic. On the contrary at the end of his journey the hero becomes morally stronger. His narrative shows he is desperate, but conscious of his strength. The invisible man is driven underground, but he is getting ready for a jump [...] In order to understand the novel correctly it is important to bear in mind that the narrator is ironic and even more – self-ironic. To live on, to realize his capacities he must leave the hole and come back to other people. Where he will go having rejected so many things, is hard to say (it is hard for the writer as well – probably that is why he is keeping silence for almost thirty years). It is clear however, that [...] his flight is caused by his urgent need for renewal, and it becomes the cornerstone for his rebirth.[32]

Chakovsky's attempts to analyse the novel in the context of African American literary tradition is not limited to Wright–Ellison relations: the critic finds much in common between Ellison and Jean Toomer, as well as James Weldon Johnson, in that all of them were inspired by African American folklore.[33]

29 Tatiana L. Morozova, 'The Defeat of a Lonely Conqueror: American Julien Sorel', in Yassen Zasurskiy, ed., *Twentieth-Century USA Literature: A Typological Study* (Moscow: Nauka Publ., 1978), 489–92 (in Russian).

30 Chakovsky refers to Part IV of Robert Bone's book *The Negro Novel in America* (1958), 'The Revolt against Protest'.

31 Sergei A. Chakovsky, 'Racial Conflict and the Twentieth-Century USA Literature', in Zasurskiy, ed., *Twentieth-Century USA Literature: A Typological Study*, 305 (in Russian).

32 Ibid., 307.

33 Ibid., 302; see also Sergei A. Chakovsky, 'African Americans and the USA Literature', in Alexander N. Nikoliukin, ed., *American Literature Coming of Age* (Moscow: Nauka Publ., 1981), 275, 285, 287 (in Russian).

The role of folklore in Ellison's work is another issue that Soviet critics start to discuss from the mid-1970s onwards. Ellison was lauded in the USSR for his interest in folklore, because it gave an opportunity to insert him in the cultural matrix sanctified by Marx and Lenin: folklore as 'the closest approximation to *narodnost*' [folk spirit], 'emphasizing internationalism embedded in people's cultures everywhere'.[34] Tamara Denisova (1934–2015), a leading scholar of American literature from the Ukrainian Academy of Sciences, commented in her book on the post-war American novel on Ellison's profound interest in jazz, which she classed as 'folk Negro culture'. Comparing writer's work to jazz improvisation, she writes,

> Ellison offered a theory about the character and peculiarities of the Negro culture. Let us sum up his basic concept: the writer must know very well the culture of the past, both 'highbrow' and popular, and work on the basis of classical and folk culture. And here it becomes clear that he used to be a jazz musician – because jazz is one's own variation of the common melody, it unites the individual and the common body, freedom and necessity. The jazz soloist, just like the writer, generalizes the common experience of his people while striving at self-expression.[35]

By the end of the 1970s, existentialism, folklore and social criticism became the guidelines for the critical interpretation of Ellison's work. The next decade, the 1980s, however, was incredibly scant in terms of critical writings – a paradox, taking into account the fact that, by this time, *Invisible Man* was included by the Soviet critics in the top three twentieth-century black novels (together with Wright's *Native Son* and Baldwin's *Another Country*). The 1980s did nonetheless bring two small but interesting publications: a critical review of Robert O'Meally's book *The Craft of Ralph Ellison* (1980) in a bibliographical journal of the Soviet Academy of Sciences,[36] and a write-up of the celebrations in the USA on

34 Foley, *Wrestling with the Left*, 81. See also ibid., 79–82.

35 Tamara N. Denisova, *Contemporary American Novel* (Kiev: Naukova Dumka Publ., 1976), 177–8 (in Russian).

36 Liudmila I. Zhelokhovtseva, review of Robert G. O'Meally, *The Craft of Ralph Ellison* (Cambridge, MA: Harvard University Press, 1980), *Referetivnyi zhurnal*, series 'Literaturovedenie' [*Bibliographical Journal*, series 'Literary studies'], 1 (1983), 159–62 (in Russian).

occasion of the thirtieth anniversary of Ellison's novel.[37] The latter describes the new Random House anniversary edition of *Invisible Man*, informs the readers that the novel has gone through thirty-seven editions and was translated into fifteen languages, and cites several paragraphs from Ellison's direct speech about his second novel. The small item from the news section is based on the article from the *New York Times*, and it is striking that Russia is mentioned in that *NYT* source piece:

> The author's wife, Fanny, who magically finds just about everything he has written in their home files, says that a request came in for a Polish edition just before martial law was declared in Poland. He says that the Russians are aware of his writings, but that if a translation exists in Russian, he hasn't seen any edition.[38]

Communications with Ellison and Translations of His Work, 1970–1989

The *NYT*'s reference to Russia may be rooted in the growing interest in Ellison's work in the Soviet Union that the novelist would have perceived in the 1970s and early 1980s. At that time, Soviet scholars of American literature made at least two attempts to reach Ralph Ellison. The first one was made by Raisa Orlova, who maintained wide and active contacts with American writers and academics – this practice was rare in the USSR, which remained a closed-off country even after Stalin's death. In the mid-1970s, Orlova began her two-way study of American writers' attitudes to Russian literature and of Soviet writers' ideas about American literature. To make the book *Bridges: Russian–American Literary Relations*, she wrote over fifty letters to American writers and critics between October and December 1974, and between February and May 1975. Among these was a letter to Ralph Ellison:

37 'Anniversary of the Novel', *Inostrannaia Literatura* 2 (1983), 250–1 (in Russian).

38 Herbert Mitgang, '*Invisible Man*, as Vivid Today as in 1952', *New York Times* (1 March 1982), 13, <https://www.nytimes.com/1982/03/01/books/invisible-man-as-vivid-today-as-in-1952.html>, accessed 12 August 2019.

> 19 November 1974.
>
> Dear Mr. Ellison,
>
> I'm but one of many readers and admirers of *Invisible Man* in this country. My field is American writing. One of my pupils[39] defended her doctorate on Ralph Ellison works, she lives in Tbilisi, Georgia (we also have one).
>
> All this is an awkward attempt of an introduction. And a preface to asking of a favor. I have begun a new work (I had published several books on American literature), – 'American writers in Russia', in this connection I put a question to a group of American writers and would highly appreciate it, if you would answer: what was a role of Russian literature in your life? Your writer's and reader's life (in case it may be separated)?
>
> Is it possible to develop some remarks you made in an interview at 1955 (republished in *Shadow and Act*) about *Notes from the Underground* and, especially, about *The Overcoat*?
>
> Thanking you in advance, with all the best wishes.
>
> I sincerely hope that we'll have at last *Invisible Man* in Russian! (Only in the last two years we had *The Sound and the Fury* and *Light in August*.)
>
> R. Orlova.[40]

Although Ellison was not among Orlova's personal acquaintances, having got her letter he nonetheless wrote a concise but quite informative answer:

> Dear Miss Orlova:[41]
>
> It pleases me to know that you and other students of literature are interested in my novel I.M. I, too, would like to see it translated into Russian.

39 This pupil is Tamara K. Senkevich (see above).

40 Raisa Orlova, letter to Ralph Ellison, 19 November 1974, Library of Congress, Ralph Ellison papers, I:62, folder 7 (a copy of the letter is also in the personal archive of Maria N. Orlova, folios 69–71). Raisa Orlova's letter, which was written in English, is quoted with minor edits, for sense, made by me. The Russian translation, by Valeria D. Medvinskaya, was published by Valeria Abrosimova in *Literature of the Americas* 6 (2019), 374.

41 I have transcribed this letter from a typed draft in the Library of Congress archive – the edits in square brackets are Ellison's own. There is also a draft of this letter in

> The work of 19th century Russian writers has always been very important in my life, especially when I began to write, for the depiction of Russian society as found in the works of Tolstoy, Turgenev, Dostoevsky and Gorky offered me many insights into ways of interpreting social events as they unfolded in the U.S. I think of Dostoevsky as perhaps the greates[t] of all novelists and I continue to learn from his work. I am also aware of Pushkin and Chekov [sic], along with other masters of Russian literature.
>
> Notes from Underground was especially important in the writing of I.M. I think a look at the two works would make further comment unnecessary. For the narrator of I.[M]., despite differences in culture, race and nationality, [is] also an underground man.
>
> The Overcoat I found entertaining but I gained more insight and learned certain approaches to fictional material from Gogol's Dead Souls, which I rank as on[e] of the world's great novels.
>
> I hope that these few words will be useful to you in your work.
>
> Again, I thank you for writing and am sinc yrs [Ralph Ellison.]

Orlova managed to get ten letters from American authors via Soviet post before her emigration from the USSR, but the major part of the correspondence didn't reach its destination – very possibly this was the case with Ellison's reply itself. Unfortunately, Orlova's project remained unrealized and her book was never published: she and her husband Lev Kopelev, a historian of German literature, dissident and human rights activist, had to emigrate in 1980. It's not known if Raisa Orlova ever received Ellison's answer, even if it were mailed, after she had left the USSR; most probably not, as no trace of it has been found in her archive to date.

Another attempt to contact Ellison was connected with the endeavour to translate his novel. On 16 and 20 September 1977 *Literaturna Ukraina*, the newspaper of the Ukrainian Union of Writers, published 'Battle Royal'. The translation into Ukrainian was made by Oksana Bedzyk-Galitska, a research assistant at Taras Shevchenko Institute of Literature of the Ukrainian Academy of Sciences; her grandfather Dmitry Bedzyk (1898–1982) and her father Yuri Bedzyk (1925–2008) were well-known Soviet Ukrainian writers.

---

pencil in the same location. The letter is undated and it is possible that no version of it was ever mailed. Ralph Ellison, draft letter to Raisa Orlova, Library of Congress, Ralph Ellison papers, I:62, folder 7. I am very grateful to Andrew Davenport and Paul Devlin who supplied me with the archived Ellison–Orlova correspondence.

After the publication in *Literaturna Ukraina* – so presumably some time in the early winter of 1977, although she did not date her letter – Oksana wrote to Ralph Ellison:

> Dear sir!
>
> Receive my New Year greetings and my best wishes to you.
>
> Not long ago I accidently run into your story 'Battle Royal'. It impressed me so that I made an immediate attempt to translate it into Ukrainian. The story was published in a local literary newspaper and roused widespread interest to its author and his work. I am eager to continue the work and now began to translate the whole your novel 'Invisible Man'. Unfortunately I have no other your works.
>
> As for me I was born [in] 1947 in Kiev and graduated from Kiev University in 1971. Since then I work in the Ukrainian Literature Institute [of the] Academy of Sciences [of the] Ukrainian SSR. I have two year old son and my husband [is a] mathematician.
>
> With respect Oksana Bedzyk-Galitska.[42]

In the USSR in 1977, sending a letter to the USA to an American writer was not an ordinary or easy thing to do. The letters going abroad to the 'capitalist countries' were usually inspected and very often failed to reach the addressee; in cases where they did reach the destination, it took months to deliver them. Most probably Oksana Bezyk-Galitska asked someone to take the letter to the United States – maybe an official from the Soviet Embassy. Somehow or other the Ellisons got the letter from the Ukrainian correspondent, and Fanny Ellison resent it to the Random House Executive editor Albert Erskine with the following comment:

> 26 June 1978.
>
> Dear Albert:
>
> I was to have sent this to you in May but it got lost in the madness of trying to get out of N. Y. It is a communication concerning the translating effort by a Ukrainian and she, or he, needs to be advised about rights and procedure.

42 Oksana Bedzyk-Galitska, Letter to Ralph Ellison, undated (c. early winter 1977), Library of Congress, Ralph Ellison papers, Foreign Rights and Translations 1952–78, I:53, folder 5. Oksana Bedzyk-Galitska's letter, which is undated, was written in English and I have transcribed it maintaining the author's orthography. I express sincere gratitude to Tessa Roynon for supplying me with the archived documents that made this reconstruction possible.

> When it has been taken care of, will you please have the correspondence returned to us.
>
> Thanks and regards, [Fanny Ellison][43]

Carolyn Reidy from the subsidiary rights department wrote to Oksana Bedzyk-Galitska quite a discouraging letter, asserting to the Ukrainian admirer of Ellison that her publication was a copyright infringement:

> 31 October 1978.
>
> Dear Oksana Bedzyk-Galitska:
>
> Some time ago you wrote to Mr. Ralph Ellison concerning his book, *Invisible Man*. In your letter you mentioned that you published Mr. Ellison's story 'Battle Royal' in Ukrainian in a local newspaper.
>
> Although we would be pleased to see *Invisible Man* translated into Ukrainian and published in your country, we are somewhat distressed that Mr. Ellison did not receive any prior notice of this publication or monetary compensation for it. As you no doubt know, it is customary for an author to receive payment of some kind when his work is translated into a foreign language.
>
> If you have found a publishing house which is interested in publishing *Invisible Man* in its entirety in Ukrainian, we would like to hear further from you and would like to arrange a license for such publication. Mr. Ellison's book has been translated throughout the world and continues to be considered one of the America's greatest twentieth-century novels.[44]

These demands, however, didn't have any legal basis. Although in 1973 the USSR joined the Geneva 1952 version of the Universal Copyright Convention, according to the agreement signed, the copyright was not retroactive: only foreign works first published after 27 May 1973 outside of the USSR were to be copyrighted in the Soviet Union.

Carolyn Reidy reported to Fanny Ellison when the task was completed:

43 Fanny Ellison, Letter to Albert Erskine, 26 June 1978, Library of Congress, Ralph Ellison papers, Foreign Rights and Translations 1952–78, I:53, folder 5.

44 Carolyn Reidy, Letter to Oksana Bedzyk-Galitska, 31 October 1978, Library of Congress, Ralph Ellison papers, Foreign Rights and Translations 1952–78, I:53, folder 5.

> 1 December 1978.
>
> Dear Mrs. Ellison:
>
> Some time ago you sent to Mr. Albert Erskine a short letter plus a copy of the Ukrainian newspaper which had published parts of the *Invisible Man*. This has recently surfaced here and, as you can see, I have written to the woman who wrote to you about the matter .... When we hear from Oksana Bedzyk-Galitska, I will let you know.[45]

But in fact neither the Ellisons nor Random House staff ever heard again from Oksana Bedzyk-Galitska, who presumably gave up on her idea to translate *Invisible Man*. Her former colleagues now hardly remember this descendant of two famous writers, who worked in the Ukrainian Academy of Sciences at a minor position for a very short period of time and soon left for Israel with her family. All their ties with her were broken entirely.

The Ukrainian translation project had failed, but perhaps not coincidentally, when it came to the first translation of Ellison's fiction into Russian, the whole thing started with the same piece: 'Battle Royal'. This particular episode used to be regarded as the best choice – it was an impressive anti-racist text that could be read (as indeed Ellison had first published it, in the *Horizon* journal in 1947), as an accomplished short story. It was rendered into Russian by the famous translator of American and British literature, Victor Golyshev. Golyshev recollects that in 1980 Progress Publishers was considering the possibility of translating the *Invisible Man* in their series 'Library of American Literature', but finally the publishers preferred Richard Wright.[46] Instead of the *Invisible Man*, therefore, Golyshev had to translate *The Man Who Lived Underground* for Wright's *Selected Works* (1981). 'Battle Royal', prepared by Golyshev as a trial translation, entered the Russian collection of Ellison's short stories entitled *King of the Bingo Game*, that appeared in 1985, in the very beginning of *Perestroika* ['restructuring'] – Mikhail Gorbachev's period of reforms.

45 Carolyn Reidy, Letter to Fanny Ellison, 1 December 1978, Library of Congress, Ralph Ellison papers, Foreign Rights and Translations 1952–78, I:53, folder 5.

46 Victor Golyshev, personal communication, 15 September 2017.

The first (and so far the last) book edition of Ellison in Russian was published in the famous popular series of pocket-sized books 'Biblioteka Inostrannoi Literatury' [Library of Foreign Literature]. The book included ten of his short stories taken from various American periodicals and collections of 1941–64, together with the essay 'Hidden Name and Complex Fate'.[47] The edition was prepared by the critic Mikhail B. Landor, son of a reputed literary historian Tamara L. Motyliova. In his foreword, Landor praised Ellison's novel, gave a thoughtful analysis of the short stories and stressed that Ellison's work was lauded by William Faulkner, Robert Penn Warren, Langston Hughes and other prominent writers. The short stories were rendered into Russian by the best translators of American and British literature: Victor Golyshev, Andrei Sergeev, Vladimir Oryol, Inna Bernstein, Vladimir Boshnyak and Alexey Zverev. In 1991, one of these short stories, a fragment from the *Juneteenth* (translated by Rostislav Rybkin) entered two anthologies,[48] while 'Hidden Name and Complex Fate', translated by Oleg Alyakrinsky, was included in the two-volume anthology *American Writers on American Literature*.[49]

The Teaching, Studying and Translation of Ellison, 1980s–2000s

Before the 1980s, African American literature in general remained out of view in Soviet universities. Some works of Richard Wright, Langston Hughes, W. E. B. Du Bois and James Baldwin from time to time appeared in the reading lists for students majoring in American literature, but

47 Ralph Ellison, *King of the Bingo Game*, multiple translators, ed., Mikhail Landor (Moscow: Izvestiia Publ., 1985) (in Russian).

48 Victor Veber, ed., *Holy Night: A Collection of Tales by Foreign Writers* (Moscow: Politicheskaya Literatura Publ., 1991), 213–22 (in Russian); Rostislav Rybkin, ed., *Sonny's Blues: A Collection of Short Stories by Foreign Writers on Music and Musicians* (Moscow: Muzyka Publ., 1991), 262–72 (in Russian).

49 Alexander N. Nikoliukin, ed., *American Writers on American Literature* (Moscow: Progress Publishers, 1982) (in Russian).

Ellison's works weren't taught. Steven Kellman, an American professor who went via Fulbright to Tbilisi State University for the spring semester of 1980, was among the pioneers who started to teach Ellison in the Soviet universities. Remembering his experience in Soviet Georgia, Professor Kellman describes the atmosphere of the late Brezhnev era: he arrived in Tbilisi soon after the USSR invaded Afghanistan. The US started to boycott the Moscow Olympics, and classes were delivered under strict surveillance – they were both recorded and monitored.[50]

Kellman taught his course of American literature to 'about a hundred eager students'. (No wonder the students were excited: in 1980 an American professor teaching in a Soviet university was an extraordinary event.) Ellison's novel, as well as some other texts selected for teaching, were unavailable in Georgian libraries, but the students read books their mentor 'brought in through diplomatic pouch', passing them to each other. Unexpectedly teaching Ellison in Breznev's USSR became an important experience for him and his students:

> I was struck by how, in the United States, where everything is available, little is valued, whereas in a closed society every scrap of writing becomes precious. [...] During private conversations later, students expressed their gratitude to Ellison for conveying so vividly the alienation they were feeling. [...] Though, set in a small Southern town, a college much like Tuskegee, and New York City, *Invisible Man* is very much an American novel, crucially shaped by the racial history of the United States, Georgians were able to respond to the universality of the quest to carve out a meaningful identity in a society intent on erasing one's individuality. I have taught *Invisible Man* many times since in the United States, and American students are in awe of its literary achievement, but perhaps not with the same urgency that Georgians felt back in 1980.[51]

Having come back to the US, Steven Kellman wrote a letter to Ralph Ellison telling him about the enthusiasm of his Georgian students for the novel. Ralph Ellison wrote back thanking him for the news brought from behind the Iron Curtain:

50 Steven Kellman, email to Paul Devlin (17 September 2019). I am very grateful to Professor Kellman for his permission to use his text and to Professor Devlin for sharing it.

51 Ibid.

> March 28, 1982.
>
> Dear Mr. Kellman:
>
> Thanks for letting me know that I have readers in Soviet Georgia, and for your role in increasing their number. It gives me some of that delayed pleasure which I imagine one receives upon learning that a message launched years before in a sea-borne bottle was actually fished up along a faraway shore and enjoyed by a sympathetic reader. Till now whenever I thought of the possibility of any of my writings finding readers in Russia it was in terms of hunting with a shotgun in thick cover. You fire the gun's broad pattern of pellets in the direction of what is at best a vaguely seen target, and if you are told of the results in the form of royalty payments – well, that's history. But if you missed, or were unable to hear a thud or count a kopek – that, without question, is mystery. And a mystery of international publishing wrapped up in a political enigma at that! Thanks to you, at least some of that mystery has been dispelled. [...] Several writer friends have informed me of their having met Soviet writers who were familiar with my novel, but none were able to tell me how this had come about or if there was an edition of *Invisible Man* available in Russian.[52]

The situation with teaching Ellison in the universities began to change during the 1980s: *Invisible Man* and sometimes an essay or two from *Shadow and Act* were often included in the reading lists for the students majoring in American literature in the biggest universities (such as Lomonosov Moscow State University, Leningrad State University and universities in Kazan, Minsk and Kiev). In the mid-1980s the course of contemporary American literature at the Philological Faculty of MSU (Moscow State University) was delivered by Professor Tatiana Venediktova, a well-known scholar of American Romanticism, poetry and the contemporary novel. Her course required extensive reading of American prose and poetry of the 1940s–80s in the original, since very few works from the reading list were translated into Russian at that time. Ralph Ellison's novel was on the list, and the students (including myself) had to read it in the reading room of the Library of Foreign Literature. So that is how I, then a four-year student majoring in American literature, learned about Ellison and his *Invisible Man*. This was in 1985.

52 Ralph Ellison, Letter to Steven Kellman, 28 March 1982, in *The Selected Letters of Ralph Ellison*, eds, John F. Callahan and Mark C. Conner (New York: Random House, 2019), 768–9.

The analysis of the novel offered by Professor Venediktova seemed to me the most inspiring topic of the semester, and I therefore chose Ellison for my final graduation paper. Four years later, in the PhD dissertation I defended in 1991,[53] I concentrated on the series of oppositions which represented the basic dualism of Ellison's world: false/true; social/personal; persona/personality; alienation/community feeling; official history/folklore (verbal art, music). The most interesting seemed to be the opposition of the 'senescent' bourgeois Western civilization – and an emergent hybrid culture created by the peoples of non-European descent (African Americans, Native Americans), that for a certain period of time remained at the pre-bourgeois stage of their history in the New World, before their integration in the modern industrial civilization. As a result, these peoples arguably acquired a very particular vision of their country, its destiny and its culture. This view and some elements of the poetics used to express these attitudes had, to my mind, much in common both with postmodernist discourse and with Latin American 'magic realism'. I regarded Ellison as a pathbreaker in this respect and argued that some elements of his multifaceted novel echoed the works of very different younger black writers of the 1950s–1980s: Ishmael Reed, Toni Morrison, James Alan McPherson, Toni Cade Bambara, Ernest J. Gaines, Leon Forrest.

In 1998, the Belarusian scholar of American and African American literature, Yuri V. Stulov, a professor at Minsk State Linguistic University, included Ellison in his bio-bibliographical dictionary *100 American Writers* (first published in 1998).[54] The book contains brief biographical data, a critical bibliography and a publication history of Ellison's works; its second, revised and enlarged version (published in 2019) included the 2010 edition of *Three Days before the Shooting …* prepared by John Callahan and Adam Bradley. Yuri Stulov offers a critical appraisal of *Invisible Man* and characterizes it as a masterpiece of the twentieth-century American literature:

53 Olga Surova (Panova), 'Ralph Ellison and the Blackamerican Literature of the 1950s–1980s'. PhD dissertation (Moscow, 1991) (in Russian).

54 Yuri V. Stulov, *100 American Writers* (Minsk: Vysshaia Shkola Publ., 1998), 322–4; ibid., 2nd rev. and enlarged edn, 2019, 372–4 (in Russian).

> In literary history Ellison remains the author of only one novel; however he in many aspects defined the evolution of African American literature in the 1960s-1980s. His existentialist hero stands close to the narrator from Dostoevsky's *Notes from Underground*; the novel explores the problem of identity quest – an underlying theme of African American literature in the 1950s – and demonstrates the disastrous effects of the inability to affirm self-identity. [...] Being black, he is doomed to remain an 'invisible man' rejected by the racist society. At the same time 'invisibility' provides him with an existential freedom of action. The poetics of the novel are remarkable: elements of realism, naturalism, surrealism and folklore are closely intertwined. Ellison's style is characterized by an outstanding poetic force and powerful impact. His creative work unites European and African American literary traditions. His aesthetic views are close to those of James Baldwin.[55]

Yet overall, in the post-Soviet period thus far, Ellison's oeuvre and their legacies haven't got the critical appraisal they obviously deserve. Although Ellison has achieved the status of a great American twentieth-century classic, the conspiracy of silence still goes on. Thus, for example, in volume VI of the definitive *History of the USA Literature*[56] dedicated to twentieth-century literature, while Ellison is very briefly mentioned several times in chapters written by different scholars, there is not one paragraph devoted to him and his works. The volume does include chapters, however, on the Harlem Renaissance, Jean Toomer, Zora Neale Hurston, Langston Hughes, Richard Wright and African American drama.

After the 1991 publications of Ellison's fiction, the next one came over twenty years later – in 2013. It became possible thanks to Alexander Livergant, editor-in-chief of *Inostrannaya Literatura* magazine, an experienced and very professional translator and an expert in modern British and American literature, who for a long time had a special interest in Ellison's novel. In late 1990s Livergant was thinking of translating *Invisible Man* into Russian together with his friend Victor Golyshev. They tried to get a fellowship to go to New York City to work in the New York Public Library, to see Harlem, to get acquainted with the localities and to better

55 Ibid., 2nd edn, 372–3 (in Russian).

56 Maya M. Korevena, Ekaterina A. Stetsenko, Andrey F. Kofman and Alexandra P. Urakova, eds, *History of the USA Literature* (Moscow: Institute of World Literature of the Russian Academy of Sciences Publ., 1998–2013).

understand Ellison's cultural, mythical, political and literary allusions. However, they failed to get money for the project. Victor Golyshev described the situation as follows.

> Long ago Livergant suggested: 'Let's translate Ellison's *Invisible Man*!' – but it came to nothing after all. Probably we failed to find a publisher. Or maybe we were not insistent enough, or went into some other project. Somehow or other finally it was just a big nothing.[57]

In 2011, Alexander Livergant proposed the publication of several chapters from the *Invisible Man* in *Inostrannaya Literatura*, to be translated by me. Ksenia Starosel'skaya, an experienced translator, checked and edited my translation; when it was ready, the next difficulty to overcome was the copyright problem. It was not easy to get permission from the copyright holder, but we were luckier than Oksana Bedzyk-Galitska. We had to wait for almost two years while sending requests and negotiating details. Finally, thanks to Alexander Livergant's efforts we succeeded, but had to shorten the publication (initially the text was twice as long). To replenish the material we decided to accompany the fragments from the novel with two nonfictional pieces – Saul Bellow's essay on Ralph Ellison (a very nice and lively sketch), and Ellison's 1955 interview 'The Art of Fiction' for the *Paris Review*. This was the second piece from the *Shadow and Act* collection to be translated into Russian – after 'Hidden Name and Complex Fate'. As for the novel, we chose several episodes: the Prologue, the narrator's first acquaintance with Tod Clifton at a Brotherhood meeting; Clifton selling Sambo dolls, Clifton's death and his funeral with the narrator's rousing speech; and the emergency meeting with Brother Jack and the other Brotherhood leaders.[58] So far, however, Russian readers haven't got the full translation of the novel.

In 2018 I signed an agreement with a prestigious Russian academic book series 'Literaturnye pamiatniki' ('Literary Monuments'), for the

57 Victor Golyshev, personal communication, 15 September 2017.

58 Ralph Ellison and Saul Bellow, 'Literary Guide. "Invisible Novel" by Ralph Ellison', ed., trans. and with an introduction by Olga Panova, *Inostrannaia Literatura* 1 (2013), 203–64 (in Russian).

editorial project 'Ralph Ellison, *Invisible Man*'. It is my hope that the scholarly, annotated edition of Ellison's masterpiece will be published in Russian after all, sometime in the next two or three years.

Bibliography

Abrosimova, Valeria N., 'Raisa Orlova's *Bridges*: *Russian–American Literary Connections* Half a Century Later', *Literature of the Americas* 6 (2019), 297–378 (in Russian). DOI: 10.22455/2541-7894-2019-6-296-378. <http://www.litda.ru/images/2019-6/LDA-2019-6_296-378_Abrosimova.pdf>, accessed 17 July 2020.

'Anniversary of the Novel', *Inostrannaia Literatura* 2 (1983), 250–1.

Bedzyk-Galitska, Oksana, Letter to Ralph Ellison, undated (c. early winter 1977), Library of Congress, Ralph Ellison papers, Foreign Rights and Translations 1952–78, I:53, folder 5.

Brown, Deming, *Soviet Attitudes towards American Writing* (Princeton, NJ: Princeton University Press, 1962).

Chakovsky, Sergei A., 'African Americans and the USA Literature', in Alexander N. Nikoliukin, ed., *American Literature Coming of Age* (Moscow: Nauka Publ., 1981), 274–91 (in Russian).

——, 'Racial Conflict and the Twentieth-Century USA Literature', in Yassen Zasurskiy, ed., *Twentieth-Century USA Literature: A Typological Study* (Moscow: Nauka Publ., 1978), 285–312 (in Russian).

Crossman, Richard, ed., *The God that Failed* (New York: Harper, 1949).

Denisova, Tamara N., *Contemporary American Novel* (Kiev: Naukova Dumka Publ., 1976) (in Russian).

Elistratova, Anna A., 'Spiritual Crisis of the USA Young Generation in the American Novel', in Ivan I. Anisimov, Anna A. Elistratova, Roman M. Samarin and Georgiy P. Zlobin, eds, *Contemporary USA Literature* (Moscow: Academy of Sciences of the USSR Publ., 1962), 23–43 (in Russian).

Ellison, Fanny, Letter to Albert Erskine, 26 June 1978, Library of Congress, Ralph Ellison papers, Foreign Rights and Translations 1952–78, I:53, folder 5.

Ellison, Ralph, *Invisible Man* (New York: Signet Books, 1953).

——, 'Juneteenth', trans. Rostislav Rybkin, in Rostislav Rybkin, ed., *Sonny's Blues: A Collection of Short Stories by Foreign Writers on Music and Musicians* (Moscow: Muzyka Publ., 1991), 262–72 (in Russian).

——, 'Juneteenth', trans. Rostislav Rybkin, in Victor Veber, ed., *Holy Night: A Collection of Tales by Foreign Writers* (Moscow: Politicheskaya Literatura Publ., 1991), 213–22 (in Russian).
——, *King of the Bingo Game*, ed., Mikhail Landor (Moscow: Izvestiia Publ., 1985) (in Russian).
——, Letter to Raisa Orlova (draft, undated), Library of Congress, Ralph Ellison papers, I:62, folder 7.
——, Letter to Steven Kellman, 28 March 1982, in *The Selected Letters of Ralph Ellison*, eds, John F. Callahan and Mark C. Conner (New York: Random House, 2019), 768–9.
——, 'The World and the Jug', in Ralph Ellison, ed., *Shadow and Act* (New York: Vintage, 1995), 115–47.
—— and Saul Bellow, 'Literary Guide. "Invisible Novel" by Ralph Ellison', ed., trans. and with an introduction by Olga Panova, *Inostrannaia Literatura* 1 (2013), 203–64 (in Russian).
Foley, Barbara, *Wrestling with the Left: The Making of Ralph Ellison's* Invisible Man (Durham, NC: Duke University Press, 2010).
Golyshev, Victor, email to Olga Panova, 15 September 2017.
Kellman, Steven, email to Paul Devlin, 17 September 2019.
Korevena, Maya M., Ekaterina A. Stetsenko, Andrey F. Kofman and Alexandra P. Urakova, eds, *History of the USA Literature* (Moscow: Institute of World Literature of the Russian Academy of Sciences Publ., 1998–2013).
Mendelson, Moris O., *Contemporary American Literature: A Public Lecture Held on 20 April 1947 in the Moscow Conference Hall* (Moscow: Pravda Publ., 1947) (in Russian).
——, *Contemporary American Novel* (Moscow: Nauka Publ., 1966) (in Russian).
—— and Alexander S. Muliarchik, eds, *The Main Currents of Contemporary American Literature* (Moscow: Nauka Publ., 1973) (in Russian).
——, Alexander N. Nikoliukin and Roman M. Samarin, eds, *Contemporary Literary Criticism in the USA. Debates over American Literature* (Moscow: Nauka Publ., 1969) (in Russian).
Mitgang, Herbert, '*Invisible Man*, as Vivid Today as in 1952', *New York Times* (1 March 1982), 13.
Morozova, Tatiana L., 'The Defeat of a Lonely Conqueror: American Julien Sorel', in Yassen Zasurskiy, ed., *Twentieth-Century USA Literature: A Typological Study* (Moscow: Nauka Publ., 1978), 361–91 (in Russian).
Muliarchik, Alexander S., ed., *American Literature and the Social and Political Struggle, 1960s–Early 1970s* (Moscow: Nauka Publ., 1977) (in Russian).
——, 'Critical Realism in the Postwar American Novel', in Maya Tugusheva, ed., *Twentieth-Century American Literature: A Soviet View*, trans. Ronald Vroon (Moscow: Progress Publishers, 1976), 100–20.

——, 'Development Trends of the Postwar American Novel as Treated by the Literary Criticism of the USA', in Moris O. Mendelson, Alexander N. Nikoliukin and Roman M. Samarin, eds, *Contemporary Literary Criticism in the USA: Debates over American Literature* (Moscow: Nauka Publ., 1969), 274–305.

——, 'The Writer and Contemporary America', in Alexander S. Muliarchik, ed., *American Literature and the Social and Political Struggle, 1960s–Early 1970s* (Moscow: Nauka Publ., 1977), 6–41 (in Russian).

——, 'Youth Movement and the American Novel of the Early 1970s', in Alexander S. Muliarchik, ed., *American Literature and the Social and Political Struggle, 1960s–Early 1970s* (Moscow: Nauka Publ., 1977), 79–105 (in Russian).

Nikoliukin, Alexander N., ed., *American Literature Coming of Age* (Moscow: Nauka Publ., 1981) (in Russian).

——, ed., *American Writers on American Literature* (Moscow: Progress Publishers, 1982) (in Russian).

——, 'The Topic of the Negro Protest', in Moris O. Mendelson and Alexander S. Muliarchik, eds, *The Main Currents of Contemporary American Literature* (Moscow: Nauka Publ., 1973), 218–19 (in Russian).

Orlova, Raisa D., Letter to Ralph Ellison, 19 November 1974, Ralph Ellison papers, Library of Congress, Washington DC, I:62, folder 7.

——, 'Richard Wright: Writer and Prophet', in Maya Tugusheva, ed., *Twentieth-Century American Literature: A Soviet View*, trans. Ronald Vroon (Moscow: Progress Publishers, 1976), 384–410.

——, 'Voices of the Negro Revolution', *Voprosy literatury* [*Questions of Literature*] 1 (1966), 136–58 (in Russian).

Panova, Olga, 'Exotic Visitor: Claude McKay in the Soviet Union', *Literature of the Americas* 6 (2019), 220–56 (in Russian). DOI: 10.22455/2541-7894-2019-6-220-256. <http://www.litda.ru/images/2019-6/LDA-2019-6_220-256_Panova.pdf>, accessed 11 June 2020.

——, 'Richard Wright's Might-Have-Been Travel to the USSR', *Literature of the Americas* 3 (2017), 176–228 (in Russian). DOI: 10.22455/2541-7894-2017-3-176-228. <http://www.litda.ru/images/2017-3/LDA-2017-3_176-228_Panova.pdf>, accessed 11 June 2020.

Pesis, Boris, 'Towards Rear Guard', *Kniga i revoliutsiia* [*Book and Revolution*] 29–30 (1930), 16–18 (in Russian).

'Plan of Activities Directed at the Strengthening of anti-American Propaganda for the Union of the Soviet Writers of 1 April 1949', in D. G. Nadzhafov and Z. S. Belousova, eds, *Stalin and Cosmopolitanism. Documents of the Agitprop of the CP USSR Central Committee, 1945–1953* (Moscow: MFD Publ.; Materik Publ., 2005), 346–8 (in Russian).

Reidy, Carolyn, Letter to Fanny Ellison, 1 December 1978, Library of Congress, Ralph Ellison papers, Foreign Rights and Translations 1952–78, I:53, folder 5.

——, Letter to Oksana Bedzyk-Galitska, 31 October 1978, Library of Congress, Ralph Ellison papers, Foreign Rights and Translations 1952–78, I:53, folder 5.

Senkevich, Tamara K., 'On the Problem of Alienation in Ellison's Novel *Invisible Man*', in *Scholarly Reports of the Academy of Sciences of the Georgian Soviet Socialist Republic*, 58/2 (1970), 497–500 (in Russian) with abstracts in English and Georgian.

——, *Problems of the Contemporary Negro Novel in the USA, 1940–1952, and* Invisible Man *by Ralph Ellison*, PhD dissertation (Tbilisi, 1971) (in Russian).

——, 'Ralph Ellison and His Novel *Invisible Man*', *Academic Papers of Tbilisi Pedagogical Institute of Foreign Languages* 11–12 (1972), 392–403 (in Russian).

Startsev, Abel, 'To Harlem, to Harlem!', *Oktiabr'* [*October*], 4–5 (1931), 236 (in Russian).

Stulov, Yuri V., *100 American Writers* (Minsk: Vysshaia Shkola Publ., 1998; 2nd rev. and enlarged edn, 2019) (in Russian).

Surova (Panova), Olga, 'Ralph Ellison and the Blackamerican Literature of the 1950s–1980s', PhD dissertation (Moscow, 1991) (in Russian).

Tugusheva, Maya, ed., *Twentieth-Century American Literature: A Soviet View*, trans. Ronald Vroon (Moscow: Progress Publishers, 1976).

'The Young People of the Sixties and Literature about Them. A Roundtable Discussion', *Inostrannaia Literatura* 12 (1965), 249–52 (in Russian).

Zasurskiy, Yassen, ed., *Twentieth-Century USA Literature: A Typological Study* (Moscow: Nauka Publ., 1978) (in Russian).

Zhelokhovtseva, Liudmila I., review of Robert G. O'Meally, *The Craft of Ralph Ellison* (Cambridge, MA: Harvard University Press, 1980), *Referetivnyi zhurnal*, series 'Literaturovedenie' [*Bibliographical Journal*, series 'Literary studies'], 1 (1983), 159–62 (in Russian).

Zverev, Alexey M., 'Social Struggle of the 1960s and the Literature of the USA', in Alexander S. Muliarchik, ed., *American Literature and the Social and Political Struggle, 1960s–Early 1970s* (Moscow: Nauka Publ., 1977), 42–78 (in Russian).

CHRISTA BUSCHENDORF AND NICOLE LINDENBERG

7 Ellison in East and West Germany: Early Reception in a Divided Country

ABSTRACT:
This chapter on Ellison's reception in the Cold War explores the radically different reactions to his work on both sides of the Iron Curtain. The focus is on the new discipline of American Studies as documented in journals, monographs and literary histories from the mid-1950s to the 1970s. Whereas in West Germany (as well as in Austria and Switzerland) Ellison is widely praised for his accomplished style and existential humanism, he is criticized or even ignored for his lack of progressive political thinking in East Germany. The chapter also discusses the Ellisons' experiences in the 1954 Cold War setting of the Salzburg Seminar and the couple's trips to West Germany. As Ellison's unpublished notes for the Seminar reveal, he insisted on the crucial contributions of black history and culture to the complexity of the American character. Finally, there is a brief discussion of the 1954 German translation of *Invisible Man* and its 2019 revision.

In the literary field of African American writers, Ralph Ellison has held a unique position. More than any other black novelist, Ellison has evoked stark controversies focusing on the question of whether or not he was a progressive, let alone radical, representative of his group. Since the publication of *Invisible Man* in 1952, Ellison has aroused continuous and oftentimes fierce battles between the author's admirers and critics, the former celebrating his artistic accomplishments and his humanist worldview, the latter condemning his lack of radicalness and political engagement. Over the decades, the US-American debate about Ellison's work has also been shaped both by the changing cultural and political context and by the shifting theoretical paradigms in the discipline of literary studies. Studying Ellison's reception outside the United States poses yet another question, namely, to what degree and in what manner the various countries' different cultural and political contexts have impacted the reading of Ellison.

Readers outside of the USA are involved in the disputes of their own cultural agenda, and they position themselves (whether consciously or unconsciously) in the intellectual field in which they seek recognition; thus, their interpretations may reveal much more about the political conditions that shape their approach than about Ellison's standing in the history of American literature. This becomes evident in the stark difference that Ellison's early reception exhibits in the two German states in existence between 1949 and 1989: the German Democratic Republic (GDR – the 'East') and the Federal Republic of Germany (FRG – the 'West'). Obviously, the political borderline between the communist *Ostblock* und the capitalist *Westblock* determined the respective attitudes vis-à-vis the United States and its culture. Consequently, we observe much greater differences in the reception of Ellison between East and West Germany than between West Germany and Austria and Switzerland. In fact, the latter are quite insignificant, and therefore we will focus almost exclusively on the two German states and the impact the opposing ideologies had on German readers, especially on scholars of American Studies.

As to the bibliographical basis of Ellison's early reception in Germany, we are fortunate to be able to draw on previous studies, most notably on Jacqueline Covo (1975), Karl-Wilhelm Dietz (1979) and Rolf Franzbecker (1979). While we make use of the material they present, we differ in our approach. In her chapter on Germany, Covo focuses on the reviews of the first German translation of *Invisible Man* by Georg Goyert (the renowned translator of James Joyce); it was entitled *Unsichtbar* meaning 'to be invisible' and was published by S. Fischer Verlag in 1954. In contrast to Covo's reception study, Dietz's monograph, one of the early West German PhD dissertations on African American literature, is divided into two parts: a history of the reception of *Invisible Man* and an interpretation of the novel. Dietz presents major trends of the reception of *Invisible Man* both in the United States and in German-speaking countries from the first reviews to the scholarly works in the 1970s. However, he is more interested in the changing perspectives of the scholarship on Ellison's novel than on the specific cultural and political contexts framing the reception in various countries. Instead, Dietz presupposes an international community of scholars that builds upon and critically assesses each other's research.

So does Rolf Franzbecker. His bibliographical report focuses on Richard Wright, Ralph Ellison and James Baldwin as 'the three great novelists of this century who in all likelihood will also be known to European and German readers'.[1] Covering research published before the spring of 1977, Franzbecker seeks to define major trends in international Ellison criticism. He distinguishes three diverging schools: first, the universalist and integrationist school that claims *Invisible Man*'s universalism as well as the more controversial assertion of its rootedness in 'mainstream' American literature and Western culture; second, the sociological and communist school; and third, the new school of black aesthetics. The universalist and integrationist approaches, embraced mostly by white scholars, concentrate on the humanist contents and aesthetic qualities of the novel. Meanwhile the sociological and 'racial-ideological approach' (to quote Franzbecker in reference to the American Marxist critic Ernest Kaiser (1970)), which was favoured by 'black militants', of which the 'Marxist Kaiser school' can be regarded as 'symptomatic',[2] criticizes the novel's and Ellison's (non-)political stance. In a note, Franzbecker states parallels between the Marxist thrust of Kaiser's critique and the arguments of the East German scholars Karl-Heinz Schönfelder and Karl-Heinz Wirzberger.[3] But since the author is not interested in distinguishing national trends of Ellison criticism, he pays no further attention to the Marxist criticism of GDR scholars. In terms of method, our essay is closest to Angelika Schmitt-Kaufhold's study of the reception of North American literature in German-speaking countries after 1945, especially with regard to her insistence on juxtaposing West German and Austrian positions with the communist viewpoint of East Germany. Yet, as Schmitt-Kaufhold covers all of American literature after 1945, she does not deal extensively with Ellison.

What the focus on the early Ellison reception in East and West Germany reveals will not come as a surprise: namely, that the political

1 Rolf Franzbecker, unter Mitarbeit von Peter Bruck und Willi Real, *Der Moderne Roman des amerikanischen Negers: Richard Wright, Ralph Ellison, James Baldwin* (Darmstadt: Wissenschaftliche Buchgesellschaft, 1979), VIII. All translations from the German are our own unless otherwise noted.

2 Ibid., 54.

3 Ibid., 144 n56.

divide is minutely reflected in the clear-cut division between the universalist school favoured by West German (as well as Austrian and Swiss) critics and the Marxist school prominent in East Germany. What deserves attention, however, is the degree to which this ideological divide determines Ellison's recognition: whereas he is most highly esteemed by literary critics in the West, he is widely neglected or even ignored in the East. The stark contrast of the academic reception of Ellison in East and West Germany can also be traced in the history of the first German translation of *Invisible Man* which will be discussed in the first section of our essay. This is followed by an outline of Ellison's travels to Austria and West Germany that, again, raises the question of his reception and self-representation as a humanist.

The 1950s: The First German Translation of *Invisible Man*, and the Ellisons' Visits to Austria and West Germany

The first reactions to Goyert's German translation of Ellison's *Invisible Man* appeared in more than sixty reviews published in Austrian, Swiss and West German newspapers, weeklies, journals and radio programmes in 1954.[4] These were followed by a smaller wave of reviews, when Fischer Verlag (Frankfurt am Main) reissued *Unsichtbar* [*Invisible*] – by then considered a 'classic' – in 1969.[5] Fischer had published a special edition of the unchanged, unabridged Goyert translation in 1959; further editions issued by various publishing houses in West Germany and Switzerland that appeared in the years 1984, 1987, 1995 and 1998 indicate that Ellison had resonated with the general reading public. However, Goyert's translation received mixed reviews. Covo observes:

4 Jacqueline Covo, *The Blinking Eye: Ralph Waldo Ellison and His American, French, German and Italian Critics, 1952–1971* (Metuchen, NJ: Scarecrow Press, 1974), 89–98; 168–72.

5 Ibid., 98–100; 172–3.

> Given the ambitiousness of the stylistic undertaking, the quality of the translation becomes all-important, but those critics who do mention it seem divided in their opinions, some feeling that Goyert was precise as well as subtle, others on the contrary finding his prose stilted and inadequate to its task.[6]

The challenge for the translation of Ellison's masterpiece is that the essence of *Invisible Man* is based on African American culture and folklore.[7] In his 1981 article, Soi-Daniel W. Brown argues that Goyert's translation does not grasp this essence: he offers compelling examples of omissions of animal allegory and of the dozens in *Unsichtbar* that ultimately take away 'the interpretive potential that is evident in the original'.[8] Goyert also prevents any in-depth understanding of Ellison's novel by mistranslating or obliterating all references concerning the blues. The final pivotal sentence of the prologue reads: 'Weshalb war ich so ängstlich? Man habe Geduld mit mir' [What is the reason that I was so afraid? Be patient with me]. *Ängstlich*, to be anxious or afraid, is not an equivalent to the term *blue* used by Ellison.[9] Brown draws the conclusion that

> Goyert was not culturally attuned enough to make the proper interpretation of that final question. It also appears that he did not entertain the idea that the novel which he was translating was an extended, literary version of the blues.[10]

6 Ibid., 94.

7 See Soi-Daniel W. Brown, '*Invisible Man*'s Appearance in Germany: An Analysis of Potential Critical Response to the German Translation', *Amerikastudien / American Studies* 26/2 (1981), 213–18.

8 Ibid., 218.

9 Ibid., 214.

10 Ibid. For more than sixty decades, then, readers who relied on the German translation had no chance to grasp Ellison's skilful use of the vernacular. As late as 2019, Aufbau Verlag published a thoroughly revised version of Ellison's novel by translator Hans-Christian Oeser under the title *Der unsichtbare Mann* [*The Invisible Man*]. Oeser corrects many of Goyert's mistakes and takes account of numerous allusions to African American folklore. It also took decades before other works of Ellison were translated into German. In 1999, a collection of short stories, *Flying Home und andere Geschichten* [*Flying Home and Other Stories*], translated by Manfred Allié and Gabriele Kempf-Allié, edited and with an introduction by John F. Callahan, was published by Ammann Verlag (Zürich), followed by a translation of *Juneteenth* by the same translators in 2000.

It is important to note that the unawareness of black culture that Goyert displays in his translation is rather common among German intellectuals in the 1950s. Unintentionally, this ignorance contributes to the tendency in the West to claim Ellison for an apolitical universalist perspective. Moreover, universalism and existentialism are integral to Western philosophy in the 1950s and function as a basic argument against Marxism in the Cold War.

Ellison's attendance at the famous Salzburg Seminar in American Studies in 1954 brought him in close contact with the Cold War's political battles. Until 1955, Austria was divided – as Germany had been until 1949 – into four occupation zones ruled by France, Great Britain, the USA and the USSR. Salzburg was in the American zone and the renowned Americanist Henry Nash Smith, in his contemporary account of the first two Salzburg Seminars in 1947 and 1948, points to the 'presence of an American army of occupation'.[11] The official agenda of the Seminar was part of the comprehensive American re-education programme, namely, as Smith expressed it somewhat vaguely, to 'bring Europe into contact with America'.[12] Smith's article emphasizes a democratic atmosphere in the encounters between American intellectuals and European students, embraced by the latter who had been socialized with propaganda. However, as Reinhold Wagnleitner explains in his study *Coca-Colonization and the Cold War*, the exchanges were closely watched by United States officials.[13] In fact, the 'mild criticism of the United States [which] had been voiced in the stimulating discussions during the first session in 1947 caused the secret service to intervene'.[14] According to Wagnleitner, this indicated a 'control of the Salzburg Seminar by the US Army, which amounted, more or less, to ideological conformity'.[15] The consequence was a 'ban' of supposed communists, which even included the exclusion of one of the

11 Henry Nash Smith, 'The Salzburg Seminar', *American Quarterly* 1/1 (1949), 31.

12 Ibid., 36.

13 Reinhold Wagnleitner, *Coca-Colonization and the Cold War: The Cultural Mission of the United States in Austria after the Second World War*, trans. Diana M. Wolf (Chapel Hill and London: University of North Carolina Press, 1994), 164–5.

14 Ibid., 164.

15 Ibid., 165.

founders of the Seminar, Clemens Heller, as well as Alfred Kazin and F. O. Matthiessen, the famous Harvard professor, who had taught literature at the first Salzburg Seminar in 1947.

Interestingly, it was through Kazin as well as Saul Bellow that Ellison had initially heard about the Salzburg Seminar.[16] From 22 August to 18 September 1954, Ellison joined the University of Chicago historian Avery Craven, the Cornell economist Robert Ferguson and the Harvard musicologist Allen Sapp at the Seminar. Another participant was the political scientist Max Lerner, 'a former war correspondent now a Brandeis University professor as well as a newspaper columnist known for his commitment to civil rights'.[17] Lerner wrote: 'One reason the venture works … is that no one can suspect it of being an engine of American propaganda. It is wholly free-wheeling',[18] but whether Ellison would have agreed with Lerner's confidence in the Salzburg Seminar, we do not know. According to Rampersad, the Ellisons 'joined gladly in the missionary role of the enterprise'.[19] As for Ellison's role of American missionary to post-war Europe, after the publication of his so-called 'Cold War narrative' *Invisible Man*, he was beyond reproach about his own Leftist past. In *Race, Ralph Ellison and American Cold War Intellectual Culture*, Richard Purcell even argues that 'Ellison's presence at the seminar, juxtaposed to Matthiessen's expulsion, sheds light on many of his Cold War activities, which brought him in close proximity to the CIA-funded CCF'.[20]

Ellison's notes and course descriptions reveal that he meant to debate the role of literature in the recognition and the emergence of an 'American character'. In a letter to Dexter Perkins, the Salzburg organizer, Ellison had

16 See Lawrence P. Jackson, *Ralph Ellison: Emergence of Genius* (New York: John Wiley and Sons, 2002), 409–10, and George Blaustein, *Nightmare Envy and Other Stories: American Culture and European Reconstruction* (New York: Oxford University Press, 2018), 22 n41.

17 Arnold Rampersad, *Ralph Ellison: A Biography* (New York: Alfred A. Knopf, 2007), 301.

18 Ibid.

19 Ibid.

20 Richard Purcell, *Race, Ralph Ellison and American Cold War Intellectual Culture* (New York: Palgrave Macmillan, 2013), 75.

offered his understanding of his task by underlining that he felt 'neither the necessity to attack nor defend' America before Europeans: 'I am interested only in helping them to discover the complex truth of American reality'.[21] As Rampersad stresses, this complex truth involved the special position Ellison had as a black man 'teaching American culture to Europeans skeptical about America and its often boastful claims about liberty and justice'.[22] Ellison made sure that the courses he offered reflected both the American literary canon and the black experience. For the sixty participants out of the total number of sixty-four students from the whole of Europe who enrolled in his Main Lecture, entitled 'The Role of the Novel in Creating the American Experience', Ellison prepared the following 'lecture outline', which reveals that for him the 'complex truth of the American reality' – as presented in fiction – consisted in acknowledging the problematic of racism:

> (Factors influencing the form of our 19th and 20th century fiction, stressing the works of Melville, Twain, Hemingway, Faulkner).
>
> Discussions will include:
>
> Rhetorical Problems of the American Novel –
>
> as a Medium of Communication
>
> as a Definition of Experience
>
> as a Gauge of Democratic Health
>
> as Projector of the American Image
>
> as The Search for Identity
>
> as Reflecting The [sic] Racial Situation and the Problem of Value.[23]

Purcell notes that Ellison included Matthiessen in his lectures in that 'the grouping of authors, period and geography point to' the eminent literary

21 Ralph Ellison, Letter to Dexter Perkins, 28 January 1954, Ralph Ellison papers, Library of Congress, I:173, folder 1.

22 Rampersad, *Ralph Ellison*, 302.

23 Ralph Ellison, Speeches, Lectures and Interviews, Ralph Ellison papers, Library of Congress, I:173, folder 1.

critic.[24] Yet in contrast to Matthiessen, 'Ellison sought to complicate the nature of America's literary inheritance and continuity with history' by also 'dealing with the presence of slavery', and by raising the question, 'how did chattel slavery and racism determine the USA's reception and possibilities of literary expression?'[25] Ellison's intention to introduce Europeans to the significance that black experience and aesthetics have for 'the American character' becomes even more obvious in his course description of the 'Main Seminar Topic[:] The Background of American Negro Expression – Folklore, Writing and Music':

> Discussions will include:
>
> A Definition of the Slave's Vision of American Reality
>
> Early Twentieth-Century Negro Writing as a Search for Identity
>
> The 1940s: Negro Fiction and the Crisis of Negro Sensibility
>
> Recent Novels: Fiction and the New Face of Freedom
>
> Music: The Blues, Jazz, Spirituals (illustrated by Recordings and Tape recordings), with Special Attention to Southwestern Jazz: Count Basie, Benny Moton, Andy Kirk, George E. Lee, Jimmy Rushing, Charlie Christian.[26]

Evidently, Ellison was not prepared to present to his Salzburg students a sanitized portrait of the United States and its history. To him, both the injustices of slavery and racism as well as the viewpoint of the slave and his descendants were intrinsically tied to the 'American character'.

In all lectures and seminars Fanny Ellison was present; her letters uncover that she was wondering 'what [the students] *really* think and … feel', and that she was surprised, for example, at the 'excessive deference and uninterrupted politeness toward the professors and their wives'.[27] However, the students' civility did not prevent an occasional rise of tensions. Confronted with a declaration by one of the French students that 'Negro writers' ought

24 Purcell, *Race, Ralph Ellison and American Cold War Intellectual Culture*, 77.

25 Ibid.

26 Ralph Ellison, Speeches, Lectures, and Interviews, 1945–1993, Ralph Ellison papers, Library of Congress, I:173, folder 1.

27 Quoted in Rampersad, *Ralph Ellison*, 302.

to write in 'a Negro manner', Ellison – in a 'fiery attack' – accused the Frenchman of 'European romanticism'.[28] While Ellison's political stance was neither so radical as to attract the attention of the CIA, nor so conformist that he acted as a mouthpiece of US propaganda, his teaching at the Salzburg Seminar was certainly far from being apolitical.

After the Seminar the Ellisons visited Munich and Heidelberg on their way to Ulm, where on 20 September 1954 they met another Fischer Verlag author, the young German writer, Paul Schallück. Brigitte Bermann Fischer had paired Ellison with Schallück for a reading tour through Germany, which promoted the Fischer Verlag's publication of the German translation of *Invisible Man*. On 2 June 1954, Bermann Fischer had written to Ellison that *Unsichtbar* 'has not only received many wonderful and positive critics', but also 'seems to penetrate with all power into those who have read it'. She continued by pointing to Schallück's 'genuine' 'enthusiasm' for *Unsichtbar*, adding that the German author 'has written an extensive review which shows his admiration and penetration into the depths of your book' and that they had 'decided to multiply this review and spread it among the German book-sellers'. Bermann Fischer then proposes the joint reading tour in the hope that Ellison would agree to 'this somewhat unusual project' that, as she stresses, would promote his book in Germany. Her proposals as to where the readings could take place indicate a preference for academic institutions that would guarantee an educated audience particularly fascinated by American culture: the Seminar of American Studies in Munich, attached to Munich University and the Geschwister Scholl Hochschule in Ulm, 'a sort of American College which was just opened', as she describes it.

28 Ibid., 303. Occasional visits to Salzburg restaurants are evoked in what Blaustein calls Ellison's 'postwar parable, which appears in the posthumous novel *Three Days before the Shooting* … [in which] a white American journalist named Welborne McIntyre recalls his "first trip to peacetime Europe"' (see Blaustein, *Nightmare Envy and Other Stories*, 17). A Salzburg restaurant is the setting of 'a cartoonish and overwrought scene of tangled national identifications' (18). Blaustein continues, 'What triggers the memory [of McIntyre], in fact, is a French intellectual's irritating request that McIntyre explain the "real" America. [The story …] grew out of Ellison's own experiences in postwar Europe. Like McIntyre […], Ellison considered himself a custodian of the national image and the national literature' (18).

She continues: 'This school is a very open-minded place where American life and thought is fostered. In both places you will find a very interested and unprejudiced audience of students and young people'.[29]

For reasons unknown, the reading at Munich University did not come about; Rampersad only chronicles readings in Ulm, Frankfurt and Cologne. Moreover, on the whole, the Ellisons' expectations were not met. In their correspondence, the couple describe the 1954 lectures as 'a completely anti-climactic experience',[30] and in her letter to Vilgot Sjomar – a Swedish journalist the Ellisons had met at the Salzburg Seminar – Fanny even goes so far to state that she and Ralph 'regretted it'.[31] In Frankfurt, for instance, an announcement in the local Tageszeitung *Frankfurter Allgemeine Zeitung* documents that Schallück introduced Ellison's debut novel and read from his own new novel *Die unsichtbare Pforte* [*The Invisible Gate*]. In contrast to what Bermann Fischer had hoped for, the reading took place in a bookstore and thus before a general audience rather than students. In fact, the 'very interested … audience' that Bermann Fischer had promised turned out to be disappointing:

> They applauded politely and went home. After the stimulation and vitality of the Salzburg experience this was, indeed, deadening. But we were assured again and again by the parties in charge that this was what the German audiences liked and wanted, that they were contented and curious to see the men, hear their voices even though they may not have read their novels.[32]

It was not only the audience that disappointed the Ellisons, however. Fanny's letters to her mother reveal that they did not like Germany, which was more heavily marked by the Nazi era and the effects of the war than Austria. Looking back, Fanny vividly remembers her feeling of 'apprehension' in her first encounter of post-war Germany in 1954:

29 Brigitte Bermann Fischer, Letter to Ralph Ellison, 2 June 1954, Library of Congress, Ralph Ellison papers, Foreign Rights and Translations 1952–78, I:153, folder 5.

30 Quoted in Rampersad, *Ralph Ellison*, 304.

31 Ibid., 303.

32 Fanny Ellison, Letter to Vilgot Sjoman, 3 December 1954, Library of Congress, Ralph Ellison papers, I:173, folder 1.

> Perhaps the Nazi element was very active then and I remember resenting very much seeing the town of Dachau represented in the Octoberfest parade and one old woman in particular who wore the costume of her region with much pride and danced along waving her arms to the music, bowing and smiling at everyone. When we had gone to Frankfurt we'd had our encounters with the Prussian arrogance, the weather was bleak and damp, there was noise of hammering and steam shoveling everywhere, the city was practically rebuilt again. We hated it too.[33]

In an earlier letter, Frankfurt is described as 'ugly' and the people, especially the women, 'are almost always quite big, unhandsome and with no sense of style. Their faces are coarse and unpleasant. This is the generation who went through the hardships of the war and they show it'.[34]

It is interesting to note that at some point Ellison must have met the German Africanist Janheinz Jahn, who gained fame for his translations

33 Fanny Ellison, Letter to Willie Mae Brock McConnell, 26 July 1956, Library of Congress, Ralph Ellison papers, I:1, folder 12. The importance of Fanny Ellison's letters to her mother came to our attention in the talk on 'The Intimate Spaces of Artistry: Ralph and Fanny Ellison's Creative World' that Dr Lena Hill delivered at the (Re)Reading Ralph Ellison Symposium at Goethe University Frankfurt, 20 July 2019. We would like to express our deep gratitude to Dr Hill for sharing the manuscript's innovative archival material with us. In addition, a trip the Ellisons took to Wiesbaden may have inspired the following passage in *Three Days*, in which Daddy Alonzo Hickman renders his version of the life of the 'crazy' woman who had claimed his adopted son Bliss as her own child: 'And I heard she was at a place called Wiesbaden where she enjoyed herself losing a lot of money' (Ellison, *Three Days before the Shooting …*, 352, 354). Moreover, Ellison was an avid reader of Dostoevsky and his notes for *Invisible Man* show that he had read Dostoevsky's novella *The Gambler* (see Barbara Foley, *Wrestling with the Left: The Making of Ralph Ellison's* Invisible Man (Durham, NC: Duke University Press, 2010), 417). Its setting is the fictional town of 'Roulettenburg', where the novella's first-person narrator, like Dostoevsky himself, becomes addicted to gambling. It is usually assumed that Wiesbaden served as the model for 'Roulettenburg', as it was in this famous nineteenth-century spa that Dostoevsky played roulette for the first time. It is perhaps owing to his keen interest in the biography and the fictional world of one of his favourite authors that Ellison himself made a stop in Wiesbaden's notorious casino.

34 Fanny Ellison, Letter to Willie Mae Brock McConnell, 3 October 1954, Library of Congress, Ralph Ellison papers, II:5, folder 3.

of (neo)African literature.[35] Dietz states that the part of Jahn's library, which was acquired by the Institut für Ethnologie und Afrika-Studien of the University of Mainz, includes a copy of *Unsichtbar* signed by Ellison, in which he expressed his gratitude for an interview given in Frankfurt.[36] So it may well be that Jahn listened to Ellison, when he read a passage of *Invisible Man* on the evening of 21 September 1954, in the bookstore Amelang, opposite the house in which Goethe was born in 1749.

Two years later, in 1956, the Ellisons paid a second visit to Germany, in which they stopped only very briefly in Frankfurt and Munich on their way from London (where Ralph had attended the PEN congress), back to the American Academy in Rome. This short trip would not be worth mentioning were it not for a notable change of perception. Now that Germany was two more years into its 'economic miracle' [*Wirtschaftswunder*], the atmosphere seems to have been more relaxed and friendly. In a letter to Mozelle Murray, Fanny expresses the Ellisons' pleasant surprise and delight at the nice room in the Hotel Wolff as well as the friendly people and the good beer and food in the Bavarian city. In a letter to her mother Fanny recalls that 'last time we'd been in Munich was for the Octoberfest of '54 and we disliked it so. I even dreaded returning this time, although I said nothing to Ralph'.[37] But this time Munich 'turned out to be exceedingly lovely and the people were all so nice, treating us not as tourists but strangers whom they wished to feel welcomed'.[38] As Fanny confesses, 'I don't know what the difference was, except within ourselves'.[39]

35 See Heinz Rogge, 'Die amerikanische Negerfrage im Lichte der Literatur von Richard Wright und Ralph Ellison', *Die Neueren Sprachen* n.s. 7 (1958), 116.

36 Karl-Wilhelm Dietz, *Ralph Ellisons Roman Invisible Man: Ein Beitrag zu seiner Rezeptionsgeschichte und Interpretation mit besonderer Berücksichtigung der Figuren-, Raum- u. Zeitgestaltung* (Frankfurt am Main, Bern and Las Vegas: Lang, 1979), 230 n81.

37 Fanny Ellison, Letter to Willie Mae Brock McConnell, 26 July 1956, Library of Congress, Ralph Ellison papers, I.1, folder 12.

38 Fanny Ellison, Letter to Mozelle Murray, 31 July 1956, in *Trading Twelves: The Selected Letters of Ralph Ellison and Albert Murray*, ed., John F. Callahan (New York: Modern Library, 2000), 140.

39 Fanny Ellison, Letter to Willie Mae Brock McConnell, 26 July 1956, Library of Congress, Ralph Ellison papers, I:1, folder 12.

In July 1959, the thirtieth congress of the international PEN association opened in Frankfurt, with Ellison serving as chief American delegate. Ellison's attendance marked his third and last visit to Germany. Each participant received as a present a numbered copy of the Charter of the association in the thirty-five languages 'of all the nations [then] represented within PEN'.[40] The political core of the Charter's mission is expressed in the PEN members' pledge 'to do their utmost to dispel race, class and national hatreds and to champion the ideal of one humanity living in peace in one world'.[41]

Yet, in the historical and official documentation of the congress in Frankfurt, Ellison himself is somewhat of an invisible man. The photographs of the event kept at the Institute for the History of Frankfurt do not capture him. He is not visible, for example, in the packed auditorium during the opening ceremony held at the Paulskirche on 20 July 1959. In the official documents Ellison's name appears only once, namely in the list of participants that designates him the delegate of the New York Center of PEN USA.[42] As an author of the Fischer Verlag, he probably participated in the cocktail party that this publishing house gave at the Hotel Frankfurter Hof on 22 July 1959.[43] Furthermore, Ellison's spirit seems to pervade the two literary sessions in the programme, which discussed the role and state of 'Imaginative Literature in the Age of Science'. The two American contributions to the sessions that are printed in the official report of the congress, Eric P. Mosse's talk on 'The Symbol of the Frontier',[44] and an untitled contribution by Leon Edel,[45] both make use of the trope of

40 PEN International, *Die Charta des Internationalen P.E.N. The Charta of the International P.E.N. Charte du P.E.N. International* (Frankfurt am Main: Ullstein, 1959).

41 Ibid.

42 PEN Zentrum, ed., *XXX. [thirtieth] Kongress des internationalen P.E.N. Frankfurt am Main. 19. bis 25. Juli 1959. Programm* (Roetherdruck Darmstadt), 50.

43 Ibid., 21.

44 PEN Zentrum, ed., *XXX. [thirtieth] Kongress des internationalen P.E.N. Frankfurt am Main. 19. bis 25. Juli 1959. Schöne Literatur im Zeitalter der Wissenschaft. Imaginative Literature in the Age of Science. La Création Littéraire a L'Age de la Science. Bericht. Report. Compte-Rendu* (Frankfurt am Main and Berlin: Propyläen-Verlag, 1960), 83–9.

45 Ibid., 156–62.

invisibility. While Edel urges the writer in the age of science to recognize not only the visible, but 'the invisible as well',[46] Mosse closes with the admonition that:

> This [...] is the canvas and the perspective on which the creative writer should live: dedicated to the precious loneliness of his work; sucked into the reckless stream of his daily life; and still never losing sight of the invisible stars above the clouds.[47]

However, whereas the invisibility addressed in Ellison's novel refers to the injustice of America's caste system, Edel and Mosse, very much in the 1950s spirit of humanism, allude to philosophical, non-political implications of invisibility.

Contrasting Receptions of Ellison in East and West Germany

In his article on the reception of American literature in Austria, Harro Heinz Kühnelt makes the important point that the small number of translations of American authors published in Austria is no indication of the degree to which they are known and read, because the German translations published in West Germany and Switzerland 'were widely available and well-known'.[48] Obviously, this was not the case in the GDR. On the other hand, given the modest amount of translations of American literature published in the GDR, the number of translations of African American literature was relatively high.[49] Therefore it is all the more

46 Ibid., 162.

47 Ibid., 89.

48 Harro Heinz Kühnelt, 'Die Aufnahme der nordamerikanischen Literatur in Österreich', in Horst Frenz and Hans-Joachim Lang, eds, *Nordamerikanische Literatur im deutschen Sprachraum seit 1945: Beiträge zu ihrer Rezeption* (München: Winkler Verlag, 1973), 204.

49 See Dagmar Frost, 'Zur Rezeption afroamerikanischer Literatur in der Amerikanistik der DDR', in Christian Freitag, Dagmar Frost, Michael Hoenisch and Werner Sollors, eds, *Bibliographie amerikanistischer Veröffentlichungen in der DDR bis 1968* (Berlin: John F. Kennedy-Institut für Nordamerikastudien, Freie Universität Berlin, 1976), 126.

significant that no translations of Ellison ever appeared in the GDR. By contrast, for example, James Baldwin's *Go Tell It on the Mountain* (1953) was published in West Germany by Rowohlt in 1966 (as *Gehe hin und verkünde es vom Berge*, translated by Jürgen Manthey), and two years later the same translation was launched by the East Berlin publisher Volk und Welt, with an afterword by Karl-Heinz Schönfelder. This was followed by several East German translations of Baldwin's essays and plays.[50]

A bibliography cataloguing East German publications between 1945 and 1969 that echo 'the culture and the struggle of freedom of North American Negroes' confirms the disregard for Ellison in GDR publishing. It lists several East German translations of works by African Americans, for example, works by Langston Hughes, Richard Wright, Paul Robeson and James Baldwin, but not a single one by Ellison.[51] In addition, the early literary criticism published about a decade later than the first reviews – so in the mid-1960s – clearly reflects that the border separating the two German states was the frontier between two opposing political systems whose enmity dominated global politics. In order to understand the fundamental differences of the reception of African American literature in general (and Ellison in particular) in East and West Germany, it is necessary to take a look at the development of the academic discipline of American Studies and its political function in the two Cold War frontier states.

As Rudolf Haas claims in his survey of the reception of American novels in West Germany from 1945 to 1965, the climate of reception after World War II was incomparable to any other constellation in the history of literary impact, because the 'preconditions for establishing influential

50 Peter Freese, 'Some Remarks on the Reception of James Baldwin's Work in the Federal Republic of Germany', in Jakob Kollhöfer, ed., *James Baldwin: His Place in American Literary History and His Reception in Europe* (Frankfurt am Main: Lang, 1991), 13; Friederike Hajek, 'Historical Aspects of the Reception of James Baldwin in the German Democratic Republic', in Köllhofer, *James Baldwin*, 43.

51 Ursula Dibbern and Horst Ihde, 'Das Echo der Kultur und des Freiheitskampfes der nordamerikanischen Neger in der DDR, 1945–1969 – eine Bibliographie', *Zeitschrift für Anglistik und Amerikanistik* 20/4 (1972), 429–42.

cultural centers were especially favorable'.[52] In the context of re-education, the activities of United States cultural institutions provided, for example, an important supply of literature on American history and culture in the numerous libraries of the Amerika-Häuser. The High Commissioner for Germany (HICOG) 'played a significant role in the founding of the German Association for American Studies'.[53] These cultural education programmes not only reacted to the backlog produced by the information gap that arose between 1933 and 1945, but also promoted the enhanced interest in the United States as the leader of the Western allies.[54] The eagerness of West Germans to appropriate the 'spirit of freedom' associated with American cultural products corresponded with the enthusiasm the first generation of teachers and students of American Studies displayed vis-à-vis American literature and culture. According to one of the prominent early scholars of American Studies, Ursula Brumm, the most important figures of the first generation of Americanists were:

> the German and European emigrants who had spent their exile in America and returned to Europe after the war. [...] By the bitter fate of exile, they had America thrust upon them, came to know it, and learned to understand it, even love it, and after their return taught America to Europeans.[55]

52 Rudolf Haas, 'Über die Rezeption amerikanischer Romane in der Bundesrepublik 1945–1965', in Frenz and Lang, *Nordamerikanische Literatur im deutschen Sprachraum seit 1945*, 20.

53 Hans-Jürgen Grabbe, '50 Jahre Deutsche Gesellschaft für Amerikastudien', *Amerikastudien / American Studies* 48/2 (2003), 163.

54 Haas, 'Über die Rezeption amerikanischer Romane in der Bundesrepublik 1945–1965', 20.

55 Ursula Brumm, ' "Fifty years ago": Memories of the Beginnings', in Ulla Haselstein and Berndt Ostendorf, eds, *Cultural Interactions: Fifty Years of American Studies in Germany* (Heidelberg: Universitätsverlag Winter, 2005), 2 (underlining in original). For a detailed history of the beginnings and the development of the German Association of American Studies, founded in 1953, supported substantially by the United States, see Grabbe, '50 Jahre Deutsche Gesellschaft für Amerikastudien'. See also Philipp Gassert, 'Between Political Reconnaisance [sic] Work and Democratizing Science: American Studies in Germany, 1917–1953', *Bulletin of the German Historical Institute Washington, DC* 32 (2003), 33–50, for the problems deriving from 'a high degree of personal and intellectual continuity with the time before 1945' (33).

In contrast to the favourable conditions that allowed American Studies to thrive in the first decades of the Federal Republic, in the German Democratic Republic the discipline encountered immense difficulties, including how to supply university libraries with American literature in the original.[56] Compared to the number of professorships and departments dedicated to American literature and culture in West Germany, East German American Studies was rather small in size and scope. Moreover, according to the renowned GDR Americanist Eberhard Brüning, the representatives of American Studies were often met with suspicion, and the disciplinary isolation they experienced could be frustrating.[57] After all, considered 'the most important and farthest developed country of capitalism',[58] the USA was defined as 'main enemy of socialism';[59] consequently, the attitude towards the United States was largely determined by 'the guidelines fraught with ideology as offered by the state and the single political party'.[60] Within American Studies, however, black literature as the alleged expression of a group belonging to the suppressed class held a special status; in fact, 'for American Studies in the GDR African American literature was a declared focus', and given the relatively modest number of editions of American literature, 'the percentage of African American literature must be called considerable'.[61]

56 Eberhard Brüning, 'Die Amerikanistik an der Universität Leipzig (1950–1990) – 40 Jahre Gratwanderung eines ungeliebten Faches', in Rainer Schnoor, ed., *Amerikanistik in der DDR: Geschichte – Analysen – Zeitzeugenberichte* (Berlin: trafo Verlag, 1999), 79; Rainer Schnoor, 'Amerikanistik in 40 Jahren DDR: Eine wissenschaftshistorische Skizze', in Schnoor, *Amerikanistik in der DDR*, 31–2.

57 Brüning, 'Die Amerikanistik an der Universität Leipzig (1950–1990)', 71.

58 Gudrun Bahls and Wolfgang Wicht, 'Amerikanistik an den Hochschulen und Schulen der DDR zwischen zentralistischer Steuerung und Emanzipation', in Schnoor, *Amerikanistik in der DDR*, 61.

59 Brüning, 'Die Amerikanistik an der Universität Leipzig (1950–1990)', 69.

60 Ibid., 67.

61 Frost, 'Zur Rezeption afroamerikanischer Literatur in der Amerikanistik der DDR', 126.

In her article 'Reading American Literature in the G. D. R.', Catrin Gersdorf 'provide[s] an idea of how "America" was read in socialist East Germany':[62]

> Although the language became less aggressive and the censoring of American culture less rigorous after [...] the G. D. R. was diplomatically recognized by the U.S. [1974], the general intention to withhold all information counterproductive to the official image of America as a stronghold of imperialist exploitation, racist oppression and cultural decadence remained a constant in the ideological rationalization of socialism.[63]

Gersdorf quotes from an article whose author, characterizing the function of American Studies in the GDR, wholeheartedly propagates the party line.[64] Referring to the twenty-fourth convention of the Communist Party of the Soviet Union in 1969, Werner Scheffel, a well-known 'hardliner',[65] echoes the party's pressing appeal to enhancing the efforts to fight US imperialism as the main enemy of all peoples. As one of the consequences of this necessity, Scheffel names the growing importance of 'the work of Americanists in the socialist countries':[66]

> The most urgent task consists of tearing apart the veil of deception hiding the true face of US-American imperialism, to expose the politics of aggression by pointing out its effects, as well as to illustrate that the exploitation, terrorization and manipulation of its own population is systemic.[67]

Given the specific political function allotted to American Studies in the ideological battle of the German Democratic Republic against

62 Catrin Gersdorf, 'Reading American Literature in the G. D. R.', in Alfred Hornung, Reinhard R. Doerries and Gerhard Hoffmann, eds, *Democracy and the Arts in the United States* (Munich: Fink Verlag, 1996), 312.

63 Ibid.

64 Ibid., 311, 311 n2.

65 Schnoor, 'Amerikanistik in 40 Jahren DDR: Eine wissenschaftshistorische Skizze', in Schnoor, *Amerikanistik in der DDR*, 39.

66 Werner Scheffel, 'Zu einigen Aufgaben der Amerikanistik im Kampf gegen die ideologische Diversion des USA-Imperialismus', *Zeitschrift für Anglistik und Amerikanistik* 20/4 (1972), 371.

67 Ibid., 381.

the United States, the great efforts undertaken to control the publication of American literature becomes understandable. Surveyed by the main office for the book trade and publishing in the ministry of culture, the 'prepublication reviewing'[68] involved statements by editors of the publishing houses as well as expert references often provided by American Studies scholars. 'People in the English Departments … were in close contact with editors in the three major presses for foreign literatures: Verlag Philipp Reclam jun. Leipzig, Verlag Volk und Welt, Berlin, and Aufbau-Verlag Berlin und Weimar'.[69] As Anna Rapp demonstrates in her PhD dissertation, which documents the processes of administrative printing permissions for African American texts in the GDR in great detail, the procedure of evaluation that determined whether the work of an African American author was published in the GDR underwent many bureaucratic changes, and it was also continuously modified according to shifts in politics.[70] Notwithstanding such changes, the criteria determining the selection of publications remained the same. Most importantly, there was the guideline of Lenin's theory of the two cultures in capitalist societies, according to which there is always a division between the reactionary forces and the suppressed classes.[71] In the case of the United States the latter were designated as the '"other" America'. Consequently, the emphasis of East German American Studies was on the struggles of the working class as they were addressed, above all, in American literature of the 1930s, the so-called Red Decade.

As the African American fight against racism was constructed as part of the global class struggle, moreover, texts by black authors were also seen in the tradition of the proletarian protest of the early 1930s.[72] In addition

68 Gersdorf, 'Reading American Literature in the G. D. R.', 313.

69 Ibid.

70 Anna Rapp, 'Der "Simple Jedermann" und die "Schwarze Rose": Afroamerikanische Texte in Druckgenehmigungsverfahren der DDR', unpublished PhD dissertation (Westfälische Wilhelms-Universität Münster, 2016).

71 Eberhard Brüning, 'Probleme der Rezeption amerikanischer Literatur in der DDR', *Weimarer Beiträge: Zeitschrift für Literaturwissenschaft, Ästhetik und Kulturtheorie* 25/4 (1970), 175; Rapp, 'Der "Simple Jedermann" und die "Schwarze Rose"', 8.

72 Friederike Hajek, 'Multiculturality in the German Democratic Republic and the Reception of African-American Literature', in Klaus J. Milich and Jeffrey M. Peck, eds, *Multiculturalism in Transit: A German–American Exchange* (New York and

to the focus on the subject of class struggle, there was in East German literary criticism a strong emphasis on the aesthetics of realism that mainly derived from the writings of Georg Lukács.[73] Based on reflection theory [*Widerspiegelungstheorie*] it held that the material conditions of a given society could best be represented by socialist realism. While there was an obvious preference for African American authors who had manifested a closeness to the Communist Party of the USA (CPUSA), or had engaged in other organizations of the Left, such as the John Reed Club,[74] it was also the individual literary work that had to pass the test. But even when the permission for publication was granted, the translation was usually accompanied by an afterword that provided, as Rapp calls it, a 'GDR construct of Afro-America'[75] and a reading in unison with the communist interpretation of US capitalism.

From the two opposing ideological viewpoints in East and West Germany, then, emerged two different canons of American literature in general and of black literature in particular. Lloyd L. Brown and John Oliver Killens, for example, who were regarded as writers in the tradition of the proletarian novel and, consequently, were considered classics of African American literature in East Germany, were hardly ever mentioned by critics in the West; at the same time, authors canonized in the West were in the East either seen ambivalently, like Richard Wright and James Baldwin, or ignored altogether. The most prominent case of neglect of black authors in the GDR is certainly Ralph Ellison. It seems surprising that East Germans refused to acknowledge even the early phase of Ellison's development. After all, there are his 'close ties to the Party' in the 1930s,[76] his 'attraction … to Marxist political theory', even if 'soon rejected',[77] as well as his respective

Oxford: Berghahn, 1998), 111; Rapp, 'Der "Simple Jedermann" und die "Schwarze Rose"', 9.

73 Horst Frenz and John Hess, 'Die nordamerikanische Literatur in der Deutschen Demokratischen Republik', in Frenz and Lang, *Nordamerikanische Literatur im deutschen Sprachraum seit 1945*, 172.

74 See Rapp, 'Der "Simple Jedermann" und die "Schwarze Rose"', passim.

75 Ibid., 5.

76 Rampersad, *Ralph Ellison*, 93.

77 Ralph Ellison, 'Introduction to *Shadow and Act*', in John F. Callahan, ed., *The Collected Essays of Ralph Ellison* (New York: Modern Library, 2003), 58.

publications, for example, in the *New Masses* between 1939 and 1942, 'when he was trying his wings as a Marxist critic'.[78] However, as Maria Diedrich pointed out in her balanced assessment of Ellison's position vis-à-vis the CPUSA 'his accusations against communists in *Invisible Man* must be called the most detailed, fiercest, and most influential in African American literature'.[79] Moreover, critics in the GDR may have been aware of the fact that at the time Ellison was exposed to harsh criticism by African American writers and intellectuals, for example by Killens and Brown, who accused him of having betrayed the black working class.[80] In a violent attack, published in a special issue on Ellison in the renowned US journal *Black World* in 1970, the American Marxist critic Ernest Kaiser blamed him even for being:

> an Establishment writer, an Uncle Tom, an attacker of the sociological formulations of the Black freedom movements, a defender of the criminal Vietnam War of extermination against the Asian (and American Black) people, a denigrator of the great tradition of Black protest writing.[81]

To transgress (as these critics saw it) both against the command of political commitment and the aesthetic norm of realism was probably too severe a breach of the rules.

In the 1950s, two journals were founded that presented research in the field of American Studies in East and West Germany: the East German *Zeitschrift für Anglistik and Amerikanistik* [*Journal of British and American Studies*] and the West German *Jahrbuch für Amerikastudien* [*Yearbook of American Studies*]. The former (*ZAA*), a quarterly that was first published in East Berlin in 1953, covered the broad spectrum of British and American literature from the beginnings to the present as well as the history of the English language and linguistics. Thus the number of articles, reviews and

78 Foley, *Wrestling with the Left: The Making of Ralph Ellison's* Invisible Man, 110.

79 Maria Diedrich, *Kommunismus im afroamerikanischen Roman: Das Verhältnis afroamerikanischer Schriftsteller zur Kommunistischen Partei der USA zwischen den Weltkriegen* (Stuttgart: Metzler, 1979), 303.

80 Ibid., 347.

81 Ernest Kaiser, 'A Critical Look at Ellison's Fiction and at Social and Literary Criticism by and about the Author', *Black World* 20 (December 1970), 95.

titles in the section of received books dedicated to American literature was small and reflects the institutional marginality of this subfield within the discipline of English philology. The first contributions on black literature appeared in the *ZAA* in the mid-1960s.

East German literary critics who relied on the concept of 'the other America' and the principle of socialist realism were inclined to dismiss Ellison (and sometimes also Baldwin) as a bourgeois author. In his 1968 article on Killens in the *ZAA*, Horst Ihde, from Humboldt University in East Berlin, juxtaposed Killens with Baldwin and Ellison, calling both of the latter 'an extraordinarily rewarding object of interpretation for idealistic literary interpretation'.[82] This was an ironic allusion to the type of criticism common in the West that would analyse literature independently of the social conditions that produced it.

The first article on African American literature that appeared in the *ZAA* in 1965 was a comprehensive assessment of the work of James Baldwin by Heinz Wüstenhagen. But despite this critic's doubts about Baldwin's compatibility 'with what [he] considered the social responsibility of a writer who was a representative of a suppressed and discriminated-against people',[83] Baldwin was to become 'one of the best if not the best known Afro-American writer in the GDR'.[84] In contrast to Baldwin, who notwithstanding the criticism he received was commonly recognized as a brilliant writer, Ellison hardly ever profited from such aesthetic acknowledgement.

Another reason why Ellison is not mentioned in GDR articles on black literature – with the notable exception of the American literary critic and Marxist activist Annette Rubinstein, whose 1966 and 1968 reports on contemporary African American authors in GDR journals do include Ellison – is the emphasis East German critics tend to put on the interrelation between literature and politics. Most American Studies articles in the *ZAA* (or in other journals or newspapers) answer to the Marxist expectation to discuss

82 Horst Ihde, '"Black Writer's Burden": Bemerkungen zu John Oliver Killens', *Zeitschrift für Anglistik und Amerikanistik* 16/2 (1968), 117.

83 Hajek, 'Multiculturality in the German Democratic Republic and the Reception of African-American Literature', 114.

84 Friederike Hajek, 'Historical Aspects of the Reception of James Baldwin in the German Democratic Republic', 33.

literary texts as 'reflecting' political history. For example, in an early GDR contribution on black literature on the 'American Negro' freedom struggle, Rolf Recknagel mentions Shirley Graham [Du Bois], Robert Hayden, John Killens, Lloyd Brown and Langston Hughes.[85] Methodologically similar topics discussed in the *ZAA* are, for example, Ihde's article on the contribution of black slaves to the culture of the United States,[86] Brüning's essay on the 'Black Liberation Movement' and the American drama,[87] and an essay on the October Revolution and American literature by Wirzberger.[88] Ellison's reticence with regard to political activism definitely did not make him a likely candidate for the Marxist perspective on literature that dominated in the GDR.

One of the pioneer West German contributions on black literature happens to be an extensive, informative article on Ellison published in a journal of modern philology in 1958. The author, Heinz Rogge, expresses what was to become the typical universalist and integrationist evaluation of Ellison in West Germany by pointing out that in his novel this author advances to the 'core of [his] life task, namely to explore human existence', and that thus 'the title of the book [*Invisible Man*] becomes a symbol for the modern human being in general'.[89] Rogge also emphasizes the influence of European authors upon Ellison, naming Goethe, Thomas Mann, Balzac, Dostoevsky, Turgenev and Kafka.[90] The start of the West German *Jahrbuch für Amerikastudien* (*JbAS*), first published in 1956, was closely linked to the foundation of the German Association for American Studies

85 Rolf Recknagel, 'Der Befreiungskampf der amerikanischen Neger im Spiegel der Literatur', *Die Nation*, Berlin 8 (1958), 563–82.

86 Horst Ihde, 'Der Beitrag des Negersklaven zur Kultur in den USA', *Zeitschrift für Anglistik und Amerikanistik* 19/1 (1971), 5–35.

87 Eberhard Brüning, '"The Black Liberation Movement" und das amerikanische Drama', *Zeitschrift für Anglistik und Amerikanistik* 20/1 (1972), 46–58.

88 Karl-Heinz Wirzberger, 'Die Oktoberrevolution und die amerikanische Literatur. Rückschau und Ausblick', *Zeitschrift für Anglistik und Amerikanistik* 16/2 (1968), 229–56.

89 Heinz Rogge, 'Die amerikanische Negerfrage im Lichte der Literatur von Richard Wright und Ralph Ellison', *Die Neueren Sprachen* n.s. 7 (1958), 105–7.

90 Ibid., 108–9.

(GAAS) in 1953.[91] Like the GAAS, the journal, exclusively devoted to the study of American culture, enjoyed the constant support of the American Embassy.[92] Even so, the fact that it was launched as a yearbook, started publishing two issues per year in 1974, and became a quarterly as late as 1979, shows that even in West Germany it took American Studies some time to establish itself as a new discipline.

In the *Jahrbuch für Amerikastudien*, the first articles on black literature appeared in the early 1960s. However, the authors were Americans who participated in transatlantic academic exchanges. Thus, in the *JbAS*, Ellison is first discussed in an article by US-based academic Edward Clark on 'Images of the Negro in the American Novel'. In his contribution, which was based on a talk he had given at a conference for English teachers at Marburg in June of 1959, Clark juxtaposes 'the Negro as a stereotype or a symbol' as he appears in novels written by Melville, Twain and Faulkner (as well as in Richard Wright's *Native Son*), with a new image, namely, 'the Negro as a believable human being, one who in his complex humanness enters our imagination as a real person'.[93] '[S]uch a Negro', Clark declares, 'appears in 1952. [...] The novel is *Invisible Man* by Ralph Ellison'.[94] Adhering to the universalist approach, Clark explains that Ellison tells 'the story of that most basic of human quests, the quest for selfhood, the discovery of one's identity so that one can go on to self-fulfillment'.[95] In the following volume of the *Jahrbuch*, Charles H. Nichols, who at the time taught at the Amerika-Institut of the Free University of West Berlin, also criticizes white authors, especially Twain and Faulkner, for not having 'attempted to

91 Grabbe, '50 Jahre Deutsche Gesellschaft für Amerikastudien', 160; Alfred Hornung, 'From the *Jahrbuch für Amerikastudien* to the Quarterly *Amerikastudien / American Studies* – 1956–2005', *Amerikastudien / American Studies* 50/1–2 (2005), 12–13.

92 Hornung, 'From the *Jahrbuch für Amerikastudien* to the Quarterly *Amerikastudien / American Studies* – 1956–2005', 17.

93 Edward Clark, 'Images of the Negro in the American Novel', *Jahrbuch für Amerikastudien* 5 (1960), 178.

94 Ibid., 179.

95 Ibid.

empathize with the experience of being a Negro in America'.[96] Among the 'Negro novelists of sensitivity and power',[97] Nichols, like Clark, focuses on Ellison, whose critique of 'the white American's "Manichean fascination with the symbolism of whiteness and blackness" '[98] he shares. Clark's and Nichols' appraisals of Ellison accord with the opinions of West German Americanists. But in addition, the West German scholars would further emphasize the universalist approach by underlining the aesthetic quality of Ellison's style, ranking him among the best contemporary American writers. They would no longer necessarily discuss him in the context of the representation of black life, but rather would integrate him in studies dealing with more general themes of 'identity', 'initiation', 'the quest' and so on. For example, in her 1964 article on the critique of the American way of life in the contemporary novel, Ursula Brumm, while defining Ellison as a representative of minority literature, underlines that:

> in his novel the theme of the existence of the Negro is subordinated or pigeonholed to another theme, the search for 'identity.' […] From this point of view, the Negro problem is part of the general task of the spiritual-individual existence of human beings – a sign of maturity [that] Negro literature achieves with this novel by Ellison.[99]

Similarly, Heiner Bus in his 1970 discussion of the 'hero' figure in modern American novels, nominates Ellison and Baldwin besides Norman Mailer, J. D. Salinger, Bernard Malamud and Saul Bellow as examples of a particularly fruitful period for the American novel, which he locates in the years 1948 to 1953.[100] In his 1971 survey of the development of the image of the metropolis in the modern American novel from the nineteenth century to the present, Heinz Ickstadt discusses Ellison's *Invisible Man* together

96 Charles H. Nichols, 'Color, Conscience and Crucifixion: A Study of Racial Attitudes in American Literature and Criticism', *Jahrbuch für Amerikastudien* 6 (1961), 45.

97 Ibid.

98 Ibid., 39.

99 Ursula Brumm, 'Die Kritik des *American Way of Life* im Roman der Gegenwart', *Jahrbuch für Amerikastudien* 9 (1964), 32.

100 Heiner Bus, 'Die Figur des "Helden" im modernen amerikanischen Roman: Ein Forschungsbericht', *Jahrbuch für Amerikastudien* 15 (1970), 208.

with such American classics as Dreiser's *Sister Carrie*, Fitzgerald's *The Great Gatsby* and Dos Passos's *Manhattan Transfer*. To Ickstadt, the invisibility that the individual experiences in the city merges with the specific invisibility of the black hero in Ellison's novel in a society that sees him only according to its own prefabrications.[101] Dieter Meindl, meanwhile, in discussing the resurgence of the American first-person novel in the 1950s, stresses the narratological aspects of Ellison's novel and its contribution to the tendency of the post-war era to focus on the individual. He pays less attention to its implications for the collective life of African Americans.[102]

The same trend to interpret *Invisible Man* from the perspective of the post-war philosophy of existentialism and humanism – one that necessarily leads to a depoliticization of Ellison's novel – can be observed in monographs on American fiction, published in non-socialist contexts, in the early and mid-1970s. Like Meindl, the Swiss scholar Fritz Gysin examines 'American Negro Fiction' under formal and structural aspects, namely as phenomena of the genre of the grotesque.[103] More common is research with a focus on thematic aspects. In his study of journeys of initiation of young adults in the modern American novel, for example, Peter Freese claims that *Invisible Man* owes its aesthetic form and representative significance to the fact that at its core lies (in US scholar Ellin Horowitz's words) 'the ancient initiation of the great going down into the darkness of symbolic death and the resulting resurrection'.[104] Freese's interpretation underlines the assessment typical of West German literary critics at the time that, due to his use of symbolism and myth, Ellison should be aligned with white mainstream authors rather than with his black contemporaries. In a similar

101 Heinz Ickstadt, 'Gesichter Babylons: Zum Bild der Großstadt im modernen amerikanischen Roman', *Jahrbuch für Amerikastudien* 16 (1971), 61–2.

102 Dieter Meindl, 'Zur Renaissance des amerikanischen Ich-Romans in den fünfziger Jahren', *Amerikastudien / American Studies* 19/2 (1974), 210.

103 Fritz Gysin, *The Grotesque in American Negro Fiction: Jean Toomer, Richard Wright, and Ralph Ellison* (Bern: Francke, 1975).

104 Ellin Horowitz's 1964 article is quoted in Peter Freese, *Die Initiationsreise: Studien zum jugendlichen Helden im modernen amerikanischen Roman* / mit einer exemplarischen Analyse von J. D. Salingers *The Catcher in the Rye* (Neumünster: Karl Wachholtz Verlag, 1971), 64.

study, entitled 'Odyssey to the Self', the Austrian Arno Heller interprets representations of the search for identity in the American novel.[105] He praises Ellison for no longer being merely 'the spokesperson of a race, but a free shaper of universal human experience', thereby having connected 'Negro literature to the great American tradition of the novel and thus to world literature'.[106] Brigitte Scheer-Schäzler, meanwhile, in a 1971 PhD thesis, investigates the construction of space in a broad range of contemporary American novels. The only black author included is Ellison, whose invisible man she interprets as a 'hero in the realm of the underground' thus emphasizing the relevance of the literary tradition of Dostoevsky.[107]

As these examples illustrate, the combination of the universalist or integrationist approach and New Criticism's emphasis on literary form that was favoured in the West, not only depoliticized Ellison, but also stripped him, as it were, of his blackness, that is to say of his rootedness in black culture and history. This depoliticization was at the same time a precondition of catapulting him to the rank of world literature. Ellison himself appreciated this categorization, when in 'The Art of Fiction: An Interview' he famously remarked 'the Germans, having no special caste assumptions concerning American Negroes, dealt with my work simply as a novel'.[108] It is understandable that he valued the rise in literary status bestowed upon him, even though it ironically led to making him 'invisible' as a black author. However, we may assume he would have agreed with the astute judgement of Martin Christadler, who in the group of the early West German critics stands out by arguing that the common polarization used in the discussion about *Invisible Man* and *Native Son*, the juxtaposition of

105 Arno Heller, *Odyssee zum Selbst: Zur Gestaltung jugendlicher Identitätssuche im neueren amerikanischen Roman* (Innsbruck: Verlag des Instituts für Sprachwissenschaft der Universität Innsbruck, 1973), 14.

106 Ibid., 72.

107 Brigitte Scheer-Schäzler, *Konstruktion als Gestaltung: Interpretationen zum zeitgenössischen amerikanischen Roman*. Salzburger Studien zur Anglistik und Amerikanistik, vol. 2 (Vienna and Stuttgart: Wilhelm Braumüller Universitäts-Verlagsbuchhandlung GmbH, 1975), 65.

108 Ralph Ellison, 'The Art of Fiction: An Interview', in John F. Callahan, ed., *The Collected Essays of Ralph Ellison* (New York: Modern Library, 2003), 217.

art versus protest, was one-sided and did not do justice to Ellison's work. Ellison, he claimed:

> drew both upon the social criticism and the documentary intentions of the protest novel and, with regard to the novel's structure and texture, on the achievements of the symbolistic novel. Ellison's interest in modern methods of representation did not at all prevent him from analyzing and exploring, in a very precise and impressive manner, black-and-white relationships, the relation of the black minority to political power in a society shaped by a white majority.[109]

With the establishment of Black Studies first in the United States, documented by Werner Sollors in a bibliography published in *JbAS*,[110] and a few years later in West Germany, a shift occurs away from the universalist or integrationist approach. From the mid-1970s onwards, then, there is in West Germany a growing awareness of the vastness of the field of Black Studies documented, for example, in the research report of Manfred Pütz,[111] combined with a rising tendency to analyse black writers in the context of the African American experience and tradition, as, for example, in seminal work by Berndt Ostendorf.[112] In the case of devoting a study to several African American authors, the 'classic' triad of Wright, Ellison and Baldwin remains popular until the subfield of Black Studies opens up significantly in the 1980s.

109 Martin Christadler, 'Ralph Ellison: *Invisible Man*', in Hans-Joachim Lang, ed., *Der amerikanische Roman: Von den Anfängen bis zur Gegenwart* (Düsseldorf: August Bagel, 1972), 368.

110 Werner Sollors, 'Black Studies in the United States: A Bibliography', *Jahrbuch für Amerikastudien* 16 (1971), 213–22.

111 Manfred Pütz, '"Black Literature" in der neueren Kritik', *Die Neueren Sprachen* n.s. 22/3 (1973), 159–61.

112 See, for example, Berndt Ostendorf, 'Black Poetry, Blues, and Folklore: Double Consciousness in Afro-American Oral Culture', *Amerikastudien / American Studies* 20/2 (1975), 209–59; Berndt Ostendorf, 'Ralph Ellison's "Flying Home": From Folktale to Short Story', *Journal of the Folklore Institute* 13 (1977), 185–99, and Berndt Ostendorf, 'Ralph Waldo Ellison: Anthropology, Modernism, and Jazz', in Robert O'Meally, ed., *New Essays on* Invisible Man (Cambridge, UK: Cambridge University Press, 1988), 95–122.

The different perspectives on Ellison can also be observed in the literary histories published in the two German states. Typical of the West German reception is the chapter on the American novel in the twentieth century in Rudolf Haas's history of American literature that contains a section on 'Afro-American Fiction'.[113] Haas quotes extensively from Ellison's National Book Award speech, in which he positions himself within the tradition of the mainstream American novel. In conclusion, Haas argues 'how closely especially Ellison is connected to the totality of American life and American literature and how important it is to place "black literature" in this "context"'.[114] The passage on 'Afro-American Fiction' starts out with Richard Wright, focuses on Ellison, refers to Baldwin only as a playwright and mentions neither Du Bois nor Killens.

In the GDR, the Americanists Schönfelder and Wirzberger published a survey of American literature in 1968. In contrast to Baldwin, Ellison receives only a brief entry, in the fifth chapter, on 'the critical bourgeois realism after World War II'.[115] While Wirzberger characterizes *Invisible Man* as a very 'artful, mostly symbolic novel', his critique reflects the expectation that a literary work should be didactic by explicitly offering solutions to real-life problems. The novel fails, Wirzberger states, 'with respect to indicating ways how to overcome this situation so fatal to the Negro; it hardly leaves any possibility for active intervention'.[116] Chapter VI on 'the progressive American literature from the thirties to the sixties', pays tribute only to the following black writers: Wright, Killens and Du Bois (as the author of the Mansart trilogy of historical novels).

In an essay based on a talk given at the German Academy of the Sciences in East Berlin in 1966, Wirzberger offered a survey of African American literature in the context of American history, with a focus on

113 Rudolf Haas, *Amerikanische Literaturgeschichte* 2 (Heidelberg: Quelle & Meyer, 1974).

114 Ibid., 336.

115 Karl-Heinz Schönfelder and Karl-Heinz Wirzberger, *Literatur der USA im Überblick: Von den Anfängen bis zur Gegenwart* (Leipzig: Verlag Philipp Reclam Jr., 1968; 1977; Frankfurt am Main: Röderberg-Verlag GmbH, 1977), 390–415, on Ellison: 410–11, on Baldwin: 411–14.

116 Ibid., 411.

problems of the civil rights movement.[117] On the one hand he addresses Ellison's lack of political activism by referring to his black critics such as Killens, 'who are not happy that he does not support the fight of the civil rights movement more actively and openly and who would rather see him on the forum of public debate than behind the screen of academic institutions'.[118] On the other hand, Wirzberger acknowledges that Ellison's novel, 'although falling behind the attitude of protest characteristic of *Native Son*, has [...] opened new ways of literary representation and coming to terms with the Negro problem'. What follows is a remarkable passage of high aesthetic praise culminating in the following sentence:

> By turning the means of expression calculatedly, systematically and continuously into a decisive factor of realizing his project, Ellison achieves that relatively high level of language mastery which since then has become obligatory also for other contemporary Black American writers.[119]

Wirzberger's praise of Ellison's aesthetic qualities is clearly an exception. As mentioned above, Ellison's political activism, or the lack thereof, was generally an important criterion for critics in East Germany, while it was hardly ever mentioned in West German discussions.[120] The most extraordinary example of the conscious neglect of Ellison's work in the GDR is Brüning's literary history. Produced as a handbook for teachers, it consists of brief biographical and bibliographical entries on American authors, arranged alphabetically. In his list of ten famous twentieth-century African American writers, Ellison is missing, even though there is no question that Brüning was aware of the quality of Ellison's work.[121] The discrepancy

117 Karl-Heinz Wirzberger, *Probleme der Bürgerrechtsbewegung in der amerikanischen Prosaliteratur der Gegenwart* (Berlin: Akademie Verlag, 1967).

118 Ibid., 12–13.

119 Ibid., 13.

120 With the exception of the critical intervention of Klaus Ensslen, Hartmut Keil and Michaela Ulich, 'Sprache und Ideologie: konservative Sprachmuster liberaler Intellektueller in den USA um 1950', *Zeitschrift für Literaturwissenschaft und Linguistik* (LiLi), Beiheft 4 (1976), 106–155, and Klaus Ensslen, *Einführung in die schwarzamerikanische Literatur* (Stuttgart: Kohlhammer, 1982).

121 Eberhard Brüning, *Nordamerikanische Schriftsteller: Biographisches und bibliographisches Handbuch* (Berlin: Ministerium für Volksbildung der DDR, Hauptabteilung Lehrerbildung, 1976). He even alludes to Ellison's importance

between Wirzberger's laudatory remarks and Brüning's silence may have to do with the different audiences they address: what was acceptable or even desirable in a report before the scientific community of the Academy of Science was unwanted before a broader public, let alone in a handbook for school teachers. Excepting these fine distinctions, the scholarly reception of Ellison in East and West Germany demonstrates the strong interdependence between the political conditions shaping the reception process and the resulting assessment of the author. In the case of Ellison, we see a perfect analogy between the different ideological frameworks and the interpretations of *Invisible Man*. The subsequent discrepancy between dismissing Ellison for his alleged lack of progressive agenda and the correlating absence of socialist realism in the East, and praising the same author for a universalism that supposedly transcends his blackness and the correlating literary symbolism in the West, perfectly reflects the divergence between the two opposing political systems.

The German Reception of Ellison after Reunification

In the late 1970s, when Dietz and Franzbecker shared an international perspective in their bibliographical reports, most studies on American literature and culture published in German-speaking countries were still written in German, including their own. Yet it is certainly true that from early on German-speaking scholars would refer diligently to the research published in the United States, whereas Americans have tended to pay less attention to scholarship produced outside North America, even when it is written in English. But notwithstanding a certain imbalance in mutual recognition, we may assume that for the last three to four decades

in a review of Maria Diedrich's monograph on communism in the African American novel: see Eberhard Brüning, Review of Maria Diedrich (1979) and Rolf Franzbecker (1979), *Zeitschrift für Anglistik und Amerikanistik* 29/3 (1981), 269–71.

there has existed an Ellison scholarship written in English that, although still dominated by US-American research, is international. The question then arises to what degree more recent scholarship is still shaped by the specific national context of the respective country of its origin.

In contrast to the first decades of the reception of Ellison, after the end of the Cold War the research located in German-speaking countries has certainly merged more and more with general trends of international scholarship. But at the same time, the current US-American academic debates on Ellison still differ from their counterparts in a reunited Germany because they tend to be highly political in nature. The issues discussed in the United States usually refer to internal political controversies, above all to the question still fervently debated as to whether or not Ellison's work contributes to the struggle of anti-black racism.

Besides Gender Studies, Black Studies has been a particularly thriving subfield within German American Studies since the 1980s. Since then topics and themes have greatly diversified, and while Ellison has preserved his status as a classic African American author, he has not retained the high ranking he had obtained in the West in the first twenty years of his reception. On the other hand, the field's steadily growing expertise in black culture and vernacular has led to an increasingly differentiated and nuanced perspective on Ellison among German Black Studies scholars. In contrast to the earlier East German approach, Ellison is no longer automatically rejected for an alleged lack of progressive political thinking; and in contrast to the former West German view, he is no longer accepted on the basis of a supposed transcendence of ethnicity that somehow expresses a much-hailed universalism. Rather, it seems, the time has come to acknowledge that the 'complexity' that Ellison so fervently claimed to be characteristic of US society also characterizes his work.

Oeser's 2019 revised translation of *Invisible Man* also marks a significant change in the novel's reception. By correcting numerous inaccuracies and amending cardinal omissions of Goyert's translation, Oeser not only improves the first German version in a general sense, but, more importantly, he is attentive to Ellison's allusions to core elements of African American culture such as the blues or playing the dozens. Thus the German reader finally has the opportunity to recognize Ellison's literary style as rooted both in black folklore and vernacular culture as well as in the myths and symbols of the tradition of white American and European fiction.[122] However, there remains a desideratum: what Oeser's translation does not yet convey sufficiently is the specific and varied character of black vernacular that Ellison displays in *Invisible Man*. To transpose black speech into German has admittedly been a major challenge of translating African American literature. It may take the new generation of German intellectuals with African or African American family roots, who grew up with German as the official language but who also speak their parents' languages and vernacular, to produce creative versions of the vernacular in African American texts. Such translations would not only be closer to the originals, but they would also be evidence of a Germany much more diverse than the nation in which Goyert, and Oeser in turn, were socialized.

Bibliography

Bahls, Gudrun and Wolfgang Wicht, 'Amerikanistik an den Hochschulen und Schulen der DDR zwischen zentralistischer Steuerung und Emanzipation', in Rainer Schnoor, ed., *Amerikanistik in der DDR: Geschichte –Analysen – Zeitzeugenberichte* (Berlin: trafo Verlag, 1999), 51–65.

Blaustein, George, *Nightmare Envy and Other Stories: American Culture and European Reconstruction* (New York: Oxford University Press, 2018).

Brown, Soi-Daniel W., '*Invisible Man*'s Appearance in Germany: An Analysis of Potential Critical Response to the German Translation', *Amerikastudien / American Studies* 26/2 (1981), 213–18.

Brüning, Eberhard, 'Die Amerikanistik an der Universität Leipzig (1950–1990) – 40 Jahre Gratwanderung eines ungeliebten Faches', in *Amerikanistik*

122 While most critics consider Oeser's revision a considerable improvement on Goyert's version, they nevertheless generally wished for a completely new translation (see, for example, Scalla, hr2-kultur, radio programme broadcast 16 April 2019). Yet we should keep in mind that it is the publisher's decision whether to provide merely for a revision or to invest in a new translation.

in der DDR: Geschichte – Analysen – Zeitzeugenberichte (Berlin: trafo Verlag, 1999), 67–85.

——, '"The Black Liberation Movement" und das amerikanische Drama', *Zeitschrift für Anglistik und Amerikanistik* 20/1 (1972), 46–58.

——, *Nordamerikanische Schriftsteller: Biographisches und bibliographisches Handbuch* (Berlin: Ministerium für Volksbildung der DDR, Hauptabteilung Lehrerbildung, 1976).

——, 'Probleme der Rezeption amerikanischer Literatur in der DDR', *Weimarer Beiträge: Zeitschrift für Literaturwissenschaft, Ästhetik und Kulturtheorie* 25/4 (1970), 175–86.

——, Review of Maria Diedrich (1979) and Rolf Franzbecker (1979), *Zeitschrift für Anglistik und Amerikanistik* 29/3 (1981), 269–71.

Brumm, Ursula, '"Fifty Years Ago": Memories of the Beginnings', in Ulla Haselstein and Berndt Ostendorf, eds, *Cultural Interactions: Fifty Years of American Studies in Germany* (Heidelberg: Universitätsverlag Winter, 2005), 1–5.

——, 'Die Kritik des *American Way of Life* im Roman der Gegenwart', *Jahrbuch für Amerikastudien* 9 (1964), 23–35.

Bus, Heiner, 'Die Figur des "Helden" im modernen amerikanischen Roman: Ein Forschungsbericht', *Jahrbuch für Amerikastudien* 15 (1970), 208–20.

Christadler, Martin, 'Ralph Ellison: *Invisible Man*', in Hans-Joachim Lang, ed., *Der amerikanische Roman: Von den Anfängen bis zur Gegenwart* (Düsseldorf: August Bagel, 1972), 333–69.

Clark, Edward, 'Images of the Negro in the American Novel', *Jahrbuch für Amerikastudien* 5 (1960), 175–84.

Covo, Jacqueline, *The Blinking Eye: Ralph Waldo Ellison and His American, French, German and Italian Critics, 1952–1971* (Metuchen, NJ: Scarecrow Press, 1974).

Dibbern, Ursula and Horst Ihde, 'Das Echo der Kultur und des Freiheitskampfes der nordamerikanischen Neger in der DDR, 1945–1969 – eine Bibliographie', *Zeitschrift für Anglistik und Amerikanistik* 20/4 (1972), 429–42.

Diedrich, Maria, *Kommunismus im afroamerikanischen Roman: Das Verhältnis afroamerikanischer Schriftsteller zur Kommunistischen Partei der USA zwischen den Weltkriegen* (Stuttgart: Metzler, 1979).

Dietz, Karl-Wilhelm, *Ralph Ellisons Roman* Invisible Man*: Ein Beitrag zu seiner Rezeptionsgeschichte und Interpretation mit besonderer Berücksichtigung der Figuren-, Raum- u. Zeitgestaltung* (Frankfurt am Main, Bern and Las Vegas: Lang, 1979).

Ellison, Fanny, Letter to Mozelle Murray, 31 July 1956, in *Trading Twelves: The Selected Letters of Ralph Ellison and Albert Murray*, ed. John F. Callahan (New York: Modern Library, 2000), 136–41.

——, Letter to Vilgot Sjoman, 3 December 1954, Library of Congress, Ralph Ellison papers, I:173, folder 1.

——, Letter to Willie Mae Brock McConnell, 3 October 1954, Library of Congress, Ralph Ellison papers, II:5, folder 3.

——, Letter to Willie Mae Brock McConnell, 26 July 1956, Library of Congress, Ralph Ellison papers, I:1, folder 12.

Ellison, Ralph, 'The Art of Fiction: An Interview', in John F. Callahan, ed., *The Collected Essays of Ralph Ellison* (New York: Modern Library, 2003), 210–24.

——, *Flying Home und andere Geschichten* [*Flying Home and Other Stories*], with an introduction by John F. Callahan, translated into German by Manfred Allié und Gabriele Kempf-Allié (Zürich: Ammann, 1999).

——, 'Introduction' to *Shadow and Act*, in *The Collected Essays of Ralph Ellison*, ed., John F. Callahan (New York: Modern Library, 2003), 49–60.

——, *Juneteenth. Roman* [*Junteenth: A Novel*], with an introductory afterword by John F. Callahan, translated into German by Manfred Allié und Gabriele Kempf-Allié (Zürich: Ammann, 2000).

——, Speeches, Lectures, and Interviews, 1945–1993, Library of Congress, Ralph Ellison papers I:173, folder 1.

——, Speeches, Lectures, and Interviews, 1945–1993, Library of Congress, Ralph Ellison papers I:173, folder 2.

——, Speeches, Lectures, and Interviews, 1945–1993, Library of Congress, Ralph Ellison papers I:173, folder 4.

——, *Three Days before the Shooting …* (New York: Modern Library, 2010).

——, *Unsichtbar* [*Invisible*], Deutsch von Georg Goyert (Berlin and Frankfurt am Main: S. Fischer Verlag), 1954.

——, *Unsichtbar* [*Invisible*], aus dem Amerikanischen, Deutsch von Georg Goyert, Ungekürzte Sonderausgabe (Berlin; Frankfurt am Main: G. B. Fischer Verlag, 1959).

——, *Unsichtbar* [*Invisible*], Deutsch von Georg Goyert (Berlin; Frankfurt am Main: S. Fischer Verlag, 1969).

——, *Unsichtbar* [*Invisible*], mit einem Nachwort von Ralph Ellison, Deutsch von Georg Goyert, das Nachwort übersetzt von Helma Schleif (Herbstein: März Verlag, 1984).

——, *Unsichtbar* [*Invisible*], mit einem Nachwort von Ralph Ellison, aus dem Amerikanischen von Georg Goyert, das Nachwort übersetzt von Helma Schleif (Reinbek bei Hamburg: Rowohlt, 1987).

——, *Der unsichtbare Mann* [*The Invisible Man*], aus dem Amerikanischen von Georg Goyert, das Nachwort wurde von Helma Schleif übersetzt (Zürich: Ammann, 1995).

——, *Der unsichtbare Mann* [*The Invisible Man*], Deutsch von Georg Goyert. Reinbek bei Hamburg: Rowohlt, 1998.

——, *Der unsichtbare Mann*: Roman [*The Invisible Man: A Novel*], mit einem Nachwort des Autors, aus dem Amerikanischen von Georg Goyert, vollständig neu überarbeitet von Hans-Christian Oeser (Berlin: Aufbau Verlag, 2019).

—— and Albert Murray, *Trading Twelves: The Selected Letters of Ralph Ellison and Albert Murray*, ed., John F. Callahan (New York: Modern Library, 2000).

Ensslen, Klaus, *Einführung in die schwarzamerikanische Literatur* (Stuttgart: Kohlhammer, 1982).

——, Hartmut Keil and Michaela Ulich, 'Sprache und Ideologie: konservative Sprachmuster liberaler Intellektueller in den USA um 1950', *Zeitschrift für Literaturwissenschaft und Linguistik* (LiLi), Beiheft 4 (1976), 106–55.

Foley, Barbara, *Wrestling with the Left: The Making of Ralph Ellison's* Invisible Man (Durham, NC: Duke University Press, 2010).

Franzbecker, Rolf, with Peter Bruck und Willi Real, *Der Moderne Roman des amerikanischen Negers: Richard Wright, Ralph Ellison, James Baldwin* (Darmstadt: Wissenschaftliche Buchgesellschaft, 1979).

Freese, Peter, *Die Initiationsreise: Studien zum jugendlichen Helden im modernen amerikanischen Roman / mit einer exemplarischen Analyse von J. D. Salingers* The Catcher in the Rye (Neumünster: Karl Wachholtz Verlag, 1971).

——, 'Some Remarks on the Reception of James Baldwin's Work in the Federal Republic of Germany', in Jakob Kollhöfer, ed., *James Baldwin: His Place in American Literary History and His Reception in Europe* (Frankfurt am Main: Lang, 1991), 11–32.

Frenz, Horst and John Hess, 'Die nordamerikanische Literatur in der Deutschen Demokratischen Republik', in Horst Frenz and Hans-Joachim Lang, eds, *Nordamerikanische Literatur im deutschen Sprachraum seit 1945: Beiträge zu ihrer Rezeption* (München: Winkler Verlag, 1973), 171–99.

—— and Hans-Joachim Lang, eds, *Nordamerikanische Literatur im deutschen Sprachraum seit 1945: Beiträge zu ihrer Rezeption* (München: Winkler Verlag, 1973).

Frost, Dagmar, 'Zur Rezeption afroamerikanischer Literatur in der Amerikanistik der DDR', in Christian Freitag, Dagmar Frost, Michael Hoenisch and Werner Sollors, eds, *Bibliographie amerikanistischer Veröffentlichungen in der DDR bis 1968* (Berlin: John F. Kennedy-Institut für Nordamerikastudien, Freie Universität Berlin, 1976), 126–42.

Gassert, Philipp, 'Between Political Reconnaisance [sic] Work and Democratizing Science: American Studies in Germany, 1917–1953', *Bulletin of the German Historical Institute Washington, D.C.* 32 (2003), 33–50.

Gersdorf, Catrin, 'Reading American Literature in the G. D. R.', in Alfred Hornung, Reinhard R. Doerries and Gerhard Hoffmann, eds, *Democracy and the Arts in the United States* (Munich: Fink Verlag, 1996), 311–17.

Grabbe, Hans-Jürgen, '50 Jahre Deutsche Gesellschaft für Amerikastudien', *Amerikastudien / American Studies* 48/2 (2003), 159–84.

Gysin, Fritz, *The Grotesque in American Negro Fiction: Jean Toomer, Richard Wright, and Ralph Ellison* (Bern: Francke, 1975).

Haas, Rudolf, *Amerikanische Literaturgeschichte* 2 (Heidelberg: Quelle & Meyer, 1974).

——, 'Über die Rezeption amerikanischer Romane in der Bundesrepublik 1945–1965', in Horst Frenz and Hans-Joachim Lang, eds, *Nordamerikanische Literatur im deutschen Sprachraum seit 1945: Beiträge zu ihrer Rezeption* (München: Winkler Verlag, 1973), 20–46.

Hajek, Friederike, 'Historical Aspects of the Reception of James Baldwin in the German Democratic Republic', in Jakob Köllhofer, ed., *James Baldwin: His Place in American Literary History and Its Reception in Europe* (Frankfurt am Main, Bern, New York and Paris: Peter Lang, 1991), 33–43.

——, 'Multiculturality in the German Democratic Republic and the Reception of African-American Literature', in Klaus J. Milich and Jeffrey M. Peck, eds, *Multiculturalism in Transit: A German–American Exchange* (New York and Oxford: Berghahn, 1998), 111–18.

Heller, Arno, *Odyssee zum Selbst: Zur Gestaltung jugendlicher Identitätssuche im neueren amerikanischen Roman* (Innsbruck: Verlag des Instituts für Sprachwissenschaft der Universität Innsbruck, 1973).

Hornung, Alfred, 'From the *Jahrbuch für Amerikastudien* to the Quarterly *Amerikastudien / American Studies* – 1956–2005', *Amerikastudien / American Studies* 50/1–2 (2005), 12–52.

Horowitz, Ellin, 'The Rebirth of the Artist', in Richard Kostelanetz, ed., *On Contemporary Literature* (New York: Avon, 1964), 330–46.

Ickstadt, Heinz, 'Gesichter Babylons: Zum Bild der Großstadt im modernen amerikanischen Roman', *Jahrbuch für Amerikastudien* 16 (1971), 60–76.

Ihde, Horst, 'Der Beitrag des Negersklaven zur Kultur in den USA', *Zeitschrift für Anglistik und Amerikanistik* 19/1 (1971), 5–35.

——, '"Black Writer's Burden": Bemerkungen zu John Oliver Killens', *Zeitschrift für Anglistik und Amerikanistik* 16/2 (1968), 117–37.

Jackson, Lawrence P., *Ralph Ellison: Emergence of Genius* (New York: John Wiley and Sons, 2002).

Kaiser, Ernest, 'A Critical Look at Ellison's Fiction and at Social and Literary Criticism by and about the Author', *Black World* 20 (1970), 53–59, 81–97.

Kühnelt, Harro Heinz, 'Die Aufnahme der nordamerikanischen Literatur in Österreich', in Horst Frenz and Hans-Joachim Lang, eds, *Nordamerikanische Literatur im deutschen Sprachraum seit 1945: Beiträge zu ihrer Rezeption* (München: Winkler Verlag, 1973), 200–24.

Meindl, Dieter, 'Zur Renaissance des amerikanischen Ich-Romans in den fünfziger Jahren', *Amerikastudien / American Studies* 19/2 (1974), 201–18.

Nichols, Charles H., 'Color, Conscience and Crucifixion: A Study of Racial Attitudes in American Literature and Criticism', *Jahrbuch für Amerikastudien* 6 (1961), 37–47.

Ostendorf, Berndt, 'Black Poetry, Blues, and Folklore: Double Consciousness in Afro-American Oral Culture', *Amerikastudien / American Studies* 20/2 (1975), 209–59.

——, 'Ralph Ellison's "Flying Home": From Folktale to Short Story', *Journal of the Folklore Institute* 13 (1977), 185–99.

——, 'Ralph Waldo Ellison: Anthropology, Modernism, and Jazz', in Robert O'Meally, ed., *New Essays on* Invisible Man (Cambridge, UK: Cambridge University Press, 1988), 95–122.

PEN International, *Die Charta des Internationalen P.E.N. The Charta of the International P.E.N. Charte du P.E.N. International* (Frankfurt am Main: Ullstein, 1959).

PEN Zentrum, ed., *XXX. [thirtieth] Kongress des internationalen P.E.N. Frankfurt am Main. 19. bis 25. Juli 1959. Programm* (Darmstadt: Roetherdruck).

——, ed., *XXX. [thirtieth] Kongress des internationalen P.E.N. Frankfurt am Main. 19. bis 25. Juli 1959. Schöne Literatur im Zeitalter der Wissenschaft. Imaginative Literature in the Age of Science. La Création Littéraire a L'Age de la Science. Bericht. Report. Compte-Rendu* (Frankfurt am Main and Berlin: Propyläen-Verlag, 1960).

Pütz, Manfred, '"Black Literature" in der neueren Kritik', *Die Neueren Sprachen* n.s. 22/3 (1973), 159–61.

Purcell, Richard, *Race, Ralph Ellison and American Cold War Intellectual Culture* (Basingstoke and New York: Palgrave Macmillan, 2013).

Rampersad, Arnold, *Ralph Ellison: A Biography* (New York: Knopf, 2007).

Rapp, Anna, 'Der "Simple Jedermann" und die "Schwarze Rose": Afroamerikanische Texte in Druckgenehmigungsverfahren der DDR', unpublished PhD dissertation (Westfälische Wilhelms-Universität Münster, 2016).

Recknagel, Rolf, 'Der Befreiungskampf der amerikanischen Neger im Spiegel der Literatur', *Die Nation*, Berlin 8 (1958), 563–82.

Rogge, Heinz, 'Die amerikanische Negerfrage im Lichte der Literatur von Richard Wright und Ralph Ellison', *Die Neueren Sprachen* n.s. 7 (1958), 56–69, 103–17.

Rubinstein, Annette, 'Amerikanische Negerschriftsteller heute', trans. Helmut Heinrich, *Sinn und Form* 20/5 (1968), 1264–74.

——, '"Befähigt, für die Menschheit zu sprechen", Literaturbrief aus den USA', trans. Marta Feist, *Neues Deutschland* 21/71, 10 (1966), 2.

Scalla, Mario, hr2-kultur, radio programme broadcast 16 April 2019.

Scheer-Schäzler, Brigitte, *Konstruktion als Gestaltung: Interpretationen zum zeitgenössischen amerikanischen Roman* (Vienna and Stuttgart: Wilhelm Braumüller Universitäts-Verlagsbuchhandlung GmbH, 1975).

Scheffel, Werner, 'Zu einigen Aufgaben der Amerikanistik im Kampf gegen die ideologische Diversion des USA-Imperialismus', *Zeitschrift für Anglistik und Amerikanistik* 20/4 (1972), 370–91.

Schmitt-Kaufhold, Angelika, *Nordamerikanische Literatur im deutschen Sprachraum nach 1945: Positionen der Kritik und Kriterien der Urteilsbildung* (Frankfurt am Main and Bern: Lang, 1977).

Schnoor, Rainer, 'Amerikanistik in 40 Jahren DDR: Eine wissenschaftshistorische Skizze', in Rainer Schnoor, ed., *Amerikanistik in der DDR: Geschichte – Analysen – Zeitzeugenberichte* (Berlin: trafo Verlag, 1999), 29–50.

——, ed., *Amerikanistik in der DDR: Geschichte – Analysen – Zeitzeugenberichte* (Berlin: trafo Verlag, 1999).

Schönfelder, Karl-Heinz and Karl-Heinz Wirzberger, *Literatur der USA im Überblick: Von den Anfängen bis zur Gegenwart* (Leipzig: Verlag Philipp Reclam Jr, 1968, 1977; Frankfurt am Main: Röderberg-Verlag GmbH, 1977).

Smith, Henry Nash, 'The Salzburg Seminar', *American Quarterly* 1/1 (1949), 30–7.

Sollors, Werner, 'Black Studies in the United States: A Bibliography', *Jahrbuch für Amerikastudien* 16 (1971), 213–22.

Wagnleitner, Reinhold, *Coca-Colonization and the Cold War: The Cultural Mission of the United States in Austria after the Second World War*, trans. Diana M. Wolf (Chapel Hill and London: University of North Carolina Press, 1994).

Wirzberger, Karl-Heinz, 'Die Berliner Anglistik und Amerikanistik zwanzig Jahre nach der Wiedereröffnung der Humboldt-Universität. 1. Die Berliner Amerikanistik', *Zeitschrift für Anglistik und Amerikanistik* 15/2 (1967), 152–65.

——, 'Die Oktoberrevolution und die amerikanische Literatur. Rückschau und Ausblick', *Zeitschrift für Anglistik und Amerikanistik* 16/2 (1968), 229–56.

——, *Probleme der Bürgerrechtsbewegung in der amerikanischen Prosaliteratur der Gegenwart* (Berlin: Akademie Verlag, 1967).

Wüstenhagen, Heinz, 'James Baldwins Essays und Romane: Versuch einer ersten Einschätzung', *Zeitschrift für Anglistik und Amerikanistik* 13/2 (1965), 117–57.

MICHIO ARIMITSU AND RAPHAËL LAMBERT

8 Ralph Ellison and African American Literature in Post-World War II Japan: Making Blackness Visible

ABSTRACT:
In 1957, Ralph Ellison went to Japan to attend the PEN International Congress. The following year, Hashimoto Fukuo published a partial translation of *Invisible Man*. Though Ellison's visit drew little attention from the Japanese media at the time, Hashimoto's translation of Ellison's masterpiece helped African American literature become relevant and meaningful – no longer 'invisible' – for a significant number of readers in the nation. In the early 1960s, a group of dedicated scholars and translators led by Hashimoto went on to edit *Kokujin bungaku zenshu*, a monumental thirteen-volume anthology of African American writings. The anthology, featuring Hashimoto's full translation of *Invisible Man*, was as critically acclaimed as it was commercially successful. This chapter demonstrates how Hashimoto and other intellectuals of the post-war era, including the future Nobel Prize laureate Ōe Kenzaburō, understood African American literature and succeeded in promoting it as a front runner of world literature.

> 僕は低周波数で諸君の代言をしてるのかしれないではないか?
> *Who knows but that, on the lower frequencies, I speak for you?*
> Ralph Ellison, *Invisible Man* (1952), translated into Japanese by Hashimoto Fukuo in 1961

In the late August of 1957, Ralph Ellison left Italy. The African American novelist had spent the two previous years in Rome as a fellow at the American Academy.[1] Before his eventual return to the US, he travelled to Japan, where he was to attend the twenty-ninth international PEN Congress. The meeting was to gather over 160 delegates and observers from more than twenty countries.[2] Touted as the first to be held in

1 See Arnold Rampersad, *Ralph Ellison: A Biography* (New York: Alfred A. Knopf, 2007), 343.

2 'Kichōna nanika wo motome te: Kokusai pen taikai, seiō kara 66 nin nyukyō', *Yomiuri Shimbun* (31 August 1957), 5; 'Kokusai pen taikai e no kitai', *Mainichi shimbun* (1 September 1957), 1; 'Kokusai pen taikai kaikai shiki', *Mainichi shimbun*

Asia, the PEN in Tokyo was to examine and promote the 'reciprocal influences of the literatures of the East and the West on contemporary writers both in relation to esthetic values and to their ways of life'.[3]

The organizers of the PEN Congress seem to have done all they could do to create a cosmopolitan, culturally hybrid event where every participant would feel welcome regardless of their ideology, nationality, culture, religion, race or skin colour. Elizabeth Janeway, Vice President of the PEN at the time, fondly recalls cocktail parties, performances of *kabuki* and *noh* 'with a special libretto written (in English and French)' and 'a most wonderful garden party with a band that greeted us with jazz and [which] then swung into the traditional accompaniments to various geisha and folk dances'.[4]

Despite the PEN's aspirations for open, depoliticized dialogues about literature and culture, however, there was no denying that tensions and conflicts haunted the meeting. For instance, the Korean delegate In-sŏb Zŏng lambasted Japan for its imperialist past. Western colonialism was also harshly rebuked by the then Pakistani ambassador to Japan.[5] Moreover, the media coverage of the Congress was far from balanced. While the few recognized stars of the literary world received lavish treatment, many were ignored and left out of the picture.[6] The main subject of this chapter, Ralph

(2 September 1957), 1. Throughout this essay, all transliterations and translations from the Japanese are our own unless otherwise indicated. In bibliographic citations and the bibliography, the titles of primary works in Japanese are translated into English, but those of secondary works are not. Also, throughout this essay the names of Japanese authors are written (as per Japanese convention) with the family name first, unless the publication is either written in or already translated into English. In the bibliography, the family name is also listed first.

3 Elizabeth Janeway, 'The PEN in Tokyo', *New York Times* (6 October 1957), 294.

4 Ibid.

5 Ibid.

6 Yamaya Saburō, 'Surudoi hihan no kageni "satori": Pen taikai ni rainichi sutainbekku shi', *Asahi shimbun* (8 August 1957), 6; 'Ajia de hatsu no kokusai pen taikai', *Asahi shimbun* (15 August 1957), 3; 'Pen taikai ni tsudoru hito to sono chosho', *Asahi shimbun* (30 August 1957), 6; 'Kokusai pen taikai e no kitai', *Mainichi shimbun* (1 September 1957), 1; Tamura Taijirō, 'Medatanu hito wo wasureruna', *Asahi shimbun* (28 August 1957), 6.

Ellison, was a perfect case in point. There was not a single reference to him in the mainstream media; he was in effect as invisible in Japan as the protagonist narrator of his magnum opus, *Invisible Man* (1952).

Interestingly, Ellison did not complain about his invisibility during his visit to Japan. Though we know very little about his trip, he seems to have enjoyed his fourteen-day stay in Tokyo and Kyoto. While he deemed the PEN Congress itself 'simply another convention',[7] he was charmed by Japan and enthused to his friend Albert Murray, 'Japan was so exciting that if I could go back tomorrow I'd leap'.[8] Likewise, he wrote to his wife, 'I find the country much more fascinating than Italy and would like to return'.[9]

What fascinated Ellison most was Japan's cultural hybridity: 'They've taken the Western way, especially the American, and done something of their own with it'.[10] Impressed by the nation's traditions that resiliently survived the devastations of World War II and by how uniquely the Japanese mixed them with the Western influence, Ellison also remarked on the Japanese cultural affinity with nature: he admired 'the manner they bind up the wounds of an injured tree'.[11] Moreover, after 'trading' his old camera 'for a Nikon 35 mm fl.8', a deal that he considered as 'the best part of the trip', Ellison apparently enjoyed taking numerous photos in colour to help himself retain the vivid memories of what he saw and experienced.[12]

Although Ellison seems to have enjoyed his short stay in Japan without encountering explicitly racist behavior, one cannot help wondering what caused the African American author's complete absence in the nation's

7 Ralph Ellison, Letter to Fanny Ellison, 20 September 1957, in *The Selected Letters of Ralph Ellison*, eds, John F. Callahan and Marc C. Conner (New York: Random House, 2019), 505.

8 Ralph Ellison, Letter to Albert Murray, 3 October 1957, in *Selected Letters*, ed., Callahan and Conner, 511.

9 Ralph Ellison, Letter to Fanny Ellison, 29 September 1957, in *Selected Letters*, ed., Callahan and Conner, 509.

10 Ralph Ellison, Letter to Albert Murray, 3 October 1957, in *Selected Letters*, ed., Callahan and Conner, 511.

11 Ralph Ellison, Letter to Fanny Ellison, 29 September 1957, *Selected Letters*, ed., Callahan and Conner, 509.

12 Ralph Ellison, Letter to Albert Murray, 3 October 1957, in *Selected Letters*, ed., Callahan and Conner, 511.

media. In this chapter, we will demonstrate that his invisibility in Japan had to do with a certain perception of American literature still prevalent in the nation at the time. Ellison's invisibility, we argue, was a telling sign that Japanese readers in the late 1950s still generally perceived American literature as a segregated tradition that could not be readily represented by or associated with a black author. It was only after Ellison's visit that African American literature came to be recognized as a significant tradition. Our goal is to historicize this change in post-war Japan, an incredible transformation of African American literature from a state of invisibility into what Japanese readers came to see as a beacon of world literature in the mid-twentieth century.

According to Ōta Saburō, who published a quantitative history of the translation of foreign literature into Japanese right before the PEN Congress, a total of 31,201 foreign literary texts had been translated into Japanese from 1868 to 1955: 8,716 of these were from French literature, 7,751 from Russian, 5,508 from English and 4,235 from German.[13] American literature came in fifth with 2,653, less than half the number of the translations from English literature.[14] In other words, by 1957, American literature had yet to have a prominent share in the Japanese literary market. Nevertheless, writer Itō Sei boldly declared that the realities of the literary marketplace in Japan were changing fast: 'From the end of the nineteenth century to the twentieth century, France and Russia led the literature of the world; now it seems America has taken over their place'.[15]

Even though the popularity of American literature and the critical acclaim for it steadily increased in post-war Japan, American authors of colour, in particular, had yet to find their place in the hearts and minds of most Japanese readers in 1957. For instance, in his profile of the American delegation published in a nationally syndicated newspaper just a month prior to the Congress, Tatsunokuchi Naotarō, a professor of American literature at Waseda University and the founding president of the American

13 Ōta Saburō, 'Tōkei kara mita honyaku bungaku', *Yomiuri Shimbun* (26 August 1957), 3.

14 Ibid.

15 'Gendai amerika bungaku zenshū', *Yomiuri shimbun* (15 August 1957), 2.

Literature Society in Tokyo, presented the image of American literature as still exclusively white by leaving out Ellison from the group.[16]

To be sure, Ellison was not completely unknown in Japan even at the time. In fact, by the time of his visit, Hashimoto Fukuo was already working on the translation of *Invisible Man*, and a significant number of readers there knew that this novel had won the National Book Award in 1953 – thereby outshining Steinbeck's *East of Eden* and Hemingway's *The Old Man and the Sea*. Moreover, a handful of aficionados had been passionately reading *Invisible Man* in the original along with other African American literary texts, seriously discussing their significance and relevance for themselves and for the Japanese as a whole. One cannot help but wonder whether Ellison would have been as invisible and inaudible in the Japanese media during the PEN Congress had the translation come out before the summer of 1957. As an indirect way to answer this hypothetical question, this chapter will show that Hashimoto's partial translation finally published in 1958, followed by a full version collected in the thirteen-volume *Kokujin bungaku zenshū* [*The Complete Anthology of Black Literature*] (1961–3), soon made Ellison and his writings conspicuously visible. Moreover, Hashimoto and his colleagues' collective translations of black literature as well as their critical and editorial work succeeded in constructing an African American literary canon specifically for the readers in Japan, and in making it a tradition profoundly relevant to them. The first two sections of this chapter will thus focus on how and why Hashimoto and other pioneering Japanese literary scholars of the 1950s brought Ellison and other African American writers out of obscurity into the limelight. The bold endeavour of these early scholars and translators of black literature would eventually bear fruit in the aforementioned thirteen-volume anthology in the early 1960s. This impressive feat of cultural translation proved instrumental in establishing Ellison's and other African American authors' reputations in Japan.

In the third section, we will then examine how the trailblazing work of these Black Studies scholars inspired up-and-coming intellectuals such as future Nobel laureate in literature Kenzaburō Ōe. An insatiable reader of

16 Tatsunokuchi Naotarō, 'Pen taikai ni kuru hitobito. No. 2 amerika', *Mainichi shimbun* (6 August 1957), 3.

African American literature, the young Ōe eagerly emulated black authors in themes and styles. As he immersed himself in black literature in the late 1950s and the early 1960s, he found a parallel between the marginalization of the African American community and the existential conditions of the Japanese in the mid-twentieth century. In particular, it was through the Ellisonian tropes of invisibility and diversity that Ōe eventually forged a more original and complex interpretation of the African American experience, which then helped him to think self-reflexively on what it meant to be 'Japanese' in the aftermath of World War II. Ellison's influence on Ōe evidences the capacity of African American culture to produce meaning far beyond its national or racial boundaries.

'*We* Are Still in the Underground': Reading Ellison as a Global Existential Humanist in 1950s Japan

Before demonstrating how Ellison's visit to Japan in 1957 marked a watershed moment in terms of the reception of African American literature there, we need to go back in time. Even before 1957, Ellison had actually begun to acquire followers and admirers in Japan – a few but keen – especially after the National Book Award success. Two months after the 1953 winner was announced, Ryō Namikawa (1905–84) wrote to Ellison from Tokyo: 'I have read your splendid book *Invisible Man* just now and found it is extremely interesting'.[17] Namikawa introduced himself as a translator of American literature whose previous works included Mark Twain's *Life on the Mississippi*, John Dos Passos's *USA*, Upton Sinclair's *Lammy Budd* series, Claude McKay's *Home to Harlem*, Sholem Asch's *Mary*, and most recently Ann Petry's *The Street*. The prolific translator told Ellison that he had been looking for another book to work on for the past year and that he was now '*trembling with surprise and earnest desire to translate your*

17 Ryō Namikawa, Letter to Ralph Ellison, 15 March 1953, Library of Congress, Ralph Ellison papers, 'Foreign Rights and Translations', I:153, folder 6.

"Invisible Man" immediately'.[18] Ellison wrote back on 20 May, telling the prospective translator that he 'would be very interested in seeing it done'.[19] Unfortunately, the project got stranded when Namikawa somehow failed to find a publisher for the translation.[20]

Despite this earlier failure to release a Japanese version of *Invisible Man*, Namikawa's enthusiasm was shared by a handful of other Japanese readers at the time. In January 1954, Ōhashi Kenzaburō (1919–2014), who would become one of the most influential post-World War II Japanese critics of American literature, penned the first review of *Invisible Man* in Japanese.[21] This was the first of several that Ōhashi would write on African American literature, and it is particularly important as it set the future tone of readings not only of Ellison but more broadly of the African American literary tradition in post-war Japan.

In the review, Ōhashi told his readers that he had learned several important lessons about race, America, and identity formation by reading Ellison's novel. He began by admitting his 'meager knowledge of blacks',[22] whom he had regularly seen but barely interacted with during his eight-month sojourn in New Orleans several years before. At the time, he was studying at Tulane University on an exchange programme made possible by the GARIOA programme (Government Aid and Relief in Occupied Areas). By his own account, Ōhashi would often observe black people from a measured distance as he sauntered along the shores of the Mississippi, where he saw their 'shabby huts', or as he walked through the city's uptown, observing a stark difference between the houses inhabited by white people and those by black residents.[23] The Japanese sojourner remembered black

18 Ibid. (emphasis in original).

19 Ralph Ellison, Letter to Ryō Namikawa, 20 March 1953, Library of Congress, Ralph Ellison papers, Foreign Rights and Translations', I:153, folder 6.

20 Albert Erskine, Letter to Fanny Ellison, 26 March 1953, Library of Congress, Ralph Ellison papers, 'Foreign Rights and Translations', I:153, folder 6.

21 Ōhashi Kenzaburō, 'Kokujin sakka rarufu erisun—Sono "mienai ningen" ni tsuite', *Kindai bungaku* 9/4 (1954).

22 Ibid., 56.

23 Ibid., 55–6.

Americans as 'bizarre', but at the same time he also thought they somehow evoked in him a 'childish sense of nostalgia'.[24]

Despite, or perhaps because of 'a full realization of the limitations, errors, and biases' in his own understanding of black people, Ōhashi learned by reading *Invisible Man* that various identities in terms of political ideology, nationality, race, class, education or geography could both unite and separate individuals and groups in complex and confusing ways.[25] To begin with, as a visiting researcher from an occupied country, Ōhashi considered himself an alien in the US, so he felt a definite sense of distance between himself and Ellison, just as he had with the black Americans he had seen in Louisiana. At the same time, Ōhashi also remarked on the intra-racial difference between the college-educated and well-read African American author hailing from the Southwest – Ellison was from Oklahoma – and those 'seemingly ignorant' black folks living in the 'shanties' of New Orleans.[26] And yet, Ōhashi also came to believe that Ellison, despite his education and geographic background, inescapably shared with the formally uneducated black folks in the Deep South a common racial identity that anti-black discrimination created and perpetuated. Alluding to Richard Wright's existentialist novel of 1953, *The Outsider*, Ōhashi described Ellison and the residents of the black ghetto in New Orleans as having not so much a shared cultural heritage as a socially enforced status as 'outsiders'.[27]

Writing the essay just a few weeks before the historic *Brown v. Board of Education* decision of May 1954, Ōhashi wondered if the earlier interracial struggles for social justice in the progressive era of the 1930s had done enough for African Americans. He understood that black Americans had only nominal 'civil rights', for the reality of racial discrimination was evident even (or especially) in the foreigner's eyes. It was clear that 'their personalities were not fully seen by white people'.[28]

24 Ibid., 55.
25 Ibid., 56.
26 Ibid.
27 Ibid.
28 Ibid.

Ōhashi also realized that blatant racism in the South was not the only problem that perpetuated social inequality and black invisibility. In his view, 'sociology', a discipline he considered as 'very much of the twentieth century',[29] also played a vital role in stripping black people of their humanity and rights as American citizens. Mixing the aforementioned existentialist figure of Wright in his later career – and emphatically not his early sociologically inflected naturalism – with the Ellisonian trope, Ōhashi argued that the so-called 'scientific perception' of the black people dehumanized them by reducing them into 'outsiders' and 'invisible men'.[30]

In his interpretation, Ōhashi understood Ellison as being satisfied neither with civil rights – which remained too abstract in the sense that African Americans could not fully exercise them – nor with the sociological gaze, which often objectified African Americans as mere data. The so-called 'scientific lens of sociology', Ōhashi explained to his readers, was too ideologically rigid to allow somebody like Ellison 'to explore the problem of human interiority dynamically'.[31] Ōhashi thus identified Ellison's endeavours as an 'attempt, by black people who suffered in the past and continue to suffer in the present, to produce a new humanist manifesto concerning the blind spots of contemporary human beings'.[32]

Understanding Ellison as a quintessential existentialist on a global scale, Ōhashi evoked what he called 'the frequently used Ellison–Kafka analogy', a comparison that praised both writers for their unique representations of the human condition in the twentieth century.[33] However, no sooner did he mention the analogy than Ōhashi highlighted what he viewed as a signal difference between the African American author and the German-speaking Jewish writer in Prague: Ellison could be at times as abstract as Kafka, he admitted, but a combination of the biological (the 'black blood') and the socio-historical (a 'desire for national integration') 'anchored' the African American author's pursuit of the otherwise vague

29 Ibid., 56–7.
30 Ibid.
31 Ibid.
32 Ibid.
33 Ibid., 59.

and 'unstable notion of humanity'.[34] Foregrounding what he recognized as Ellison's dual mode of identification (racial and national affiliation), Ōhashi thus praised Ellison's historically situated humanist endeavour over and beyond that of Kafka.

In his celebration of the African American author, Ōhashi understood race/blackness loosely as a social and cultural construct that was partially but inevitably informed by one's blood. While thus clinging ambivalently to the biological understanding of race, he nevertheless argued that 'the problem [of being an invisible outsider] is no longer a problem specific to blacks'.[35] Through black people's 'invisibility', he continued, 'Ellison was exploring the "invisibility" of all those who lived in twentieth-century America'.[36] Extending the metaphorical reach of invisibility even beyond the national boundary, Ōhashi further interpreted the Ellisonian project as forming a vital front in the exploration of the 'universal invisibility of all human beings'.[37]

Near the conclusion of his essay, Ōhashi rhetorically enacted this metaphorical transracialization and transnationalization of the trope of invisibility. While pondering the significance of *Invisible Man*'s ending, where the eponymous narrator hibernated in the underground, the Japanese reader saw himself standing next to the African American protagonist: '*We* are still in the underground'.[38] This pronominal articulation of the 'we' imaginatively placed Ōhashi in the shared space with the invisible man (and by extension with Ellison and other African Americans), performatively constructing a common liminal positionality despite all the undeniable differences between them.

In the literature section of the newspaper *Asahi shimbun* published on 30 May 1957, three months before Ellison's visit to Japan, Ōhashi published another article on black literature.[39] In this text featuring photographic

34 Ibid., 57, 59.

35 Ibid., 57.

36 Ibid.

37 Ibid.

38 Ibid., 60 (italics added).

39 Ōhashi Kenzaburō, 'Amerika kokujin sakka no shōsetsu: Ningen de aru toiu shuchō', in *Asahi shimbun* (30 May 1957), 8.

images of Ellison and Wright, he argued that African American authors had recently begun to transcend the black–white dichotomy. Without citing James Baldwin by name, Ōhashi implicitly disagreed with his 1949 essay, 'Everybody's Protest Novel'. While Baldwin pointed out that the protest fiction of Richard Wright in particular ironically denied the humanity of black folks, Ōhashi reiterated his assessment of black literature of three years before, and defended both Wright (of *The Outsider* if not of *Native Son*) and Ellison, insisting that they had already 'liberated themselves from social and political issues', albeit to the extent that they could do so in the politically charged present.[40] In other words, in Ōhashi's evaluation, Baldwin was by no means the only African American writer exploring the 'true humanity', or the 'matters of the interiority of the self', which had been previously neglected in African American literature by its emphasis on anti-racist protest.[41]

As he did in the earlier article, Ōhashi here criticized the sociological reading of African American literature. However, this did not mean he endorsed a New Critical or an unabashedly 'apolitical' approach. On the contrary, his fascination with this group of black texts and writers derived from his genuine interest in their capacity (or their perceived potential) to negotiate the conflict between the social and the individual, the tension between the political and the literary. It was this aspect of African American literature that Ōhashi and many subsequent readers of Ellison, Wright and Baldwin in Japan related to and appreciated. The following declaration epitomized the general interpretation of African American literature in post-war Japan: 'The contemporary black writers' effort to reclaim their humanity signals a great leap for black literature, but at the same time, it also shows their power to participate in the broader field of human literature'.[42] Ōhashi thus interpreted and translated the black experience in the US into something universally relatable and meaningful, even for the Japanese in this era.

40 Ibid.

41 Ibid.

42 Ibid. See also Nukina Yoshitaka, 'Gendai kokujin bungaku tenbō', *Eigo kenkyū* 54 (1965), 20–3.

Following Namikawa's foiled attempt in 1953, Hashimoto had secured the rights to translate *Invisible Man* by 1957, before Ellison came to Japan for the PEN Congress. Another prolific literary translator, Hashimoto had previously worked on, among others, Katherine Mansfield's letters, Herman Melville's *Typee*, James Fenimore Cooper's *The Last of the Mohicans*, Steinbeck's *In Dubious Battle* and Wright's *The Outsider*. He had read *Invisible Man* as early as 1954, and had already published a short review of the novel. By that point, Hashimoto had most likely read Ōhashi's aforementioned article and described Ellison as a 'new type of writer, a very modern man', a new black voice who could 'possibly outshine his senior, Richard Wright'.[43] In Hashimoto's summary, the novel was 'a long chronicle that begins with a black man's discovery of his racialized fate as an invisible man and ends with another discovery that he is doubly invisible as an individual', one whose life was marginalized not just by race but also by the larger forces of history and society.[44]

Just like Ōhashi, Hashimoto extended and transported the Ellisonian metaphor beyond the colour line and the national border. Unlike Ōhashi, however, Hashimoto was much more specific about the political nature of the invisibility of the Japanese in the post-war era. If African Americans had been historically invisible to white Americans (and sometimes to themselves) because of anti-black racism in the US, Hashimoto claimed that the post-war Japanese had similarly become 'invisible men in the eyes of Americans'.[45] What Hashimoto had in mind was a recent thermonuclear bomb test in the vicinity of Bikini Atoll that had just exposed the crew of a Japanese tuna-fishing boat to radiation fallout. In the aftermath, the US adamantly refused to issue an official apology (though it offered financial assistance to the victims) and continued testing nuclear bombs (despite

43 Hashimoto Fukuo, 'Ralph Ellison *no Invisible Man*: 1953 *nen no* National Book Award *jyushō sakuhin*', *Jiji eigo kenkyū* 9/6 (June 1954), 58. In his 'Afterword' to *Mienai ningen* [*Invisible Man*], (Tokyo: Shoshi Patria, 1958), which is his translation of Ellison's novel, Hashimoto refers to Ohashi's earlier review (see Hashimoto, *Mienai ningen*, 259).

44 Ibid.

45 Ibid.

30 million signatures calling for it to stop).[46] Reading *Invisible Man* in the aftermath of such a tragedy must have been an eye-opening revelation, for Ellison's story (in the eyes of many) followed a classic template of an American jeremiad that celebrates the founding ideals of the US while simultaneously and loudly critiquing its current shortcomings.[47] This was a book that eloquently articulated and amplified the Japanese reader's own ambivalence towards the nation that had only recently become an ally after the bloody and protracted war.

In the 'Afterword' to his belated translation of the first half of *Invisible Man*, which finally came out in 1958, Hashimoto apologized to his readers for taking so much time. He also told his readers that he felt 'guilty', as he was one of the very few who noticed that the African American author had been 'overshadowed' by his white compatriots during his visit to Japan the year before, but had done nothing about it.[48] Hashimoto regretted not even having gone to see Ellison in person because of his shyness and lack of confidence that he could converse smoothly in English.

In the rest of the text, Hashimoto remarked on Ellison's reputation in France, referring in particular to Sartre's praises for *Invisible Man*. As for his own evaluation of the novel, he wrote that 'Ellison, though a Negro writer, is not just addressing the specific situation of the black race or America's domestic situation, but also honestly representing a large number of human beings who are becoming "invisible" '.[49] Echoing Ōhashi, Hashimoto argued that Ellison and Wright were 'adding something new to twentieth-century literature by gazing at the problems of contemporary people through the eyes sharpened by the living experience of blacks as outsiders'.[50] Hashimoto defined this 'something new' by quoting at length from Ely Houston, a white hunchbacked character in Wright's *The Outsider*, who provides the protagonist with a memorable reformulation of Du

46 Nick Kapur, *Japan at the Crossroads: Conflict and Compromise after Anpo* (Cambridge, MA: Harvard University Press, 2018), 16.

47 Sacvan Bercovitch, *The American Jeremiad* (Madison: University of Wisconsin Press, 1978).

48 Hashimoto Fukuo, 'Afterword', in *Mienai ningen* (1958), 259.

49 Ibid.

50 Ibid., 260.

Boisian double-consciousness. Using the words borrowed from Wright, Hashimoto identified the invisible man as an embodiment of a 'psychological man' with a 'double vision', who might well serve as 'centers of knowing' for all human beings.[51]

While Hashimoto perceived an undeniable commonality between Wright and Ellison, he also pointed out a 'fundamental difference' in their perspectives.[52] Highlighting the former's involvement and subsequent rejection of communism, Hashimoto argued that Wright was an author who tried to 'know things through his brain'.[53] In contrast, Ellison was to be understood as a writer trying to 'know things with all his body'.[54] Despite his admitted lack of expertise in music, Hashimoto therefore made a point of foregrounding the multi-sensory dimension of Ellisonian writing by specifically drawing his readers' attention to *Invisible Man*'s audible and aural expressivity. From the meditation on the craft of Louis Armstrong in the prologue to scenes suffused with blues and jazz motifs, Hashimoto pointed out that readers 'can feel [music] in this novel'.[55] Though he conflated various genres (jazz, spirituals and blues), Hashimoto accurately grasped and conveyed to his Japanese readers the rich expressive ambivalence of black music, encouraging them 'to hear in the novel the conflicted and confused voices of black love and hate, dejection and rebellion, submission and revolt, and gloominess and cheerfulness'.[56]

Unlike Ōhashi, Hashimoto had never been to the USA. His contact with African Americans, therefore, seems most likely to have been limited to his reading books on black history, culture and literature. His autobiographical writings suggest that Hashimoto learned about race and racism in the US through such texts as Scott Nearing's *Black America* (1929), and eventually more directly through literary works written by African

51 Ibid. Hashimoto cites the passage in his own translation. The original (including the US spelling of 'centers') is found in Richard Wright, *The Outsider* (New York: Harper Perennial, 2003), 163–4.

52 Hashimoto, 'Afterword', in *Mienai ningen*, 260.

53 Ibid.

54 Ibid.

55 Ibid., 262.

56 Ibid.

Americans.[57] The lessons of the black Americans, in turn, led him to reflect on various forms of discrimination in his own country that had hitherto felt remote or incomprehensible to him. This pattern – of learning about black people in the US and then becoming aware of the domestic history and realities of discrimination – is observed in many subsequent readers' encounters with African American literature in Japan.

When the Negro Became Vogue in Japan: The Discursive Construction of *Kokujin bungaku* [Black Literature] from the Late 1950s to the Early 1960s

While Hashimoto's real-life encounter with African Americans may have been limited or virtually non-existent, there were indeed many Japanese citizens in the post-war era who came into direct and regular contact with African Americans. As Michael Cullen Green has noted, tens of thousands of African American soldiers were stationed in Japan during the occupation (from 1945 to 1952). At any point during this tumultuous period in East Asia (extended by the Korean War of 1950 to 1953), there were roughly 10,000 to 15,000 black soldiers (and more if one includes their dependants) in Japan, with the peak of 40,000 in late 1945.[58] Because the main tasks of the low-ranking African American servicemen were confined to driving trucks, serving as guards, or engaging in or supervising manual labour, Green points out that the first American soldiers that came into regular contact with the Japanese citizens were often black.[59]

Despite the long-standing hopes for Afro-Asian solidarity that some African American intellectuals and activists had embraced since Japan's

57 See, for instance, Hashimoto Fukuo, 'Sabetsu to henken wo kangaeru kai' e no kitai', in *Hashimoto Fukuo chosakushū*, vol. 1 (Tokyo: Hayakawa Shobō, 1989), 193.

58 Michael Cullen Green, *Black Yanks in the Pacific: Race in the Making of American Military Empire after World War II* (Ithaca, NY: Cornell University Press, 2010), 39, 45.

59 Ibid., 52–5.

victory over Russia in 1905, and in spite of a significant number of romantic relationships between Japanese women and African American soldiers, Green observes that the contact between the Japanese and black GIs, in general, remained ambivalent, tense or even violent.[60] The mixed feelings the Japanese held towards black soldiers stationed in Japan during the occupation and the Korean War are recounted or fictionally explored by well-known Japanese writers such as Matsumoto Seichō, Kojima Nobuo and – as we shall discuss later – Ōe Kenzaburō.[61]

While Green's account of Japanese ambivalence towards African American soldiers is compelling, it overlooks a heterogeneous group of students, activists and intellectuals who sought to forge imaginary and/or actual connections, networks and solidarities with African Americans. Namikawa and Hashimoto should be counted among this group whose cultural work has until recently been marginalized or neglected in the historiography of Japan–US relations.[62]

The life and work of Nukina Yoshitaka (1911–85) is an exemplary case in point. Back from World War II, the war veteran often witnessed the realities of interracial animosity and violence amid the occupying forces in Kōbe. Soon after Nukina got involved in *Nihon minshushugi bunka renmei*, or *bunren* (Japan Democratic Culture League), a post-war radical democratic

60 Ibid., 2.

61 See Michael Molasky, *The American Occupation of Japan: Literature and Memory* (London: Routledge, 1999): 86–97; Kim Jiyoung, *Nihon bungaku no 'sengo' to hensō sareru 'amerika': senryō kara sengo reisen no jidai e* (Tokyo: Minerva Shobō, 2019), 296–351; William Bridges, 'In the Beginning: Blackness and the 1960s Creative Nonfiction of Ōe Kenzaburō', *positions* 25/2 (2017), 323–49.

62 Koshiro Yukiko and Yuichiro Onishi have recently reconstructed some of the 'transpacific strivings' of these Japanese citizens, whose dreams of freedom was to transform the world beyond what was deemed possible within the narrow confines of US-led 'Cold War racial liberalism'. See Koshiro, 'Beyond an Alliance of Color: The African American Impact on Modern Japan', *positions* 2/1 (2003), 183–215, and Onishi, *Transpacific Antiracism: Afro-Asian Solidarity in 20th-Century Black America, Japan, and Okinawa* (New York: New York University Press, 2013), 2–5, 130, 144. See also Furukawa Hiromi and Furukawa Testushi, *Nihonjin to afurikakei amerikajin: Nichibei kankeishi ni okeru sono shosō* (Tokyo: Akashi Shoten, 2004).

activist organization, he also grew disappointed with intellectuals in Tokyo who were indifferent and often completely ignorant of black struggles for freedom and autonomy. Hence in 1954, he decided to found *Kokujin kenkyū no kai* (or ANS, the Association of Negro Studies) in Kōbe, which was later renamed *Kokujin kenkyū gakkai* (Japan Black Studies Association).[63]

What made Hashimoto, Nukina and a handful of other early scholars of black history and culture in post-war Japan different from most Japanese in the era, even from those who had direct and regular physical contact with African Americans, was the intensity and persistence with which they read and analysed *kokujin bungaku* (black literature). Indeed, they virtually invented a unique language and an interpretive framework through which a body of texts produced by writers of African descent were to be read and understood in the aftermath of World War II. Their efforts crystallized not only in the birth of the ANS/Japan Black Studies Association, but also in the creation of the monumental anthology *Kokujin bungaku zenshū* [*The Complete Anthology of Black Literature*].

Kokujin bungaku zenshū was arguably as ambitious as Alain Locke's *New Negro* (1925) or Nancy Cunard's *Negro: An Anthology* (1934). Yet, although widely read by general readers, the anthology has hardly ever been examined closely by scholars of African American literature in Japan, let alone by scholars of the tradition elsewhere.[64] In any case, in our brief history of the reception of *Invisible Man*, the significance of this anthology, which devoted its ninth and tenth volumes to Hashimoto's translation of *Invisible Man*, cannot be emphasized enough.

Ironically, the idea of the anthology was conceived as a result of an unfortunate setback. Soon after the first half of *Mienai ningen* [*Invisible Man*] by Hashimoto came out in 1958, the publisher suddenly went bankrupt, foiling the translator's plan to complete the project. Two years later,

63 See Nukina Yoshitaka. 'Kokujin kenkyū no kai no koto', *Gendai to shisō* 25 (September 1976), 104–6; Onishi, *Transpacific Antiracism*, 108–11; Katō Tsunehiko, 'The History of Black Studies in Japan: Origin and Development', *Journal of Black Studies* 44/8 (2013), 829–45.

64 The only serious scholarship on this subject to this day is Kiriko Nishida, 'Showa sanjyu nendai no nihon ni okeru "kokujin bungaku" to sono renkan: Kijima Hajime no "sengo shi," "minshu," "jyazu"', *Hikaku bungaku* 57 (2014), 66–79.

in April of 1960, Hashimoto was still looking for a prospective publisher for the second half of the translation. It was around this time that he was unexpectedly put in charge of orchestrating the publication of *Kokujin bungaku zenshū*. The project began when Hashimoto proposed the translation of a few African American novelists and poets – Wright, Ellison and Langston Hughes among others – to Hayakawa Kiyoshi (1912–93), the then president of a young publishing company founded in 1945. Hayakawa made a surprising counter-offer to Hashimoto in early 1960 by suggesting that they make an anthology consisting of no fewer than twelve volumes. The enterprising publisher, Hayakawa, believed that the 'publication of a few black authors would be largely ignored, but that a complete anthology would be a bestseller in this day and age when black jazz is popular in Japan'.[65] Hashimoto balked at the idea at first but eventually took on the challenge. Working closely with fellow Japanese scholars of black literature and culture such as Hamamoto Takeo, Saitō Kazue and poet/translator Kijima Hajime, Hashimoto put his heart and soul into the editing of the anthology. Coinciding with the intensification of the Civil Rights movement, it was compiled between 1961 and 1963 and helped bring about what Nukina would later recall as a shift from 'complete indifference to the Negro problem' to 'a kind of Negro vogue' in the 1960s.[66]

In editing these volumes, Hashimoto widely consulted specialists of American literature in Japan, including Ōhashi.[67] Also vital in the process was Robert Bone's recently published *Negro Novel in America* (1958), a critical history of the tradition which provided many scholars and readers of African American literature in Japan with a better understanding of said tradition at a time when their access to primary sources was limited.[68]

65 Hashimoto Fukuo, *Hashimoto Fukuo chosakushū* [*The Collected Works of Hashimoto Fukuo*], vol. 1 (Tokyo: Hayakawa Shobō, 1989), 192–3; Hashimoto Fukuo, 'Amerika bungaku tono kakawari', in *Hashimoto Fukuo chosakushū*, vol. 1 (Tokyo: Hayakawa Shobō, 1989), 299–300.

66 Nukina Yoshitaka, 'Gendai niguro amerika jin – "Maegaki" toshite', in Japan Black Studies Association, ed., *Amerika kokujin kaihō undo – Atarashii niguro gunzō* (Tokyo: Miraisha, 1966), 7.

67 Ibid., 257.

68 Ibid.

It is also important to note that Tokyo-based Hashimoto's group started to join forces with Nukina's Association of Negro Studies in Kōbe while editing this anthology; the ANS graciously provided the bibliography of all the publications related to black literature and culture in Japanese for the thirteenth volume (or the supplement).[69]

In the 'Afterword' of the first volume of the anthology, Hashimoto explained that in addition to accepting the misleadingly bold label 'complete anthology' the editors also hesitated to use the phrase *kokujin bungaku* ['black literature'], for it could mean either African American literature or more broadly 'literature written by Negroes'. Indeed, serious scholars and translators of black culture and literature in Japan like Nukina, Ōhashi and Hashimoto grappled with the nuances and historical specificities of such labels as 'black', 'Negro' or 'negro'.[70] In his critical essay placed at the very beginning of the thirteenth volume of the anthology, Ōhashi, for example, wrote about the name *kokujin bungaku* (as distinguished from 'American literature') and admitted that it was as frustrating as it was necessary – it would be needed until the day when 'American literature' would be sublimated into a more capaciously integrated multiracial and multicultural tradition.[71]

Because of their limited expertise and resources, Hashimoto and his team decided to narrow down the scope and set strict criteria for *Kokujin bungaku zenshū*. On the one hand, the texts had to be written by African American authors about black characters; on the other hand, the aesthetic value of these texts had to be as high as those of any canonical white

69 Hashimoto Fukuo, ed., *Kokujin bungaku zenshū*, supplementary vol. (Hayawaka Shobō, 1963), 294–317.

70 Hashimoto Fukuo, Ōhashi Kenzaburō, Hamamoto Takeo, Kijima Hajime, Yamamuro Shizuka and Haniya Takao, 'Kokujin bungaku wo kataru', *Kindai bungaku* 17/9 (1962), 20–33 and 17/10 (1962), 25–38.

71 Ōhashi Kenzaburō, 'Kokujin bungaku to amerika bungaku', *Kokujin bungaku zenshū*, supplementary vol. (Hayakawa Shobō, 1963), 32–3. As a noted scholar of Faulkner, Ōhashi also saw a dialectical relationship between Ellison and the white Southern author as they endeavoured, each in their own ways, to articulate the complex inner selves of human beings and to reconstruct what it meant to be 'American'.

American authors.[72] Under this guideline, the editors took great pains and showed remarkable critical acumen in their selection of the texts to be featured in their ambitious anthology.

The inclusion of Ellison was crucial for this project. Hashimoto's translation of *Invisible Man* was not the only work by the author to appear in the anthology. The eighth volume – a collection of short stories – included 'Flying Home', and the eleventh volume featured his essay, 'Society, Morality and the Novel'. Finally, the importance of Ellison was also palpable in the editors and translators' critical essays featured in the last and final volume. For instance, Hamamoto, the co-editor who did much of the administrative work, contributed a short critical essay on *Invisible Man*. He explained to his readers that the 'painful experience of enslavement could perhaps be grasped only by black people alone' and that 'their relationship to white people might also be too complex and subtle to be understood fully by us foreigners'.[73] 'Just because we are the same human beings', he continued, 'it does not mean we can readily understand the black experience through shallow humanism or ideological analysis of class stratification'.[74]

Hamamoto more or less reiterated Ōhashi and Hashimoto's earlier interpretations and identified *kokujin bungaku* as a dual exploration of blackness and humanity: *Invisible Man* was to be read simultaneously as a 'bold and successful black experimental novel' and 'a text that has made a new step forward in the history of world literature in the sense that it has addressed an extreme condition of humanity, unseen outside of the black American experience'.[75] Additionally, despite his high hopes for the future career of Ellison, Hamamoto also worried that Ellison hadn't published a second novel. After reading the latest short story, 'And Hickman Comes'

72 Hashimoto Fukuo, 'Atogaki' [Afterword], in *Kokujin bungaku zenshū* [*The Complete Works of Black Literature*], vol. 1 (Hayakawa Shobō, 1961), 255–6, 258.

73 Hamamoto, Takeo, 'Rarufu erisun: Sono shucho to jikken', *Kokujin bungaku zenshū*, supplementary vol. (Hayakawa Shobō, 1963), 157.

74 Ibid.

75 Ibid., 158.

(1960), he wondered if 'Ellison might be running the risk of pushing himself to a dead-end by always dwelling on extreme conditions'.[76]

In retrospect, Hayakawa's bold promotional acumen and the tireless work of Hashimoto's team led to the spectacular commercial and critical success of *Kokujin bungaku zenshū*. The publication of these volumes served as an introduction to African American literature tailored to the needs of Japanese readers.[77] By 1968, most of the volumes that constituted the anthology went into their third printing. In 1974, roughly ten years from its success with *Kokujin bungaku zenshū*, the Hayakawa publishing company released a pocket-sized edition of *Invisible Man*, a cheaper and more accessible edition, to meet the popular demand for the novel. In the 'Afterword', Hashimoto told the readers that he had barely got the details of the novel right in 1958. This time, he was able to improve upon the translation and include a much more detailed biography of Ellison, thanks largely to the publication of *Shadow and Act* (1964), an anthology of Ellison's essays and interviews. Moreover, Hashimoto was also able to supplement Ellison's biography by consulting Marcus Klein's *After Alienation: American Novels in Mid-Century* (1964) and Constance Webb's *Richard Wright: A Biography* (1968). He also acknowledged his debts to Saitō Tadatoshi, who had written chapter-by-chapter outlines and glossary of the novel in Japanese for a joint venture of the Japanese publisher, Eichosha, and Penguin Modern Classics. The Eichosha-Penguin Books box set included the paperback edition of the novel in English with a booklet containing Saitō's commentaries. In its Preface, Saitō in turn recognized his debts to Hashimoto's earlier translations.[78]

Thanks to the tremendous efforts and ambitious vision of the group led by Hashimoto, several texts by Ralph Ellison, as well as a constellation of other African American texts, suddenly became not only visible and readable but also relevant and popular in post-war Japan. Just as the Civil

76 Ibid., 165; upon Ellison's death in 1994, thirty-one years later, Hamamoto would write a moving obituary, 'Mōhitotsu no territori e no tabidachi: rarufu erison shi no fu ni sesshite', *Eigo seinen* 140/5 (1994), 32–3.

77 Oda Makoto, 'Taihen na shigoto', *Nihon dokusho shimbun* (16 December 1963), 4.

78 Saitō Tadatoshi, ed., *Invisible Man: Ralph Ellison, Eichosha Commentary Booklet* (Tokyo: Eichosha-Penguin Books, 1967), 3.

Rights movement was gaining momentum, Hashimoto and his collaborators' cultural translation and criticism made it possible for the non-English speaking Japanese readers to intellectually and emotionally relate to African American literature and to grasp its global significance. According to Kiuchi Tōru, there were sixty publications (books, academic papers, essays, newspaper articles, reviews and translations) with an exclusive focus on African American literature from 1927 to 1957, the year before Hashimoto's partial translation of *Invisible Man* came out. In the following three decades (from 1958 to 1988), the number soared to 1,471. Hashimoto and his peers created this turning point when African American literature became in their view the front runner of world literature, with Ellison's *Invisible Man* playing the leading role.[79]

The Japanese Artist and the Racial Mountain: Ōe Kenzaburō's Early Diversity Training through *kokujin bungaku* in the 1960s

Ōe Kenzaburō was one of many Japanese who joined the growing campaign to make black literature visible and meaningful in post-war Japan. Making his debut in the late 1950s, Ōe was a voracious reader of contemporary literature from around the world. In addition to white European and American authors, the fledgling writer also showed a keen interest in *kokujin bungaku*, a tradition that was for him represented by the writings of Wright, Ellison, Baldwin and Chester Himes, whom he read first in English, and subsequently in translation as they became available. Ellison's tropes of invisibility and diversity, in particular, left an indelible mark on Ōe, and as we will demonstrate shortly, helped him reformulate his understanding of Japan–US relations.

In July 1961, for instance, Ōe dramatically recalled what he described as 'a recent period of intensely reading black literature'. He continued:

79 Kiuchi Tōru, ed., *Kokujin bungaku shoshi* (Tokyo: Taka Shobō yumi puresu, 1994).

> It was around the time when the Conference of Afro-Asian Writers was started that I began reading nothing but black literature and works concerning Africa, like a man who had been washed onto a deserted island with only those books in his hands.[80]

Up until recently, this publicly proclaimed investment in *kokujin bungaku* has been generally overlooked by Ōe scholars within and outside Japan. As Takao Ichijyō and more recently William Bridges have compellingly argued, most critics have only paid attention to the stereotypical – one-dimensional and frankly racist – representations of blackness in the early writings of Ōe. They underestimated or casually dismissed the more nuanced and vital influence of black literature on the Japanese writer.[81]

As we have noted in the previous sections, *kokujin bungaku* in Japan during the late 1950s and the early 1960s was still a new and elastic category whose contours and meanings were being subjected to impassioned reading and revision by a small group of Japanese readers and translators, such as Ōhashi, Nukina and Hashimoto. These pioneering scholars and readers of the black tradition(s) in Japan were no longer satisfied with representations of blackness by white authors. They had begun to peruse a heterogenous body of texts produced by writers of African descent as soon as they became accessible within the economic and geographical constraints of post-war Japan.

When Ōe wrote about his immersion in *kokujin bungaku*, he was responding to these fellow readers in Japan. While listening to their interpretations of the significance of black literature, he was also trying to make sense of it in his own terms. As a result, he was sometimes off the mark (from today's point of view). For instance, he rather uncritically blurred the line between black Africa and black America in his reflection on *kokujin bungaku* when he repeatedly evoked the term *Négritude*, a diasporic vision based on an essentialist notion of blackness specific to Francophone writers

80 Ōe Kenzaburō, 'Rukeisha no dokusho', *Tosho* 143 (July 1961), 2–3. For the significance of 1961 Conference of Afro-Asian Writers for Ōe, see Nishida Kiriko, 'Sengo nihonbungaku ni okeru afurika rikai to sono tenki: Ajia afurika sakka kaigi kinkyu tōkyō taikai no imi', *Chōiki bunka kagaku kiyō* 20 (2015), 27–46.

81 Ichijyō Takao, *Ōe Kenzaburō, shiga naoya, nonfikushon: Kyojitsu no ōkan* (Tokyo: Izumi Shoin, 2012), 15–24, 138–60; Bridges, 'In the Beginning: Blackness and the 1960s Creative Nonfiction of Ōe Kenzaburō', 323–49.

of African descent, in his writings about Wright and Ellison, even though these African American writers had little investment in the idea.[82]

Given the limited resources available and the ongoing debate about the internal diversity and difference even among black intellectuals and ordinary black folks at the time, such a cultural misreading was to be expected. Much more important than Ōe's inability to historicize and properly identify the cultural and political contexts of various texts written by authors of African descent is the rationale behind his avid reading of these texts in the first place. Even before the intense 'period of reading nothing but black literature' began in early 1961, Ōe had already read Wright's *The Outsider*.[83] While the earlier reading of Wright had left a deep impression on the Japanese writer in terms of literary technique and dexterity, after having witnessed the *Anpo* struggles of 1960 (the series of protests against the renewal of the bilateral Japan–US Treaty of Mutual Cooperation and Security), Ōe noticed a qualitative difference in his more recent re-reading of Wright: 'What shook me more intensely was the aspect of black literature as protest literature'.[84] Ōe quoted from *Native Son* and told the readers that Wright's protest against racism 'thrilled him and filled him with aesthetic impulse because of the rendition of political subjugation in terms of sexual violence'.[85] As Ichijyō reminds us, the early Ōe's fascination with so-called 'sexual men', whose sense of alienation and passivity distinguished them from more active 'political men', found their counterpart in Bigger Thomas.[86]

If Bigger represented for Ōe the black voice of protest under subjugation, Ellison's invisible man spoke to the Japanese writer on a different if no less resonant register. In May of 1960, when the *Anpo* struggles were going on, Ōe published a 160-page novel entitled *Kodokuna seinen no kyuka* [*The Holiday of a Lonely Young Man*]. Ichijyō has described this text as a

82 For instance, see Ōe Kenzaburō, 'Fukashi ningen to tayōsei – Amerika ryokōsha no yume: V' [Invisible Men and Diversity: A Dream of a Traveller to America], *Sekai* 263 (1967).

83 Ōe, 'Rukeisha no dokusho', 3.

84 Ibid.

85 Ibid.

86 Ichijyō, *Ōe Kenzaburō*, 139–41.

'jazz novel' because of its numerous allusions to jazz and jazz musicians like Charlie Parker.[87] This critically and commercially unsuccessful novel in Ōe's transitional period was marked by what the writer Hino Keizō called at the time a 'frivolous and up-tempo style of writing', a new style for Ōe that Ichijyō has identified as his creative experiment with jazzy improvisation.[88] In terms of plot, the novel adapted and combined some key narrative threads from both *The Outsider* and *Invisible Man*. Just as the figures of the Wrightian outsider and the Ellisonian invisible man were interchangeable for Ōhashi and Hashimoto, Ōe superimposed one African American trope on the other and made his Japanese protagonist an amalgam of an outsider who comes to feel as if he were a *toumei ningen* (an invisible man). Although Ōe used the adjective *toumei* (literally, 'transparent') rather than *mienai* – the word Hashimoto used for his translation of 'invisibility' – the figure unmistakably referred to Ellison's nameless protagonist. As Ōe's 'invisible' hero (or rather unlikable antihero) visits a jazz café, he muses:

> I longed for black jazz musicians. They are anonymous like me. There is a black writer named Ralph Ellison. The first page of his story with a black protagonist begins with a line that says, 'I am an invisible man'. I longed for that anonymous rebel, and that feeling was also connected to my longing for jazz musicians.[89]

During the 1960s, Ōe repeatedly evoked the Ellisonian metaphor of invisibility and insisted that the Japanese, unlike the antihero of his 1960 novel, overcome it by embracing social responsibility and diversity without sacrificing individuality.[90] In the essay 'Invisible Men and Diversity' (1967), Ōe chronicled his three-month sojourn in the US in 1965, an experience that radically changed his perceptions of the former enemy nation. Beginning with a rather abrupt question, 'What have the

87 Ibid., 151.

88 Ibid., 152–3.

89 Ōe Kenzaburō, *Kodoku na seinei no kyuka* [*The Holiday of a Lonely Young Man*] (Shincho sha, 1960), 56–7.

90 For instance, Ōe used the figure to talk about the loneliness of Japanese women who left their home in the countryside to work in cities. See 'Kongetsu no kotoba: "Mienai ningen" no hanzai' [The Crime of Invisible Human Beings], *Fujin kōron* (April 1966), 51–4.

black people been to the Japanese?',[91] the essay critically measured the distance and the proximity of the Japanese self and its black Other in the US. Wondering if 'we have seen the very essence of humanity in black people', Ōe continued to ask whether the Japanese had ever seen their own 'yellow faces' reflected in the 'transparent shadow' of black folks, whose existence had been made 'invisible' by white America.[92]

Interestingly, the readers quickly learn that the first of these questions was not raised by the Japanese author himself; it was instead posed by a Korean student studying at Morehouse, the historically black college that Martin Luther King, Jr had once attended. As Ōe tells us, he made a mistake of speaking to the student in Japanese when they ran into each other in Atlanta. Struck by his faulty identification of the 'yellow face', Ōe modified and expanded the first question and now asked, 'What are the Koreans to the Japanese? And the Chinese and the Americans to us?' As one might expect, these questions about the Self and the Other finally led Ōe to ask, 'And what are the Japanese to the Japanese themselves? To the Japanese, are the Japanese today "visible men" or "invisible men"?'[93]

'Invisible Men and Diversity' was also an account of Ōe's participation in Henry Kissinger's Harvard International Summer Seminar in 1965. That year, the participants discussed, among other things, the significance of *Invisible Man*, a text that the Japanese writer happened to consider as 'arguably the best novel of post-World War II American literature'.[94] To Ōe's delight, Ellison was the last guest speaker of the programme.[95] The actual meeting of the two writers, however, was something of an anticlimax. To Ōe, Ellison looked 'gloomy and blue' (*kokoroguraku, yuutsuna*), reminding him of the somber tone of the invisible man at the beginning of the novel. Ōe unflatteringly described Ellison as 'almost like a sick and aging sea lion'.[96] In his mind, Ellison drew a sharp contrast to the members of the Congress of Racial Equality (CORE), whom he had met earlier; unlike

91 Ōe, 'Fukashi ningen to tayōsei', 137.
92 Ibid.
93 Ibid.
94 Ibid., 138.
95 Ibid.
96 Ibid.

Ellison, these younger activists seemed to him full of energy and wit and hence more relatable.

Nevertheless, Ōe, unlike Hashimoto, approached the African American author during an after-party. To the Japanese author's relief, 'behind the shadow of Ellison's gloominess lay hidden the type of deep kindness that only those with honest hearts could see'.[97] Looking back on their encounter, Ōe thought to himself that Ellison was:

> [an] upper-middle-aged man with a long career as a brilliant intellectual, but that he was also someone (like the invisible man) who retained the raw trauma of having once been blindfolded and made to participate in a prizefight as an insecure black boy. He was still that boy who had been forced to continue running as a black person must.[98]

When Ōe had Ellison's attention to himself for a few minutes, he told the older American novelist that 'in the words of his hero concerning diversity, I found the greatest hint regarding not only the black problem in the United States, but also all the problems related to the Japanese people as well'.[99] Ellison's reply was noncommittal: 'For me, the problem of diversity is a significant challenge'.[100] As is often the case when meeting one's idol in person, Ōe had mixed feelings about his encounter with the aging African American author even though he had long admired *Invisible Man* for its critique of homogeneity and conformity. While Ōe eventually understood the deep kindness hidden beneath Ellison's apparent gloominess, he clearly felt ill-at-ease with Ellison's apparent lack of interest in the ongoing fight for justice and civil rights for African Americans. This is evident from Ōe's depiction of Ellison's stand-offish attitude. While drinking gin and 'dancing peculiar dances' together with Ellison into the wee small hours, Ōe caught a glimpse of a late-night TV report about a continuing riot

97 Ibid.

98 Ibid., 139. Despite Ōe's rather facile identification of the invisible man with its creator, Ellison denied that his short story 'Battle Royal' (1947), which later became the first chapter of *Invisible Man*, was ever based on a personal experience. See, for instance, Lawrence Jackson's *Ralph Ellison: Emergence of Genius* (New York: Wiley and Son, 2002), 370.

99 Ōe, 'Fukashi ningen to tayōsei', 139.

100 Ibid.

in Watts, the southern Los Angeles neighbourhood he was to visit before leaving for home. Ōe did not describe Ellison's reaction to the stunning piece of news, leaving readers to wonder whether Ellison cared at all or was too weary to react to yet another expression of black outrage.

Five weeks later, Ōe arrived in Watts after a short visit to the headquarters of the Student Non-Violent Committee (SNCC) in Atlanta, where he interviewed John Lewis, a legendary civil rights activist who, as the Japanese writer duly noted, had by then already been jailed thirty-nine times.[101] In Watts, Ōe was struck by the stark difference between the real black people and the media's representations of them. An African American municipal worker in charge of rebuilding the neighbourhood explained to him the meaning of Watts's destruction during the riot.[102] Hearing this worker's account of what had happened confirmed to Ōe that the mainstream media such as *Life* magazine, whose photographic records captured and disseminated numerous images of black rioters on the street, misrepresented the ordinary black folks in the neighbourhood as if they were 'invisible men and women', and reduced them as a group to the sensational stereotype of the angry and violent mob for white consumption.[103]

As the citation of the Ellisonian trope here attests, Ōe, during his first trip to the US, had tried to make sense of black people, black–white relationships, and everything else related to race and racism in the United States primarily through the lens of *Invisible Man* (and supplemented in part by his reading of *Freedom Summer*, written by the white civil rights activist, Sally Belfrage). Not surprisingly, therefore, Watts reminded him of the Harlem riot scene in Ellison's novel. Drawing the reader's attention to the invisible man's ambivalent observation about the riot's instigator, Ras the Destroyer, Ōe ended the essay thus:

> hoping to cultivate the power of imagination so that the reader will be able to come close to understanding the concrete situation of the riot, and by training his eyes so that he will not see black people as 'invisible human beings' but as *jittai* [substantial existence] characterized by their diversity.[104]

101 Ibid., 142.
102 Ibid., 144.
103 Ibid., 144–5.
104 Ibid.

'Only by making such an effort', he declared, 'could we find a way to prevent ourselves from becoming invisible'.[105]

Roughly sixty years after Ōe's first call for the Japanese to defy invisibility (of themselves and others) and recognize diversity in all human activities and relations, the word *daibaashitti* (the transliteration of the word 'diversity' in Japanese) and its Japanese translation, *tayosei*, are actively promoted or bandied about everywhere in the nation. Though these catchwords have encouraged Japanese society to make various forms of disparities and marginalization visible, and therefore targets of intervention and reform, such positive attitudes are more often than not serving only as a *tatemae* (a calculated public stance), failing to tackle the messy and difficult task of guaranteeing the equality and rights of marginalized individuals and groups.

Given this reality, the idea of diversity in Japan, first imported and explored through the writings of Ellison and other African American writers, needs to be revisited and reexamined.[106] From today's point of view, even the earlier conception of diversity that Ōe advocated after his intense and repeated readings of African American authors seems not capacious enough, as it was too male-centred and focused too narrowly on nationality. In other words, the idea of diversity itself needs to be updated, expanded and truly diversified.

Re-reading *Invisible Man* in Twenty-First-Century Japan

The small group of citizens who launched Black Studies in post-war Japan may not have imagined that their intellectual work would grow and one

105 Ibid.

106 According to *Nihon kokugo daijiten* (dictionary), the use of the Japanese word '*tayosei*' dates back as early as 1935, but the English word 'diversity' and its transliteration '*daibaashitti*' have become popular only since the early 2000s. See Nakamura Yutaka, 'Basic Concepts, Historical Transitions and Significance of Diversity and Inclusion', *Takachiho ronsō* 52/1 (2017), 74.

day be recognized as part of a vital academic field both in the US and in Japan. As for Ōe, he may not have imagined that his ruminations on Ellison's notion of diversity – as an antidote against political indifference and social irresponsibility – would be revived as a buzzword in twenty-first-century Japan.

The translation of African American literature into Japanese has continued and indeed steadily increased. Since the late 1970s, however, there has been a notable change in who has been translated. Whereas the African American texts popular in Japan during the 1950s, 1960s and most of the 1970s were written mostly by male authors (with the notable exception of Ann Petry and Zora Neale Hurston), black female novelists and poets such as Toni Morrison, Alice Walker and Nikki Giovanni have received more and more critical attention and increasingly become visible faces of the tradition.[107]

Just as African American authors – both male and female – continue to expand, complicate and diversify the worldviews and self-conceptions of the readers in Japan, the recently published new translation of *Invisible Man* by Matsumoto Noboru in 2004 is itself highly significant. This hardcover version, moreover, which is based on Hashimoto's translation, was born again in a new paperback edition in December 2020, due to a growing interest in the Black Lives Matter movement. This latest edition will certainly help a new generation of readers and writers to rediscover Ellison's powerful language, tropes and visions – those that once inspired their parents or their grandparents as they struggled to articulate and address their own problems (whether they were social or existential, or both). Who knows but that, on the lower or higher frequencies, Ellison might again be heard to speak for contemporary readers and writers in Japan?

107 Kiuchi Tōru, Robert J. Butler and Yoshinobu Hakutani, eds, *The Critical Response in Japan to African American Writers* (New York: Peter Lang, 2003).

Bibliography

'Ajia de hatsu no kokusai pen taikai', *Asahi shimbun* (15 August 1957), 3.
Bercovitch, Sacvan, *The American Jeremiad* (Madison: University of Wisconsin Press, 1978).
Bridges, Will, 'In the Beginning: Blackness and the 1960s Creative Nonfiction of Ōe Kenzaburō', *positions* 25/2 (2017), 323–49.
——, *Playing in the Shadows: Fictions of Race and Blackness in Postwar Japanese Literature* (Ann Arbor: University of Michigan Press, 2020).
Edwards, Brent Hayes, *The Practice of Diaspora: Literature, Translation, and the Rise of Black Internationalism* (Cambridge, MA: Harvard University Press, 2003).
Ellison, Ralph, *Collected Essays of Ralph Ellison*, ed., John F. Callahan (New York: Modern Library, 2003).
——, *Invisible Man* (New York: Random House, 1952).
——, Letter to Albert Murray, 3 October 1957, in *The Selected Letters of Ralph Ellison*, eds, John F. Callahan and Marc C. Conner (New York: Random House, 2019), 511–13.
——, Letter to Fanny Ellison, 20 September 1957, in *The Selected Letters of Ralph Ellison*, eds, John F. Callahan and Marc C. Conner (New York: Random House, 2019), 505–6.
——, Letter to Fanny Ellison, 29 September 1957, in John F. and Marc C. Conner, eds, *The Selected Letters of Ralph Ellison* (New York: Random House, 2019), 507–10.
——, Letter to Ryō Namikawa, 20 March 1953, Library of Congress, Ralph Ellison papers, 'Foreign Rights and Translations', I:153, folder 6.
——, *The Selected Letters of Ralph Ellison*, eds, John F. and Marc C. Conner (New York: Random House, 2019).
Erskine, Albert, Letter to Fanny Ellison, 26 March 1953, Library of Congress, Ralph Ellison papers, 'Foreign Rights and Translations', I:153, folder 6.
Furukawa, Hiromi, 'Atogaki', in Kokujin kenkyū no kai, ed., *Amerika kokujin kaihō undō: Atarashii niguro gunzō* (Tokyo: Miraisha, 1966), 315–19.
—— and Testushi Furukawa, *Nihonjin to afurikakei amerikajin: Nichibei kankeishi ni okeru sono shosō* (Tokyo: Akashi Shoten, 2004).
'Gendai amerika bungaku zenshū', *Yomiuri shimbun* (15 August 1957), 2.
Green, Michael Cullen, *Black Yanks in the Pacific: Race in the Making of American Military Empire after World War II* (Ithaca, NY: Cornell University Press, 2010).
Hamamoto, Takeo, 'Mōhitotsu no territori e no tabidachi: rarufu erison shi no fu ni sesshite', *Eigo seinen* 140/5 (1994), 32–3.

Hashimoto, Fukuo, 'Atogaki' [Afterword], in *Kokujin bungaku zenshū* [*The Complete Works of Black Literature*], vol. 1 (1961), 255–65.

——, *Hashimoto fukuo chosakushū* [*The Collected Works of Hashimoto Fukuo*], 3 vols (Tokyo: Hayakawa Shobō, 1989).

——, 'Kokujin bungaku no tenkan', in *Kokujin bungaku no sekai* (Tokyo: Miraisha, 1967), 122–33.

——, trans., *Mienai ningen* [*Invisible Man*], by Ralph Ellison (Tokyo: Shoshi Patria, 1958).

——, trans., *Mienai ningen* [*Invisible Man*], by Ralph Ellison (1961), *Kokujin bungaku zenshū*, 12 vols, general editor, Hashimoto Fukuo, vols 9–10 (Tokyo: Hayakawa, 1961–3).

——, trans., *Mienai ningen* [*Invisible Man*], by Ralph Ellison, 2 vols, Pocketbook edn (Tokyo: Hayakawa Shobō, 1974).

——, 'Ralph Ellison *no Invisible Man*: 1953 *nen no* National Book Award *jyushō sakuhin*', *Jiji eigo kenkyū* 9/6 (June 1954), 58–9.

——, 'Rarufu erison no tachiba' ['Ralph Ellison's Positionality'], in *Kokujin bungaku no sekai* [*The World of Negro Literature*] (Tokyo: Miraisha, 1967), 154–6.

——, '"Sabetsu to henken wo kangaeru kai" e no kitai', in *Hashimoto Fukuo chosakushū*, vol. 1 (Tokyo: Hayakawa Shobō, 1989), 193–4.

——, Ōhashi Kenzaburō, Hamamoto Takeo, Kijima Hajime, Yamamuro Shizuka and Haniya Takao, 'Kokujin bungaku wo kataru: Part I & II', *Kindai bungaku* 17/9 (1962), 20–33 and 17/10 (1962), 25–38.

Ichijyō, Takao, *Ōe Kenzaburō, Shiga naoya, nonfikushon: kyojitsu no ōkan* (Osaka: Izumi Shoin, 2012).

International PEN Bulletin of Selected Books 8/2 (1957), 39–53.

Jackson, Lawrence, *Ralph Ellison: Emergence of Genius* (New York: Wiley and Son, 2002).

Janeway, Elizabeth, 'The PEN in Tokyo', *New York Times* (6 October 1957), 294.

Jiyoung, Kim, *Nihon bungaku no 'sengo' to hensō sareru 'amerika': Senryō kara sengo reisen no jidai e* (Tokyo: Minerva Shobō, 2019).

'*Kaihō*', *Kokujin kenkyū* 25 (March 1965), 42–3.

Kapur, Nick, *Japan at the Crossroads: Conflict and Compromise after Anpo* (Cambridge, MA: Harvard University Press, 2018).

Katō, Tsunehiko, 'The History of Black Studies in Japan: Origin and Development', *Journal of Black Studies* 44/8 (2013), 829–45.

'Kichōna nanika wo motomete: Kokusai pen taikai: Seiō kara 66 nin nyukyō', *Yomiuri shimbun* (31 August 1957), 5.

Kiuchi, Tōru, ed., *Kokujin bungaku shoshi* (Tokyo: Taka Shobō yumi puresu, 1994).

——, Robert J. Butler and Yoshinobu Hakutani, eds, *The Critical Response in Japan to African American Writers* (New York: Peter Lang, 2003).

'Kokusai pen taikai e no kitai', *Mainichi shimbun* (1 September 1957), 1.
'Kokusai pen taikai: Dai yonnichi', *Yomiuri shimbun* (6 September 1957), 5.
'Kokusai pen taikai kaikai shiki', *Mainichi shimbun* (2 September 1957), 1.
Koshiro, Yukiko, 'Beyond an Alliance of Color: The African American Impact on Modern Japan', *positions* 2/1 (2003), 183–15.
Matsumoto, Noboru, trans., *Mienai ningen* [*Invisible Man*], by Ralph Ellison, 2 vols (Tokyo: Nanundō, 2004).
Molasky, Michael, *The American Occupation of Japan: Literature and Memory* (London: Routledge, 1999).
Nakamura, Yutaka, 'Basic Concepts, Historical Transitions and Significance of Diversity and Inclusion', *Takachiho ronsō* 52/1 (2017), 53–84.
Namikawa, Ryō, Letter to Ralph Ellison, 15 March 1953, Library of Congress, Ralph Ellison papers, 'Foreign Rights and Translations', I:153, folder 6.
Nishida, Kiriko, 'Sengo nihonbungaku ni okeru afurika rikai to sono tenki: Ajia afurika sakka kaigi kinkyu tōkyō taikai no imi', *Chōiki bunka kagaku kiyō* 20 (2015), 27–46.
——, 'Showa sanjyu nendai no nihon ni okeru "kokujin bungaku" to sono renkan: Kijima Hajime no "sengo shi," "minshu," "jyazu"', *Hikaku bungaku* 57 (2014), 66–79.
Nukina, Yoshitaka, 'Gendai kokujin bungaku tenbō', *Eigo kenkyū* 54 (1965), 20–3.
——, 'Gendai niguro amerika jin – "Maegaki" toshite', Japan Black Studies Association, ed., *Amerika kokujin kaihō undō – Atarashii niguro gunzō* (Tokyo: Miraisha, 1966).
——, 'Kokujin kenkyū no kai no koto', *Gendai to shisō* 25 (1976), 102–8.
Oda, Makoto, 'Taihen na shigoto', *Nihon dokusho shimbun* (16 December 1963), 4.
Ōe, Kenzaburō, 'Fukashi ningen to tayōsei – amerika ryokōsha no yume V' [Invisible Men and Diversity: A Dream of a Traveller to America], *Sekai* 263 (1967), 137–45.
——, *Kodoku na seinei no kyuka* [*The Holiday of a Lonely Young Man*] (Shincho sha, 1960), 56–7.
——, 'Kongetsu no kotoba: "Mienai ningen" no hanzai' [The Crime of 'Invisible Human Beings'], *Fujin kōron* (April 1966), 51–4.
——, 'Kurai kawa omoi kai' [A Dark River, Heavy Oars], in *Ōe Kenzaburō zensakuhin* [*Complete Anthology of Ōe, Kenzaburō*], vol. 2 (Tokyo: Shinchōsha, 1966), 5–22.
——, 'Rukeisha no dokusho' [The Readings of an Exile], *Tosho* 143 (July 1961), 2–3.
——, *Sakebigoe* [*The Cry*] (Tokyo: Kōdansha, 1963).
——, 'Shiiku' [Prize Stock], in *Shishano ogori* [*Lavish are the Dead*] (Tokyo: Bungeishunjyusha, 1958).

Ōhashi, Kenzaburō, 'Amerika kokujin sakka no shōsetsu: Ningen de aru toiu shuchō', *Asahi shimbun* (30 May 1957), 8.
——, 'Kokujin bungaku to amerika bungaku', in *Kokujin bungaku zenshū*, supplementary vol. (Hayakawa Shobō, 1963), 32–3.
——, 'Kokujin sakka rarufu erison – Sono "mienai ningen" ni tsuite', *Kindai bungaku* 9/4 (1954), 55–60.
Onishi, Yuichiro, *Transpacific Antiracism: Afro-Asian Solidarity in 20th-Century Black America, Japan, and Okinawa* (New York: New York University Press, 2013).
Ōta, Saburō, 'Tōkei kara mita honyaku bungaku', *Yomiuri shimbun* (26 August 1957), 3.
'Pen no daihyō. Beikoku no sakka: jyon sutainbekku shi', *Mainichi shimbun* (1 September 1957), 1.
'Pen taikai ni tsudoru hito to sono chosho', *Asahi shimbun* (30 August 1957), 6.
'Pen taikai tojiru', *Yomiuri Shimbun* (6 September 1957), 5.
Rampersad, Arnold, *Ralph Ellison: A Biography* (New York: Alfred A. Knopf, 2007).
Saitō, Tadatoshi, ed., *Invisible Man: Ralph Ellison, Eichosha Commentary Booklet* (Tokyo: Eichosha-Penguin Books, 1967).
Tamura, Taijirō, 'Medatanu hito wo wasureruna', *Asahi shimbun* (28 August 1957), 6.
Tatsunokuchi, Naotarō, 'Pen taikai ni kuru hitobito. No. 2 amerika', *Mainichi shimbun* (6 August 1957), 3.
'Tenbō: Kankoku deno aru honyaku no hanashi', *Kokujin kenkyū* 19 (1963), 35.
Wright, Richard, *The Outsider* (New York: Harper Perennial, 2003).
Yamaya, Saburō, 'Surudoi hihan no kageni "satori": Pen taikai ni rainichi sutainbekku shi', *Asahi shimbun* (8 August 1957), 6.

MARC C. CONNER

Afterword: How Ralph Ellison Speaks to the World

Ralph Ellison is perhaps the most resolutely American writer there has ever been. His championing of a commitment to what his Invisible Man calls 'the principles' of the American founding and the American concept is a dominant theme that runs throughout all his writings. But Ellison's Americanness has always been a fraught and contrary congeries of ideas. Ellison first gave expression to his complex stance towards America at the end of his 1944 story, 'In a Strange Country'. The protagonist, Mr Parker, a black American sailor who has been beaten by white fellow American soldiers, is taken in by the Welsh countrymen, welcomed into their pub, and invited to participate in their music and fellowship. Here he has a realization of the equality and democracy that music both provides and demands, of the 'expansiveness', 'unity' and the 'deeper humanity' – beyond race, beyond nation – that their common commitment to music evinces. When they sing 'The Star-Spangled Banner', he is moved to tears: 'For the first time in your whole life, he thought with dreamlike wonder, the words are not ironic'. This is the defining image of Ellison's complex patriotism: a black man who has been unjustly beaten by whites, who wants to reject America yet finds he cannot, and ultimately struggles to affirm the very nation that he simultaneously wishes to reject. It is no accident that he has this realization while standing on the shore of another country.

This ambivalence becomes the stance of the Invisible Man, who at the end of a nearly 600-page journey into the heart of darkness of America, ends that novel with a very complex and nuanced affirmation of the American promise that is nearly as much rejection as it is affirmation: 'So it is that now I denounce and defend', he says, and continues:

> I condemn and affirm, say no and say yes, say yes and say no. I denounce because though implicated and partially responsible, I have been hurt to the point of abysmal pain, hurt to the point of invisibility. And I defend because in spite of all I find that I love. In order to get some of it down I *have* to love.

This is what undergirds, and complicates, his understanding that his grandfather's advice meant to affirm 'the principle on which the country was built and not the men'. It also constitutes Ellison's own stance towards the American promise – what he frequently describes as 'the American contradiction' – the tragi-comic American conflict between the 'sacred documents' of its founding and the lived reality of its history. In his 1967 lecture on 'the novel as a function of democracy' Ellison characterized the USA as 'only a partially achieved nation', and in a speech of 1983 he described his effort as an African American writer to be 'to add his individual voice to the futuristic effort of fulfilling the democratic ideal'. America, for Ellison, was always a work in progress.

It is important always to recognize how dialectic Ellison's attitude towards America was, how, like his Invisible Man, he would affirm and condemn, denounce and defend, say yes and say no. This is why his much-admired forebears and peers in the enterprise of American fiction included the Twain of *Huckleberry Finn* and the Fitzgerald of *The Great Gatsby*, whose texts are core expressions of the American consciousness that embody a complex stance towards America that mirrored and expressed Ellison's own. Hence in 1958, in response to *Time* magazine publishing an erroneous description of Ellison as 'self-exiled in Rome', Ellison wrote in a letter to the magazine's editor that he was 'too vindictively American' to be in exile. 'I am [...] too full of hate for the hateful aspects of this country', he wrote, 'and too possessed by the things I love here to be too long away'.

'Vindictively American' – the phrase suggests the anger and sense of retribution Ellison felt towards his country, and in many ways his grand, unfinished second novel, *Three Days before the Shooting ...* is filled with that sense of being vindictive towards America. That vast epic seeks to call the nation to account for its sins, the sins of rejecting what Ellison calls in that tome, 'the whiteness hidden in blackness, or blackness concealed in the whiteness', its inextricably mixed and motley racial, cultural and historical identities. To quote again his Invisible Man's guarded optimism about America: 'America is woven of many strands; I would recognize them and let it so remain'.

Ironically, this is precisely what makes Ellison a global writer, and one whose vision and values have a particular warrant for the twenty-first century. In my introduction to the essay collection, *The New Territory*, I suggest that Ellison is an especially relevant voice for our current moment, and labelled him 'the cultural prophet of twenty-first-century America'. Other critics have expressed similar sentiments: Ross Posnock presciently stated in 2003 that 'we are only now beginning to catch up with Ralph Waldo Ellison', while Timothy Parrish memorably declared in 2012 that 'Ellison was forever addressing an America that is still unrealized'. But Ellison's vision of what America could be goes beyond a merely national vision. For the America that Ellison described, hoped for, and, in his more positive vistas, predicted, is simultaneously a global, international and polyglot world that goes far beyond national borders and provincial identities. Ralph Ellison speaks not just for twenty-first-century America, but also for a global vision that has purchase on virtually every nation, religion, political entity and culture in the world.

It was in the spirit of such a vision that Tessa and I, in concert with the Ralph Ellison Society and supported by the Ralph and Fanny Ellison Foundation (as well as the Rothermere American Institute and TORCH at Oxford), conceived and organized the International Ralph Ellison Symposium at Oxford in September of 2017. As Tessa explains in the introduction to this volume, our starting point was that Ellison's status as a wholeheartedly American author was at risk of becoming somewhat over-determined. The way his work speaks simultaneously to a global and local audience and experience – precisely what Ellison himself signifies in 'In a Strange Country', when the American character attains illumination and understanding from his Welsh companions – had yet to be properly acknowledged. We sought in this symposium to build on the Ellison seminars, conferences and symposia that have been convened in the past decade in various locations in the United States (at Washington and Lee University, at Lewis and Clark College, at the Library of Congress, in Oklahoma City, and at the annual American Literature Association conferences) by hosting a major symposium outside of the United States.

Tessa's affiliation with Oxford provided an ideal location, and the resulting programme and conversations proved a model of international scholarly exchange and understanding.

What emerged from the symposium is the profound relevance of Ellison's writing and thought for, quite frankly, the entire world. Scholars came from France, Germany, Japan, Russia, South Africa, the United States, and many other places to share their perspectives on Ellison. As a US scholar of Ellison's work, I found this confirmation of the global impact of his writing to be a revelation and a delight. I have long argued that Ellison is perhaps the author who has the most to teach us about our current historical moment – I have written that he is the author who would have best understood the emergence of Barack Obama as America's first black president, and I have said that he is probably the only author who would have perfectly understood the emergence of Donald Trump as the next president. This symposium confirmed exactly that impression.

It was a natural decision to bring together many of the participants in the symposium along with other Ellison scholars throughout the world to produce a collection of essays on the powerful theme of 'Global Ralph Ellison'. For we felt this array of perspectives was crucial to help us all understand the broader reaches of Ellison's work, to see once more on how many frequencies Ellison does indeed speak for us, for all of us in this increasingly globalized world. The essays in this book's first part demonstrate the resolutely transnational nature of Ellison's intellectual formation, by using the new archival material to highlight the global nature of his reading and thinking. Those in its second part begin the task of constructing a global history of the reception of the Ellisonian oeuvre, by illuminating the role *Invisible Man* has played in four different nations' still-evolving conceptions of their own histories and identities. And at a time when America's own stance towards its borders and towards migration has been especially fraught, an approach to an American author that brought into relief his global dimensions seemed particularly apt.

Tessa and I brought the volume into its final shape during the first six months of 2020, while the Covid-19 pandemic raged across the world. We were keenly aware that our project demonstrates exactly what the pandemic has made so clear: that we are all connected, that the new globalism means that what happens in one corner of the world can have tragic consequences in corners far, far away. Reading and responding to our contributors from Russia, France, Japan, Germany, the United Kingdom, the United States and South Africa has been a profound opportunity to reflect on the sister- and brotherhoods that join us together across distant lands. Our interconnectedness and co-dependence have never been more starkly apparent, and perhaps more than at any time in human history has it been brought home to us all, that we rise or fall to the world's challenges together.

At the same time, we conclude this book in the tragic shadow of the murder of George Floyd and the subsequent protests, marches and unrest that ensued in the wake of this terrible event. The calls for justice and equality were not confined to the United States, but resonated throughout the world, once again confirming the global reality in which we live and the extent to which we are all implicated in racial injustice and inequality. Martin Luther King Jr's oft-quoted words – that 'injustice anywhere is a threat to justice everywhere' – have never felt so urgent. Once again, we see how Ellison prophesied the world in which we struggle today. The police killing of Tod Clifton in *Invisible Man* prompts a march, a protest and then a devastating riot, in which grief mingles with outrage in scenes strikingly parallel to those we've witnessed throughout America and the world in recent weeks.

In the funeral procession for Tod, there arises from the crowd first the voice of an old man, and then an accompaniment on a euphonium horn, and together they give voice to the African American freedom hymn, 'There's Many a Thousand Gone'. As the Invisible Man listens to the song, he seeks out the face of the singer from which it emerges and tries to plumb the depths of his identity and experience, finding kinship in a stranger in their mutual experience of grief and outrage:

> I looked into the face of the old man who had aroused the song and felt a twinge of envy. It was a worn, old, yellow face and his eyes were closed and I could see a knife welt around his upturned neck as his throat threw out the song. He sang with his whole body, phrasing each verse as naturally as he walked, his voice rising above all the others, blending with that of the lucid horn. I watched him now, wet-eyed, the sun hot upon my head, and I felt a wonder at the singing mass. It was as though the song had been there all the time and he knew it and aroused it. [...] Something

> deep had shaken the crowd, and the old man and the man with the horn had done it. They had touched upon something deeper than protest or religion. [...] The song had aroused us all. It was not the words, for they were all the same old slave-borne words; it was as though he'd changed the emotion beneath the words while yet the old longing, resigned, transcendent emotion still sounded above.

This achingly beautiful scene has always moved me powerfully. Today it seems to evoke the outrage and despair of our present moment, while also giving artistic voice to that outrage and channelling it towards the hope that, in some way or fashion, we can translate the world's betrayal of brother- and sisterhood into its fulfilment. This is the same hope that Ellison ascribed to the writing of this novel, when he asserted that 'a novel could be fashioned as a raft of hope [to] help keep us afloat as we tried to negotiate the snags and whirlpools that mark our nation's vacillating course toward and away from the democratic ideal'. This volume is a small contribution to that ongoing raft of hope, without which, I fear, we truly do face despair at the injustice we inflict upon our fellow human beings.

Yes, ultimately this volume is an expression of profound hope. Ellison's work is animated by that spirit of hope, a hope that is always tempered by his steely and clear-eyed understanding of the brutality and injustice that humanity perpetrates every day. Yet his commitment to giving shape to human experience, and to using the art of fiction to both challenge and invoke the highest promises of humanity, marks Ellison once again as an author who is particularly necessary to our world today. The spirit of this volume is well expressed in the PEN charter that he received in 1959, when (as Christa Buschendorf and Nicole Lindenberg discuss in Chapter 7), he participated in the organization's thirtieth congress in Frankfurt:

> Members of PEN should at all times use what influence they have in favor of good understanding and mutual respect among nations; they pledge themselves to do their utmost to dispel race, class, and national hatreds and to champion the ideal of one humanity living in peace in the world.

Marc C. Conner, June 2020

Notes on Contributors

MICHIO ARIMITSU is Associate Professor at Keio University, Japan. He has published articles on the haiku-inspired poetry of Richard Wright, Amiri Baraka and Sonia Sanchez as well as on Katherine Dunham's indelible influence on *ankoku butoh* [a dance of darkness], the avant-garde performance created by Hijikata Tatsumi in post-World-War-II Japan. His current book projects include a cultural history of African American haiku-making as well as the discursive construction of African American literature in Asia in the Cold War era.

CHRISTA BUSCHENDORF was Professor and Chair of American Literature and Culture at Goethe University Frankfurt from 1998 to 2015; in summer 2019 she was Harris Distinguished Professor at Dartmouth College. She published on the American reception of Schopenhauer, on the afterlife of antiquity in the USA, and on ancient myths in American poetry. Currently, she is exploring the approach of relational sociology in (African) American Studies. Among her recent publications on black literature and culture are articles on Edward P. Jones, W. E. B. Du Bois, Shirley Graham Du Bois, and Frederick Douglass; she edited conversations with Cornel West on *Black Prophetic Fire* (2014) and *Power Relations in Black Lives: Reading African Literature and Culture with Bourdieu and Elias* (2018).

MARC C. CONNER is the President of Skidmore College in Saratoga Springs, New York. His books include *The Selected Letters of Ralph Ellison* (edited with John Callahan, Random House, 2019), *Screening Modern Irish Fiction and Drama* (edited with R. Barton Palmer, Palgrave Macmillan 2016), *The Poetry of James Joyce Reconsidered* (University Press of Florida, 2012), *The New Territory: Ralph Ellison and the Twenty-First Century* (edited with Lucas Morel, University Press of Mississippi, 2016), *Charles Johnson: The Novelist as Philosopher* (edited with Will Nash, University Press of Mississippi, 2007), and *The Aesthetics of*

Toni Morrison: Speaking the Unspeakable (University Press of Mississippi, 2000). He has published and lectured widely on diasporic Modernism, and serves as founding member and secretary/treasurer of The Ralph Ellison Society.

BRYAN CRABLE is Professor in the Department of Communication at Villanova University and is the founding director of the Waterhouse Family Institute for the Study of Communication and Society (WFI). He is the author of *Ralph Ellison and Kenneth Burke: At the Roots of the Racial Divide* (University of Virginia Press, 2012), a book included in the Mellon Foundation's American Literatures Initiative. He is also editor of the collection *Transcendence by Perspective: Meditations on and with Kenneth Burke* (Parlor Press, 2014), and the author of the forthcoming book, *White Sacraments: The Rhetoric and Rituals of Blackness*. In addition to scholarly book chapters and reviews on Ralph Ellison, his essays have appeared in leading rhetoric journals, including *The Quarterly Journal of Speech, Rhetoric Society Quarterly, Rhetoric Review* and *Argumentation and Advocacy*.

SAM HALLIDAY teaches in the School of English and Drama at Queen Mary University of London. He is the author of *Science and Technology in the Age of Hawthorne, Melville, Twain and James: Thinking and Writing Electricity* (2007) and *Sonic Modernity: Representing Sound in Literature, Culture and the Arts* (2013). His article 'Cinema and Cinematicity in Ralph Ellison's *Three Days before the Shooting* …' is forthcoming, and he is currently working on a book provisionally entitled *A Ralph Ellison Directory*.

RAPHAËL LAMBERT is Professor of African American Literature and Culture in the Department of American and British Cultural Studies at Kansai University in Osaka, Japan. He has published essays in *Journal of Modern Literature, Critique: Studies in Contemporary Fiction, Transition: The Magazine of Africa and the Diaspora*, and *The African American Review*. His latest essay, 'From Édouard Glissant's "The Open Boat" to the Age of Mass Migration', appears in the collection *Cosmopolitanisms, Race, and Ethnicity: Cultural Perspectives* (De Gruyter, 2018), and his book, *Narrating the Slave Trade, Theorizing Community* (Brill Press) came out in 2019.

NICOLE LINDENBERG was a lecturer at the University of Münster from 2016 to 2021. She studied English and Philosophy at Goethe University Frankfurt and the University of Wisconsin-Madison; from 2014 to 2015, she was a fellow at the Kluge Center at the Library of Congress. Currently, she is working on her PhD thesis, which draws on Pierre Bourdieu's sociology to investigate the theme of passing in Ellison's unfinished second novel, and on a forthcoming volume of Ellison's 'Notes' for *Three Days before the Shooting* …. Her articles '"You have to leave home to find home": Charismatic Violence and Split Habitus in Ralph Ellison's Unfinished Second Novel' and '"What if movie is Bliss's own life?": The Symbolic Violence of the Movie in Ralph Ellison's Unfinished Second Novel' were published in 2018. She co-organized (with Luvena Kopp and Stephan Kuhl) the (Re)Reading Ralph Ellison Symposium, Frankfurt, July 2019.

OLGA PANOVA is Professor at the Department of Foreign Literature, Faculty of Philology, Lomonosov Moscow State University and Lead Researcher at the Sector of Modern European and American Literature, A. M. Gorky Institute of World Literature of the Russian Academy of Sciences. She is editor-in-chief of the scholarly journal on New World literary history, *Literature of the Americas*. As such she edited 'Ralph Ellison: Contemporary Studies', the special section of *Literature of the Americas* 5 (2018).

ARETHA PHIRI is Senior Lecturer in the Department of Literary Studies in English at Rhodes University and has been a research fellow at the Stellenbosch Institute for Advanced Study (STIAS) in South Africa (2017–19). Her research examines the intersectional interactions of race, ethnicity, culture, gender and sexualities in comparative, transnational and transatlantic considerations of identity and subjectivity, with a focus on African American, American and contemporary African (diaspora) literature. She has been a visiting fellow at the Institute for Black Atlantic

Research (IBAR) and the Centre for the Study of International Slavery (CSIS) in the UK as well as a research fellow at the National Humanities Center (NHC) in North Carolina, USA. She has published in various accredited journals including *English Studies in Africa*, *Safundi*, *Agenda*, *English in Africa*, *Cultural Studies*, *European Journal of English Studies* and the *Journal of American Studies*. She is also the editor of *African Philosophical and Literary Possibilities: Re-reading the Canon* (Lexington Books, 2020).

STEPHEN RACHMAN is Associate Professor of English at Michigan State University, where he is Director of the American Studies Program and Co-Director of the Digital Humanities and Literary Cognition Laboratory. He is the editor of *The Hasheesh Eater* by Fitz Hugh Ludlow (Rutgers University Press) and a co-author of the award-wining *Cholera, Chloroform, and the Science of Medicine: A Life of John Snow* (Oxford University Press) and co-editor of *The American Face of Edgar Allan Poe* (Johns Hopkins University Press). He has written numerous articles on Poe, literature and medicine, cities, and popular culture. He is currently completing a study of Poe entitled *The Jingle Man: Edgar Allan Poe and the Problems of Culture*.

TESSA ROYNON is in her final year as Senior Research Fellow at the Rothermere American Institute, University of Oxford, where she teaches American and world literatures, and classical reception studies. She also works as the founding Librarian at The Swan School in Oxford. She is the author of *The Cambridge Introduction to Toni Morrison* (Cambridge University Press, 2012); *Toni Morrison and the Classical Tradition: Transforming American Culture* (Oxford University Press, 2013), which was awarded the Toni Morrison Society Book Prize in 2015; and *The Classical Tradition in Modern American Fiction* (Edinburgh University Press, 2021). She is the editor (with Daniel Orrells and Gurminder Bhambra) of *African Athena: New Agendas* (Oxford University Press, 2011), and (with Daniel Orrells) of the special issue, 'Ovid and Identity in the Twenty-First Century' (*International Journal of the Classical Tradition* 26/4 (2019)).

Index

RACE AND RESISTANCE ACROSS BORDERS IN THE LONG TWENTIETH CENTURY

This series focuses on the history and culture of activists, artists and intellectuals who have worked within and against racially oppressive hierarchies in the twentieth century and beyond, and who have then sought to define and to achieve full equality once those formal hierarchies have been overturned. It explores the ways in which such individuals – writers, scholars, campaigners and organizers, ministers, and artists and performers of all kinds – locate their resistance within a global context and forge connections with each other across national, linguistic, regional and imperial borders.

Disseminating the latest interdisciplinary scholarship on the history, literature and culture of anti-racist movements in Africa, the Caribbean, the United States, Europe, Asia and Latin America, the series foregrounds, through a cross-disciplinary approach, the transnational and intercultural nature of these resistance movements. The series embraces a range of themes, including but not limited to antislavery, intellectual and literary networks, emigration and immigration, anti-imperialism, church-based and religious movements, civil rights, citizenship and identity, Black Power, resistance strategies, women's movements, cultural transfer, white supremacy and anti-immigration, hip hop and global justice movements.

The series is affiliated with the Race and Resistance Research Programme at The Oxford Research Centre in the Humanities (TORCH), University of Oxford. Proposals are invited for sole- and joint-authored monographs as well as edited collections. We welcome projects in a wide range of fields, including but not restricted to history, political science, anthropology, literature, cultural studies and media studies.

Published Volumes:

Dominic Davies, Erica Lombard and Benjamin Mountford (eds): Fighting Words: Fifteen Books that Shaped the Postcolonial World
2017. ISBN 978-1-906165-55-0. hb
2019. ISBN 978-1-78997-422-5. pb

Dominic Davies: Imperial Infrastructure and Spatial Resistance in Colonial Literature, 1880–1930
2017. ISBN 978-1-906165-88-8.

Claudia Gualtieri (ed.): Migration and the Contemporary Mediterranean: Shifting Cultures in Twenty-First-Century Italy and Beyond
2018. ISBN 978-1-78707-351-7.

Charlotte Baker and Hannah Grayson (eds): Fictions of African Dictatorship: Cultural Representations of Postcolonial Power
2018. ISBN 978-1-78707-681-5.

Rachel Knighton: Writing the Prison in African Literature
2019. ISBN 978-1-78874-647-2.

Tessa Roynon and Marc C. Conner (eds): Global Ralph Ellison: Aesthetics and Politics Beyond US Borders
2021. ISBN 978-1-78997-494-2.

www.ingramcontent.com/pod-product-compliance
Lightning Source LLC
Chambersburg PA
CBHW070639310726
48982CB00001B/330

9781789974942